CultureShock!

A Survival Guide to Customs and Etiquette

Australia

Ilsa Sharp

Marshall Cavendish
Editions

This 8th edition published in 2012 by:
Marshall Cavendish Corporation
99 White Plains Road
Tarrytown NY 10591-9001
www.marshallcavendish.us

First published in 1992 by Times Editions Pte Ltd, reprinted 1993; 2nd edition published in 1994, reprinted 1995 (thrice), 1996; 3rd edition published in 1997, reprinted 1997, 1998, 1999 (twice); 4th edition published in 2000, reprinted 2000; 5th edition published in 2001, reprinted 2002, 2003 (twice), 2004; 6th edition published in 2005; 7th edition published in 2009.

Other Marshall Cavendish Offices:
Marshall Cavendish International (Asia) Pte Ltd. 1 New Industrial Road, Singapore 536196 ■ Marshall Cavendish International (Thailand) Co Ltd. 253 Asoke, 12th Flr, Sukhumvit 21 Road, Klongtoey Nua, Wattana, Bangkok 10110, Thailand ■ Marshall Cavendish (Malaysia) Sdn Bhd, Times Subang, Lot 46, Subang Hi-Tech Industrial Park, Batu Tiga, 40000 Shah Alam, Selangor Darul Ehsan, Malaysia

Marshall Cavendish is a trademark of Times Publishing Limited

ISBN: 978-0-7614-8065-5

Please contact the publisher for the Library of Congress catalogue number

Printed in Singapore by Times Printers Pte Ltd

Photo Credits:
All black and white photos from the author except pages 3, 31, 40, 60, 244, 290 (Brian Balen), pages 19, 46, 221, 238, 282, 319 (Siva Choy), page 219 (City of Canning), pages 15, 23, 25, 196, 249, 295 (John Halliwell), page 252 (Philip Little), page 269 (Richard Simpson, courtesy of *Daily News*, Western Australia), page 21 (Jan Weller) and pages 20, 47, 117, 239, 320 (Frank Weller). All colour images from Getty Images.
■ Cover photo: Art Directors & Trip

All illustrations by TRIGG

ABOUT THE SERIES

Culture shock is a state of disorientation that can come over anyone who has been thrust into unknown surroundings, away from one's comfort zone. *CultureShock!* is a series of trusted and reputed guides which has, for decades, been helping expatriates and long-term visitors to cushion the impact of culture shock whenever they move to a new country.

Written by people who have lived in the country and experienced culture shock themselves, the authors share all the information necessary for anyone to cope with these feelings of disorientation more effectively. The guides are written in a style that is easy to read, and cover a range of topics that will arm readers with enough advice, hints and tips to make their lives as normal as possible again.

Each book is structured in the same manner. It begins with the first impressions that visitors will have of that city or country. To understand a culture, one must first understand the people—where they came from, who they are, the values and traditions they live by, as well as their customs and etiquette. This is covered in the first half of the book

Then on with the practical aspects—how to settle in with the greatest of ease. Authors walk readers through how to find accommodation, get the utilities and telecommunications up and running, enrol the children in school and keep in the pink of health. But that's not all. Once the essentials are out of the way, venture out and try the food, enjoy more of the culture and travel to other areas. Then be immersed in the language of the country before discovering more about the business side of things.

To round off, snippets of basic information are offered before readers are 'tested' on customs and etiquette of the country. Useful words and phrases, a comprehensive resource guide and list of books for further research are also included for easy reference.

CONTENTS

PREFACE

I would like to think that this book may help explain Australia to newcomers and visitors and thus bridge any 'culture gaps', improving the chances of mutual empathy and friendship. It is my particular, personal wish that Australia and Asia should draw closer together.

I hope, too, that the book will help Australians understand themselves and what it is that makes their culture unique, by holding a mirror up to them and asking them to see themselves through outsiders' eyes.

Finally, I must beg Australia's pardon if any of my interpretations have been skewed somewhat by my own 'Sandgroper' bias, due to being located at Perth, despite my best efforts to avoid such imbalance, and for any other inadvertent 'greenhorn' errors.

Ilsa Sharp
Perth, Western Australia
2012

ACKNOWLEDGEMENTS

This book would not have been possible without the help of the Australian people in general, or of many published writers already well established in the field of 'Australia-watching', besides numerous friends and acquaintances. If I have inadvertently omitted anyone's name, my sincere apologies.

I particularly want to acknowledge my debt to several reference works (for details of publishers, etc., refer to 'Further Reading' at the back of the book):

- *The Penguin Australian Encyclopaedia*
- *The Little Aussie Fact Book*, Margaret Nicholson
- *A Dictionary of Australian Colloquialisms*, G A Wilkes
- *The Macquarie Dictionary of Australian Quotations*
- *The Macquarie Book of Events*
- *The Lucky Country*, Donald Horne

Permissions

- *The Daily News*, Western Australia—Barry Thornton, Deputy Editor, for the meat pies picture.
- John Timbers of John Timbers Studio, London, for his photograph of Dame Edna Everage.
- Quotations from the *Macquarie Dictionary of Australian Quotations*, reprinted with permission of the publisher, The Macquarie Library Pty Ltd.

In Perth, Western Australia

- Siva Choy, for patience beyond the call of marriage, yet again.
- Dan (gardening buddy), Cally (walking buddy), Troy and Marina Nelson, for too much to list here, besides a smooth landing in Oz.
- Sandra and John Theseira, for much besides food, but the food *was* good!
- Danny and Jocelyn Stacey, also Denise and much-missed Joyce, for unfaltering mateship.
- Loyola D'Souza.
- Eliza Ghani.
- Titus and Sandra Wumkes, our mates in the hills.
- Brian Balen, for counsel, hospitality and his photos.

- Adil Mistry, for deep thoughts, and being a 'plant buddy'.
- Sam and Winnie Davamoni, for companionship, hospitality and fun birding.
- Members of the Australian Eurasian Association of Western Australia, for fellowship and good times, including Harvey Fitzgerald and Kay Klass, George Bentley, Colin Clark, Eddie and Barbara Fernandez, Patrick Cornelius, Priscilla and Max Clutton, Jim D'Oliveiro, Royston St. Maria and family, Teresa and Bernard Noronha, Maureen Lewis, Derek, Yvonne and Elsie Nunis; and including the late Ivan and Veronica Fitzgerald, Uncle Ivan and Peter Richards, Maurice and Estelle Pestana, Ivy and Harry Klass.
- Brian and Vivien Ward.
- The late Herman Aroozoo.
- Wilma and the late Len Bridge.
- Winston and Betty Walters.
- Dev Govindasamy, a mine of information.
- Gina Knight, for being a bright spirit. Danielle Pender, for dancing magic.
- Faridah Ali.
- Tony Shotam.
- Marilyn Hardoon.
- Herbert and Angela Teo.
- Alfonso and Pat Soosay.
- Carlose Eapon.
- Ismail and Geraldene Ahmad.
- Manjeet Kaur.
- Narinder Kaur.
- Our cousins Dhevika Rani and her mother, Yasotha.
- Matthew and Joyce Chin.
- Gudrun and Edward Benjamin.
- Edmund and Janice Teo.
- The late Lorna Ollson.
- John O'Brien.
- Hema and Claudia Peiris, and the late Lucia Peiris.
- Rudy and Chris Riduan.
- The late Roland Sharma.
- Helen Stirling, Steve Rattenbury, Sreetha Rajalingam and Roger White, our faithful house-sitters.

- Frank and Yolanda Caddy; Stephanie, Wayne, Shamone and Courtney Eade; Ashok, Neelam, Manav and Aditya Bhalla, our neighbours.
- Alastair Annandale, quintessential Aussie.
- Sarjit Singh Gill, cobbler-philosopher.
- Kerryn Franklin.
- Kenny and Anne Barker.
- David Morrison, my patient boss for a while.
- Steve Quill.
- Chris Lewis and Pam Lanzell, for help and hospitality.
- Janis Hadley.
- Lorraine McMillan and Babs Lawson.
- Dr Eric Tan, former Chancellor, Curtin University of Technology, and Honorary President, WA Chinese Chamber of Commerce.
- The Chung Hwa Association.
- Professor Garry Rodan and staff, Asia Research Centre and School of Social Sciences and Humanities, Murdoch University.
- Greening Australia (WA), for helping me to understand the land and the plants.
- *The Western Australian*, Syndication Department.
- Members of Birds Australia (WA) for good times outdoors.
- Committee members, Singapore-WA Network (SWAN).
- The WA Singapore Business Council (WASBC) and its former President Mrs Cecilia Wee.
- Ishar Multicultural Centre for Women's Health, its former Director, Shobhana Chakrabarti, and staff.

Outside Western Australia
- The Weller Family, Netherlands, for photos and fun.
- John Halliwell, UK, for photos and solid practical help.
- The late Hugh Mabbett, sorely missed friend and adviser.
- Christine Moulet and Ted Knez, Canberra.
- Liz Blyth, Queensland.
- David and Amanda Landers, Sydney.
- Peter and Betty Game, and Babe Mitchell-Dawson of Melbourne; the late Ian Newton of Sydney; James Osborne of Diamond Beach Casino Hotel, Darwin; Tony and Chris

Lewis of Balfe's Hill Farm, Tasmania; Tourism Australia (formerly the Australian Tourism Commission), the various State Tourism Commissions, at home and in Singapore, and Qantas—for looking after me so well on my Australian travels 1985–1991.

- Philip Conn of Singapore, Barry Whalen of Hong Kong, David Townsend of Canberra, Jonathan Stone of Adelaide and Bruce Wilson of Melbourne, for my very first introductions to Australia, way back when.
- Iain Finlay and Trish Sheppard, Sydney, for times past.
- Angus Finney, Sydney, for showing me Tasmania, and for being himself.
- The late Arshak, and Sophie Galstaun, Sydney.
- Kenny Minogue, Darwin, for introducing me to the sounds of Gondwanaland.
- Peter Dawson, Darwin.
- Peter Saltmarsh, Darwin, for showing me wild Australia.
- Bronwen and Gareth Solyom, Tasmania/Indonesia/Hawaii.
- Sally Taylor, USA/France, for friendship and advice.
- Zainon Ahmad, New Straits Times, Malaysia, for publishing my Letter from Australia columns in the 1990s.

In Singapore
- Members of the Singapore Australian Business Council, and staff of the Australian High Commission and Austrade.
- Margaret and Ben Cunico.
- Beth Kennedy.
- Michael de Kretser.

This book is dedicated with respect and
affection to Australia,
a country which has had the foresight to welcome
the strangers knocking at her door,
and the courage to embark on an experiment
with multiculturalism.

MAP OF AUSTRALIA

PACIFIC
OCEAN

GULF OF
CARPENTARIA

Darwin

NORTHERN
TERRITORY

Cairns

WESTERN
AUSTRALIA

AUSTRALIA

QUEENSLAND

SOUTH
AUSTRALIA

INDIAN
OCEAN

Brisbane

Perth

NEW SOUTH
WALES

GREAT
AUSTRALIAN
BIGHT

Adelaide

Sydney

Canberra

VICTORIA

Melbourne

BASS STRAIT

SOUTHERN SEA

FIRST IMPRESSIONS

CHAPTER 1

'A wilful, lavish land—
All you who have not loved her,
You will not understand.'
—Australian poet Dorothea Mackellar (1885–1968),
from 'My Country', a hymn to the Australian land that
newcomers should read in its entirety

FIRST IMPRESSIONS ARE OFTEN CLOSER TO THE TRUTH than later, more compromised, qualified and considered views. What strikes you first about Australia may not be the whole story, but it is a good outline to fill in later. I've written about likely first impressions here in the order of the most powerful impressions made, not necessarily with any logical linkage topic-wise.

GEOGRAPHY: LAND AND LIGHT

It was April 1989. We had just made our first landfall as migrants to Australia, in grand old-fashioned style aboard a (Russian) cruise ship and carrying masses of goods and chattels including our precious fax machine, at Fremantle docks in Western Australia. An Australian customs officer was suspiciously snooping through our bags. Spotting a huge camera lens, he said, "Phew! What's that?" "Oh," said my husband, "that's a wide-angle lens." He gazed at us with dreamy sun-washed eyes, and said laconically, "Yeah, right, well, you'd certainly be needing that here, wouldn't you?"

He knew and we knew that Australia is, well, big—very big. Pretty hard to frame with most average wide-angle lens, in fact. 'A wide brown land' as it has famously been called by Aussie poet Dorothea Mackellar in her poem *My Country*'. Perhaps the very first things you notice about Australia are to do with the land, and with that legendary light, that blistering sun shafting out of a brilliant blue sky immodestly naked of any white clouds at all. Everything looks bright and sharp-edged, as though you have just 'photo-shopped' the Contrast element in a photo already shot through some kind of polarising filter.

My Tamil-Malayalee (South Indian) husband comes from tiny, crowded island-nation Singapore, one of the most densely urbanised countries on the planet, so perhaps unsurprisingly (even though his idea of an 'outdoors expedition' is to drive his car through open bush without ever getting out), he says the thing he loves most about Australia is the way the horizon stretches endlessly before him, unblemished by a single skyscraper, or any other building for that matter. And indeed it does. Open 'empty' land is an enduring image of Australia.

With this comes the sense of distance—'the tyranny of distance' is another cliche often aptly applied to Australia. It's not that easy to grasp that Australia, including the offshore southern island of Tasmania, is more than seven and a half million sq km (or almost three million sq miles) in area, which means it is as big as the USA (without Alaska) and

The 'tyranny of distance'—the road stretches as far as the eye can see—is typical of Australia.

24 times the size of Great Britain. If you are in Perth, Western Australia, you don't just 'run over' to Sydney, or vice versa; it's just like going 'overseas'. You might as well 'run over' to Asia—it's closer.

So Australians are nonchalant about driving a few hours to visit the 'rellies' (relatives) for 'tea' (read 'dinner') or for a routine business meeting 'just up the road'. If they tell you the destination is 'a cut lunch and waterbag' away, better beware, because that will be quite a distance. And they are very car-bound. This is a land of big highways, articulated long-distance truck juggernauts and routine speeds of 110 kmph. Americans will recognise it.

PEOPLE: STRAIGHT-TALKING, EASY-GOING, APPAREL-CHALLENGED

The next most likely first impression will be of a chatty, friendly people who are also prone to straight-talking unembellished with niceties, and who don't seem to worry much about what they are wearing—or not wearing. In the neighbourhood shops, on the street or in the bus, you will be amazed at how long you have to wait for service while the counter-person has a little chat with the person in front of you in the queue, or at how easily you can strike up a friendly conversation with strangers, or get help from them. The message is 'slow down, talk to me.'

The same generous smiles are wheeled out in negative situations too. There is a general acceptance for example, that you, the customer, will not get upset just because the counter-person tells you with a sweet smile and a shrug, "Oh, sorry, we ran out of those last night/last week/last month" even though they are clearly listed on the stocklist/menu. The plumber or repair man who didn't keep his appointment but turns up two days later will beam broadly, "Yeah, sorry mate, had a few things to do." This is a recurring scenario. Why get upset?

Turning on the radio or television will give some of you a heart attack as you register some reporter savaging the Foreign Minister face to face without any respect for his position or title, referring to him as a 'you pompous dope' (true!) or just 'Steve' or just witness fairly extreme nudity and lewd acts on the TV (especially on the SBS channels) at the relatively early hour of 8.30pm. The language heard all around you on the streets may seem very raw, liberally doused with the 'F...' word. Don't come to Australia for respect for authority, modesty or linguistic restraint. But sometimes, it's liberating to be as rude as you can be in Australia. Watch Parliament and enjoy a good fight.

White people without shoes, strolling the streets shirtless or virtually in their underwear are all particularly puzzling to migrants and refugees newly arrived in Australia from what used to be called 'Third World' countries. And why does one see so many incidents of sheer rage, shouting scenes, what should be private quarrels, open and public on the streets? Who knows. Some trace it to a violent history in a rugged land.

LANGUAGE

The unique 'Strine' or 'Austrayan' use of the English language is really in your face from the minute you land. From the moment you struggle with whether the restaurant dress code means a G-string-style bikini bottom or rubber ('Japanese') sandals by 'No Thongs' (the latter actually) or make a fool of yourself taking an entire dinner service of crockery to a party where you have been asked to bring 'a plate' (of food, you dummy!) to 'tea' (gotcha, it's dinner not tea!), this issue will plague you for a long time to come. No, you do not 'root' for your favourite footy team—unless you want to 'cop' an obscenity rap—instead you 'barrack' for the team. Consider the car-yard placard that says 'You Beaut Utes, Lay-Bys' and translate: 'Excellent Utility Vehicles (a small truck with a front cabin and an open back 'tray' section for carrying light loads), no-interest hire purchase deals available', is an approximation.

'Catchya' is also a favourite parting shot which might seem a bit mysterious to some—short for 'Catch you later.'

Another aspect of language that strikes many non-Western arrivals is Australians' extreme preoccupation with 'politically-correct' forms, for lack of a better term. Banish all thought of continuing to use terms like 'handicapped' (change to 'disabled', 'differently abled' or 'challenged');

'blind' ('visually impaired' or 'visually challenged'); 'spastic' (just 'disabled' will do); chairman (always 'chair-person'); 'husband', 'wife', 'spouse', 'girlfriend', 'boyfriend' ('partner' works for everybody, including gays—homosexuals if you don't understand 'gay'—but leads to some confusion when you are not sure whether or not a business partner is meant!); 'natives' ('indigenous Australians', 'traditional owners', 'the first people', or just 'Aboriginals'); 'prostitute' ('sex worker', 'working girl').

As another example, a particularly daft term used by the jargon-ridden social services industry is CALD, standing for Culturally And Linguistically Diverse. It's really code for 'Wog' or 'Non-white'. If you are white and Anglo-Celtic, you are supposed to answer the question on official forms, 'Are you from a CALD background?' with 'No'. But who on earth has determined that a white Anglo-Celtic background cannot be both culturally and linguistically diverse? The same goes for NESB, or Non-English Speaking Background: even if you come from well-spoken India or Singapore, you are supposed to say, yes, you are NESB, another code-word for 'Foreign'.

The Irony of It All

In Western Australia, it has always given me some malicious pleasure to watch educated left-liberal leaning white Australians squirming as they try to remember what is the acceptable term for an iconic and ubiquitous local 'shaggy-haired' black-trunked plant once tagged the 'Blackboy'—in deference to Aboriginal Australians, this word has been dropped by many for its racial undertones, in favour of the more anodyne 'Grass Tree' or even the original Aboriginal word 'Balga'. But the irony is, you'll hear most Aboriginals refer to it quite happily as a 'Blackboy' because that's the European word they first learned for it and that's fine with them.

ACCENT

With the language comes the accent, quite contagious. Soon you too will be raising your voice at the ends of sentences, greeting people "G'day" ('Good-die') and asking "What toime (time) is it?" as naturally as Kath Day-Knight in the now defunct *Kath and Kim* TV series (a riveting comic essay in class differences within 'egalitarian' Australia; the girls return soon in *The Kath & Kim Filum* movie).

But another thing that you will notice in your first few weeks is the sheer variety of accents on the streets; multicultural Australia is right there, upfront – after all, 27 per cent of the nation now is overseas-born, and 26 per cent of those born in Australia have at least one parent born overseas. Asia (excluding the Middle East) is a major source of permanent settlers, providing 48 per cent of the 2009-2010 total, compared with Europe's 18.5 per cent (not including special business, working, refugee or humanitarian visas). Your taxi-driver speaks with the thick accent of an Iraqi or maybe a one-time Yugoslav; the doctor's receptionist or the pestering telemarketer on the phone has an Indian lilt to their voice; your real estate agent has a distinct French accent; your house-cleaner or part-time 'ironing lady' is Polish; and that TV journalist, isn't he a South African? The voices of a future Australia waft across the breeze to you from behind flapping black chadar cloaks and veils on the street, from the African drums rehearsal in a community hall, the chants wafting out of the nearby Sikh *gurdwara* (temple) and the posh hotel dinner meeting hosted by prosperous local Chinese businessmen.

CUSTOMS

Every society has its hidden codes. In Asia, your gentle hosts will never criticise you for not taking your shoes off when you enter their home, but by not doing so, you separate yourself from them and their culture for ever. In Australia of course, you're considered a bit weird if you do take them off, and no Australian will voluntarily take them off on entering your home either. But Australia too has its unspoken rules and if you don't spot them, you could seem rude. When you first arrive, you will probably notice some of these little rules quite early on. Like visitors leaving not just the room, but the house itself to smoke, out in the backyard. Like picking up your cups and plates after you have eaten in someone's home and taking them to the kitchen sink at least, possibly also offering to wash them up (no maids here, see?). Like bringing a bottle of 'booze' or 'grog' (wine or beer) when you come over for dinner, maybe a 'plate' (of food), especially if 'pot-luck

On the Flip Side

Paradoxically, in this largely helpful society, nobody bothers much nowadays about standing up for a 'lady' on the bus, or opening a door for her—a recent correspondence in the Western Australian newspaper indicated that it was now the bus company's official policy that asking anybody, including youngsters, to stand up for anybody else, even the infirm elderly, was 'discriminatory'. So you might be thought odd—or worse, on the make—if you stood up for a woman on the bus or train.

dinner' has been suggested. Like men attending to the barbecue, women mucking around in the kitchen doing salads and things. And maybe, sometimes still, a separation of the party into men talking sport and women talking, well, yes, sigh, children and things. Like not talking money and possessions too loudly—generally, not 'spruiking' ('selling') your own achievements too much. Like splitting the bill and remembering to buy a 'shout' (round) of drinks if your mate does 'shout you'. Like remembering to check if a restaurant is solely 'BYO' (Bring Your Own) and making sure you've brought a bottle of wine along with you if it is. Like signalling considerately well in advance of changing lanes when driving. Like stopping to offer help to fellow motorists in distress. Or flashing your headlights to let other oncoming motorists know that there is a speed camera or a 'booze bus' (breath testing for alcohol consumption) just ahead of you. And making sure that you pass your unexpired parking coupon on to an incoming motorist as you leave the carpark—they would do the same for you.

An American Observation

American Nana Ollerenshaw married an Australian and moved to Australia in 1965 at the age of 22. The following piece appeared in *The Weekend Australian* in 2005. Nana concedes that Australia has changed much since the time she moved here, but many of her observations still stand nonetheless.

'My brother spelled Sydney with an 'i' and some of my parents' friends thought I would never be seen again. "Do they have supermarkets?" they asked (when I moved to Australia)...

(Continued on the next page)

(Continued from previous page)

I ardently compared Australia with the US, prefacing every statement with 'In America, we...' until a forthright family friend put a stop to it...

At parties, men and women divided as neatly as a meat cleaver separates cuts, the men talking sport and politics, the women shopping and babies. I had no one with whom to discuss Jane Austen. I laughed at words such as 'crook' and 'strides' and at expressions like 'come a cropper'. And how could 'directly' mean 'not immediately'? I learned not to say 'I'm stuffed', nor did I say 'fall on your fanny'. In the US, 'fanny' means your 'butt', but they call it, euphemistically, your seat. The Puritan heritage lingers. Other differences, apart from language, were single-storey brick houses, corner pubs, memorial statues, the hard, white merciless light (which poet John Betjeman said was 'like being inside a diamond'), the hang of gum leaves, new stars, bizarre animals.

From four seasons I changed to two. From a country of mountains and rivers I went to flatness and a place where heat and light became weapons of nature. As a teacher I was dumbfounded by the emphasis given to sport. I knew I was different. I felt serious among Australians, unable to be light-hearted. I was ruled by an internal clock but they just let the day happen... I have changed too, almost an Australian, unrecognisable to my own people. The sight of an Akubra, the sound of a dry laconic voice in an overseas airport would catch my breath... So we are turned. Like chameleons we take on the colours that surround us.'

UPSIDE-DOWN LAND: NATURE AND ENVIRONMENT

For anyone who enjoys nature and the outdoors, the first encounter with Australia is also full of wonder and delight at the extraordinary, truly unique nature of the Australian environment. First of all, for everyone from the northern hemisphere and temperate climes there is the simple oddity of being 'down under', where going south suddenly means getting colder, and where December becomes summer, July winter. A summer around 27°C or so (over 80°F), you quickly discover, is 'mild.'

You are confronted with curious fauna and magnificent flora found nowhere else in the world.

Yes, there really are Kangaroos, Wombats and Wallabies, Goannas and Blue-tongues! Only now that you are actually on 'Terra Australis' is it brought home to you that Australia's biota boasts a natural diversity and 'endemism' (uniqueness) equal to any tropical rain forest (with which Australia is also endowed) and priceless in global terms. Of Australia's more than 20,000 species of flowering plant, about 93 per cent are not found anywhere else (are 'endemic'), while about 89 per cent of Australia's marsupial animals (like the kangaroos) and 73 per cent of other Australian animals are unique to the continent. The monotremes (platypus and echidnas) are found only in Australia and New Guinea.

It is hard to mistake the look, and resin-laden smell, of an Australian 'gum' (Eucalyptus) forest, the soft-white peeling trunk of a Paperbark tree, or the nose-twitching aroma of a Lemon-scented Gum, for trees from anywhere else, any more than you would mistake the hysterical cackling of Australia's Kookaburra bird or the screech of a Cockatoo or Lorikeet for the more melodious song of a European Blackbird or Songthrush. Around my suburban home in Western Australia, the chortling and burbling of Magpies, the menacing cawing of big black Australian Ravens, the shrill piping of the perky Magpie Lark, the chatter of the aggressive tail-flicking black and white 'Willie Wagtail' fantail, the happy chirrups of Honey-eaters, the sore-throated screech of the pink and grey Galahs and the urgent squawking of a bevy of black Carnaby's Cockatoos overhead, all say 'Australia' to me in a very special way. And another thing that strikes you about Australia is the relative tameness of the wild birds, which will come very close to humans at times; that's mainly because almost nobody harasses them, and cagebird culture is not as developed as it is in, say, Asia.

You may be struck too by the devotion ordinary Australians show to their wildlife. Consider highway signs warning motorists to drive slowly because there may be ducks or kangaroos crossing. And the amazing spectacle of 1,000 volunteers up to their chests in bone-chilling sea water as they struggle to keep a school of 100 beached whales alive for hours on end (in Western Australia, 2005, and many times since). At times like these, Australian altruism seems nothing less than noble.

Among your keenest first impressions will surely be the feeling that almost every Australian must be a gardening fanatic, as you stroll along suburban streets endlessly lined with flower-laden gardens and swaying trees, all clearly lovingly nurtured. You are almost certain to catch the national horticultural fever. In your garden or in the local park, and along the street verges, may be various species of red-flowered Bottlebrush or Grevillea plant, perhaps a soft green Tea tree or gracious Peppermint tree, a phallic-flowered Banksia or if you are very lucky, a Grass-tree with its flower spear erect. None of them looks like a European tree and one of the first things a new arrival may learn to his or her cost is that Australian gardening conditions are mostly utterly unlike any others. If you have been used to temperate northern-hemisphere or tropical gardening, prepare for a shock. Your rules simply do not apply. With a bit of help from the innumerable Australian TV gardening programmes programmes (The ABC's *Gardening Australia* at the top of the pile), after some years, you may finally understand that native Australian plants are uniquely adapted to their own environment, meaning they may not need as much water, and may actively hate too much nitrogen-rich fertiliser (although this is over-simplifying); they may flower happily in winter and spring but disappear in summer. Beginners who get stuck with recalcitrant coastal sands such as those on the Perth plains of Western Australia will wage battles with constant loss of water during a vicious 38–40°C (100–104°F) summer, until they learn about soil wetting agents and the greatest saviour of all, mulch, mulch and more mulch (soil-coverings of wood-chips, stones etc.). In the summer, hanging baskets will grow 'crusts' on the soil surface, with water running off them as if from a duck's back, never reaching the plant's roots. The cure? Guess what, a solution of ordinary dish-washing liquid (although there are also specially tailored commercial soil-wetting preparations to consider).

It's all an intriguing learning curve, then, but the thing is, you are in Australia and it is like nowhere else.

THE BASICS

CHAPTER 2

'One seems to ride for ever and to come to nothing,
and to relinquish at last the very idea of an object.
Nevertheless, it was very pleasant.
Of all the places that I was ever in this place
seemed to be the fittest for contemplation.'
—British novelist Anthony Trollope,
in his documentary *Australia and New Zealand*, 1873

THE LAND OF AUSTRALIA

No matter how urban or suburban the Australian is, the land of Australia lies in his or her subconscious, whether as a sensation of joy, reverence or fear.

Nobody can live in Australia without being affected by the land, the landscape and the extraordinary ecosystem it nourishes. In his own strange way, the Australian white is linked with the land, just like the Australian Aboriginal. The land is his mother too. Only he does not articulate this half-sensed emotion as clearly in his culture as do the Aboriginals.

You see this subconscious leitmotif reflected in the landscape paintings (except for the very early colonial ones, which rather desperately rendered Australian scenery much like English pastures and oak forests), the cinema and the great literature of white Australia. In the formative early years of Australian cinema during the late 20th century, it was characteristic for movies to linger on the land, long and lyrical. Seen from the outside, particularly from the white, Western point of view, Australia's is a uniquely harsh, intimidatingly vast and seemingly empty environment, hostile to human life. But the Aboriginal would not agree.

The Basic Facts of the Land

First, let us get to grips with the immensity of Australia. It is about the size of the USA if you exclude Alaska; 24 times the size of the British Isles. In absolute figures, it is

7.7 million sq km (almost 3 million sq miles) in area. The mainland distance east-west is 3,983 km (2,475 miles), north-south, 3,138 km (1,950 miles). The Western Australian capital of Perth and the Northern Territory capital of Darwin are closer to Asia than to any other Australian city.

A continent in its own right, Australia lies across the Tropic of Capricorn in the southern hemisphere, sandwiched between the Indian and Pacific oceans. Antarctica is just 2,000 km (about 1,243 miles) to the south. 'Australia' derives from the Latin *Australis*, meaning 'southern land'. Much is made of the Southern Cross constellation as a nationalistic symbol, which features on the Australian flag, since this magnificent group of five stars can only be viewed from the most southerly positions in the southern hemisphere.

This is the driest continent on Planet Earth, with recorded temperatures of up to 53°C (127°F) in places, frequently ravaged by wildfire. People still die in Australia's deserts. A year's reading of the newspapers is sure to yield a clutch of such incidents, even today. There are sad place names dotted over the continent recalling the trials of early explorers— names like 'Lake Disappointment' for a dry lake.

But there are great variations in climate and landscape, from the lush tropical north with its end-year monsoonal 'wet', rainforests and mangrove swamps, to the chilly temperate forests of the south and the ski slopes of New South Wales and Victoria. Australia is also among the world's nations considered most vulnerable to climate change, with 'extreme weather events' ever more frequent: Perth in the west is becoming more humid, making its hot summers even less tolerable, while to the east, Melbourne in Victoria sweltered through temperatures around 45°C (113°F) in January 2009, its hottest since 1908, and in September 2010 – February 2011, massive floods hit wide swathes of Victoria, causing the evacuation of thousands and more than A\$2 billion in damage to agriculture alone. Long-term, Australia's coastal urbanisation could be threatened by rising sea levels.

Be that as it may, even a venerable source like the Economist Intelligence Unit (EIU) rates Australian cities as among the world's most liveable. In the EIU's Liveability Index

The distinctive 'Three Sisters' rock formation is part of New South Wales' iconic Blue Mountains.

of 2011, with Melbourne winning top ranking, above Vienna and Vancouver, followed by Sydney (6), Perth (8) and Adelaide (9). The Aussie cities rated largely, said the EIU, because of good infrastructure, low population density, relatively low crime and plenty of recreational activities.

Australia still remembers with respect the ill-fated Burke and Wills expedition of 1860, which attempted to cross the continent from south to north; Burke and Wills died of starvation during a terrifying journey.

Rocks and Ranges

Australia was once part of a prehistoric super-continent named Gondwanaland that first started to fracture about 150 million years ago. Out of its parts were formed Australia, Antarctica, South America, Africa, India, Madagascar and New Zealand. Australia broke off from Gondwanaland between 70 and 45 million years ago. This makes Australia a very old continent indeed, with a geological history dating to the Pre-Cambrian period of 600 million years ago; the landforms of Europe and the USA, in contrast, evolved only up to 65 million years ago. With no volcanic activity or other land-forming events for the past 80 million years, the scenery you encounter in Australia is the original prehistoric landscape, undisturbed.

It is largely a flat continent, one of the flattest land areas on the globe, with major exceptions like the Great Dividing Range of the east, running from north Queensland down into Victoria in the south, which includes tablelands, alps, plateaux and mountains—the famous Atherton Tableland of Queensland, the Blue Mountains of New South Wales and the Grampians of Victoria, for example. Australia's highest peak is Mount Kosciusko in the Snowy Mountains of New South Wales, at 2,230 m (7,316 ft).

There are some very strange and dramatic excrescences on the otherwise flat Australian vistas, the most famous of these being the 335-m (1,099-ft) tall Ayers Rock monolith, rising straight out of a central plain. The vivid red Olgas, rock monoliths described by an early explorer as 'monstrous pink haystacks', are in the Northern Territory, in the same Uluru National Park as Ayers Rock.

Others include the Pinnacles, about 200 km (124 miles) north of Perth in Western Australia—platoons of natural limestone obelisks standing up to 2 m high (almost 7 ft)—and the ancient sandstone formations of the Bungle Bungle range in the remote Kimberley region of north-west Western Australia, rising 450 m (1,476 ft) above the grasslands.

THE COUNTRYSIDE

Close to 90 per cent of Australians live in capital cities or towns. Few live or even work in rural or outback regions such as the arid, dusty 'Red Centre' around the famous outback town of Alice Springs.

It is still possible to capture the old romance: cattle-drover 'cowboys' silhouetted through a shimmering veil of dust, marshalling great rivers of cattle over treeless bush (go see Baz Luhrmann's 2008 movie *Australia*), one-street towns and two-house stations stuck on lonely plains, the occasional cry of 'Coo-ee!', the old Aboriginal bush cry connecting humans separated by great distance, adopted by the whites. ("Neighbours? He doesn't even live within coo-ee of her!").

But rural Australia is bleeding. The young are leaving for the pleasures of the city. Those who stay are battling bank loans and the loss of overseas markets for their produce (wool is a key example), in addition to regular natural disasters like drought, fire, floods and, in the far north, cyclones. And the creeping menace of salinity, ironically caused by the white farmers' own agricultural practices, unsuited to this unique land—government scientists predict that some 17 million hectares (42 million acres) of Australian land will potentially become saline drylands by 2050. Depression and suicide in the countryside are the flip-side of the apparent rural idyll.

Doctor in the Air

Life in outback Australia stimulated the establishment of the world's most impressive aerial medical service, better known as The Royal Flying Doctor Service. An Australian-born Presbyterian missionary, John Flynn—'Flynn of the Inland' they called him—was the founder in 1928 of this voluntary organisation funded by government grants and other contributions. The service uses a sophisticated radio network to link outback stations with its hospitals and planes.

Fire!

The Australian ecology is built to burn. The Aboriginals have always known this and have used fire as an instrument for controlling and benefiting their environment. Fire disasters are a regular occurrence in the hot summers. The 'Black Thursday' of 1851 in Victoria, the 1939 'Black Friday' fires in Victoria and the 'Ash Wednesday' fires of 1983 in South Australia and Victoria, were terrible examples, with 70 lives lost in the last-mentioned of these. In January 2005, more than 40,000 hectares (about 99,000 acres) turned into an inferno that killed nine people, on the Eyre Peninsula of South Australia. And in January 2009, amid temperatures soaring to a record high of over 47°C, hundreds of lives were lost in the fastest moving bushfires the state of Victoria had ever seen, creating new and sombre records.

The worst fires often occur at times of drought. The extremely high temperatures reached in the Australian summer combine explosively with native plants like the oil-bearing eucalypts, which act much like petroleum thrown on the flames. Hot winds from the north do the rest. But fire seems also to stimulate new plant growth.

In recent years, the finger has often been pointed at arsonists, as much as at Nature—recent research suggests that as many as half of Australia's destructive bush fires may have been set deliberately. The totality of such fires cause an estimated A$ 77 million of damage every year, quite apart from lives lost. It's frightening to note that by definition, fire-fighting is a job that attracts pyromaniacs and so unsurprisingly perhaps, many arsonists are found among fire-fighters, with a very good understanding of exactly how to set a really dangerous fire too. Among those who are not pyromaniacs, the motives cited are stunningly banal: most arsonists seek attention or recognition, excitement or relief from boredom, are expressing anger, or just fancy a spot of mindless vandalism. Arsonists' lives apparently are characterised by family relationship problems and the breakdown of normal social interactions, employment and academic performance.

Needless to say though, setting fires in the summer when the fire-risk has been declared high (via a 'Total Fire Ban'), is a criminal offence. This means neither campfires nor even home barbecues are safe: in February 2011, a few sparks from a DIY enthusiast's home angle-grinder tool during a Total Fire Ban were enough to ignite an inferno that destroyed 72 homes, in Western Australia. Australia has developed magnificent volunteer networks such as the State Emergency Service to combat fires, or even to aid householders during storms. These wonderful folk will turn out of bed at night virtually on call.

The Flora

The 'flagship' plants of Australian botany are of course the eucalypts, a genus classified within the Myrtle family, especially the smoother-barked versions known popularly as 'Gums'.

Eucalypts have a tall and spindly look, with foliage sparsely dispersed along scarecrow branches, that is quite distinctive. They also give off a very special resinous aroma that says 'Australia' as soon as it reaches the nose on a summer's breeze. Or, as with the Lemon-scented or Peppermint

The author in bushland, a gum in the background.

versions, their leaves may yield a wonderful perfume when crushed between the fingers.

There are also the Stringybark eucalypts of the east, with their rough barks, and the largely tropical Ironbarks. The giant Karri forests of south-west Western Australia are the second tallest in the world after the California redwoods. The Jarrah, from the same region as the Karri, has a fine red-grained timber often found as polished flooring in older Western Australian homes. In

Gum trees can produce delicate and attractive blossoms.

Tasmania are some the finest stands of cool temperate rainforest in the world, featuring pine and beech species as well as myrtles that largely predate the mainland gums, originating as they do in the Gondwanaland era of about 60 million years ago. Hence the constant 'greenie' protest against logging in Tasmania.

One of the loveliest sights of the Perth summer is the flowering of countless Jacaranda trees (actually South American imports from way back when), clouds of lavender-blue.

My husband got quite excited one December day in Perth, telling me, 'Look, we've got our very own Christmas tree, on the front verge!' It was a Bottlebrush, ablaze with tall red flower 'candles', yet another myrtle.

In the same Myrtle family again—there are 1,300 species of myrtle in Australia—are the Paperbarks, sometimes referred to in Australia by their genus name, Melaleuca, and quite often identified by their peeling, papery bark. Other familiar myrtles are the Tea trees, which fall within the Leptospermum genus, including the Lemon-scented Tea tree.

Every Western Australian spring, about October–November, tourists and residents alike are presented with the most spectacular display of gorgeous wildflowers in the countryside and in the bush. It is literally a case of the desert blooming, in profusion.

Be aware too that there are many unwelcome 'guests' among Australia's flora—foreign plants brought by ignorant settlers, that can do great harm to Australia's unique ecology. There are

A National Symbol

A famous national symbol, of course, is the Wattle, in the genus Acacia, part of the Mimosa family, with its familiar yellow blossoms often cascading in drooping golden showers. There are 900 species of wattle in Australia.

dedicated self-appointed 'weed police' everywhere to lecture you on this, but if you could see the damage that imports such as the Water Hyacinth, Lantana, Patersons Curse and the Blackberry have done, to name only a few, you might have some sympathy for their concerns.

Roos and Devils

Australia's long isolation from the rest of the world has contributed to the evolution of some extraordinary life-forms unique to the continent. The existence of the ancient supercontinent of Gondwanaland can be traced from the fact that there are some related species to be found in New Guinea and in South America.

The grey kangaroo at Yanchep Park in Western Australia.

The best-known oddities in Australia are of course those egg-laying, nipple-less mammals, the monotremes—just three of them, being the Duck-billed Platypus and two species of Echidna, also known as Spiny Anteaters—and the pouched marsupials, with the Kangaroo the best-known example.

A less well-known feature of some marsupials is the fact that they have bifurcated penises, nobody knows why. One Aussie zoo director experimenting with the breeding of endangered marsupials said to me, 'Well, maybe we have double the chance of success!'

There are 19 marsupial families, encompassing not only kangaroos and wallabies, but also arboreal animals like the Koala (*not* 'koala bear', please, a misnomer) and possums, various mice and rats, wombats and 'native cats' (which look more like mongooses than cats). Half of Australia's 250 species of mammals are marsupials.

The Wombat is a wondrous beast, stocky and powerfully built, like a small bear, weighing in at about 40 kg (88 lbs). Somewhat less cuddly is the Tasmanian Devil, a smallish

Cute at a wildlife park, but the Tasmanian devil's jaws can crunch bone.

Possums are harmless but they can keep you up at night if you have one
holed up in the roof space of your home.

black-and-white carnivorous marsupial endemic to Tasmania,
which makes the most appalling screeching and grumbling
noises, feeds on almost anything, including carrion, and is
equipped with jaws that could reduce the thickest bone to
shredded-wheat consistency.

Some of the kangaroo-type marsupials have marvellous
names, like the Potoroo, the Wallaroo, the Quokka (found
only on Western Australia's Rottnest Island, off Perth—the
island's name means 'Rats' Nest' in Dutch and refers to the
Quokkas) and the Pademelon.

Possums you may get to know better than you would prefer.
Although essentially harmless, they are the bane of many a
householder's life since it is their habit to hole up in ceiling
and roof spaces of ordinary homes, even in the city, scrabbling
around and making an awful racket at night.

All native animals are protected under federal law in
Australia. However, killing of wild kangaroos, populations of
which are thriving and multiplying, is licensed for 'culling'
purposes from time to time. Farmers in particular treat these
great macropods as vermin, because they compete with
domestic livestock for grass fodder. The issue of kangaroo
harvesting is charged with emotion in Australia.

A Brace of Trivia

Just for interest: the platypus may look cute, but in fact, the male has a nasty pair of poisonous spurs on his ankles, and the name 'koala' is Aboriginal for 'He who does not drink'—the koala gets most of its moisture from the leaves it chews, although actually, it does very occasionally drink liquids. Belying their looks, koalas are not particularly cute, being bad-tempered and sullen, slow-moving animals most of the time.

Sadly, many of these unique animals are threatened by unexplained recent outbreaks of disease—one wonders if it must be something human beings have done to them or their environment. Tasmanian devils are now plagued by putrefying cancerous facial tumours (the animal was put on the Endangered Species list for the first time in May 2008, its population having halved between 1995 and 2005), while platypus have fallen prey to a disease producing skin lesions and attacking internal organs, koalas are prone to chlamydia bacteria, possibly have been for many years, and wombats often collide with cars.

Emus and Galahs

There are 867 species of bird in Australia. When the first white settlers arrived in 1788, one of them, surgeon Arthur Bowes Smyth, remarked that as his ship hove into what was to be Sydney Harbour: 'The singing of the various birds among the trees, and the flights of the numerous parraquets, lorrequets, cockatoos and maccaws, made all around appear like an enchantment.'

Here again, you see the traces of Gondwanaland, with the Australian Emu closely related to other flightless birds like the South African ostrich and New Zealand's kiwi, for example.

Other unique avifauna include the Black Swan. This reverse-image bird, seen in northern hemispheric terms, has caused awful trouble for the Japanese, since their word for swan can only refer to a white bird.

Of course, of all the Australian birds, the 'laughing' Kookaburra is perhaps the most widely known. It is quite a cheeky bird. The few times I have been out to use the public barbecue pits in Perth's King's Park, there have always been a couple of these quite large and handsome birds sitting

The Magpie-Lark is an attractive and familiar Australian bird.

beside me on my log seat, hinting that they would like to be offered a few slivers of meat, please. In Western Australia, they are unwanted guests, being eastern states birds not native to the West.

Very Australian too are the 56 species of parrot (only five of them found elsewhere in the world), from the brightly coloured Rosella and exotically multi-hued Rainbow Lorikeet, to the black-capped, yellow neck-ringed, green 'Twenty-eight' or Ring-necked Parrot, and the familiar Cockatoo.

There are more cockatoos, however, than just the white-bodied sulphur-crested one so commonly seen in Western aviaries (protected but considered a pest by most Australians). There are, for instance, handsome black cockatoos like the Palm Cockatoo of Queensland and the Carnaby's Cockatoo unique to Western Australia, besides the red-headed cockatoo ('Gang-Gang') and the pink-and-grey Galah (pronounce with the stress on the 'lah', quickly swallowing the first half of the word).

The poor galah has entered Strine-talk as a synonym for idiocy—in expressions like 'Mad as a gumtree full of galahs.' If you wish to express your contempt for someone, you could refer to them as 'a silly galah'.

We must not forget the Fairy Penguins, resident on Victoria's Phillip Island; their nightly 'parade' is a big tourist draw.

Personal favourites of mine are the stately Pelican found

almost everywhere, the majestic 1.5-metre tall Brolga crane, symbol of the Northern Territory, the delicate little Honey-eaters sucking nectar from the red Grevillea flowers in my garden, the cackling Wattle-bird with his dangling red neck lappets and the large crow-like black and white Magpie whose bell-like chortling always means 'home' to me when I am in Perth.

Scalies and Slimies

There are some fairly dramatic lizards in Australia—450 species, including the large dinosaur-like Goanna, or Monitor Lizard (good eating), the dragon-lizards (Agamidae) such as the histrionic Frill-necked Lizard of the north, and the much smaller, ceiling-walking house Gecko. But the reptiles that attract the most attention are snakes and crocodiles.

Snakes admittedly are more alarming in Australia than almost anywhere else: of the approximately 172 species in the country (140 on land, 32 in the sea), the poisonous outnumber the harmless ones. And some are among the most dangerous in the world—the Giant Brown Snake and the Taipan of the north, the Tiger Snake of the south-east, the Copperhead and various types of Sea Snake. However, there are only about 15 of these very dangerous snakes.

There are some scary tales about species like the Brown Snake or the Red-bellied Black Snake not only standing their ground against humans, but even attacking or chasing them, in the breeding season. You should certainly give any snakes sighted a wide berth.

Crocodiles are the stuff of Australian legend and a fascinating link with Earth's prehistory. Thanks to conservationist policies which have granted them complete protection in Australia since the early 1970s, their number has increased dramatically; some estimates now put the population of the Estuarine or Saltwater Crocodile at about 100,000, probably more.

The focus of public fear and awe is the 'Saltie', which will take human beings if they are at hand—and has done so on several highly publicised occasions. The reality is about 15 fatal crocodile attacks in the 20 years between 1985 and 2005, although the total number of attempted killings is greater of course. Crocs are efficient killers. The

Daredevil feeding of crocs.

animal grips larger prey in its jaws and then takes it below water to drown it in a 'death roll', rolling over and over in the process, then stores the body underwater before eating it a few days later. The danger to humans has probably been increased by tourist operators who bait crocodiles by hanging carcases like chickens high above the water from large boat decks, thus teaching the beast to leap ever higher. The average small fisherman's boat then becomes no problem for the crocodile.

The seemingly lumbering 'saltie' can move at impressive speed on land, and hide so well as to become invisible when stationary. When touring by land, especially in coastal swamps and even on the river banks of northern Western Australia, the Northern Territory and Queensland, you should take special care, and think twice before swimming. Also, try not to do the same thing at the same time every day (like filling the camp kettle from the river every day at 5pm) and keep moving camp; crafty crocs stalk their prey for days before they attack, to learn your schedules first.

Ocean swimming brings other terrors. Shark attacks are a real risk. But as with the crocs, fatalities are comparatively low. In the last 20 years, sharks have killed 24 people in Australian waters, with Western Australia leading the scoreboard in recent years.

The Ferals, and Other Unwelcome Guests

Feral domestic animals—in other words, humankind's animals left to go wild in the bush and desert—are some of the great banes of the Australian ecology and a constant reminder of the ignorance of the early white settlers.

(By the way, as an aside, you will frequently hear the word 'feral' used in a different context in Australia: it is a derogatory term used to dismiss contemptuously all somewhat left-wing, 'hippie', unconventional people, such as 'greenies', who protest against things or live alternative lifestyles. Often the implication of this use of 'feral' is that the person referred to is not only wild and out of control but also dirty, unwashed, unemployed and on welfare).

There are feral buffalo, horses and donkeys, rabbits, feral birds too, such as mynahs and starlings, and perhaps most startling of all, dogs and cats. If you are a newcomer, do not approach 'pussycats' seen in the countryside with the same affectionate trust you might offer your best friend's pet cat. It could turn out to be a snarling tiger-like thing if it is a 'feral'. The heavier ferals, such as the buffalo, which love to wallow in muddy ground, and wild ponies, do immense damage to natural bush vegetation and soils, particularly in the case of hoofed animals.

Another legacy of thoughtless white Australia is the rabbit. Rabbits came with the First Fleet in 1788 but really took off when some new arrivals were imported in the mid-19th century. Their multiplication to near-plague proportions and the damage they can do to agriculture by devouring pastureland grasses provoked the erection of thousands of kilometres of 'rabbit-fences' across the land. The disease myxomatosis was introduced after World War II and successfully controlled the rabbits for some time, although now, the animals are developing resistance to the infection. The latest strategy has been deliberate introduction of rabbit calcivirus which miraculously does not harm any other Australian animals.

Still worse than the rabbit has been the European fox, which was introduced for nothing better than the pleasure of the hunt, in the 1840s. This predator has had a disastrous impact on Australia's many unique small mammals.

Toad Tales

One notorious introduction occurred in relatively recent times, to the nation's great shame: the cane toad, also known as the giant or Queensland toad, was introduced to northern Queensland in 1935, from its South American homeland via a stopover in Hawaii. Americans will be familiar with this creature. The idea was that the toad would control beetle pests in Queensland's economically important sugar cane plantations.

The toad in fact did not do this job very well, but spread widely across the north and began to eat native animals as well. Because this noxious beast has poison glands in its skin, it is also dangerous to native predators which may take a fancy to it.

Proving that human behaviour is any time more bizarre than any animal can produce, there are reports from the USA of drug fiends actually licking live cane toads for kicks afforded by its poison glands; in Australia, it is suggested that Queenslander drug-freaks may be smoking dried toad-skin as a hallucinogen.

Certainly, there is a mass of folklore surrounding the cane toad. In fact, the cane toad has become a cult object in Australia, regarded with perverse affection. A brilliantly hilarious and surprisingly informative, award-winning documentary called *Cane Toads* has been made. Hire it at your local video shop in Australia; this is a 'must-see' item of really offbeat Australiana. There is even an underground political newspaper in Queensland named after the toad and political satirists regularly cartoon unpopular Queenslander politicians as cane toads. Meanwhile the toad marches on and in 2009, even remote Western Australia was nervously eyeing its northern border as the cane toad invasion drew closer and closer.

The Thylacine that Got Away

One of the great zoological puzzles of Australia is the Thylacine, also known as the Tasmanian Tiger or the Marsupial Wolf, the largest carnivorous marsupial known to the world. It is extinct—or is it?

The last known tiger died in Hobart Zoo, Tasmania, in 1936. White settlers put a bounty on surviving tigers from about 1830 and shot it to extinction when it took to hunting their sheep.

But claims of sightings are regularly made today, often in south-western Western Australia, where the Thylacine may have roamed thousands of years ago—and one of these was seriously discussed and published in the eminent British science magazine, *The New Scientist*, during the 1980s. For the moment, searching for, and reporting on, the Thylacine remains one of Australia's more delightfully silly preoccupations – for a thriller movie based on exactly that idea, catch *The Hunter* (starring Willem Dafoe, and released some time 2011-2012). For your own expedition, it's just a pity that the A$1.5 million bounty offered in 2005 by the then national news weekly, *The Bulletin*, for a live capture is no longer on offer. But not content with waiting for this, some at the Australian Museum have actually been talking about cloning the Thylacine from a thylacine pup the Museum has preserved in alcohol, collected in 1866, thus bringing the creature back to life.

Sea, Surf, Sun

White Australians love the seas around their land even more actively than they do the land. Which is amazing, considering all the nasty things in those seas—sharks, crocodiles, jellyfish, sea snakes and so on. Unfortunately, there are also other man-made hazards nowadays: the waters off Sydney's famous Bondi Beach, for example, are badly polluted.

Australians who cannot swim are few and far between. So if you are a newcomer and cannot yet swim, start taking lessons to become one of the crowd.

Australian surf life-savers are one of the great macho images of the nation—muscled, bronzed and noble—and perhaps deservedly so. From its formation in 1907 up to 2011, more than 600,000 people had been saved by Surf Life Saving Australia, the country's largest volunteer organisation of its kind. This is vastly more than the Australian death toll in the two world wars.

The surfing fraternity in Australia has developed an elaborate subculture with its own language, publications and values. Do not let your young son get too involved in this essentially male, macho mystique if you want him to stay at school and pass exams.

Australians have a deep love for the sea. Many enjoy spending time at the beach, taking in the ocean air and the easy pace of life.

Dicing with Death

Expatriate Australian author John Pilger has said that it is the constant effort of peering through the sun that makes the Australian face look so 'laconic', with its lopsided smile and permanent squint. Certainly, there are a lot of glazed blue-grey eyes set in wrinkle-tracks to be seen in Australia (including Pilger's own).

Right up to the turn of the 20th century, the typical Australian exhibited a strong streak of paganism, laced with hedonism, when it came to beaches, stripping down at the slightest excuse to catch a suntan. Owning a tan has always been an essential part of the Australian Dream. There are beaches that allow women to indulge in bare-breasted 'topless' bathing, just to help the tanning process along, further bolstering the pagan image. You are not supposed to stare.

This culture survives but it is looking more and more antique as a new generation grows up that has been carefully trained at school to 'slip, slap, slop' sunblock cream liberally over their bodies, to swim in whole-body suits, and to don a large cap with a 'desert-fighter' or 'Foreign Legion' style protective flap hanging down the back of the neck. The message has got through that the sun-worshipping culture is dangerous.

And with good reason. Skin cancer is an ever-present bogey. The skin cancer rate in Australia is the highest in the world, three times that in the USA and six times that in Britain—skin cancers account for about 80 per cent of all new cancers diagnosed each year and the deadliest form of skin cancer, Melanoma, is the fourth most common cancer in the country, with more than 10,000 new cases every year. And it is in the younger active years that the foundation for cancer apparently is laid. Two in three Australians will develop skin cancer before the age of 70 and Australians are four times more likely to develop a skin cancer than any other cancer. Many Aussies sport deeply gouged, scarred arms where cancers have been cut out. I am told that some are sitting in hospital with their scalp-skin rolled down to graft into new noses or foreheads. Get more information at http://www.health.gov.au/internet/skincancer/publishing.nsf/Content/home

Australia is just too close to the infamous 'Ozone Hole' over the southern pole, and its classic blue skies do nothing to filter harmful ultra-violet (UV) rays. Fair skin, blue eyes (watch out for cataracts) and plentiful moles or freckles are high-risk factors. Apart from regularly applying water-resistant sun-block cream (with Sun Protection Factor or SPF 30 + or more) to exposed areas of your body, it is important to cover as much of your body as possible when outdoors, wear sunglasses and a hat. Avoid the sun between 10am and 3pm. Amazingly, you will still see many foolish Aussies working bare-chested in summer sun or baking half-naked on the beach, but don't follow in their footsteps. Hug the shade, with the proviso only that Vitamin D deficiencies are also not uncommon in Australia and you do need a few minutes of sun on the skin daily, at safe times, to promote that vital bone-constructing vitamin; if you are dark-skinned, you will need quite a bit more daily sun than a 'whitey' to accumulate Vitamin D.

The bad news is that it is also possible to get the worst form of skin cancer—melanoma—on parts of the body not exposed to the sun. The back is a danger spot, as few people can see what is going on there. Get a friend to check regularly for any obvious changes. The good news is that skin cancers are easily detected early—they are visible—and very curable, and because Australia is very aware of the problem, the survival rates there are among the highest in the world. Simply watch out for changes in your skin. Few skin cancers are painful. The most important thing is to train children in self-protection against the sun from an early age.

At the risk of sounding sexist, women particularly should avoid the Australian sun; the drying and wrinkling effect on the skin can age them by many years. One Aussie medic's test on a 25-year-old surfing life-saver at the beach, who had spent half his life on the beach, rated the youngster's skin with a medical age of 60.

When I am in Australia, I find I need extra moisturiser. Anyone who has lived in a humid tropical climate suffers from flaky skin when at first suddenly deprived of moisture in Australia. The most uncomfortable thing is the way your lips crack up; most Australians carry a stick of lip salve about with them to deal with this..

Needless to say, you also need very 'serious' sunglasses, the sort that really do filter harmful rays such as ultra-violet (i.e. offering 100 per cent UV absorption), fully polarised, of the cool-dude 'wrap-around' design (about 35 per cent of UV light creeps in around the sides of most 'sunnies'), preferably with an endorsement sticker from the Cancer Council Australia and an 'EPF' (Eye Protection Factor) of 10 (= 99 per cent protection). Note that there is some argument about how early and how much children should wear sunglasses though; they may need some exposure to UV in order to develop protection against it.

The fun part of sun protection is the typically Australian penchant for hats. For real protection, you need a broad-brimmed one, but within that parameter, there are so many wonderful choices, from 'dinky-di' Aussie bushranger hats, with the famous Akubra at the pinnacle of the genre, to charming straw hats with bedecked ribbons and applique flowers, and huge confections for special occasions like the Melbourne Cup race day, weddings or a classy picnic. (The elite's favourite, the whimsical, flimsy 'fascinator', an apology for a hat, won't offer you any sun protection – see the Melbourne Cup picture between pp 276-277. I'd never heard of a fascinator before coming to Australia, but you see them everywhere at the nation's 'blue ribbon' (top-notch) social events).

Atoning for Past Sins

Just as white Australia has a debt to repay to the Aboriginals, so it also has quite a bit of explaining to do about what it has done to the Australian environment. In both areas, a severe case of guilty conscience is tangible throughout the nation.

Through the combined ravages of habitat clearance, mining extraction and introduced predators and competitors, at least 20 native species of animals have been lost during the period of European settlement. About 65 species, close to a quarter of the total, are still considered under threat.

Although Australia to the casual observer seems a wild and largely untouched land, it is in fact dreadfully scarred by the hand of humankind. Groundwater has been polluted by chemicals; more than half the land requires soil-rehabilitation measures to combat salinity, acidification and erosion.

In reaction to the past, the average young Australian or schoolchild is now well versed in basic environmentalist responsibilities. Small children will lecture you on not using plastic bags, or on recycling aluminium 'tinnies'. (South Australia was the first state to announce a total ban on the use of plastic bags, operable by 2008, and the signs are that this ruling may soon spread through the whole nation, to combat the difficulties of plastic-bag disposal and the threat such bags allegedly pose to wildlife).

Supermarket shelves are crammed with 'environmentally friendly' goods, including items such as non-phosphate, biodegradable washing powders and dishwashing liquids, and recycled, unbleached toilet rolls or tissue packs. (A wry cartoon by Aussie Mark Lynch has two elderly suburban housewives peering suspiciously at the recycled-paper toilet rolls and remarking doubtfully, 'I don't think my Eric would be too keen on toilet paper that's been used before.') At the checkout counter, they will pack your purchases in paper bags if possible (others may charge for plastic bags). Many responsible shoppers now make a point of taking their own, canvas or woven, shopping bags to substitute for supermarket plastic bags.

Every neighbourhood has its sorted recycling bins for glass, cans, newspapers, old clothing, etc. Local councils arrange for sorted garbage pick-ups, gardening groups teach you how to compost organic waste. There is nothing you cannot recycle if you want to.

Australia was one of the first countries to outlaw leaded petrol and ozone-depleting chlorofluorocarbons (CFCs), and is a leader in substituting the much cleaner liquefied petroleum gas (LPG) for conventional gasoline in vehicles, over about a quarter of the transportation sector. The country is of course a major LPG producer.

Solar energy is another exciting form of alternative fuel—a fifth of Western Australian households use solar water heaters, a figure growing to almost three-quarters in the sunny Northern Territory, but overall the national penetration rate is surprisingly low, below 10 per cent.

Australia's Labor government ratified the Kyoto 'Greenhouse Gas' Treaty in December 2007, but climate change and renewable energy remain hotly contested battlefields in Australia: get some background from the seminal *Garnaut Climate Change Review* (2008) and its 2011 Update by respected Australian economist and former Ambassador, Professor Ross Garnaut, at www.garnautreview.org.au/

A Darker Shade of Green

Over the past three decades, a vociferous, energetic and sometimes militant 'Green' movement has grown up to wield considerable political power in Australia. No Australian politician can really afford to adopt an obviously 'un-Green' position nowadays.

Almost every day, it seems, running battles are fought between environmentalists and mining companies, sawmill and plywood companies, housing and tourism developers, and so on. The 'greens' will man barricades, harass nuclear or fishing vessels in port, tie themselves to trees, bury themselves up to the neck in the ground before advancing bulldozers, you name it. They are committed, serious, and emotional. Unfortunately, the atmosphere often is one of confrontation rather than discussion.

The major conservationist players are the Australian Conservation Foundation (ACF), the Wilderness Society (born in Tasmania, now national), and Greenpeace, particularly active on issues like whale and dolphin protection and nuclear energy, as well as the state-based Conservation Councils.

There are myriad other groups at the state and local levels, besides many less politicised nature-rambling clubs.

Environmentalist politicians such as Tasmania's Senator Bob Brown, recently retired leader and a key founder of the Australian Greens Party, established in 1992, cut their teeth on a number of issues, but most notably on the Franklin River controversy of the early 1980s. The federal Labor Party's support for the environmentalist position on the proposed dam on the Franklin River, one of Tasmania's most dramatic wilderness regions, swung the 'green vote' behind it at the 1983 elections which brought it to power—the dam was scotched. The green lobby also succeeded in getting the north Queensland rainforest and Kakadu National Park in the Northern Territory declared World Heritage sites. Battles are still periodically fought over the uranium mining potential in Kakadu.

SURVIVAL SENSE

Survival in Australia's remote outback and deserts is a skill that really needs to be learned; there are courses and many good handbooks to help you do so. Although the Australian environment is unique, basic survival techniques are much the same as those taught elsewhere, be it the USA, Canada, England or Asia. However, one or two tips may help the casual camper, driver or hiker who finds him or herself in a tight situation.

The 2010 federal election that confirmed Julia Gillard as Labor Prime Minister after her dramatic earlier ousting of Kevin Rudd (who then accepted the lesser post of Foreign Minister) brought a hung Parliament. The balance of power in the House of Representatives lay with a cluster of four Independents, one National Party and one Green member of parliament. Three Independents and the one Green then helped Gillard to form a fragile minority government. In the Upper House – the Senate – nine Greens hold the balance of power and can therefore amend or reject any proposed new legislation. This has given the federal Australian Greens Party under new leader Christine Milne much more say than in their previous policing/monitoring, or 'keep the bastards honest', role. As a result, Green policies perforce have dominated the Labor government's deliberations.

This was most evident in the excoriating debate during 2010-2011 of the so-called 'Carbon Tax' (really Carbon Pricing) or Clean Energy legislation, passed in November 2011 for implementation in July 2012 and intended for a three-year warm-up period before a proper Emissions Trading Scheme (ETS) is substituted. The new laws are still threatened by the Liberal Party Opposition under leader Tony Abbott (suspected by many of being a closet 'climate-change sceptic'). Abbott says he will overturn the Clean Energy laws together with their eventual evolution to an ETS if he gets in at the next election (a likely prospect). Under the new Act, carbon pollution producers will pay a price of A$23 per tonne of carbon emitted, incrementally increasing annually up to 2015, when the carbon-trading ETS market kicks in. That Australia has taken this radical step before major polluters such as the USA, China and India, has been hugely controversial. Ordinary Aussies fear the likely increased costs, particularly in domestic energy-usage bills, despite promised cash compensation for the vulnerable. But the Gillard government hopes that the new Act will drive polluters to seek out cleaner and higher-technology, renewable energy sources to replace carbon-culprits such as coal.

Fire

First, never go bush-walking if the newspapers, radio and television tell you there is a 'High' fire alert or a total fire-lighting ban. Leave longer walks till after summer is over.

If caught in a bush fire, do not panic, and do not run if you can avoid it—fires are anytime faster than you. Especially, do not run uphill, which is exactly the way fires love to go. Take shelter where you can to avoid radiated heat (more dangerous than flames or smoke), for instance in a depression such as a vehicle wheel-rut, and cover yourself with a blanket, or even just soil.

This may be hard to believe, but your chances of survival are far higher if you *stay* in your car or your house than if you run from them, even if fire is approaching. And that does not mean driving off in your car—the majority of the 2005 bushfire deaths in South Australia, for example, were of people trying to drive away from the fire.

The evidence is that your car's petrol tank will *not* explode. You need only survive the climax of the fire passing over you—a maximum of four minutes. If you panic and run, you not only get exhausted, but radiated heat will kill you. Lie low and *cover yourself*. Read more, e.g.

- www.fesa.wa.gov.au/safetyinformation/fire/bushfire/pages/travelinformation.aspx
- www.dse.vic.gov.au/fire-and-other-emergencies/teachers-and-students/publications/brochures-and-fire-notes/traveller-safety-information

The most dreadful news about wildfires in Australia is that about half of them, around 30,000 fires a year, are caused by wilful arsonists deliberately setting the bush alight, whether for their amusement or out of mental illness. The Australian Institute of Criminology publicised these figures in 2009 and also calculated that fires set by arsonists were costing the community about A$1.6 billion a year.

Snakes

First, wear long trousers and closed shoes when hiking; second do not go near snakes or provoke them.

If bitten, do not perform the old macho ritual of slashing the bite with a razor blade to bleed it and tying a tight tourniquet between the bite and the heart. This is potentially dangerous. Tight tourniquets (which should be released every 30 minutes) are used only for funnel-web spider, blue-ringed octopus and box jellyfish cases.

The important thing is to act quickly and apply firm pressure with a crepe bandage wound extensively around the bitten area; use a piece of shirt if there is no bandage. To hold the bitten limb immobile, it should be splinted using a strong stick, binding the splint over the bandage. The patient must be kept very still.

Bush Ticks

These are common in the wetter parts of the East. Their bite is not fatal but can make you very ill (e.g. Tick Typhus fever and partial paralysis).

Do not try to pull the tick out—you may create a septic wound. Just touch the tick with a hot match head, or dab it with kerosene or methylated spirit. As it backs out of your flesh, seize it with fingers or tweezers, taking care to pull the head out, not just the body.

It is possible not to know that a tick has visited you. If you have any problem walking or with body co-ordination after hiking in the bush, see your doctor. The tick may have left, but not its poison.

Leeches

Relatively harmless in themselves, leeches are bloodsuckers and may leave small open wounds which could get infected. They are found chiefly in wet areas, like rainforests. Keep bite-wounds clean. You can deter leeches with rub-on insect-repellents, but they are quite easy to remove with a touch of salt or tobacco.

Bush-Walking

You are safest if you have taken a course in map-reading. However, compasses and maps do not survival make; they can even go wrong. Ultimately, you will be thrown back on your own common sense, and whether or not you have prepared wisely.

Even in the apparently meek and mild temperate forests of the south, you must take care. For example, there is a rather horrible thing called horizontal scrub, in which vegetation has bent over and layered itself horizontally into a springy 'floor' which may in reality be several feet above the true forest floor. The unsuspecting hiker could fall through this mass and might find it very difficult to get out.

You must have with you a good water container, and preferably water too, of course. Some means of making fire should be with you. Beware of the 'I'm just going for half a day, why bother with food and water and medical kits' syndrome. If you get lost, you are really in trouble without food and water. Always carry at least some, no matter how short you intend your walk. In high temperatures, you may need about 5 litres of water a day—but do not drink unless you really need to. There is evidence that excessive drinking while walking or otherwise exercising only makes things worse. Sometimes just moistening your lips will do.

If you decide to go exploring, make sure you leave word with someone on where you are going and when you will be back.

Of course, if you have studied 'bush tucker' with the Aboriginals, you may be able to live off the land in an emergency. But better play safe and carry food ...

You should particularly be ready for violent weather changes, common in southern areas like Tasmania, but also encountered elsewhere. Sudden drops in temperature are the greatest threat.

Water purification tablets, salt, wool or string (to mark a path taken), a plastic groundsheet (which can be spread over a sunlit pit packed with vegetation around a centrally placed container, weighted with a stone over the container, and thus used to collect condensation water in the container overnight), a torch, a knife—these could all be useful. But don't take so much that it becomes a misery to carry your pack!

Geography the shape of the land itself is one of the several pillars propping up the Australian sense of self and nation; the others include history and race/culture.

Put the essentials in a body belt, always with you. It is no good having a first-aid kit if you have left it behind in your pack at camp.

If you are lost, leave messages as you walk or at your camp if you leave it—scratched in the earth, for instance. Light a smoky fire to guide rescue aircraft. Construct an SOS message with each letter at least 2.5 metres high so aircraft can see it. But before all this, whenever you go 'off the beaten track', walking or driving, leave your intended itinerary and return date with someone, such as the local park ranger, policeman, hotelier or pub-owner and stick to your timetable, so that there is someone to worry when you don't get back on time.

Last of all, don't worry, it won't happen. Take no notice of all this and do go bush-walking! It is one of the best reasons for being in Australia.

A SENSE OF NATION

Australians know how to laugh at themselves, as I have said. But try laughing at them as an outsider and you will find the ground rules have suddenly shifted beneath your feet. Such sensitivity is not unusual in young nations—and white Australia's 200 years or so *is* still young in the history of nations.

Get Wise about Gallipoli

I have said that anything is fair game when it comes to Australian humour: from cripples to Christ on the Cross. This is true. But not Gallipoli, or 'the Anzacs'...

Gallipoli? You will certainly have to get wise about Gallipoli if you wish to penetrate the Australian psyche. Anyway, you only have to stay long enough in Australia to hit the Anzac Day national holiday on 25 April to understand its importance.

No matter how small the Australian town you may chance upon on 25 April, you can be sure there will be an Anzac Day parade around the local war memorial, complete with emotional speeches, brass bands and little boys clutching their fathers' hands, both wearing the traditional cocked Digger slouch hat. ('Digger' has been the name for an Aussie soldier since World War I, but nobody seems to know for sure why, possibly because so many Aussies were miners of Australia's considerable mineral resources, including gold.)

Gallipoli was the site of a great battle during World War I, in Turkey. The only thing is, like Dunkirk, France, in World War II, it was a great defeat and retreat, not a great victory.

The British, who still remember the evacuation from the beaches of Dunkirk with pride, and perhaps the Americans, who similarly still remember non-victories like Custer's Last Stand against the Sioux Indians in the 19th century or MacArthur's retreat from the Philippines during World War II, may perhaps empathise with the Australian celebration of failure at Gallipoli.

For others, particularly 'face'-conscious Asians, it may take a little longer to get the hang of things. You may as well hear the whole story now, from me. It will save you some mystification later, when the great 25 April fuss hits you via the newspapers, television and radio. As columnist Max Harris has commented in *The Weekend Australian*: 'Australians regard an honestly won failure as the essence of success. We're a weird mob.'

Anzac Day commemorates the terrible trials of the Anzacs—the Australian and New Zealand Army Corps—in their attempts to scale and control the rugged sea-cliffs at Gallipoli, from the landing date, 25 April 1915, until their withdrawal on 19 December that year. During this time, 8,000 or so Australians (and more than 2,000 New Zealanders, as well as French soldiers and others) were killed, and 19,000 Australians were wounded. Their bravery in the face of hopeless odds won the Australian soldier an enduring reputation thereafter, to this day—one reconfirmed elsewhere, as at the battle for Singapore in 1942 and since then in Vietnam (1960s), Iraq and Afghanistan. In 2009, Mark Donaldson of the Special Air Services won Australia's first Victoria Cross for 40 years, for conspicuous acts of gallantry while under fire in Afghanistan. But by November 2011, a total of 32 Australian soldiers on the Afghan front were dead, 200 wounded, and still counting.

The real significance of Gallipoli lies not so much in the nobility of the Australians' dogged courage in attempting the almost impossible, nor in their legendary 'mateship' unto death, but rather in the fact that they were fighting for, and obeying orders from, the Imperial British government. This despite the fact that Australia had announced its intention to become independent of Great Britain in 1900 and had proclaimed the Commonwealth of Australia in 1901, holding the first federal elections that same year.

The sense of abandonment experienced at Gallipoli—it was all British war leader Winston Churchill's fault—saw the beginning of the end for Australian ties with the 'mother country', Britain. Australian director Peter Weir's epic film of 1981, *Gallipoli*, conveys this well: find a video of it if you can.

Underlying the Gallipoli celebration each year then, are not anti-Turkish feelings (on the contrary, the fashion nowadays is for survivors of both sides to embrace one another), but strong anti-British sentiment, and a feeling of 'To hell with all the others.'

The historic animosity for the British felt by the Irish, who formed a large part of Australia's original convict settlers, has reinforced this feeling. (Britons, beware of telling your favourite Irish joke in Australia before you ascertain your host's family origins). Gallipoli crystallised a sense of nation; hence its sacred-cow status when it comes to acceptable jokes. The Aussie is his own person, no Englishman in disguise, his country 24 times the size of the British Isles.

This said, some dissenting voices however have been raised against the Anzac mythology: take a look at the brave book *What's Wrong With Anzac?* by Marilyn Lake, Henry Reynolds, with Mark McKenna and Joy Damousi (New South Books, 2010).

HISTORICAL MILESTONES

Even in the 16th century, many Western explorers were convinced that 'a Great South Land' existed. Several among them found parts of Australia but did not recognise the significance of their discoveries: Dutchman Willem Jansz around Cape York Peninsula in 1606, his compatriot Dick Hartog off Western Australia in 1616, and another Dutchman, Abel Tasman, who discovered Tasmania in 1642. Others include Englishman William Dampier off the north-west coast in 1688, and Willem de Vlamingh, who discovered Perth's Swan River in 1696.

1770 ▪ Englishman Captain James Cook lands at Botany Bay and calls the eastern coastline New South Wales.

1788 ▪ The First Fleet arrives at Botany Bay under the command of Governor Arthur Phillip, with the first convict settlers from the British Isles—548 males, 188 females.

1793 ▪ Arrival of the first free settlers.

1828 ▪ First census shows 36,000 convicts and free settlers, as well as 2,549 soldiers.

Eureka!

Few outsiders have heard of the 'Eureka Stockade' incident of 1854, but most Australians are well aware of its significance in their political history. The incident is an icon of the left wing and socialist Australia, and considered to be one of the sparks that lit up Australian democracy. You can compare its meaning to that of the Storming of the Bastille for the French or the Battle of the Alamo for the Americans.

'We swear by the Southern Cross to stand truly by each other and fight to defend our rights and liberties', was the oath sworn by thousands of gold diggers gathered in protest at Ballarat, Victoria, in 1854. 'It is the inalienable right of every citizen to have a voice in making the laws he is called on to obey... taxation without representation is tyranny', the diggers declared, demanding the vote they did not have and opposing property-owning qualifications for members of Parliament. The gold diggers' uprising may well be the original reason for Aussie fighters or soldiers earning the proudly boasted name 'Diggers'. But in fact, the 25,000 diggers living at Ballarat were a multicultural lot, including immigrants from America, Ireland, Europe and China, among other places, very few of them born in Australia.

It was the rebellious diggers who adopted the Southern Cross flag as their emblem and flew it for the first time in Australia; today the Southern Cross constellation of stars is a motif integral to the national flag. You can see the diggers' original flag still proudly displayed at the Ballarat Fine Art Gallery today. Protesters for various causes occasionally still coopt the simple Southern Cross flag to their cause even today.

The Eureka Stockade was a justified gold diggers' rebellion against petty and oppressive government authority and as such it stands for the tradition of Australian resistance to authority in general. The officials governing the early Victorian goldfields were cruel in their exercise of elite power and privilege, oppressive and corrupt in their arbitrary policing and farming of the gold-digging licences.

The actual process of extracting the gold was particularly gruelling and uncertain. After a series of brutal incidents between the diggers and their oppressors, thousands of diggers rose up and declared 'war'. Led by Peter Lalor, the most militant of them marched to a predominantly Irish area called 'The Eureka' and proceeded to fortify it behind a wooden stockade. But with only a few hundred men behind the stockade on 3 December 1854, government troops made short work of their flimsy defences, rounding the stockaders up, killing 20–30 diggers and quickly declaring martial law. However, the incident was seen as a turning point in the development of Australian democracy; 13 arrested stockaders were acquitted in court in 1855, a Commission of Enquiry castigated the administration of the goldfields, and in a short time most of the miners' demands were granted, including their inclusion in parliamentary democracy. Peter Lalor was even elected to Parliament.

1840	■ Abolition of transportation of convicts to New South Wales.
1851	■ First discovery of gold, New South Wales.
1876	■ Death of Truganini, the last full-blooded Tasmanian Aboriginal.
1883	■ Silver discovered at Broken Hill, New South Wales.
1900	■ The Australian states federated; Australia announces intention to become independent from Britain.
1901	■ Census counts 3.8 million (white) population.
1902	■ Women get the vote at federal elections.
1908	■ Canberra chosen as the federal capital.
1914	■ World War I declared, Australian troops embark for Europe.
1915	■ Australian and New Zealander soldiers land at Gallipoli on 25 April but are evacuated by 18 December.
1920	■ White population now 5.4 million, according to official figures.
1932	■ Sydney Harbour Bridge opened.
1940	■ Australian troops detailed for service abroad in World War II.
1942	■ Darwin in the Northern Territory bombed by the Japanese, and Japanese submarines enter Sydney Harbour.
1947	■ Australia's new drive for immigration begins, focusing mainly on Britain and Europe at first.
1949	■ Australian citizenship comes into being and is granted to all Australians.
	■ Robert Menzies' Liberal government comes into power.
1952	■ Discovery of uranium in the Northern Territory.
1956	■ The Olympic Games held in Melbourne.
1961	■ Iron ore deposits found at Pilbara, Western Australia.
1964	■ Australia's first truly national newspaper, *The Australian*, is born.
	■ National Service was introduced, a two-year scheme. For the first time, army conscripts could also be sent anywhere, opening up the possibility of their participation in Australia's Vietnam War commitments.

The Round House, 1831, Fremantle, Western Australia. Old prison legacy from Britain.

1965 ▪ Australian infantry battalion sent to Vietnam.
  ▪ Aboriginal student activist Charles Perkins organises a seminal University of Sydney students' bus tour (known as "The Freedom Ride") of neglected, impoverished aboriginal settlements in country towns of New South Wales, exposing and filming endemic racism, also violent racial hostility from local whites, shocking the nation. The tour mirrored civil rights movements in the USA, raised consciousness, and set the scene for future reforms.

1966 ▪ Prime Minister Sir Robert Menzies, Australia's longest-serving leader (1939–1966, except for 1941–1949), retires.
  ▪ Decimal currency is introduced and the metric system of weights and measures phased in.

1967 ▪ Australians vote in a referendum to abolish all forms of discrimination against the Aboriginals.
  ▪ Convicted gambler-thief Ronald Ryan is the last person to be hanged in Australia, for stabbing a prison warder to death when trying to escape, provoking enormously emotional public protest and street demonstrations against the sentence.

The 'Great War' of 1914, World War I, traumatised, and shaped the Australian nation, as symbolised by this War Memorial at King's Park Botanical Gardens in Perth, Western Australia.

- Prime Minister Harold Holt disappears at sea off Victoria.
1968
- John Gorton, Liberal Party leader, becomes prime minister of Australia.
1969
- Bob Hawke is elected president of the Australian Council of Trade Unions (ACTU).
- Women are granted equal pay for equal work.
1972
- Labor Party wins elections under the leadership of Gough Whitlam, after 23 years in opposition, riding on the public's desire for change, and the slogan 'It's Time'.
- The 'White Australia' policy is formally ended.
- Conscription for military service is abolished in favour of a small professional volunteer army.
1973
- 18-year-olds get the vote.
- Queen Elizabeth II of Great Britain to be known as 'Queen of Australia'.
- The Sydney Opera House opens, 16 years after the initial design had been selected.
1974
- Cyclone Tracy hits Darwin in the Northern Territory on Christmas Day with wind speeds of up to 300 kmph, and inflicts terrible devastation (at least

50 deaths, 30,000 evacuated), requiring complete rebuilding of the town.

1975 ■ Dismissal of the Whitlam government by Governor-General Sir John Kerr. Malcolm Fraser's Liberal-Country Party coalition government takes power.

1979 ■ Aboriginal Land Trust now has title to 144 properties, former Aboriginal reserves.

■ ACTU calls second general strike in Australia's history.

1980 ■ Campbell Inquiry into Australian financial system.

■ Nugan Hand Bank collapses.

1982 ■ The Franklin Dam controversy erupts in Tasmania, Australia's biggest-ever 'Green' battle.

1983 ■ Prime Minister Malcolm Fraser is granted a double dissolution of Parliament, followed by an election for both houses. The Labor Party takes power under the leadership of Bob Hawke.

■ 'Ash Wednesday' bush fires devastate South Australia and Victoria—75 dead, 8,000 homeless.

■ Australia wins the America's Cup with its yacht *Australia II*.

■ Australia's first AIDS death – in late 2010, an estimated 21,000 Australians of all ages were living with the HIV virus that can lead to AIDS.

■ In December, the Australian dollar is floated for free trading, for the first time

1984 ■ Government, business and union leaders sign the 'Accord' on prices and income policy.

■ Control of Ayers Rock ('Uluru') is given to the Aboriginals of the area.

1985 ■ The Federal Treasury, as part of general financial deregulation, allows 16 foreign banks to apply for banking licences.

1986 ■ Queen Elizabeth II of Great Britain signs a proclamation while in Australia which finally clears the way for Australia's severance from the United Kingdom, expressed in the Australia Act of the same year.

■ The movie *Crocodile Dundee*, starring Paul Hogan, becomes the highest-earning film in Australian history and also the highest-earning foreign film to be shown in the USA.

1987 ■ Labor retains power at federal elections.

1988 ■ White Australians celebrate the bicentennial anniversary of the arrival of Britain's First Fleet, while Aboriginals stage a massive protest against this celebration of the white 'invasion' of Australia.

1990 ■ Labor again retains power at the federal elections.

1991 ■ In December, a coup in the ALP's inner circle ('Caucus') results in Bob Hawke's ouster by Paul Keating, as the government gears up for a tough fight in the 1993 federal elections.

1996 ■ In March, the electorate ends 13 years of ALP rule and returns John Howard's liberal government.

1997 ■ Bushfires rage across the nation.
 ■ A 370-day royal commission ends its investigation into police corruption.

1998 ■ An economic crisis in Asia and political turmoil in Indonesia adversely affect Australia's economy and psyche.

1999 ■ Federal Parliament declares the nation's 'deep and sincere regret' over past ill treatment of Aborigines, but avoids the explicit apology many Aboriginals and other Australians expect.
 ■ Historic referendum on becoming a Republic with a Parliament-appointed President replacing the Queen gets a 55 per cent 'No' vote, and the Constitutional Monarchy stays.
 ■ Australia's relationship with and role in Asia changes with Australian initiation and leadership of the United Nations-mandated Interfet peacekeeping force in newly independent, formerly Indonesian territory of East Timor.

2000 ■ On 1 July, controversial major tax reforms, including a new 10 per cent Goods and Services Tax (GST), come into force.
 ■ In September, Sydney hosts the Olympic Games and soon-to-be Gold Medallist, Aboriginal track athlete Cathy Freeman has the honour of lighting

the Olympic flame.

2001 ■ Australian cricketing icon Sir Don Bradman dies on 25 February at the age of 92.

■ The Norwegian *Tampa* vessel loaded with rescued refugees seeking asylum in Australia becomes a *cause celebre* used by the Liberal Howard government to capitalise on Australians' fear of outsiders and so ensure its own re-election with an increased majority at the Federal General Election on 10 November.

■ Prime Minister John Howard is visiting Washington, USA, when terrorist group Al-Qaeda destroys the twin towers of the World Trade Centre with hijacked aircraft; the emotions of the moment influence a subsequent much stronger Australian commitment to the traditional alliance with the USA.

■ The 66-year-old Ansett Australia domestic airline folds, shocking the nation and taking with it 16,000 direct employees' jobs.

2002 ■ On 12 October, the nation is traumatised by Indonesian terrorists' bombing of Kuta nightspots on Bali island frequented by Australians and other foreigners, killing 202 people of whom 164 were foreign nationals, including 88 Australians, and injuring another 209.

2003 ■ Australia's population passes the 20 million mark.

■ In March, the invasion of Iraq by mostly US and British forces is backed by Prime Minister John Howard, who commits Australian troops to the Iraq War.

2005 ■ Australians are horrified to witness another terrorist bombing incident on Bali island in Indonesia, targeting two separate tourist areas and killing 20, including four Australians, with another 19 Australians among the 129 injured.

2007 ■ By end-June, Australia's population has passed the 21 million mark.

■ In the run-up to a federal election, PM Howard's Liberal government launches the drastic Northern Territory Emergency Response (known as 'The Intervention') in 73 allegedly dysfunctional

Aboriginal settlements within the Territory, sending in the army after reports of widespread child abuse in the settlements; the Intervention, since modified but still supported by the current Labor government, includes many dramatic measures such as suspension of welfare payments, the compulsory acquisition of Aboriginal town lands, and alcohol supply restrictions. The move is labelled hasty, racist, punitive and paternalistic by many.

- November 24 sees the Federal General Election that ends the seven years of Liberal party Prime Minister John Howard's government, voted out in favour of Kevin Rudd's new Labor government.

2008
- On 13 February, Parliament opens with the historic occasion of government's formal Apology to the indigenous peoples of Australia for past wrongs, led by Labor Prime Minister Kevin Rudd.
- On 9 November, three of the terrorist Bali Bombers are executed by firing squad.

2009
- In February, Australia's worst bushfires ever recorded rage across 272,000 hectares of the state of Victoria, taking 173 lives, destroying more than 2,000 houses and causing an estimated A$4.4-billion worth of damage. Known as 'Black Saturday.'

2010
- In June, Labor PM Kevin Rudd is replaced by his deputy, Julia Gillard. She moves to a general election in August that results in a hung Parliament, and is forced to form a minority government dependent on Independent and Greens representatives.
- Australia's population reaches 22.5 million at the end of the year. Net migration accounted for more than half of the increase.

2011
- Serious flooding in the New Year causes an estimated A$1-billion worth of damage and impacts almost a quarter of a million people in 70 towns, killing 35, chiefly in the state of Queensland. This is closely followed by floods in Victoria causing A$2-billion of damage.

- In October-November, the world's eyes are on Australia, first when the Commonwealth Heads of Government (CHOGM) summit takes place in Perth, Western Australia, and then when US President Barack Obama visits the country for an intense 27 hours, making an internationally important speech on his intention to refocus US foreign policy on the Asia-Pacific region, with Australia as an important partner. The policy includes escalation of US military involvement in the region, with 250 marines based at Darwin in the Northern Territory, eventually growing to 2,500 troops, and more US ships calling into Western Australian ports. Many believe, despite US and Australian protestations, that this is all about containment of a rising China.

- At the end of October, major industrial disputes within the once-national airline carrier Qantas climax with Qantas grounding its entire fleet worldwide for three days, despite the presence of world leaders in Australia for the CHOGM summit. The disputes go to arbitration but the airline's future is unclear, and likely to be overseas, in Asia.

- In October-November, Parliament passes the historic 'Carbon Tax' or Clean Energy legislation, capping a lengthy and bitter Climate Change argument; the equally contentious Mineral Resources Rent Tax, previously known as the 'Super-Profits Tax', also goes through the lower house – this means that at last the big mining companies' huge profits from Australia's valuable non-renewable resources such as iron ore (mostly sold to China, and India) during the recent mining boom can be harnessed to the permanent national good by dint of a special mining tax at the federal level (as opposed to the value- or quantum-based royalties already rendered by miners to the States in which they operate).

A JIGSAW NATION

Few outsiders realise that Australia was for long no more than a collection of separately autonomous colonies. Nationhood is still a very new thing.

To make matters worse, internal communications and understanding have been hampered both by the geography of a harsh and huge terrain, almost 4,000 km (2,500 miles) from east to west, over 3,000 km (1,864 miles) north to south, and by economic stupidities that make internal transport costs as high as going overseas for a holiday.

The remnants of that early colonial structure, still expressed in the independence of the six state governments, are only now being broken down. For example, only in 1991 was a decision taken to form national bodies which would standardise legal procedures, electrical power, road systems, and the gauge used on railway lines across the country. But whether all of this will actually materialise is still in doubt. Inter-state differences have been a great block to economic progress, and to crime-busting too, for many years.

Protectionist measures block eastern potatoes reaching Western Australia, among many other examples of interstate quirks. There is a federal policy to increase competition but some states are only being dragged kicking and screaming towards that goal.

Electricians, plumbers, doctors and lawyers needed licences to work outside their home states. A rail cargo container sent east-west from Sydney to Perth was subject to four changes of locomotive, five safe working systems, six sizes of loading gauge and had to spend 12 hours at sidings for crew changes and inspections.

The states can raise some of their own revenue by taxation but their power to collect state-based income tax was grabbed by federal legislation in 1942; the Federal Government generally raises the equivalent of 80 per cent of all government spending. Regular 'blues' (fights') between the federal and state governments over a beast called 'horizontal fiscal equalisation' or the distribution of federal monies to the states, nowadays mostly in the shape of federal GST (Goods and Services Tax) revenue, are a routine feature

Different Standards

For years until 1991, sausages had differing content regulations in different states, preventing their inter-state sale. Quite often, a single product had to wear different labels and packaging in each different state. There were three definitions of bread; one state demanded that margarine be sold only in cube-shaped packages.

of the Australian political and economic landscape.

THE SPIRITUAL AUSSIE

Adherence to formal religion, especially to the church-going brand of Christianity often claimed as the 'bedrock' of Australian society by conservatives ranging from John Howard to Pauline Hanson, is declining noticeably in Australia. About 64 per cent of the population claims to be Christian but church attendance is far lower than you would expect from that figure— and looking at some of the congregations, you could be forgiven for believing that the churches only survive by grace of a large number of devoted Christians of immigrant origin, particularly from Asia. Recruitment of the younger generation is not really happening. In 2005, the number of Catholics attending Mass at Perth churches in Western Australia had fallen to its lowest level in 25 years, with less than one third of Catholics attending Mass on weekends, while the local Anglican churches were considering holding services on days other than Sundays in order to fit in with families' social and work timetables and combat declining attendance. The Catholics in Perth even went so far as to take an advertisement in the local paper *The West Australian* to cajole believers back into church. Nationwide, non-Christian religions are growing faster than Christianity and now account for 5.6 per cent of Australians (2006 Census). In the decade 1996–2006, the fastest growing faith was Hinduism, which doubled its adherents to make up 0.7 per cent of the nation, and Buddhism which also doubled and accounted for over 2 per cent of the population. Significantly, 19 per cent of Australia now professes no attachment to any religion, up 2 per cent on the 1996 figure and compared with only 7 per cent in 1971. Adherents to non-Christian religions are also more numerous in Sydney and Melbourne than anywhere else in Australia.

How Aussies See Themselves

When the Liberal Prime Minister John Howard proposed a new Preamble to the Constitution as a secondary question with the Republic Referendum on 6 November 1999 (more on this in 'The British' section), Australians roundly rejected it.

Nonetheless, the text of this ill-fated document offers some interesting insights into Australian perspective of themselves and their nation today. It was controversial in its incorporation of Aboriginal ties with the land (likely to repeated soon in a new Constitutional draft), and of the migrant contribution and in enshrining not only the concept of God but also that of 'mateship':

'With hope in God, the Commonwealth of Australia is constituted by the equal sovereignty of all its citizens.

The Australian nation is woven together of people from many ancestries and arrivals. Our vast island continent has helped to shape the destiny of our Commonwealth and the spirit of its people.

From time immemorial our land has been inhabited by Aborigines and Torres Strait Islanders who are honoured for their ancient and continuing cultures.

In every generation immigrants have brought great enrichment to our nation's life.

Australians are free to be proud of their country and heritage, free to realise themselves as individuals, and free to pursue their hopes and ideals. We value excellence as well as fairness, independence as dearly as mateship.

Australia's democratic and federal system of government exists under law to preserve and protect all Australians in an equal dignity which may never be infringed by prejudice or fashion or ideology nor invoked against achievement.

In this spirit we, the Australian people, commit ourselves to this Constitution.'

That Christian Anglo-Celtic' stereotype of Australians that even some Aussies still harbour about themselves is really wearing thin these days.

HOW AUSSIES SEE SOME OF 'THE OTHERS'

Chapters One and Two touch on some stereotyped images of Australia and Australians. In their attempt to define their own identity when it comes to other nationalities, races, creeds and cultures, obviously the Australians too harbour their own stereotypes of 'the outsider'. Understanding these may help you position yourself better when relating to Australians.

The French

There has been great hostility to the French among Australians, based mainly on France's nuclear facilities on Australia's doorstep and a general suspicion that the French are untrustworthy. Paradoxically, amid this debate, little has been said or remembered of British nuclear tests inside Australia between 1852 and 1958.

While this Francophobia is yet another legacy of Australia's British heritage, some of it stems from the famous Australian 'cultural cringe'—a feeling of inferiority when confronted with alleged European sophistication, history, culture and what-have-you. So when an Australian reviles 'the frogs', he is only getting his own back for being made to feel small because he cannot cope with a French menu. But nowadays, there is a bit of a grin behind all this abuse, and one senses that the jibing is a lot more affectionate in essence now than it used to be, that there is now more admiration for what is generally perceived as French 'style'.

The tone can sink low at times. A heading in *The Weekend Australian* (25–28 September 1993) read simply 'The Bloody French'.

The British

Better known to Australians as Poms or Pommies (believed to derive from POHM–Prisoner of Her Majesty—in reference to Britain's convict past in Australia), the British are more usually referred to as Pommy Bastards or Whingeing Poms. Aussies believe that the British specialise in the art of whingeing (which means griping, complaining or moaning) and have taken it to a high level as shop stewards dominating the Australian trade union movement.

Indeed, the New South Wales Anti-Discrimination Board reported in 1997 that 22 per cent of recent complaints emanated from Poms. However, in 2007, the Advertising Standards Bureau in Canberra overruled a complaint against the use of "Pom" in a Weetbix cereal ad featuring celebrity cricketers with the following comment: "The Board considered the nature and usual intention of the word 'Pom' when used in Australia and agreed that the term is used largely with non-hostile, playful and often affectionate intentions. The Board felt that in Australia the term 'Pom' is used in a manner that is not meant to be hostile or vilifying, but rather is consistent with Australian humour, particularly in the context of cricket."

Australian folklore says Pommies do not bathe enough. Hence the phrase 'as dry as a Pommy's towel (or bathmat)', apparently coined by comedian Barry Humphries' Barry McKenzie character.

Traditional ties have weakened considerably since Britain joined the European Economic Community and gradually dropped in her ranking as one of Australia's most important export markets. T-shirts have been emblazoned with such legends as 'Keep Australia Beautiful—Shoot a Pom' and

> 'Australians are the most morbidly small-minded, petty, nationalistic, chippy, insecure, over-sensitive houseplants ever to find their way out of the greenhouse.'
> —Anglo-Australian warfare surfaces in an editorial in England's *The Evening Standard*, reacting to Australian reports of 'Pommy whingers' in 1997

'Grow your own dope—Plant a Pom'. One of the primary reasons many Australians used to make cruel and sometimes ribald jokes about the Liberal Howard government's Foreign Minister Alexander Downer was that he seemed a mite too Anglicised and carried the accent to go with it, being a graduate of Oxford University, England, with his mother 'Lady Mary' by virtue of his knighted father. He was constantly portrayed by cartoonists as wearing fishnet stockings, in a sly reference to a once-revealed possible cross-dressing incident in his wayward youth; the implied stereotype here of course is the English pervert who has emerged from the alleged gay culture of elite English private schools (called 'public' schools in England).

The paradox in such attitudes, of course, is that the Queen of England 20,000 km (almost 12,500 miles) away, remains the Queen of Australia represented by the Governor-General, a position cloned in each of the Australian states. Futhermore, although the federated Commonwealth of Australia was proclaimed in 1901, only in 1986 did the Australia Act finally sever most ties with Britain by denying the British the power to make laws for Australia or to exercise any governmental responsibility and by removing the mechanism of legal appeal to the British Privy Council.

The Queen had a nasty moment on 6 November 1999 when Australia went to the polls on the Republic Referendum. However, some 55 per cent voted the Queen should stay, proving once again that there is nothing Australians detest more than change, and missing a historic opportunity to greet the new millennium and the centenary of federation with a brand new face.

To be fair to Australians though, a bit of fancy political footwork had succeeded in skewing the result somewhat. Instead of being asked to vote simply whether or not to have a Republic, voters were offered what many branded a 'politicians' republic' with a Parliament-appointed President. Most Australians, democratic to the core, preferred direct election of the President, and therefore rejected the proposition—not necessarily because they were anti-Republic.

The Referendum question read: 'Do you approve of an Act to alter the Constitution to establish the Commonwealth of Australia as a Republic with the Queen and Governor General being replaced by a President appointed by a two-thirds majority of the members of the Commonwealth Parliament?'

'No' said 55 per cent. But nobody could tell from this what the support for a Republic really was. Recent polls suggest not only a decline in support for the idea—amazing, considering the relatively unattractive conduct of the British Royal Family in recent times—but perhaps also general disinterest in the issue and a feeling that there are more important things to worry about. A second chance at a Republic may be a long time coming.

Americans

White Australians share many national traits and also historical experiences (such as gold rushes) with the Americans. The two nations are also military allies, together with New Zealand, under the ANZUS security treaty dating back to 1952. There are several somewhat mysterious American satellite surveillance and defence installations in Australia's remote heartland. A Free Trade Agreement between the two countries went into operation from 2005, raising issues for some in the pharmaceuticals, food labelling and creative services areas, but nonetheless cementing an already solid trade relationship: the two partners' 2010 two-way trade total was worth close to A$50 billion. The USA is Australia's fifth most important export market for goods at a value of just over A$9 billion (2010) and its second most important for services exports at just over A$5 billion (2010); the USA is Australia's biggest import source for services at almost A$10 billion, and its second largest import source for goods at over A$25 billion. That adds up to a trade deficit of almost A$21 billion on the Australian side.

The two peoples are similarly outgoing, both preferring informality, tending to be brash, loud, and wearing their opinions and emotions on their sleeves. They have both conquered a big country (Australia and the mainland USA, excluding Alaska, are almost the same size), including quite a bit of rough terrain.

White Australians too have their cowboys and, in the Aboriginals, 'Indians' (or native Americans). It is significant perhaps that one of the many delegations of helpers who have visited Australian aboriginal settlements to advise on coping with social problems like the petrol-sniffing addiction, came from America's native American reservations, where they share the same problems. The two nations also share the passionate rhetoric of freedom, human rights and democracy, despite some clay feet on both sides since the 9/11 terrorist catastrophe of 2001 in New York.

The two people's languages and their cultures—from drive-in everything and hamburgers to country-and-western music, and of course, television imports—are drawing closer every day. One Australian newspaper columnist recently complained bitterly that somebody had changed the old English word 'torch' to the American 'flashlight' behind his back when he wasn't looking.

In general, there is a feeling of natural affinity. And it must be said, of admiration on the Australian side, despite a regular chorus of complaint against American cultural infiltration. Occasionally, the admiration takes the negative form of a 'cultural cringe' in relation to American superiority as a world power. For one thing, it is generally agreed, by Australians

One of the similarities between white Australians and Americans is the rodeo.

too, that America saved Australia from a Japanese fate worse than death during World War II.

Everybody, on both sides of the argument, was delighted at the symbolically significant union of quintessential Aussie Paul Hogan ('Crocodile Dundee') with his American leading lady (and for many, the marriage of Hogan's natural heir, the late 'crocodile hunter' Steve Irwin, to his American wife Terri was about the same sort of thing). On the darker side, some Australians further to the left look askance at Australia's strong defence and security links with the USA, and at the alleged American penetration of the Australian political process. This paranoia, stoked by Prime Minister John Howard's dogged loyalty to President George W. Bush post-9/11, has diminished with PM Julia Gillard's apparent love affair with President Barack Obama since 2010.

For a fascinating exposition of this darker school of thought, see London-based Australian journalist John Pilger's controversial book, *A Secret Country*.

Italians and Greeks

Most jokes about the Italians or Greeks are quite good-humoured. After all, an awful lot of Australians can claim Italian or Greek ancestry (more than 4 per cent and 2 per cent respectively), and Melbourne in the state of Victoria is accounted the world's third biggest Greek city. The Italian accent is often caricatured publicly, as on a one-time popular advertisement on Perth television, where 'Luigi' genially instructed the viewer on how to 'Sava-Dava-Moni'. The SBS TV sitcom series *Pizza*, set in a pizza shop, was enormously popular for its somewhat politically incorrect depiction of various ethnic types from Mediterranean 'wogs' (almost a term of affection in Australia now) to a Lebanese rapper, a white Aussie 'bogan' (yob, lout), a Maori 'Kiwi' (New Zealander), a Chinese, and others. It is generally agreed that any Australian houses sporting neo-classical porticoes, pillars, columns, statues, lions and the like usually prove to belong to, or have been designed by, nostalgic Italian-Australians—from my own observation, they really do!

New Zealanders

You might imagine that Australians would feel some affinity with the 'Kiwis' of New Zealand, by virtue of being close neighbours, as well as military allies.

Not so. As far as Aussies are concerned, Kiwis are pinching Australian jobs—their passports allow them free entry to and employment in Australia (via an automatically granted 'Special Category Visa') and there are more than half a million of them in Australia—and are nearly as responsible for the rise in crime as the Vietnamese. Well, almost.

The Australians further resent the Kiwis' often revealed sense of superiority (they do not share the Australians' convict ancestry) and 'English ways'. There is really little love lost between them. Cruel jokes about New Zealanders' alleged sexual affinity for their sheep, and mimicking of their Scots-based accent (rendering 'fush' for 'fish') abound in Australian public life.

The Tasmanians

Now, this is an awkward one. Tasmanians (often jocularly referred to as Taswegians) are Australians. But you wouldn't think so from the way most mainlander Australians talk about them.

Tasmania (affectionately known as Tassie, pronounced 'Tazzie') is Australia's smallest state and an island, 240 km (150 miles) off the south-eastern corner of the mainland, with a population of less than half a million spread over more than 67,000 sq km (almost 26,000 sq miles). It's a wild and beautiful place much favoured by artists and dropouts seeking the simple life, but with some mean weather at times.

Tasmanians are a standing joke in mainland Australia. The basic premise of every Tasmanian joke is that Tasmanians are hillbillies and country bumpkins (including lonely farmers habituated to questionable sexual practices) afflicted with the mental and physical consequences of extensive inbreeding: hence the many jokes referring to them as having 'two heads', 'pointy-heads' and the like.

But Isn't Australia Racist?

I mentioned all the above as a prelude to answering the question, 'Are Australians racist?'

When I first wrote this book in the early 1990s, against a backdrop of a Labor-government Australia officially dedicated to multi-culturalism. I answered this question with 'No, they are equally rude about absolutely everybody, of whatever colour or creed.'

I also pointed out that Aboriginal Australians are the ones suffering most from any Australian racism. I asked the reader to examine his or her nation's own glass house. I pointed out that Australia's tradition of free expression opens her up to more bruising public discussions of sensitivities like race than are possible in more restricted societies.

All of this remains true, but in the context of 11 years of a Liberal government under Prime Minister John Howard replacing Labor's Paul Keating from 1996–2007, a body of opinion previously silenced unfortunately has been emboldened to speak up. Its xenophobic, sometimes racist, voice was for a while that of the former independent, now largely disgraced, Member of Parliament, Queenslander Pauline Hanson. Not, of course, that John Howard ever actively or openly espoused xenophobia or racism; but many believe he too passively stood aside from restraining such views, and so indirectly encouraged them.

The Hanson camp expressed strong opposition to Asian immigration, to financial aid and welfare grants to Aboriginals, and to certain forms of foreign investment. While Hanson apparently represented many white Australians-in-the-street—only partially educated, she herself ran a simple fish-and-chips shop—her words brought far more sophisticated toads out from under their stones. But Hanson's One Nation Party is now a thing of the past, with no federal political presence since the 2004 federal elections, and plenty of internal problems. Hanson herself left politics in 2004.

It would have been tempting to say that Hanson's political demise represents the burial of old-style racism in Australia. Unfortunately, it does not. Recent surveys show the percentage of people reporting racist incidents connected with their own ethnic background or appearance rising from about 9 per cent in 2007 to 14 per cent in 2011. The primary targets of racial abuse tend to shift from decade to decade however, depending on what is newest and strangest: back in the 1950s, it might have been the Italians or Greeks; in the 1970s, it became the Vietnamese; over the past decade, and ongoing, it has been visible Muslims and Middle Easterners, with occasional digressions to Indians; the latest phase has been a focus on the many Africans now arriving, chiefly from Somalia and the Sudan.

Perhaps the lingering fear of powerful and populous Asian neighbours, for example, is inevitable in an island nation with plenty of empty land and alluring mineral resources. Deep in the Australian psyche there remains the dread of the 'Australian way of life' being overwhelmed by 'them.' Indonesia looms large in this context and there has been enhanced mutual distrust since Australian troops moved into East Timor after the new nation's bloody passage to independence from Indonesia in 1999. The appalling spectacle of ignorant and emotional Australian reactions to the drug-trafficking conviction of Australian girl Schapelle Corby in an Indonesian court in 2005 uncovered yet again the virulent forms that this fear can take. The assumption for many was that (a) Corby was innocent, (b) she was victimised by the Indonesians and (c) the Indonesian courts were incompetent and corrupt. And they said so, abusively.

So what is it all about? Well, try to empathise. Hanson and her ilk stood for the dying throes of the old 1950s Australia. Imagine the trauma of being jolted awake from a comfortable introspective Anglo-Celtic dream and forced to make yourself a place in the world or worse, in Asia, on pain of economic death. Of suddenly not knowing or understanding your immediate neighbours, newly arrived foreigners. For disturbed people like Pauline Hanson, the rules have been changed with brutal abruptness, the golden age has evaporated, and it all seems terribly unfair—'stop the world, we want to get off!'

But rest assured, the future of Australia is not on the racists' side. Relax, do not become hyper-sensitive, keep a sense of humour, and all be well. There is still plenty of courtesy and kindness on the streets of Australia, besides also full freedom of speech and the rule of law: you can give as good as you get. And you can complain, for example to the Human Rights Commission (www.humanrights.gov.au) who are helping to spearhead a National Anti-Racism Strategy to operate from 2012-2015.

Asians

Before we talk about Australian attitudes to Asians, let us first translate the word 'Asian' into Australian: it means, almost exclusively, Chinese and Vietnamese, and perhaps sometimes Japanese too. It does not usually refer to Indians, for example. In other words, it refers to those of Mongoloid stock. Among racists, it is a euphemism for 'slant-eyes'. This is quite different of course from the meaning the word 'Asian' has acquired in, say, London or Birmingham, UK, where it is used to refer to South Asians.

Some folk in Australia are striving very hard to make the dream of integration with Asia a reality. From 1996, a special government programme had children learning Chinese, Japanese, Malay and Indonesian at school but tragically, the Howard government drastically cut funding to this programme from 2002 and Asian language studies started to decline as a result. This, coupled with an on-off attitude to funding for important Australian outreach tools such as Radio Australia, broadcasting into Asia, meant that the climate up to late 2007 did not look that good for improving cross-cultural understanding. Nonetheless, Australia's countless academic research centres and 'think tanks' specialising in strengthening Australia's links with Asia valiantly kept the fires burning until almost miraculously, a Chinese-speaking Prime Minister, Kevin Rudd, was installed after the November 2007 Federal election. Rudd's speedy allocation of an A$62-million budget to the National Asian Languages and Studies in Schools should have turned the tide. But vital momentum lost during the Howard era has not been regained: now fewer than 20 per cent of Australian students are learning an Asian language, and only a worrying 6 per cent by Year 12, the pre-university entrance examination year. Considering China is Australia's most important trading and business partner (A$105-billion in two-way trade for 2010), not to mention the political significance of near-neighbour Indonesia, this is cause for concern. Rudd is now out of power. Prime Minister Julia Gillard showed belated interest in the issue in late 2011, commissioning experts to draw up a White Paper on *Australia in the Asian Century*, for release in mid-2012.

The White Australia Policy

The White Australia policy dated back to the 1901 Restrictive Immigration Act which kept out non-European immigrants, following an influx of cheap Chinese labour to the Australian goldfields after the 1840s.

Among other things, the policy produced silly situations like the case of the twin brothers with mixed parenthood, one looking Indian and the other European. No prizes for guessing which one got in and which one didn't. And many a southern European was rejected for immigration in those days, on the grounds of being a touch too swarthy. The only Asians admitted as early

The attitudes of those times spawned a rash of consumer products like Golden Fleece Soap, which said it would 'Keep Australians White'. This policy was not abandoned till 1973. Up to that date, Australians were taught to be afraid of the 'Yellow Peril' from the north, be it Japanese or Indonesian. It takes time to shake off such grim instruction.

as the 1950s or 1960s were those who could prove direct European heritage, such as the Anglo-Indians of India or the Eurasians of Singapore and Malaysia. Sometimes it seems the Australian immigration officers making such fine decisions simply looked at the applicant's skin colour to make their final judgement.

Well-treated

Yet, curiously, I must mention here that a Chinese-Australian and Sri Lankan-Australian friend of mine, both of whom arrived in Western Australia long before 1973, have told me that they were well treated at that time, 'like guests, like a special novelty'. Even today, I can report that a Chinese friend was hosted to a welcome tea-party by his Aussie neighbours and another Chinese lady regularly exchanges cooked dishes from her kitchen for handyman fixing about her house by her Australian neighbour.

That said, quite a few Australians do believe that the Vietnamese have brought an increase in crime (proportionately, in fact, they generate less than their share of national crime), that other Asians have brought exotic diseases like tuberculosis and hepatitis B, and that migrant Asians are taking Australians' jobs. You will find similar misconceptions about immigrants in almost every country experiencing a sudden influx of them.

The Mystery of the Vanishing Abalone

Then there is the abalone problem off Western Australian coasts. For decades or more, ordinary Australians have enjoyed their annual abalone harvest, sticking firmly to the rules, or so they claim: take no more than 20 pieces per person per day and leave the small ones alone, to generate future stocks.

But in 1991, the Western Australian state government had to cancel that year's fishing season outright. There was no abalone left and it looked likely there might not be much more in future either. Who dunnit? 'The Vietnamese,' said some Aussies. 'The Chinese,' said others. 'All Asians,' said yet others. 'Not us,' chorused the Asians. It was the big boys, the Australians with the commercial interests.

Obviously, the Western Australian Fisheries Minister at that time, Gordon Hill, thought somebody not English-speaking had done it: among the measures he announced when cancelling the season was a multilingual education programme for the fishermen.

And columnist Mike Roennfeldt, writing in *The West Australian* newspaper said: 'Everyone, including the media, has been so terrified of being labelled racists that the obvious truth has been ignored. It seems to me that tippy-toeing around the fact that the whole abalone problem lies directly at the feet of Australians of Asian descent is actually being more racist than facing squarely up to the truth.'

Since 2004, the prime Western Australian abalone harvest has been even more strictly controlled with a view to future sustainability, through a mix of size and bag or catch limits, with closed seasons and closed areas announced from time to time. By the mid-21st century, some 20,000 recreational fishers were taking out abalone fishing licences every year in Western Australia alone, bagging up to 40 tonnes a year of the highest quality abalone. Australians who remember more easy-going times resent the more strictly regulated fisheries scene of today. Whatever the rights and wrongs of this case, it is a good example of why some Australians may have reservations about Asians.

A very similar thorn in Australian flesh is the Indonesian 'poaching' of Australia's valuable Trochus shell. Between 1989 and 1991, Australian patrol boats arrested 150 Indonesian vessels, mostly from Sulawesi, for fishing inside Australian waters, in a multi-million campaign to stop such fishing. A concerted campaign by Australia has had some impact: the number of illegal fishing boats intercepted has fallen somewhat in recent years, to 121 in 2007 from 365 in 2006, according to Australian records. Still, at any one time, there may be about 250 Indonesian illegal fishermen waiting 'to be processed' in Darwin's jail, up in the Northern Territory, close to Indonesian waters.

From the Indonesian fishermen's point of view, fishing off Australia, for fish and shellfish, for Trochus and for sea-slug (known as Trepang), is a centuries-old traditional right, which in many cases they had negotiated amicably with the indigenous Aboriginals. Besides, they are poor and desperate enough to just keep on coming.

To top this all off, Australians generally feel that Asian societies are reprehensible for their lack of social and political freedom, in short, for not being like Australia.

This Land is My Land (?)

There are worrying new sources of tension, such as the sudden boom in Asian, particularly Chinese, investment in not only general real estate but also large stretches of agricultural land, apparently with a view to turning them over to mining in future. It used to be the Japanese investors in Queensland property that worried everyone in the 1980s, but that phase is over (and the generation that remembers the brutal Pacific war with the Japanese during World War II is dying off). Among the many interesting statistics cited in *The Australian* during 2011, one Chinese mining giant, Shenhua Watermark Coal, paid inflated prices to acquire 43 farms in the New South Wales wheat belt between 2009 and 2011, while Singapore-based company Olam International now controls almost 45 per cent of Australia's almond plantations. Nobody seems to know what the big picture is, but the Gillard government ordered an audit of foreign land ownership in 2011, as fears rose that Australia might lose control of its land, and of its own food security.

Nonetheless, at the official level, despite frequent political scuffles with Malaysia and Indonesia over human rights, Australians carrying or taking drugs, terrorist threats, and simple good manners (such as feisty Prime Minister Paul Keating's memorably offensive reference to Malayan Prime Minister Mahathir as a "recalcitrant" back in 1993), Australia's relationship with Asia is maturing and deepening. Most ordinary Australians today understand the geo-politics of being so close to a major Southeast Asian power like Indonesia and are also well aware that they owe much of their living to a booming China hungry for their mineral resources. If nothing else, Australia's more than A$33-billion tourism industry needs Asia. Official projections see Asian visitor arrivals (excluding the Middle East) accounting for nearly half of the total growth in visitor numbers and 61 per cent in terms of expenditure up to 2020. China alone is forecast to contribute almost 28 per cent of the total growth in tourism export dollars.

The Challenge of the Crescent Moon

Islam is a topic calculated to raise the hairs on the back of many an Australian neck. This reaction stems from a blend of ignorance and blind fear. Australians are not alone in this.

People in Middle Eastern dress, especially women in veils, are too visibly different on Australian streets. The 2006 Census showed 340,000 Muslims in Australia, with only 129,000 of them born in Australia. The largest Muslim community is of Lebanese origin, more than 30,000 of them born in Lebanon. Another 23,000 Australian Muslims were born in Turkey. Afghanistan (16,000), Pakistan (just under 14,000), Bangladesh (just over 13,000) and Iraq (10,000) are other important source countries for Muslim migrants. Terrorism as manifested in Al Qaeda's September 11 attack of 2001 on New York and the Bali Bombings of 2002 and 2005, widely seen as anti-Australian, has hardly helped these communities to integrate. As in America and elsewhere, some of Australia's freedoms have been subtly eroded as a result of the security crackdown perceived as a necessary response to these incidents. Since 2002, the powers of the Australian Security Intelligence Organisation (ASIO) have moved from mere surveillance to detention and interrogation without charge and the banning of proscribed organisations, while the definitions of and penalties for terrorism and treason have been broadened, among other things. The full impact of this has been seen in the notorious case of Dr Mohammed Haneef, wrongfully arrested in 2007 (see Chapter 10).

Such measures have only served to widen the chasm between Islamic and non-Islamic Australia. It will take great patience and tolerance on both sides if this chasm is to be bridged.

It certainly was alarming to hear white Australian residents on the eastern side of Australia reacting to the prospect of a mosque being erected in their neighbourhood. They howled their opposition. Their reason: property values would slump (unfortunately possible), and 'the kiddies wouldn't be safe to walk home,' as one woman-in-the-street out it to the TV cameras, a revelation of shocking prejudice. One talk-back radio caller debating another issue declared flatly: "I reckon we should not have Arabs in this country. I reckon they are all mad."

The atmosphere has been seriously exacerbated by thoughtless Australian Muslim clerics like Sheik Taj Din al-Hilali, chief Mufti of Muslim Australia (no longer, needless to say), who in 2006 famously remarked that immodestly clothed (and unveiled) women invited rape since they were like 'uncovered meat', inviting to stray cats; or mosque cleric Samir Abu Hamza who as recently as January 2009 is alleged to have said that it was OK for husbands to slap their wives around a bit, and also to demand sex, which if taken by force, did not constitute rape within a marriage (although Australian law specifically says that it is still rape if not consensual). Prime Minister Kevin Rudd spoke for most Australians when he commented that such comments have no place in modern Australia.

Different Attitudes

Just after the conviction of Schappelle Corby in her Bali drugs case, in 2005, one of my Eurasian friends who originally came from Malaysia was casually chatting in Indonesian with an Indonesian girl at the weekend market where they run a stall together selling jewellery. An Australian white who was looking interested in their wares suddenly turned around to his wife and said, "Do you know what language that is that they are speaking? Come on, let's get out of here." Whereupon they both left in high dudgeon, pleased at the opportunity to boycott 'Indonesians'. Yet both the stall-holders were already long-time Australians.

But try telling all this to my Singapore-Malay and Muslim friend, who is married to an Australian girl of Roman Catholic Italian parentage, Cindy, and lives in Perth (which, like many other Australian cities, is well supplied with Islamic 'halal' butchers). Cindy is now a good Muslim—the couple have found a mosque in Perth to attend every Friday—and she produces fine Malaysian food every year for the Muslim feast of Ramadan, at the end of the fasting month, clad in traditional Malay dress.

Does she ever get teased or harassed about her new religion? "No, no—not at all," she smiles gently. End of conversation.

It will take time for Muslims to win greater acceptance from mainstream Australia. This is a path already successfully trodden first by the initially equally maligned Italians and Greeks, and then by the Vietnamese (Africans will be the next wave). Creative initiatives like the home-grown Australian Muslim comedy show on SBS TV, *Salam Cafe* in 2008, have helped. I like to ponder on an incident that I witnessed in 2011, when being served by a young girl in full Muslim headgear, probably a student in a part-time job, at a supermarket meats counter that definitely was not certified *halal*, the necessary religious qualification for any meat touched or eaten by a Muslim. This was interesting enough in itself, but it was really startling when she made some small error and like any other Aussie teenager, swore loudly in frustration, "Oh, Jesus!" This, I thought to myself, this is Australia, irreverent, complex, multicultural – and evolving.

Entente, But Less Cordiale

Australians know they must come to terms with Asia, for economic survival if for nothing else. Europe and the Americas have their faces turned elsewhere and are trading more with one another. Corporate Australia now understands the rules of the game well, although old habits die hard and still too many Australian exporters focus on English-speaking countries. As the English weekly *The Economist* remarked in 1989, 'The trouble is that Australians have not worked out exactly what to do with all this talk about Asia, beyond having politicians flying around the region.'

The spectacle of East Timor's descent into hell in 1999, as its people struggled to affirm their independence from Indonesia, shook the Australian nation. Australians mandated Prime Minister John Howard to initiate leadership of the UN-backed Interfet peacekeeping force that duly patrolled East Timor from September 1999 to February 2000 when UN 'blue-berets' took over.

This was the largest deployment of Australian troops (about 5,000) since the Vietnam War and, more significantly, the first time Australia had acted as a power in the region without any hand-holding from the US. A surge of Anzac-style emotion among Australians proud of their troops' conduct, has led to charges of 'triumphalism' from Indonesia, Malaysia (that familiar bête noire) and others.

Suspicions have risen over Australia's real motives. And the unseemly tug of war that has ensued in more recent years between Australia and East Timor over the rights to oilfield exploitation off East Timor and the revenue-sharing, does give ground for these suspicions. Australia's underlying relationship with Asia, notably with Indonesia and China, is edgy as a result, particularly in the context of a recently enhanced military alliance with the US.

Many Australians realise the impossibility of keeping their distance from Indonesia as the two countries become increasingly intertwined, yet are frustrated at how to manage the relationship. This dichotomy was evident when Australians' innate generosity rose to the surface as the nation rushed to donate hundreds of millions of dollars almost overnight in response to the tsunami disaster of Boxing Day, 2004, yet only six months later these very same people bayed for Indonesian blood when Schapelle Corby was convicted of drug trafficking in Bali, and shamefully, in some cases demanded their donation money back from Indonesia's tsunami-hit province of Aceh.

On the political front, there was a sea-change virtually reversing all that Paul Keating achieved when in 1995 he engineered a security treaty with Indonesia, once the Howard government came to power. With South-east Asian governments finding greater common cause with Australia in the wake of 21st century terrorism, however, the situation has mellowed somewhat, at the political level if not on the average Australian street. Australia was the host for the APEC (Asia-Pacific Economic Cooperation) group in 2007 and this is symbolic of Australia's steadily improving integration with regional Asian fora, including such groups as the Asean (Association of Southeast Asian Nations) Regional Forum and the regular Asean-Australia forum gatherings and the East Asian Summit. In February 2008, things got even better, with the Rudd Government's signing of the Australia Indonesia Framework for Security Cooperation, or the Lombok Treaty, which spells out the framework for cooperation between Australia and Indonesia in key areas such as defence, counter-terrorism, law enforcement, maritime security and emergency preparation.

Land, history and race, all these define Australia. But as in any country, so does the world of work, and the nation's attitude to it. That world, and Australians' somewhat unique attitude to it, is discussed in detail in Chapter 9. To some extent, the Australian view of work is in turn defined by the national obsession with a particular aspect of leisure – sport, both actual and spectator. And it *is* an obsession: sometimes, as a not-too sporting person ('un-Australian'!), I just want to go hide in a hole with a book at weekends, as the 'Great Sports Binge' begins across the nation, on every medium from radio to television. It's just inescapable. If you can't beat 'em, join 'em, I guess, but I'm afraid it makes me very cranky, and an inveterate 'Monday-lover.'

AFTER HOURS

Australians draw a sharp line between work-time and play-time. And they work hard at play. Their favourite form of play is sport, whether spectator or participatory. Sport—the practice and the theoretical knowledge of it—is your surest and shortest route to the heart of Australians, your safest topic of conversation with the highest and lowest in the land.

Australian politicians scramble to be associated with sporting events and to be seen as such on the TV screen. Former Prime Minister John Howard played this to the hilt, popping up every so often on telly to offer his views on the current state of cricket and 'footy' (but chiefly cricket), and so bolster his popularity ratings. He was renowned for timing his official visits to England around the time of cricket Test Matches. Sport in any case has always played an important part in Australia's concept of foreign diplomacy.

Australia's performance at major sporting events is a matter of almost political concern, and most times, the nation can hold its head high on this score. At the Beijing Olympics of 2008, Australia ranked sixth in the medal tallies, after China, the US, Russia, Great Britain and Germany, with a total medal haul of 46, including 14 Gold, 15 Silver and 17 Bronze, ranking fifth among Gold medal winners. More than half of the 46 total medals were won at swimming or diving events.

Because so much of the population is concentrated around the coastline, water sports are important—swimming, sailing, surfboarding, windsurfing, water-skiing and rowing, as well as white-water rafting.

Partly because winters are usually short and mild, many sports can be played almost the whole year round. But Australian Rules or AFL (Australian Football League) football ('Footy') and its rival, more European, football format, Soccer, have distinct seasons, with footy running in March-August (autumn-winter) and soccer in October-February (spring-summer). Cricket and Horse-racing, the other two big sports in Australia, are summer activities. With reference to the latter, it's worth repeating that you must take note that the A$6-million Melbourne Cup race (first Tuesday in November) at Flemington is a national happening of massive significance, albeit a public holiday only in Melbourne itself—do not try to talk to Australians (even overseas) about anything else on this day.

Close to A$200 million in bets flows into this one race every year. The most famous horse ever has probably been Makybe Diva, who went into the history books for being the only horse to win three Melbourne Cups, her third victory being at the 2005 race. But the 'dark horse' is the currently unbeaten Australian horse Black Caviar, a sprinter so not well suited to the 3,200-metre (two-mile) Melbourne Cup course, which she has never run.

The most famous trainer, 'King of the Cup,' is Bart Cummings, with 12 Melbourne Cup wins to his name, the latest in 2008, at the age of 71.

Tennis is popular, thanks to the stunning victories at major championships such as Wimbledon by top-calibre Australian players like Evonne Goolagong Cawley, Pat Cash, Leyton Hewitt and today's rising star, Samantha Stosur.

Golf in Australia is not the preserve of the moneyed elite as it is in so many other societies, but is enjoyed by all, at minimal cost. Fine Australian golfers have emerged regularly, veteran Greg Norman (57 now) being one of the strongest 'brand' names to hit the international sports pages.

Australia has had an international sporting presence for almost a century, at first as part of the cricketing British Empire, later as an independent member of the world community—the 1956 Olympics were hosted in Australia (Melbourne), with

Australian swimmers taking eight of the 14 available gold meals, as were the 2000 Olympics, in Sydney (16 golds for Australia).

The annual Formula One Grand Prix motor race was staged in Adelaide from 1985 to 1996, when it moved to Melbourne.

Willow and Leather

The Melbourne Cricket Club was established as early as 1838, and today's iconic 100,000-capacity Melbourne Cricket Ground (MCG) saw its first cricket match in 1854. The first-ever Test cricket fixture was played at the MCG in March 1877, with the home team Australia beating England by 45 runs. But cricket was played in Australia earlier than all these landmark dates. It seems slightly odd that a sport so strongly associated with the British Empire and the British upper classes should have rooted so easily in convict-settled Australia, as it did in colonised India too, but the game is indeed a national passion.

If you do not come from a cricket-playing nation, my advice is that you read up on this puzzling game before attempting to relate with Australia.

Since the first 'Test' match, the Test trophy has always been the 'Ashes', supposedly the 'ashes' of the dead English game at that 1877 match. Test matches were a sensitive topic for Australian sportsmen until quite recently, in 1989, when Allan Border's team won back the Ashes on tour in England—this was the first time the Australians had retrieved the Ashes in England since 1934, and they retained them right up to 2005. But in the 2005 Ashes series, the British took victory, then were trounced again by Australian in the 2006-'07 series; the Ashes trophy now sits with the British again following their victory in the 2009 and 2010-'11 series, pending what the British-hosted 2013 series brings.

Cricket pundits worldwide are familiar with great Australian cricketing names like Sir Donald Bradman (more than 28,000 runs against England in Test matches 1928–1948, and a record of 1,448 runs in one season unbeaten until 1971), Richie Benaud, Ian Chappell, Dennis Lillee, Jeff Thomson, Greg Chappell and Allan Border, and star bowler Shane Warne (also renowned for his off-field sexual exploits), bowler Glen McGrath, former national captains Steve Waugh and batsman-wicket keeper Adam Gilchrist ('Gilly'). From 2004-2011, Ricky Ponting, captain of the national team, was the face of Australian cricket, but his replacement in the captaincy now is Michael Clarke, and increasingly high-profile is batsman-bowler Shane Watson. Those wishing to catch up with cricket tales behind the scenes, might want to grab some of Ponting's books, his Captain's Diary series, published in 2007, 2008, 2009 and as The Captain's Year in 2010.

To get by with the sports small-talk that is essential to survival at the Australian dinner table, in the pub or at the neighbourhood barbie (outdoors barbecue party), you will also need to be familiar with two particularly famous cricketing incidents.

The first of these is the 'bodyline' incident in the 1932–1933 English tour of Australia, during which English bowlers were believed to have bowled directly to Bradman's body in a deliberately threatening manner. Several Australian batsmen were injured during this tour and Australian feeling against the English cricketers rose to fever pitch.

In the second incident, the boot was on the other foot, with Australia monopolising the infamy. This was the notorious 'underarm' tactic against New Zealand in 1981. Bowler Trevor Chappell, one of three famous cricketing brothers, was instructed by his captain, coincidentally also his brother Greg, to bowl underarm for the last ball of the limited-over final.

The New Zealand team at that point needed six runs from the last ball to level with Australia in this one-day match, but Chappell's stratagem effectively denied the opposition a tie with Australia—it would be impossible to hit the underarm-delivery ball hard or high enough to get time for runs while the fielders chased it. Australia's reputation for sportsmanship suffered a bashing and underarm bowling was subsequently banned, as underhand and not cricket.

The well-known subsidiary Aussie sport of 'sledging' (verbal abuse) among sportsmen aiming to lower each other's morale on-field has sadly spread to cricket, as a result of which another incident that is a current hot topic is the question of whether or not Indian player Harbhajan Singh made a racist reference on-field to dreadlocked Australian player Andrew Symonds (who has Afro-Caribbean blood), calling him a 'monkey' (earning this incident the media tag 'Monkey-gate'), at the Test Match in Sydney, January 2008.

Australian Rules Football

This virtual amalgam of rugby and soccer was invented in Melbourne in 1858. It is a lot rougher than soccer, with plenty of hand-ball, body contact, hand-passing and the like. It also seems to be characterised by extremely tight butt-hugging shorts for some reason. You will need to familiarise yourself with the commonly used term 'ruckman' for one of the key positions in any footy team: the ruckman, essentially a forward player, will usually be the tallest and fittest member of the team, in order to fill his role of leaping high into the air to tap the ball into play, vertically. One of the most famous ruckmen was a Western Australian of Aboriginal descent, Graham 'Polly' Farmer, in his sporting heyday during the 1950s and '60s. The Graham Farmer Freeway in Perth is named after him, and the freeway tunnel under Perth's Northbridge district is locally tagged 'Polly's Pipe' in his honour.

Sadly, the sport's rough-and-tumble image has spilled over into a 'yobbo' reputation of late, with endless scandals about footy players' conduct off-field, ranging from drug abuse to drunken brawls, loutish sexual harassment and even gang rape. Names like Wayne Carey and Ben Cousins have been star players, but also star 'boof-heads' (idiots).

Footy has never taken off outside of Australia, but domestically, footy is the leading ball game and an authentic item of Australiana which all visitors should experience for themselves. Loyalties focus on local clubs, which compete in a relatively recently established national competition.

However, a fierce battle is brewing between the entrenched tradition of footy and the imported, more international game of 'soccer' (which its devotees in Australia are trying hard to rebrand simply as 'football'). Unfortunately, this battle divides strongly on ethnic lines, since most of the soccer enthusiasts are first or second-generation migrants who hail from soccer-playing nations such as the former Yugoslavia, Greece, Italy,

England and South America. Soccer has even rudely been referred to by footy-buffs as 'wogball' to emphasise this ethnic dimension.

There's been a lot of action in this sport since the publication in 2003 of the Report of the Independent Soccer Review Committee, also known as the 'Crawford Report' which delved into allegations of corruption and mismanagement in the former governing body, Soccer Australia. Since only 2005, the newly formed Football Federation Australia (FFA) or 'Football Australia' has been the governing body overseeing the game. There is a national men's team, the 'Socceroos', as well as a national women's team, the 'Matildas'. The FFA launched a new national league in 2005, the 'A-League', replacing the National Soccer League that had existed since 1977. Not without some controversy, the FFA moved from the Oceania Football Confederation (of which Australia was a founding member) to the Asian Football Confederation as of 2006 on the premise that this would help to improve Australian football standards and raise the nation's chances of participating in the World Cup series in future.

And almost miraculously, it did happen: the Socceroos qualified for the World Cup in 2006, Australia's first appearance at the event since 1974. Their forced exit from the fray in the very last second of a match with Italy, thanks to a much-disputed penalty kick awarded to Italy (final score 1:0 against Australia), remains the stuff of bar-room brawls.

The America's Cup

Sailing is a favourite pastime and passion for many Australians, unsurprisingly since most urban centres cling to the coast. Having your own boat bestows far more prestige in this country than any car ever could. The laurels have long faded, but the past glories of Australia's triumph in 1983 at the world's premier sailing event, the America's Cup, still sit front of mind for most Aussie yachtsmen, as they weep into their beers at the emotional memory of it all. Competing in the USA, the Australians wrested the coveted trophy from the New York Yacht Club that had held it continuously since 1857, thanks partly to the revolutionary new winged-keel design of the Royal Perth Yacht Club's vessel Australia II, owned by West Australian businessman Alan Bond and captained by John Bertrand. The nation went simply bananas in the delirium of the triumph and the return event in 1988 brought great prosperity to the host city, Fremantle in Western Australia. But all things pass: there followed an era of New Zealand wins at the iconic race, and today the Cup is safely back with the Americans, until 2013 that is.

All a Bluff?

Strangely enough, despite the strong sporting culture that permeates the macho-skewed Australian social ethos, statistics I have discussed in Chapter 6: Tucker show that a large number of Australians are physically lazy, overweight and unfit. In the 1970s, the government launched a campaign featuring a slovenly, beer-bellied couch potato named 'Norm', who only watched sports on the small screen from his living room sofa, 'tinnie' in hand. He was berated into more physical activity with the slogan 'Life, Be In It.' But Norm remains a familiar sight today.

CHAPTER 3

'He is a very nice fellow, certainly nobody
would ever guess he was born in Australia.'
—British playwright and wit, George Bernard Shaw,
in his play *Major Barbara*, 1907

THE TYPICAL AUSTRALIAN
Image, Stereotypes and Misconceptions

I can't count how many times my decision in the late 1980s to set up home in Australia, particularly Western Australia, was greeted with curling lips and an amazed 'But, why on earth would you want to live *there*?'

This told me more about the enquirer than about Australia.

Australia seems to be one of those countries that nobody feels neutral about. Everybody has strong views, for or against. Depending on where you are coming from then, geographically, psychologically and culturally speaking, you are sure to harbour in your heart one of a well-defined range of stereotypes depicting 'the typical Australian'.

So let's clear the air first by spelling out some of these stereotypes from the start. The most widespread, unfortunately, is 'The Ugly Australian' otherwise known since about the 1960s as the 'Ocker', and nowadays within Australia, more often as the 'Bogan', who seems to come in approximately three models:

European Model

If you are of continental European origin, this means the Aussie is barbaric, loud-mouthed, ignorant and uncultured, hopelessly provincial.

He is physically outsized but mentally minuscule, somewhat naive, and nearly always extremely badly dressed (this gaffe weighs particularly hard on the minds of the

Parisian French—but anyway, the Aussie is usually more undressed than dressed). He cannot hold his wine, and has the temerity to claim that his own country produces this celestial ambrosia on a par with the French original. Worst of all, he cannot understand menus written in French. Basically, he is a peasant.

But actually, most Europeans are blissfully unaware of the existence of Australia or the Australians.

British Model

If you are British, you probably see your Antipodean cousin as a rather alarming, alien being bereft of the (hypocritical) courtesies of the mother country, far too frank (which other country could have produced a foreign minister who used the 'F…' word in public while on an official tour of South Africa [Gareth Evans], or a premier who dared to put his arm round Queen Elizabeth II of Great Britain [and Australia] [Paul Keating]?), frequently obscene; a naive colonial boy in shorts, an insular sheep-farmer sporting a big hat with corks hanging off it to keep the flies away. A bit of a simpleton, really.

You find the way he tends to 'get physical' rather terrifying, although you secretly admire it too. And the way he puts himself on first-name terms with you from the word go is quite beyond the pale. He's notorious as a bloke fond of a booze-up, most often culminating in a 'technicolour yawn' or 'chunder' (in low Australian patois, a vomiting session)—which latter he performs in a back-garden 'dunny' (outshed toilet).

The Australian accent, furthermore, is execrable by British standards and unfortunately slots the Australian firmly into 'the lower classes', since it best resembles working-class Cockney from East End London, or Irish-dialect English—take the still fairly frequent use by Aussies of 'youse' for both the singular and the plural 'you,' for example.

Many of these British images derive from the Barry ('Bazza') McKenzie comic strip, which ran for years (1963–1974) in the British satirical magazine *Private Eye*, lampooning the worst traits of an Aussie on the loose in Europe. However, a handful of erudite and intellectual Australian expatriates have done their very best to mitigate this image within their adopted homeland England, suave commentator Clive James, moral high-ground journalist John Pilger and acerbic English literature professor Germaine Greer among them.

Asian Model

If you are Asian, you probably share the European and British concern at the Australian's admittedly blunt ways, since calling a spade a spade is hardly an Asian trademark. His predilection for semi-nakedness will not have endeared him to you, either.

Faux Pas

The Aussie is notoriously oblivious to the subtleties of Asian culture and even the greatest in the land are not immune, although the former Mandarin-speaking Labor Prime Minister Kevin Rudd has gone a long way to correct this failing—recent years have seen premier John Howard himself fail to recognise a finger bowl of rose scented water politely proffered by the Indonesians at a tree-planting ceremony and tip it on the tree rather than wash his hands in it, as well as refer to the then newly installed Malaysian prime minister Dr Abdullah Ahmad Badawi as 'Dr Badawi' when even a passing knowledge of Malaysian culture would have told him that Badawi is not Dr Abdullah's name but his father's name. Aussie VIPs mispronouncing foreign names in the diplomatic environment is too common an occurrence to merit any comment.

And most likely, you have been persuaded that the typical Australian is a dyed-in-the-wool racist, besides being lazy or on the dole and totally incompetent because he can't seem to make as much money as you can—and even more irritatingly, for some reason, does not seem to *want* to make money, anyway.

He has no drive and to all intents and purposes, has parked himself in the world's KIV tray, his nation quite literally 'a basket case'.

You are also more than a little shocked and disillusioned by various 'third world' elements in the Aussie lifestyle that you did not expect in a 'developed' country like Australia: power blackouts, police, bureaucratic bungling and red tape, Aussies running around without shoes etc.

Although it is true that where there is smoke, there usually are at least a few glowing coals, in fact, many of these images derive from a hostile Asian press, egged on by Asian governments intent on preventing their best and brightest from emigrating to Australia. (The Aussie media have, however, more than held their own, exchanging insult for insult, and then some.)

The culture gap is at its widest between Australia and Asia, a cause of enduring sadness to all concerned, for Asia is where Australia is located and where Australians eventually must, willy-nilly, make their psychological, cultural and economic home. Since this book was first published, admittedly progress has been made, yet not enough. As we go to press, Australia awaits the government-commissioned *White Paper on Australia in the Asian Century* due in the second half of 2012. "The shift of economic and strategic weight to Asia has never been more profound for Australia's interests than it is now," said the Government, announcing the project in late 2011.

The Great Suburban Bore

A kind of sub-category within 'The Ugly Australian' classification is the Australian as 'The Great Suburban Bore'.

By definition, this view of the Australian can only be held by someone who thinks he himself or she herself is the opposite, i.e., sophisticated, intellectually dazzling, exciting, glamorous, etc. Well, we know what we think of people who think this of themselves, don't we? That would certainly be the Australian reaction to such pretentiousness, at any rate. The somewhat vulgar Aussie vernacular phrase for it is "A bit up himself, isn't he?". Or even more crudely, "Wankers!"

It is true that the vast majority of Australians lead simple, peaceful lives, putting great store by their homes and families, and the general philosophy of *cultiver son jardin* (with the gardening bit taken quite literally). But then, what is so reprehensible about such simple values in our troubled times?

As chief Australia-watcher Professor Donald Horne, himself a native son, has said, describing Australia as the world's first 'suburban nation' in his seminal *The Lucky Country:* 'The profusion of life doesn't wither because people live in small brick houses with red tile roofs.'

An Aboriginal artist in Bairnsdale adds the finishing
touches to his work of art. Aboriginal culture has
left its mark on Australian culture, language and
art being two significant areas of influence.

Striking buildings and architecture at Federation Square, the cultural and entertainment precinct in Melbourne.

The Sydney Opera House, a UNESCO World Heritage Site since 2007, is one of the world's most distinctive 20th century buildings, and one of the most famous performing arts centres in the world.

Cradle Mountain-Lake St Clair National Park in Tasmania. Australia is a haven for nature lovers, with spectacular rocks and ranges, lush flora and forests and unique wildlife.

Heritage and shopping: the Queen Victoria Building has played an important historical role in Sydney since its completion in 1898, and is now a lovely shopping centre with exquisite architectural features and chic shops.

Fitting into the landscape—the author on horseback in the Avon Valley, Western Australia.

Crocodile Dundee

Another, more positive, image of Australians bases itself on the 'Australian Pioneer' stereotype, one which many Australians themselves have taken to their bosom, along with sundry others, particularly the Americans. You can tell how much Aussies fancy themselves in this role by the number of them who don bush hats, cowboy hats or 'Digger'-style Aussie army hats, especially when showcasing themselves on trips abroad. The other give-away is the urban Australian's love of the tough-looking four-wheel drive (4WD) vehicle, which he may or may not really ever take into the bush. Former labourer-turned-comic actor Paul Hogan's sell-out *Crocodile Dundee* films of the 1980s did much to fuel this myth, and in more recent times, the late, larger-than-life zoo personality Steve Irwin stoked that very same fire quite efficiently, with an outsized television image (risking his own baby in the croc pool and so on) that was beamed around the world. The very latest incarnation of this type of hero probably is Aussie movie star Hugh Jackman, playing 'The Drover' in the 2008 blockbuster movie *Australia*, an almost stereotypical cattle-driver complete with hat, taciturn style and rippling muscles.

This stereotype has it that every Australian is fit, tanned and courageous in the face of hideous adversities daily encountered in the bush and deserts of a harsh continent. He is attuned to the secret voice of Nature, thanks to his Aboriginal mentors, consumes goanna steaks most dinners and spends an awful lot of time fighting bush-fires, that is, when he's not locked in mortal combat with either crocodiles or lethally poisonous serpents. He is the original frontiersman (alias Davy Crockett) reborn.

Americans really relate to this myth, because many of them live its American counterpart, nursing the idea that they are all cowboys at heart, still conquering the Wild West.

A subdivision within the Australian Pioneer category falls into the *Rural Idyll* box: here, most Australians make their living herding cattle or sheep, spending much of their time on horseback, bathed in pastoral peace and romantic sunsets.

There are all kinds of weird and wonderful events that celebrate this rural image, from outback rodeo shows to gatherings like the 'Dog in a Ute' festival at the Wheat-belt town of Corrigin in Western Australia. More than 1,000 'utes' (utility vans, with a driver's cabin at front and trailer-type freighting tray at the back—Holden does some flashy metro-styled models) assemble for this festival every year, complete with the mandatory dog in the back tray (preferably a Blue Heeler or some other Cattle Dog), to engage in entertainments like the 'Dog and Owner Lookalike' competition.

These fantasies of course completely ignore the fact that the overwhelming majority of Australians—close to 90 per cent—

in reality huddle together in urban centres clustered along the coastline, in mortal dread of the outback beyond, terribly disturbed by the thought of having to deal with the Aboriginals and blithely oblivious of their own burgeoning paunches. If anything, the nearest they have ever got to the desert is burying their heads in the metaphorical sand most of the time.

You know Australia is changing when the 2011 Census tells you that:

- Mandarin Chinese has overtaken Italian as the second most used language in Australian homes, after English;
- India is the birthplace for the largest number (13%) of recent new arrivals in Australia (between 2007-2011), more than the United Kingdom (12%), with China in third position (10%);
- Non-Christians now account for 7.2% of the total population, with followers of Hinduism increasing by 189% to 275,500 between 2001-2011;
- Those professing 'No Religious Affiliation' are the second most significant 'religious' group in the country (22%) after the Catholics (25%).

The Honey-Coloured Facts

As with all extreme stereotypes, the truth lies somewhere in between.

'The truth' is also changing rapidly, almost minute by minute, as Australia itself changes, under the impact of the geo-politics of the Australasian region, and of very varied immigration inflows, particularly from Asia.

How inadequate black-and-white statements are, about any country or culture! The truth in between is, in fact, not so much grey as honey-coloured when it comes to Australia: the country's distinguished first ambassador to China, Stephen Fitzgerald, has declared that this will be the national skin colour one day soon, thanks to Asian immigration and mixed marriages.

More than a quarter of Australia's almost 23 million people today were born outside Australia. If you include the

Australian-born who have at least one overseas-born parent, the statistic for multicultural connections gets closer to 45 per cent. As of 2009, more than 8 per cent were born in Asia. And this is not to forget the more than 500,000 original 'first Australians' or indigenous Australians—the Aboriginals.

Australia is no longer a bastion of white or Anglo-Celtic culture. This is a myth—although true that perhaps 40–50 per cent of Australians can claim Anglo-Celtic ancestry. But the Anglo-Celtic foundations were in fact undermined long ago, with the influx of southern European immigrants after World War II, notably from Italy, Greece and Eastern European countries such as Yugoslavia. The Asian influx picked up from the 1980s, and today we see more Africans and Middle Eastern nationalities such as Iraqis and Iranians, arriving, often as refugees. But as I shall explain elsewhere, the foundations cannot be ignored, even today.

SELF-IMAGE

What do Australians think of themselves? Fortunately, like their British ancestors, they are blessed with a limitless capacity for self-mockery, always a healthy trait. Home-bred intellectuals are at times far more critical than outsiders would be.

But one mocks only when the foundations are secure, and the fact is, the vast majority of Australians believe that their way of life is the best, and the right one. In fact, they mostly are blissfully unaware that there could be any other way. They see themselves as egalitarian 'battlers' against the adversities of life, and champions of the 'fair go' for all, as straight forward, not 'tricky', always poised to help their fellow men and women in any crisis.

Their biggest failing, however, is that few of them realise just how lucky they are. They take their freedoms and the welfare system for granted, among other perks of the Australian way of life. For all their detestation of the 'whinger', they themselves are capable of whingeing about the most minute infringements of their rights. They need to travel more, to bring back sobering lessons from the tightly 'guided democracies' and outright dictatorships of the developing world.

Nonetheless, call it smugness and complacency if you will, yet there is an attractive sense of security, pride and identity in the ordinary Australian's conviction that he has got it right. One of the most striking things about Australians, if you come from a more regimented background where ostentatious demonstrations of patriotism are mandatory 'or else', is that without any great pressure from anyone, they voluntarily and quite literally wave the flag every Australia Day (26 January)—on that day, traffic lanes are a-flutter with Aussie flags attached to private cars. Such demonstrations can too easily transmute into ugly jingoism of course, but you can't help admiring such simple love of country so spontaneously and proudly displayed.

The Cultural Cringe

The only chink in this armour is the famous 'Cultural Cringe'. This originates from an uncomfortable suspicion that anything British, from the original motherland, was *per se* better than home-grown Aussie stuff. In these post-British Empire days, there are now variations on this theme, focusing on Europe: I have met Australians who are obsequiously obsessed with the notion that anything French must automatically be superior, for instance. And the increasing warmth of the country's official relationship with the USA in recent years has led to extensive 'colonisation' of the Australian mind and culture by things American too. These trends are particularly evident in 'softer' fields like the arts. There is still the lurking worry that Australian-produced cinema, literature and fashions—the whole gamut of creation—may not be as good as 'the real thing', from Hollywood, Britain or France. (But no signs of an inferiority complex when it comes to dealing with Asian neighbours; while some may pay lip service to respect for Asian countries and cultures, not so deep down, the Australian rates his own as superior to theirs).

Still, 'The Cringe' has led to extensive self-flagellation in public places and is a topic of eager discussion in the Australian press, learned works and the like. It even affects the Australian economy (which is importing too many foreign goods for its own good, in preference to those made in Australia).

THE COLONIAL PAST

Such discussions will ring a clangorous bell with other 'developing' nations who share Australia's colonial past—similar debates on the worth and universality or otherwise of local literature occur from time to time in Singapore and Malaysia, for example. It's a phenomenon quite commonly seen in new young nations, although you might have thought that 100 years or so (since Australia's declared independence from Great Britain in 1900) would be long enough to get over it.

In short, he who wishes to understand the Australian mind, needs to study the country's history and to take both convicthood and the 'colonial factor' into careful account.

The Australians who called England 'home' and valued a pukka British accent are still with us today, albeit dwindling in numbers and influence (some say they are centred in Melbourne, capital of the state of Victoria). The Queen of England is still the Queen of Australia, albeit perhaps not for too much longer (perhaps only for the lifetime of Queen Elizabeth II in fact), if the Republican movement in Australia has anything to do with it (41 per cent of Australians supported a Republic in 2011—4 per cent fewer than in 2007—with about 20 per cent neutral to the issue, according to a Newspoll commissioned by the *Weekend Australian newspaper*).

Despite all the overlays deposited by post-World War II migration, the key to mainstream Australian culture still lies in the 19th century working-class London and Ireland from which the first, convict, Australians were unwillingly torn—to the extent that you still hear forms of the English language in Australia which are no longer currency in modern England itself.

I would go so far as to say that a good way to understand Australia, especially for non-Europeans, might well be to spend a couple of years in London first. A tortuous route for some, perhaps, but a worthwhile soft landing, compared with going in cold.

In this context, I continually marvel at the bravery of the thousands of Asian and other non-English speaking migrants who every year struggle to bridge the enormous cultural and linguistic chasm separating them from 'the real Australia'.

Without my own British background, I do not know how I could possibly have begun to understand Australia. But even a British grounding is still only a beginning.

THE CONVICT HERITAGE

For long, Australians' largely convict history was a source of great shame, a 'birthstain'. But feelings are more mixed nowadays and many proudly seek out their convict genealogy as a badge of 'real Australian-ness'. The unpopular Australian Islamic cleric Taj Din al-Hilali tried to press the shame button when he memorably said in 2007, referring to Muslim Australians, "We came as free people. We bought our own tickets. We are more entitled to Australia than they are." This attempted insult provoked loud guffaws among average Australians, who have a good sense of humour.

Do read historian Babette Smith's book *Australia's Birthstain* (Allen & Unwin, 2008). She attributes many strong Australian qualities to the experience of convict-hood (and remember, so many of these 'convicts' were very young working-class petty thieves pushed to crime by hunger and poverty, or else political radicals opposed to new forms of mechanisation then destroying workers' jobs): 'Laughter, often in the form of cheek, was their best, indeed their only defence. (They) literally laughed in the face of death. Their humour, laced with bravado, dry, self-deprecating, face-saving, is still a defining characteristic of the society they left behind... The convicts displayed qualities that had been honed by trying to survive in Britain: wit, daring, opportunism, the ability to keep your nerve, the courage not to weep, the stoicism to endure and the determination to find a way when everything is ranged against you.'

The Battler

The typical Australian also invariably likes to see himself as that national icon, The Battler—a working-class underdog who struggles to survive, the salt of the earth. This is the model he emulates. Hence his odd celebration of a major military defeat like the Battle of Gallipoli in 1915, during World War I, every year on Anzac Day, 25 April.

Snapshot of Australia

A snapshot of average Australia, extracted from How Australia Compares, Cambridge University Press (2nd edition, 2009) by Professor Rodney Tiffen and Ross Gittins, comparing Australia with 17 other democracies—it breaks some of the stereotypes about Australia:

- **Home Owners**

  Little change since 1960 (63%), with 69% of Australians owning their own homes by 2000, while the Irish scored 78%, the British 69%. The Aussie Dream lives on, but it's getting less affordable.

- **Booze Gurglers**

  Against a backdrop of falling alcohol consumption rates, Australians were only the seventh biggest beer drinkers and eighth wine-drinkers (2002), as well as only the tenth for overall alcohol consumption (Ireland leading the field) (2005). But Australia was tops for flavoured alcoholic drinks consumption, favoured by adolescents, the reason government raised taxes on them in 2008.

- **Agricultural & Rural**

  With 88% of its living in urban areas in 2005, Australia came third most urbanised after Belgium (97%) and the UK (90%) —and first in terms of the 61% of Aussies living in large cities (above 750,000 people).

- **Techno-savvy**

  in 2003, Australia recorded 608 personal computers per 1000 population, ranking about ninth; with 1,025 mobile phones per 1,000, Australia ranked about 13th; while Aussie Internet users in 2007 numbered 690/1000, taking 12th place. Not so impressive.

- **A Welfare State**

  In 2001, Australia was the seventh lowest spender on social and health welfare programmes, but still pretty average at 21% of GDP compared with the top spender Germany at 27.6%; Australia was less enthusiastic with its unemployment benefits, however, at 33% of GDP compared with top giver Denmark's almost 87%, but ahead of the USA's meagre 16.6%.

(Continued on the next page)

(Continued from previous page)

- **Egalitarian**
  In 2005, Australia had the ninth widest gap between the incomes of the richest and poorest, doing better than New Zealand (fifth) and the USA, the most unequal of all.
- **Rich**
  In 2005, Australia had the fourth highest percentage of the population with income below the poverty line (half of the nation's median income), at 12.4 %, compared with the USA's worse 17.1 % or the best performer, Denmark with only 5.3 %. In terms of the percentage of elderly people living in poverty, Australia was a shocking second on the list (27 %).
- **Environmentally Aware**
  The highest annual greenhouse gas emissions per person (27 tonnes of carbon-dioxide equivalent, 2005), the fourth-highest generation of municipal waste per person (2003), and the fourth highest car ownership per 1000 people (659 in 2006), almost two vehicles per three people – with train travel halving between 1970-2005 – that's Australia's record.
- **Laid Back-cum-Lazy**
  Australians now work more hours per week (44 hours for full-time workers in 2007) than anyone else in the sample countries.

The Tall Poppy

However, should the battler actually win and come out on top, achieving success, fame and money, he immediately transforms into a Tall Poppy, a most undesirable thing, begging to be cut down to size. The typical Australian tries not to shine too obviously and does not much like those who do. As a result, it's difficult if not impossible to set yourself individual excellence as a goal in Australia.

Bogans and Larrikins

'Bogans' essentially are working-class Aussies, usually male, who self-consciously celebrate a particularly earthy interpretation of Australian-ness partly in resistance to creeping Americanisation. Basically, a bogan celebrates uncouthness and is probably related to Barry McKenzie. According to an article by Stephen Lacey in *The Weekend Australian Magazine* in 2003, many bogans will sport a 'mullet' hairstyle—sort of 'normal' and short around the scalp, then descending into lank long locks at the back.

The bogans also tend to live in acid-washed jeans, tight tight shorts or 'trackie daks' (tracksuit bottoms), favour loudly checked shirts, woollen 'beanies' on their heads, and the sloppy Aussie original sheepskin wool-lined lounging boots that used to be called 'Ugg boots' until Americans patented the name and stole them. They drive Australian classics such as the Holden and hang around hard-rock pubs. Larrikins have all the 'boys will be boys', 'he's a bit of a lad' cheekiness and borderline lawlessness expected of the Australian male. Look for them among the workers on building sites, among other places.

Street-Friendly

It is true that Australians have 'country ways' for the most part; this is a large part of their considerable charm. They take a direct, simple approach to things and people, and can be quite child-like at times. Their most delightful characteristic is a willingness to talk to strangers in the street, on the bus, anywhere, and to spend time with you—they are rarely in a hurry. (This principle may not apply in the centre of Sydney at rush hour—capital cities will be capital cities.)

Singaporean journalist Chai Kim Wah nutshelled this quality neatly in a travel report during the 1980s: 'A trait I came across often (was) a readiness to give you the time of day, to be matey. It is not the American gushing-on-all-eight-cylinders friendliness, but a laid-back variety you can take or leave.'

This willingness to linger awhile also gives rise to a shortcoming in terms of modern life: Aussies sometimes do things a little slower than others, so be patient while the checkout girl at the supermarket has a nice little chat with the old lady in front of you about everything from the weather to her darling little grandchildren rolling around on the floor.

So never be afraid to greet an Aussie in the street or to talk to a taxi-driver; always take the initiative if you can, because you will inevitably be rewarded with a smile and friendly conversation. This presupposes, of course, that you can speak English. Most

Australians are not comfortable at all with foreign languages; and good English is still the key to their hearts.

Mateship

Once your friend, the Australian is characteristically your friend for life, for better or for worse. Loyalty, 'mateship', still counts for much.

And there probably can be no better friend in a physical crisis than an Australian. The Australian somehow seems to revert to the 'Pioneer' stereotype at the sight of fires, floods or crime—he will always roll up his shirt-sleeves (or more typically, take his shirt off) and charge in to help, oblivious to his own personal safety.

Proud and independent they may be—and they expect others to be likewise—but Australians do know how to band together in times of crisis and are quick to lend a helping hand to their fellowman, a habit learned in the bad old days of bush settlement. Asians, and others too, have often wrongly labelled the Australian 'individualistic'.

Selfless Friendship

I shall never forget how my Australian neighbours demonstrated this quality when a serious fire broke out in the wooden-hut village down my road in Singapore. They were first out of the block. By the time I got to the scene, having dithered around putting on the 'right' clothes and shoes, and then dousing myself in water first, the Aussies were already running in and out of the flames, stripped down to their underwear, carrying the villagers' sticks of furniture out of harm's way.

Mateship is a concept that has been seriously discussed for enshrinement in possible revisions to the Australian Constitution, and as a 'core Australian value.' It's what makes the difference even to the most conservative Australian. The same Australian who has just made disparaging remarks about Asians to white friends over the dinner table, will the next minute deck any white who insults the Asian friend and neighbour with whom he has been enjoying a pint of beer at the pub for the past few years—'cause mates are mates, see?' He himself is unlikely to perceive the paradox.

Scout's Honour

The Australian can be naive—long may he stay that way. It is only yesterday that most, even in the cities, kept their front doors open to visitors and never locked their cars. All that has changed, but it is still all too easy to take advantage of the Australian's innocence. He takes you at your word, and expects it to be your word of honour too.

As was inevitable, although lamentable, the Australians are now being pushed into the harsh real world. Already, it is not as easy as it was to walk into a bank and open an account in the name of Mickey Mouse without showing any identification whatsoever. It seems only yesterday that you could deposit a large amount of cash into a bank account and get no documentation to prove you have ever paid it in—no worries, the clerk is your mate, right? Back in the 1980s–1990s, you could set up telecoms accounts over the phone sight unseen, or leave your passport at the Immigration office without a receipt and get it back by unregistered normal mail. The two most famous Aussie catch-phrases, 'She'll be right,' and 'No worries' (apparently superseded by 'Too easy' nowadays) assumed the essence of the Latin *mañana* or Oriental fatalism at such times.

Naiveté is why Australians have had some trouble doing business in Asia. They are not used to hidden meanings behind words. As far as they are concerned, words mean exactly what they say. This attitude hardly fits them for the arcane shadow-play of business in countries like Indonesia or China.

Everyone Makes Mistakes

It's generally observable that a characteristic of the 21st century is that nobody need be to blame for anything. Nobody is accountable. Criminals have had bad childhoods, parents are overloaded, so are teachers, and so are politicians, so they all make mistakes. Nobody ever resigns, that's for sure. And few are sacked. Australians, however, were masters of this particular trick long before it became fashionable. Endearingly, they do not pile the proverbial manure onto a worker who has erred, instead they forgive, and move on. One has to admit that this is a very 'empowering' environment. The less endearing flip side of this mindset though, is that the

Australian's excessive tolerance of mistakes has led to a climate of permitted bungling, incompetence and error in many fields of life, ranging from flagrant spelling mistakes to Australian citizens mistakenly deported as illegal aliens. Because, in a fatalistic way, every Australian believes it will all be all right in the end—'She'll be right, no worries'. And besides, who wants to be a 'tall poppy' and get it right all of the time?

The Soft Underbelly

Lastly, I have observed that, contrary to the machismo pervading the nation's self-image, Australians are incredibly soppy sentimentalists. It's a short step from slap-on-the-back mateship to blubbering on each other's shoulders at the pub.

You have only to study the Australian creative style in film-making, whether for advertising or for the cinema, to be struck by its lingering, lyrical quality, its preference for tear-stained soft focus.

The Australian's shell is rough and tough, a protection born of his violent past in a harsh land; but if handled sympathetically, he will turn turtle and show you his soft underbelly.

THE SKELETON IN THE CUPBOARD

Every Australian who has been in the country for more than two generations carries a ghost on his shoulder, or has a skeleton rattling in her cupboard. For a start, are they really Australians, do they belong in the country, do they own any of it? The first Australians, the indigenous Aboriginals with something like a 60,000-year track record on this island continent, are still around to remind later settlers ceaselessly of their original tenancy of this wide brown land. And like it or not, Aboriginal culture sits in the heads of all Australians, who have acquired from the Aboriginals a deep almost spiritual reverence for their stunning land, many words and concepts from Aboriginal language and culture, the outdoor camp-fire cooking habit a.k.a. the barbecue and a host of other

Those familiar with the famous 'Singapore Girl' advertisements patented by Singapore Airlines, which fit very much into this genre, might remember that the image-creator behind them, Ian Batey, is a British-born Australian.

little quirks that have nothing to do with their largely European ancestry.

DREAMTIME AUSTRALIA: THE ABORIGINALS

If I begin simply by saying that Aboriginal matters are a minefield for the unfortunate author, you may get part of the picture.

There is no topic more sensitive in Australia—although the Anzacs and Gallipoli come a close second—than the Aboriginals. Approach the subject with caution; better shut up and listen than put your foot in your mouth.

For a country as dedicated to the pursuit of democracy and human rights—and as critical of South Africa's apartheid track record—as Australia is supposed to be, the 'Aboriginal problem' is a particularly painful Achilles heel. Every Australian, and every visitor, whether migrant or tourist, confronts 'the problem' sooner or later, and deals with it in his or her own way, sometimes with grace, but often with guilty resentment, or angry aggression.

On the other hand, it is also very easy indeed to live in Australia without getting to know any Aboriginals, even without seeing any, particularly if you live in the larger cities. For many Australians, they remain but shadows on the fringes of life, phantoms that flit through the newspaper headlines.

For Americans and Canadians conscious of their nation's lamentable track record with their own Native Americans, First Nations or Inuits, for white South Africans and for many others, Australia's problem is a case of *déjà vu*. Wherever we come from, we can probably conjure up other examples in the world which do not necessarily counterpoint only whites and non-whites; many a 'coloured' migrant race too has dominated another, weaker, similarly 'coloured' native race—in South-east Asia and elsewhere.

What is 'the problem' in Australia? Basically, it is the spectacle of an underclass, which happens to be black, disadvantaged in almost every way, pushed to the fringes of society, so demoralised that it also seems to be bent on committing mass suicide in a variety of ways. And this in the midst of relative, white affluence.

Aboriginal children in the Northern Territory outback.

They Came First

The Aboriginals themselves would prefer to be called names from their own languages: Koori in the east and south (meaning 'Our People'), Nyunga or Noongar in Western Australia, Yolngu in the Northern Territory, Anangu in central Australia and Nungga in South Australia. That's just a few of them.

These names, however, have not caught on to any great extent within white Australia, even less so in the world beyond Australia. For this reason, I am using the more conventional 'Aboriginal' in this chapter, with no insinuations attached.

But be mindful that Aboriginal identity is complex, fractured by notions of family, extended 'skin' or clan groups, language groups, and by the 'Nation' and 'Country'—territory or area of land—whence any one Aboriginal may hail. Before European settlement (many Aboriginals would call this 'the Invasion') in 1788, experts believe that there were about 700 separate Aboriginal nations speaking some 250 languages, further sub-divided into local dialects. Often, there were subtle overlaps among several groups but essentially, pre-settlement Australia was in reality a patchwork quilt of diverse societies, each with their own customs, rituals and rites collectively known as 'The Law'. Crucially, each group showed great respect for every other group's 'country', entering it only after observing certain accepted protocols seeking permission to enter. This is the reason that in Australia today, all officials, and all thinking events organisers routinely schedule a ceremony at the beginning of their event called 'Welcome to Country' in which the 'traditional owners', the indigenous Aboriginals, of the 'country' in which the event is taking place, formally welcome the 'intruders' who have come to the event, and give them permission to carry on and enter their 'country.' You will even see regularly on your home TV, an onscreen statement offering respect to the traditional owners of the site where the TV programmes are made, on Australia's most multicultural channel, SBS. To some, it may seem a tiresome knee-jerk ritual, but for Aboriginal self-respect it is vital, and by observing it, you make yourself a full member of the wider Australian 'family' and 'nation'.

'The First Australians' is the phrase most favoured among Australian liberals nowadays when referring to the original, black Australians, who may have come to Australia from South-east Asia at least 60,000 years ago. Indeed, the Aboriginals' curly hair, blue-black skins, spread noses and thick lips are reminiscent of the peoples of southern India and Papua New Guinea. My Tamil southern-Indian husband is convinced they are fellow Tamils, and prehistoric geography does make this conceivable—some of their languages even sound similar. He is often approached in the street by Aboriginals as a 'brother'.

The term 'First Australians' serves to remind all Australians, whether migrant or of many generations' standing, that they are all newcomer settlers to some degree, compared with the Aboriginals. If you are a migrant 'new Australian', do not expect Aboriginal Australians to find common cause with you as a fellow minority, not even if you happen to be black.

For the Aboriginals, post-World War II migrant settlement of Australia has simply added to their woes, adding yet more human strata above them, further blurring their claim to real ownership of the country. Immigration has pinned them even more firmly at the bottom of the social pile.

Australia's most famous old-generation Aboriginal politician, lawyer and Martin Luther King-style freedom fighter, Charles Perkins, the nation's first Aboriginal university graduate in 1965, expressed this feeling when he spoke out roundly condemning Asian immigration in the mid-1980s.

Statistical Phantoms

Aboriginals are thought to have numbered perhaps one million in the Sydney region alone when the Europeans arrived in Australia in 1788. The fact that this population had fallen to around 60,000 by 1888, as the European population zoomed above one million, speaks tragic volumes—newly imported diseases such as smallpox were partly responsible. But nobody really knows the true statistics Australia-wide, not least because Aboriginals were non-persons in census terms right up to 1967.

When the whites first arrived in Australia, they declared it an 'empty land' belonging to nobody, *Terra Nullius*, as if it were uninhabited. This was very convenient as it obviated the usual legal need to negotiate any kind of lease or treaty with traditional owners; the land could simply be taken.

Persona Non Grata

As writer John Pilger has put it in his *A Secret Country*, the Aboriginals were not accounted human but rather 'part of the fauna'. As late as 1963, Australia showed its contempt for Aboriginal human rights once again when it partnered with the British government to allow nuclear testing at three sites in Australia, one off the Western Australian coast and two others in South Australia, at Emu Field and Maralinga. These tests took place between 1952 and 1963, rendering the areas affected dangerous 'no-go' sites, yet during the entire process, scant regard was shown for the fact that aboriginal families were present in the area. A Royal Commission of Inquiry in 1984 revealed the shocking impact both on the land and on the indigenous people.

At 30 June 2006, the estimated resident Indigenous population of Australia was 517,200 or 2.5 per cent of the total population. This represented an increase of 58,700 since 2001, or 13 per cent. Projections suggest the total will swell to over 700,000 by 2021, with a 2.2 per cent growth rate, higher than the 1.4 per cent growth rate for the total Australian population. The rising trend over recent years is in part due to a real improvement in the treatment of Aboriginal Australians, and to a higher than average birth rate, but partly also to the increasing acceptability of declaring publicly one's aboriginality.

Only in 1967 did a referendum produce a 90.8 per cent popular vote to recognise Aboriginals as people who should be counted in the national census and also for whom the Commonwealth government could make laws (a decision that unfortunately for many of them, also gave them for the first time the legal right to drink alcohol). Many Australians confuse this referendum with the decision to give the vote to Aboriginal Australians, but the history of Aboriginal suffrage is in fact much more complex than that. Effectively however, Aboriginals did not have the federal, Commonwealth vote until 1962, and Queensland was the last state to grant them a State vote, in 1965.

Trauma of a Nation

The Europeans brought with them the flu, smallpox, venereal disease and many other ailments previously unknown to the Aboriginals, against which they had no immunity. The infinitely better armed settlers also hunted down the simple hunter-gatherer Aboriginals like animals, sometimes even putting out poisoned meat for them, as if for rabid dogs. They raped Aboriginal women and children. They ignored, despised or actively destroyed Aboriginal culture. This was attempted genocide, an orgy of cruelty. This is not to say that there were not incidences of whites who were ashamed of such barbarity or who strove to achieve harmony and understanding with the Aboriginals, nor that there were no individual kindnesses ever shown to the Aboriginals, but the overwhelming trend nonetheless revealed ignorance, fear, contempt and wilful destruction.

The Myall Creek Massacre

The most famous incident among a long litany of white-settler offences against the indigenous people was the 'Myall Creek Massacre' of 1838, in New South Wales state. For this wanton and brutal killing of innocent and defenceless Aboriginal women children and old men, seven of the 11 whites accused were hanged. But such justice was unusual. You will get something of a flavour of the times by watching the movie *The Tracker*. with an extraordinary performance by Aboriginal actor David Gulpilil.

The still unexorcised shame of this terrible time haunts the national psyche—as well it should, for it is by no means over yet. Although official policies of discrimination are long gone, you will still hear dreadful things said of 'the blackfella' in white society all over Australia ('blackfella' being a term more or less acceptable even among Aboriginals themselves, just as 'whitefella' is also neutral, not insulting at all); the deeper you get into the countryside, the worse the things you hear. To far too many white Australians, Aboriginals are still 'boongs' or 'abo's', the old terms of contempt now taboo in polite urban society. Even my otherwise charming Aussie friend spelled it out for me: 'They're all bludgers (the Aboriginals), that's what they are! Never worked for any land, never bought any land, just inherited it, that's all!'

Blatant cases of discrimination still surface regularly in the press. In 1989, Aboriginal university graduate and youth welfare officer, Julie Marie Tommy, successfully sued a Western Australian pub-hotel for refusing to serve her at its bar. It transpired during the case that the hotel had also set aside separate whites-only and blacks-only bars. Such scenes are repeated endlessly throughout rural Australia today.

The scandal of Aboriginal deaths in police custody erupted into the public mind, with the 1991 publication of a Royal Commission enquiry into *Aboriginal Deaths in Custody* into at least 105 unexplained Aboriginal deaths in police and prison cells. In so many cases, what may have begun as a simple arrest for drunk and disorderly behaviour has ended with sudden death. The Council for Aboriginal Reconciliation and also the post of Aboriginal and Torres Straits Islander Social Justice Commissioner were established in response to the Royal Commission's findings. Fingers have been pointed at the police over the issue of deaths in custody, but ultimately the finger points at all Australians. There seems to have been little progress since 1991. Of all deaths in prison/custody, 20 per cent were indigenous Australians in 2002; and whereas in 1991, 14 per cent of the total prison population comprised indigenous Australians, by 2011, this figure had risen to 26 per cent – very disproportionate in terms of Aboriginals accounting for barely 3 per cent of the total population of Australia.

Similarly alarming is the high rate of suicide among Aboriginals. Accurate figures are hard to come by but experts are agreed that the Aboriginal rate of suicide, most notably among young males, is at least 40 per cent higher than in the general population, and that it is increasing rapidly, whereas in traditional indigenous society, it was almost unheard of. Just as an example, in the Kimberley region of Western Australia alone, just between July 2010- July 2011, there were 10 Aboriginal suicides and many other incidents of self-harm.

Perhaps this is the right place to mention another tradition in dealings between whites and Aboriginals in Australia, similar to the 'Welcome to Country' rite: the need to apologise when forced to make reference to, or depict, Aboriginal persons who are dead. Mentioning dead people is extremely distressing to Aboriginals and you will see apologies on TV preceding almost every programme dealing with Aboriginal issues that has to show pictures of those who have passed away. It will always be appreciated if you can offer the same respect should the occasion arise, just an acknowledgement in advance that you are about to break an Aboriginal taboo, and you are sorry for it.

For Their Own Good

By the beginning of the 20th century, the best an Aboriginal could expect from life was to be relegated to an Aboriginal reserve and get some sort of a job with the white man—on a farm, a cattle station or as a domestic servant. In some states, the Aboriginal was forbidden to consume alcohol, to marry or have sex across the colour line, or to carry a firearm. The 'sex bar' didn't stop many of their white employers, however, systematically raping their female workers.

The 1930s and well beyond, into the 1960s, saw a fully articulated policy of assimilation, with or without Aboriginal consent, for mixed bloods. Out of a sort of twisted benevolence, the white authorities systematically removed Aboriginal children, particularly those of mixed blood, from their mothers 'for their own good', in an attempt to integrate them into white society and obliterate their aboriginality forever. Often, however, they were simply put into domestic servitude, akin to slavery. You need to see US-based Australian

Philip Noyce's movie of 2002, *Rabbit-Proof Fence* (starring David Gulpilil and also Shakespearean actor Kenneth Branagh as the frosty 'Protector of the Aborigines') to get some sort of feeling for the enormity of suffering that such policies caused. The movie, set in the 1930s, was based on Doris Pilkington's book *Follow the Rabbit-Proof Fence*.

The basic idea was to weed, and breed out Aboriginal genes, leaving the full-blood elders to die off peacefully, thus eliminating the Aboriginal race altogether. This was thought to be the 'kindest' stratagem for dealing with 'the problem.' Descendants of the Aboriginal children taken from their families are known as 'The Stolen Generation'; they are still searching for their families and discovering who they really are. Some experts have estimated that two thirds of all mixed blood children—thousands—were impacted by these policies, in the Northern Territory region alone, between 1912 and the 1960s. In his speech opening Parliament in February 2007, Prime Minister Kevin Rudd assessed the overall picture: "...between 1910 and 1970, between 10 and 30 per cent of Indigenous children were forcibly taken from their mothers and fathers. ...as a result, up to 50,000 children were forcibly taken from their families."

The Aboriginal Experience

A part of these dispossessed children's story is told movingly by a mixed-blood Aboriginal psychologist-writer-artist, Sally Morgan, in her book *My Place*.

A similar understanding of the Aboriginal experience is presented in *Dingo, The Story of our Mob* by Sally Dingo, a white Australian married to entertainer Ernie Dingo, a role model for young Aboriginals. The full story is told in agonising detail through the official report *Bringing Them Home: The Stolen Children Report'* resulting from the 1995 National Inquiry into the Separation of Aboriginal and Torres Straits Islander Children From Their Families.

In 1991 a special Memorandum of Understanding was signed to allow Aboriginals from 'the stolen generation' special access to Australia's official archives and records of policies resulting in the separation of families, so that they could research their own genealogy more effectively. But most have remained 'lost'.

The story of the Stolen Generation however should not be seen as pure black and white, as it were. Influential Aboriginal commentator and columnist Noel Pearson has pointed to greater complexity In his many columns for *The Australian* between 2008-2011:

Indeed, many have commented on how some of the most successful and articulate Aboriginal leaders are mixed-blood and in fact do come from a background where they were taken from their families and brought up and educated by Christian missions or white foster parents. But this has to be weighed against the deep losses of cultural identity and parental love.

Absorbing the Difference

Today's policy, first set by Gough Whitlam's Labor government in 1972, is to allow Aboriginals self-determination. In line with the wider goal of building a multicultural Australia, Aboriginals are offered a share in the benefits of modern white society through gradual (and voluntary) assimilation. Every effort is made at official levels to encourage the Aboriginals to preserve their culture.

Assimilation is no easy matter, for there can be no disputing that Aborigines are 'different'. Differences exist within their community as well, with some members originating from different tribal or language groups (although 'tribe' is not quite the right concept to apply to the highly fractured format of Aboriginal society) and others delineated more by whether they grew up in the towns or countryside and whether they are mixed or full-blood Aborigines, whether they were influenced or educated by Christian missionaries or not.

Among the Aboriginals' most striking differences with white Australians is their legendary penchant for 'going walkabout'— disappearing without warning for days, weeks or months— which gives them a reputation for being unreliable. In this they echo their nomadic ancestors, but also they will always answer the call of any major kinship event (birth, marriage, death), no matter how far away from home. Possession and property are alien concepts in Aboriginal culture, the antithesis of Western materialism. Nomads do not carry around much luggage, and share freely. They also expect the same of others, and this can sometimes make them appear too free with others' goods. Private property is an alien concept in their culture.

Even when tribal bands of Aboriginals in their natural state wandered through one another's territory, defined only by a delicate structure of oral precepts, there was never any attempt to 'conquer' one another or 'acquire' the land. So when the whites came, it never dawned on the Aboriginals that they had lost their land, since such a concept was unimaginable. Only when the whites erected fences to keep them out and filled the land with sheep and cattle, depriving them of their hunting grounds or vandalising ancient sacred sites of spiritual value, did they begin to react with hostility, but in vain.

Confinement within four walls induces virtually terminal claustrophobia in many Aboriginals, once upon a time used to ranging across some of the vastest open spaces known to humankind. That is why prison is a particularly brutal experience for them and often results in suicide. But even a home can be a challenge. When offered a neat little home, Aboriginals may opt instead to create a rough camp outdoors, in the garden. They may even destroy timber structures to use the wood for making campfires outdoors to cook on. In the view of unsympathetic whites, this looks like a perverse insistence on creating slums and an innate lack of

This reconstruction at Perth's Dumbartung Gallery depicts a typical overnight shelter—a 'humpy'—built from natural materials by wandering Aboriginals in the wild.

'civilisation'. But it also has a lot to do with seeing the stars in the heavens above as the only ceiling you really need.

Diet of Death

The European newcomers were the harbingers of Aboriginal death in many shapes and forms. They brought flour, sugar, alcohol and tobacco, among a host of other goodies that would destroy the Aboriginals' health. The most visible result for the casual observer is Aboriginal obesity. Mind you, the whites are hardly immune, thanks to fast food.

Research in the 1980s and 1990s has demonstrated that the Aboriginals' spartan original diet of berries, roots, insects and occasional fish or wild animals like the goanna lizard or the kangaroo, was far better for them. Hence also the trendy cuisine style among hip whites called 'Bush Tucker'—but more of that in Chapter 6: Tucker.

The lamentable state of Aboriginal health today is certainly one more reason for Australia to continue feeling ashamed. Heart disease, diabetes, tuberculosis, even trachoma and malnutrition, AIDS too; you name it, they've got it. Taking the remote 'outback' Kimberley region of Western Australia as just one example, the area holds only 2 per cent of the State's population yet generates two-thirds of the State's notifications of syphilis, a third of those of gonorrhoea and a sixth of those of chlamydia, mostly known to emanate from Aboriginal communities. This is more because of Aboriginals' lack of awareness of and access to screening and treatment than because they are intrinsically sexually irresponsible. Creative ideas like 'condom trees'—wilderness trees bedecked with free condom-filled containers to give wandering Aboriginals easy access to safe-sex tools—have been devised to deal with such issues, distributing about 100,000 condoms a year in the Kimberley region.

Aboriginal life expectancy in recent years is estimated at about 67.2 years for indigenous males, 72.9 years for females (compare an average 78.7 and 82.6 for all Australians). The gap is even wider for the Northern Territory and Western Australia. These rates recall the mainstream figures a century ago. These rates are also about the same as for females in sub-Saharan

Africa (with AIDS factored out) and as for males in Myanmar or Papua New Guinea. There have been small improvements over the 21st century (the statistics were worse in 2001) but not enough. This ill-health stems largely from poor diet, poor living environment and often unstable family life. Alcohol abuse, petrol sniffing and domestic violence, even incest and child abuse, are rife in Aboriginal families (not that Australian whites do not have their share) – watch Aboriginal director Warwick Thornton's 2009 movie *Samson and Delilah*, and weep.

As many others have put it before me, Aboriginal Australians live a 'Third World' life in the midst of a 'First World' nation. Their trashed out-of-town settlements resemble the worst sort of refugee camps, or the black shanty townships of South Africa. You do not want to be there on pay-day or welfare cheque handout night, when the drinking and bottle-throwing starts in the streets.

The Rights See-saw

Such conditions make it extremely difficult for Aboriginals to take advantage of the many special aid and affirmative-action schemes which now exist to help them enter mainstream Australia. They still have a very steep climb ahead of them, even despite a litany of special rights assigned to them since the 1970s, often much to the chagrin of some less compassionate white Australians.

In gradual steps, different states have, at different times since the mid-1960s, legislated first to turn over Aboriginal reserve lands to the Aboriginals themselves, and then to grant traditional ownership of vacant lands to them on application.

The acknowledged turning points were the Aboriginal Land Rights (Northern Territory) Act of 1976 and the so-called "Mabo Case" of 1992 in which the courts overturned the old *'Terra Nullius'* lie, finding that Aboriginals did have the right to make legal native title land claims, although subsequent settlement may sometimes have extinguished their title – which means of course that some of the best land may be denied to them. A Native Title Act resulted but there has been a see-saw of conflicting court judgements over time, creating a legal labyrinth. Internal disagreement among Aboriginal groups has also delayed many title agreements, including a major attempt in Western Australia during 2011-2012.

At present, something like 20 per cent of Australia is held by the Aboriginal community in some form or another—often, under agreements merely allowing non-exclusive access to Aboriginal traditional owners, a very limited form of 'ownership'. Land rights battles continue today, particularly when Aboriginal aspirations come into conflict with powerful mining and farming interests. Individual agreements pop up now and again, from State to State, but there seems to be no national blueprint on how to proceed.

The 'Aboriginal Industry' is an elaborate tangle of Federal and State policies, institutions and bureaucracies, all of them extremely worthy, but effectively congealing into a single dismaying discombobulated glob.

Because it is all so confusing, I have taken the simplest route of reproducing, just slightly edited, a 2010 factsheet from the Australian Bureau of Statistics, below, to explain some of the current situation:

In 1989, the Aboriginal and Torres Strait Islander Commission (ATSIC) was created as a nationally representative organisation of the Aboriginal and Torres Strait Islander peoples. It effectively was elected by Aboriginals. ATSIC advised governments on Aboriginal issues and advocated for its clients.

However, major change to Aboriginal and Torres Strait Islander governance came with the abolition of ATSIC in March 2005. ATSIC's functions were transferred to a mainstream Commonwealth government agency, the Department of Family and Community Services and Indigenous Affairs (which is still the key official channel for policy on indigenous affairs – see http://www.fahcsia.gov.au/sa/indigenous/overview/Pages/default.aspx). A new body, the National Indigenous Council, was appointed by the Commonwealth government as a key advisory body on Aboriginal affairs, but was abolished in 2008. In May 2010 the National Congress of Australia's First Peoples (NCAFP) was established, to be a national representative body, a national leader and advocate for recognising the status of Aboriginal and Torres Strait Islander peoples as First Nation peoples.

(A company owned by its own members, independent of government, NCAFP's first Board took up office in July 2011).

In almost all areas of Aboriginal and Torres Strait Islander affairs, the fostering of Aboriginal and Torres Strait Islander leadership has been identified as a priority, with a range of Aboriginal and Torres Strait Islander leadership programmes operating throughout Australia.

Conservative and Liberal Prime Minister John Howard explained the ATSIC closure at the time thus: "We believe very strongly that the experiment in separate representation, elected representation, for indigenous people has been a failure." In future, he said, Aboriginal programmes would be "mainstreamed" but "arrangements will be established to ensure that there is a major policy role for the Minister of Indigenous Affairs." This pretty much remains the case, but the Labor government since 2007 has overlaid it with the as yet untested extra of the new NCAFP, another Aboriginal-elected body that seems potentially to echo ATSIC. The official slogan now is 'flexibility' in arrangements, but this can all too easily mask chaos and uncertainty.

Into the void created by ATSIC's departure came some interesting new initiatives such as 'Shared Responsibility Agreements' that demanded a 'two-way street' for welfare payments, housing or other benefits given to Aboriginals; some of these have made it mandatory for Aboriginals to guarantee that their children would consistently attend school, or even simply feed their children properly and get them to shower and wash their school uniforms regularly, in return for welfare. By 2008, almost 300 such agreements had been signed between government and Aboriginals. But their future seems mired in debate over definitions and terms, and one notices that they do not get mentioned very often these days.

The centrepiece of government Aboriginal policy these days is "Closing the Gap". More about this concept ahead in this chapter, under "Turning of the Tide".

The Land Mother
Land rights are central to Aboriginality. It is hard for outsiders to comprehend the very deep and mystic way in which

Ritual spirit poles on Bathurst Island, Northern Territory.

Aboriginals feel they are bound to the land. This is not the feeling of the white farmer who loves his land through proud possession and control of it. Rather, the Aboriginals feel *they* are owned and controlled by the land. The earth is their 'mother'.

In a far-off 'Dreamtime', believe the Aboriginals, ancestral spirits, beings and other agents of Mother Earth travelled across the land creating people, places, plants and animals. You will hear a lot in Australia about Aboriginal 'sacred sites'. Once a place is declared a sacred site, it becomes extremely problematic to develop it or tamper with it in any way. A pitched battle went on for many years now over State Government development proposals for a riverside site in Perth, Western Australia, formerly a brewery, for exactly this reason (but it is now an upmarket apartment complex). The sacred sites were the halting points where the ancestral beings paused on their journeys across the land. There are many other such cases across the country.

Each Aboriginal's very identity, and position within the tribe or clan, is based on the place where he or she was born, and is linked to an ancestral being, expressed through a plant or an animal. The soil is the source of all life, and the home to which all life returns after death, for recycling into life again. There is no sense of separation from other life-forms. This tunes well with beliefs found in some of the great world religions—Hinduism and Buddhism among them—and native American philosophy too.

The Aboriginals lived in complete harmony and balance with the wild land. Their burning-back patterns were an essential part of the ecosystem, regenerating and benefiting many species of plants and animals in an ecology geared for natural fires. They took from the land only what they needed to survive.

The Culture

There is no single Aboriginal culture, but its many facets are linked by one common thread: the attachment to Nature, particularly to the land, including animals and plants. The culture is peopled by spirit beings and spirituality infuses every aspect of daily life. 'Stories', 'Story Places' and the complex concepts of both 'Dreamtime' and 'Songlines' are fundamental to the culture. For real understanding, you will have to read a whole lot more.

Magic plays an important role. Even white Australians are in some awe of customs like 'pointing the bone'—a form of curse willing an enemy to die—and 'singing', an intensive group incantation, again intended to bring injury or death to the enemy. Stories of singing-victims (black and white) falling down dead abound.

The Aboriginal system of justice was harsh, but effectively meted out by the elders of the tribe—you might be speared in the leg or, much worse, 'sung to death' for transgression of tribal laws.

Kinship and extended family are central to Aboriginal integrity. Many South-east Asians and the more traditional or Mediterranean Europeans will recognise this group-oriented social structure as similar to their own.

That is why an Aboriginal house with capacity for a family of five may well be crammed to bursting point with 50 or more, just because the 'rellies' dropped by for a while on their latest walkabout, often in connection with a family funeral. An Aboriginal never refuses family as a house guest, no matter how absurd the numbers or how difficult the resulting overcrowding. Just another sticking point with white neighbours.

Culture and wisdom were passed on through the community's rich repertoire of oral history, stories and songs—there was no writing—culminating in the formal, and often painful, initiation ceremony for children passing into adulthood. Secret knowledge of sacred things was communicated at this ceremony. Men and women have segregated secrets—'men's business' and 'women's business'. To this day, there are many such secrets still carefully kept from the uninitiated.

To get a feeling for some of the charm of the traditional societies that were erased by white settlement, you can view one remnant but still vibrant culture in Rolf de Heer's marvellous film of 2006, *Ten Canoes*, set in the tropical Arnhem Land region of the remote north (do visit the website http://www.tencanoes.com.au/tencanoes/ which is an ongoing work, with interactive elements allowing the indigenous people involved in the movie to continue their stories). This movie, the first ever to use the indigenous people's own languages in the dialogue (mediated in translation by the authentically accented English narration of Aboriginal actor David Gulpilil, whose son Jamie also acts in the movie), shows the people's intimate relationship with their land and simply tells a great, and often funny, story.

For a solid, objective overview, try the national Australian Museum's website on indigenous history and culture: http://www.dreamtime.net.au/index.cfm

One of the most respected white commentators on Aboriginal lands, lifestyles and issues is *The Australian* newspaper's Northern Australia correspondent Nicolas Rothwell (of part Czech extraction), based in Darwin. His columns in the paper are always engrossing reading, and his book *Another Country* gives very good context to the whole topic and reveals enormous empathy and 'feel' both for the landscape and the people.

The Art of Being Aboriginal

One of the most striking things about Aboriginal culture before white settlement was the existence of an estimated 250 distinct Aboriginal languages, with more than 500 dialects. More than half of these languages are now extinct.

While most of these languages, like the Aboriginals

themselves, evolved in complete isolation from outside influences, in some areas there was some cross-fertilisation: in the Northern Territory, as well as parts of north-western Western Australia. For example, ancient trading links with Indonesian fishermen seeking Australia's valuable sea-slugs and trochus shells, led to Indonesian vocabulary entering Aboriginal tongues. In parts of the Northern Territory, for example, the word for 'foreigner' is *balanda*, the Indonesian word for a Dutchman or 'Hollander'.

Aboriginal languages have left their mark on white Australia, in place-names and in everyday words, from 'billabong' to 'kangaroo'. But we can only guess at what opportunities for acquiring extraordinary knowledge have been squandered over the years of white contempt for Aboriginal culture. No research body was set up to study this fascinating kaleidoscope of cultures before the establishment in 1961 of the Australian Institute of Aboriginal Studies at Canberra.

Aboriginal culture has since been revealed as vastly more sophisticated than previously understood. On the artistic front in particular, the Aboriginals have contributed to the very definition of 'Australian-ness'.

This Reconciliation mural was painted by Melanie Evans in 1999 for display at the Pioneers Park in Fremantle, Western Australia. Melanie's people are the Mudburra from the Northern Territory although she lives in Fremantle now. The mural depicts the 'Wargul' or 'Wagyl' (Rainbow Serpent). The revered Rainbow Serpent is associated with water but also with the shaping and organisation of natural life, the land and its fertility.

Aboriginal Australian art, traditionally executed chiefly on the Aboriginals' own bodies, on cave and rock walls, and on strips of bark, has achieved international recognition in recent decades, as Aboriginal artists have learned to transfer it to canvas and transmit it through modern media such as watercolours, oils and acrylic. Especially well known are the dot-mosaic and 'X-ray' styles of painting (depicting animals complete with their skeletal structure and internal organs). The best examples are now, quite rightly, very expensive, and grace the walls of some of the world's premier galleries.

Albert Namatjira was a pioneer Aboriginal artist who scored most of his considerable success before World War II—he died in 1959. But he did it with Western-style watercolour paintings. More traditional Aboriginal art was not to win white acclaim until long after the war. Today, there are many Aboriginal artists of note in Australia keeping tribal traditions alive and also producing innovative modern works using non-traditional techniques and media.

Just as creative as the fusion with Western art media has been the recent grafting of Asian techniques like batik—wax-resist textile printing—with Aboriginal motifs, to stunning effect in some areas of the Northern Territory.

The success of Aboriginal art has already helped restore the Aboriginals' pride in themselves and their culture, quite apart from bringing them income. But a contentious issue of today raises the question of 'intellectual copyright': whether or not white-community 'borrowing' and commercialisation of Aboriginal styles and themes constitute acceptably inspired derivation, or merely plagiarist exploitation. Aboriginal art promoters today have to take a lot more care with how they market the product and how much of the resulting income they remit to the originators, the Aboriginals themselves.

A Brand New Day on Its Way?

Less well known to the outside world are Aboriginal music and dance, central elements in traditional Aboriginal culture. Here again, Western influences have produced interesting hybrids. Many Aboriginal musicians have shown a talent for pop or country-and-western styles.

Aboriginal rock painting at Nourlangie, Northern Territory.

Every year in about September–October, Aboriginal society holds its very own 'Oscars' award ceremony to recognise Aboriginal artistes, 'The Deadlys' ('Deadly' is black street lingo for 'Terrific, Awesome' etc). The Deadly Awards are handed out to Aboriginal achievers in the arts, sport and community work, with all the pomp and ceremony of an Oscars event. In existence since 1995, these awards have become more prominent since SBS TV decided to televise them in 2005. The talent showcased at the Deadlys is truly impressive.

Contact between Aboriginal and white Australian musicians has also spawned outstanding fusion bands such as the former *Gondwanaland* (now just *Gondwana*, named after the supercontinent of some 150 million years ago which, according to Continental Drift Theory, gave birth to Australia about 45 million years ago). Equally powerful is the fusion music of the all-Aboriginal group *Yothu Yindi*, led by former teacher Mandawuy Yunupingu of the Yolngu people, who in 1988 was the first tertiary graduate from the Aboriginal reserve area of Arnhem Land. To learn more, go to: http://www.yothuyindi.com.

Fusion bands like these have evolved a quintessentially Australian sound with original compositions featuring instruments as diverse as electronic synthesisers, drums and the Aboriginal didgeridoo, a very long, tube-like wind instrument carved from raw logs. The insistent, throbbing drone of the didgeridoo is the sound of Australia itself, an awe-inspiring voice from the desert speaking to the deepest, most mysterious levels of the human soul. Yet another Yunupingu of the Yolngu, singer Geoffrey Gurrumul Yunupingu, and formerly a member of *Yothu Yindi*, is the latest 'big thing' in Aboriginal music. Born blind, he released his first solo album *Gurrumul* in 2008. His singularly sweet-noted voice made it an instant hit. A lovely new voice and face is Aboriginal singer Jessica Mauboy, discovered at the age of 16 during the 2006 *Australian Idol* contest, a Darwin girl, daughter of a father with Indonesian (West Timor) ancestry and an indigenous mother. Perhaps more unexpected is the classical operatic career of Aboriginal soprano Deborah Cheetham, of the Yorta Yorta people (her mother is Aboriginal but her father Irish), who made her debut in 1997 – she recently performed her own creation, an indigenous opera called *Pecan Summer* and is now fostering Australia's first indigenous opera company, *Short Black Opera*. For added interest, she is a niece of the much loved, world-class Aboriginal singer Jimmy Little, sadly deceased in 2012.

Aboriginal dance is not just campfire stuff. Try the sophisticated *Bangarra Dance Theatre* for a fine fusion of contemporary dance with Aboriginal features and themes – visit http://www.bangarra.com.au

Among Australia's best known Aboriginal actors and dancers is David Gulpilil. If you saw the first *Crocodile Dundee* film, you will remember Gulpilil as Dundee's Aboriginal friend, but he was also outstanding in Rolf de Heer's more substantial movie of 2002, *The Tracker*, already mentioned—a subtle tale of Aboriginal wisdom set against white brutality and crudeness.

Theatre is another arena now beginning to showcase Aboriginal talents. Actor Ernie Dingo is a well-established example, and the late Western Australian playwright Jack Davis another (he died in 2000)—Jack Davis in particular conjured up the bleakness of Aboriginal life in the old days on settlements controlled by whites. His works are now considered Australian classics and are used as secondary school study texts.

Another major theatre event for the Aboriginal world was Black Swan Theatre's 2008 premiere of writer Steve Hawke's play *Jandamarra* in Western Australia. The play tells the story of an Aboriginal tracker's rebellion against his white bosses in the 1890s. His subsequent armed insurrection was doomed to end in tragedy, with Jandamarra himself tracked down and killed by an Aboriginal tracker, his head removed and sent to England as a trophy. The play carries an extra fillip of interest in that its creator, Hawke, is none other than the son of one of Australia's best known Prime Ministers, Bob Hawke (Prime Minister 1983–1991); at 19, Steve Hawke took off for northern Western Australia's rugged Kimberley region, developed close links with Aboriginal society there, and has never looked back since.

Bran Nu Dae

I was privileged to attend the 1990 premiere of Australia's first Aboriginal musical, *Bran Nu Dae* ('A Brand New Day') – now also a chirpy movie, released in 2010. The name of its creator was Jimmy Chi, the product of a Chinese father and an Aboriginal mother in the old pearling port of Broome, up in the northwest of Western Australia. The descendants of Afghan camel drivers' unions with Aboriginal women are another example of the many such exotic mixes to be found in the melting pot of Australia.

Wonderfully raucous, rumbustious and ribald, the play depicts an Aboriginal boy's flight from the city of Perth back to his outback homeland. White society, from the local Roman Catholic archbishop to well-meaning hippies, is satirised mercilessly but in a good-natured sort of way.

In the West too, the theatre group Yirra Yaakin often makes interesting waves in Aboriginal theatre world—visit http://www.yirrayaakin.asn.au/

The black protest movements of the 1950s and 1960s in the West had their impact on Aboriginal Australia and a new school of writing is now apparent as a result. One of the first and best-known Aboriginal protest writers was Oodgeroo Noonuccal, also known as Kath Walker, a formidable poetess, whose first volume of poetry, *We Are Going*, was published in 1964. Another early success was Aboriginal artist and writer Dick Roughsey, who wrote chiefly for children—works such as *The Giant Devil-Dingo* in 1973 and *The Rainbow Serpent* in 1975.

Sporting Laurels

Aboriginals have also shown exceptional talent in sports. Curiously, the very first Australian cricket team to visit England was a privately-organised all-Aboriginal team, which toured the country in 1868. (However, several of them found England's climate so inhospitable that they had to go home before time; one of them actually died.)

Most sports fans have also heard of Aboriginal tennis player Evonne Goolagong, the 1971 and 1981 Wimbledon women's singles champion. Aboriginal sportsmen have also excelled in football and boxing. Famous Aboriginal boxers include Dave Sands (1940s), bantam-weight Lionel Rose, world champion in his class at the Mexico Olympics of 1968, and Tony Mundine in the 1970s and his son today, Anthony Mundine.

Hockey player Nova Peris-Kneebone scored gold at the Atlanta Olympics in 1996, transmuting into a runner in the 2000 Olympics. And who in the world did not thrill to Australian Aboriginal athlete Cathy Freeman's triumphant raising of the torch carrying the Olympic flame at the Sydney Olympics opening ceremony in 2000, followed by her epic Gold Medal win in the 400-metre race final? Less well known on the world stage are the countless big Aboriginal names in Australian Rules Football or 'footy'—names such as David Wirrpunda, Chris Lewis and Jeff Farmer.

The author's friends and former neighbours, the Eades family in Perth, WA, are fairly typical of urban Aboriginal families: from left to right (back), mum Stephanie Eades, with son Wayne and daughter Courtney, and front, husband Wayne and daughter Shamone. Photo by Viva! Life Photography, Perth.

Black Politics

Education is the key to Aboriginal advancement, as it is for so many other disadvantaged peoples. At the moment, Aboriginal employment rates for adults are about half those for the rest of the population. The community does already have models to follow: for example, Sir Doug Nicholls, who died in 1988, a pastor, the first Aboriginal to be knighted by the Queen and also the nation's first Aboriginal Governor, of South Australia, 1976–1977.

The year 1971 also saw the first Aboriginal Member of Federal Parliament, Neville Bonner, while 1978 saw Pat O'Shane become Australia's first Aboriginal law graduate and barrister. The first two Aboriginals to be employed by the diplomatic service in the Ministry of Foreign Affairs were hired in 1982. Aden Ridgeway of the Democrats became the second Aboriginal Member of Federal Parliament, but lost his seat in

2004. The first indigenous woman ever to sit in any Australian Parliament, Carol Martin, took her seat in the Western Australian Parliament in 2001; 2006 saw Labor's Ben Wyatt elected to the Western Australian seat of Victoria Park, and 2008 brought the first female indigenous Deputy Chief Minister, Labor politician Marion Scrymgour, in the Northern Territory.

Burnum Burnum, an Aboriginal lawyer and freedom fighter, is also politically significant. He once planted the Aboriginal flag on England's white cliffs of Dover, on Australia Day 1988, to claim England for the Aboriginal 'nation'.

Burnum Burnum also masterminded the recovery of the bones of Truganini, the last full-blood Tasmanian Aboriginal (but not the last Tasmanian Aboriginal), who had died in 1876. Tasmania's Hobart Museum had put them on display up to 1947 against Truganini's express wish that her body be left undisturbed. Her ashes were at last scattered on waters close to her homeland. Many other attempts to retrieve Aboriginal bones stored as curiosities in foreign museums are still underway.

Among other activist names you will undoubtedly encounter are Gary Foley, Dr Lois O' Donoghue, Peter Yu (half-Chinese) and Pat and Mick Dodson.

But possibly the biggest, most vocal and influential voice in our times is that of Aboriginal intellectual and leader Noel Pearson, director of the Cape York Institute for Policy and Leadership that he created, a passionate and eloquent campaigner for his people who has consistently been a 'lateral thinker' with very different and new ideas on how his people can pull themselves out of the trough most of them are in. Pearson is widely believed to have been a factor behind major changes in government policy towards Aboriginals during 2007, initiated by Liberal Prime Minister John Howard. Pearson's version of 'tough love' and ruthless self criticism on behalf of his fellow Aboriginals have not endeared him to all sectors of his community, and he has been castigated for high-handedness as well as outright bad behaviour (swearing at the media etc). He has consistently and bravely pushed the line that the key to resolution of the Aboriginal dilemma is to put an end to what he calls 'passive welfare', the handout mentality, the waiting for what

Aboriginals colourfully term 'sit-down money' (i.e. money for doing nothing), that he sees as having robbed the Aboriginal community of drive and purpose. He is a strong advocate for Aboriginal self-management but only within a framework of proper responsibility for self. In a 2007 interview with the ABC TV's Lateline programme, he put this in context:

"We've got to take charge. We've got to be given back responsibility. Might I say the collapse of responsibility that we see, the wasteland of responsibility in Indigenous Australia is the consequence of government and bureaucracies and welfare organisations, including NGOs, who have intervened in Aboriginal affairs and said, "Listen, you don't have to take responsibility. You have a whole suite of rights, including the right to welfare, the right to drink, the right to party all night, the right to have the trappings of office without being accountable for any return on your role."

Many would agree with Pearson: as the then Prime Minister Rudd put it when he opened Parliament in February 2007, the 'business as usual approach' to Aboriginal issues no longer works. Australia is ready for completely new approaches to 'The Problem'.

THE MABO/WIK MESS

Aboriginal history reached a historic crossroads with the landmark 'Mabo' judgement made by the Australian High Court in June 1992—a judgement named after deceased Aboriginal land-rights negotiator Eddy Mabo. The High Court ruled that the original colonial designation of Australia as *Terra Nullius* or 'empty land', was erroneous: the Aboriginals did have valid 'native title' to much of the Australian land.

This has generated hysteria, and more importantly, uncertainty for farmers and would-be minerals exploiters. Is the average suburban backyard secure from Aboriginal land claims? Yes, the Mabo decision stated clearly that no privately-owned land is threatened.

States like resource-rich Western Australia however had concerns because vacant State land certainly was vulnerable to native-title claims and Western Australia, for one, has plenty of that; Premier Richard Court's conservative Liberal state government therefore passed its own legislation to override the High Court judgement. But even if native-title claims do not stand on occupied land, there may now be a case for financial compensation to the original 'traditional owners', the Aboriginals.

A Native Title Tribunal set up after Mabo has been hearing claims. In many cases, all the Aboriginals want to establish is their right of access to properties in connection with visiting 'sacred sites', hunting and fishing, and their right to be consulted on the future disposal of the land. To a large extent, they want not simply access to the wealth that is land, but more the 'face' of recognition and consultation, to salve the humiliating wounds of their lamentable history—Asians culturally attuned to concepts of 'face' will perhaps be the first to sympathise with that desire.

But Australians have an additional ruling to wrestle with: 'The Wik Decision' handed out to the Wik People of Cape York Peninsula, Queensland, in 1996. The High Court in this case ruled that native title can coexist with pastoral (farming) leases and can only be extinguished permanently by a special law, which has not occurred. In other words, the farmers did not have exclusive hold on the land, although it seems their rights have priority when there is a conflict. Any new decision to mine or log such land, however, must go through a negotiation process with native-title holders first.

To muddy the waters further, the Federal Court of Australia later ruled that native title could exist over coastal waters and that in some cases 'the tide of history had washed away' that title. Nobody wants to face up to the real meaning of reconciliation with the Aborigines, for at its heart lie the issues of land ownership and land use. Land, in turn, lies at the heart of Australia's wealth. But as journalist John Pilger concludes in *A Secret Country*, 'Until we white Australians give back to black Australians their nationhood, we can never claim our own.'

THE INTERVENTION

Aboriginal society has become inured to an almost endless stream of enquiries and reports dating right back to early colonial days, all focusing on 'what to do with' various

Aboriginal problems. It all seems a bit repetitive, and results in far too little change for the better. However, in the overall scheme of things, the *Little Children Are Sacred* report of 15 June 2007, produced by a Board of Inquiry into the Protection of Aboriginal Children from Sexual Abuse commissioned by the Northern Territory Government, was definitely different, both in its content and in its consequences, not least in terms of the Federal Government's almost immediate and radical reaction. The report detailed a shocking level of sexual abuse of Aboriginal children of both sexes, and at all ages, even babies, and identified the situation as a national crisis. Alcohol abuse—the addiction to 'grog' so evident in most remote Aboriginal communities—was fingered as a major contributor to the problem, besides a catalogue of other Aboriginal woes ranging from poor housing to unemployment—a point of debate still is the now suspended and largely discredited former CDEP or Community Development Employment Programme, specially crafted to give Aboriginals paid work but dismissed by many as a 'make work' scheme irrelevant to the real world and therefore to some extent disabling for Aboriginals trying to get into the real workplace.

The Australian public had for a couple of years already been forewarned by a series of increasingly strident articles and speeches from those on the ground that conditions in remote Aboriginal communities were becoming intolerable in many ways—there were continual tales of endemic substance-abuse (notably petrol sniffing) leading to permanent physical and mental disabilities among the young, of irreparable alcohol addiction (with babies affected at the breast) and premature deaths, of underage girls selling themselves for drugs, of high suicide levels, of sexual abuse, of tiny children with full-blown venereal diseases, and of rampant domestic violence. The *Little Children Are Sacred* report was simply the straw that finally broke the camel's back with its revelations of widespread, tragic and horrifying sexual abuse of children, essentially charting the ruin of a whole generation, or two.

Many sniped that John Howard's ailing Liberal government now smelled an opportunity to demonstrate leadership and inject a sense of crisis into the nation just before the upcoming

General Election, just as it had in with the its fear-mongering over the 'Tampa affair' involving a boat-load of more than 400 refugees seeking asylum shortly before the 2001 General Election (which Howard won partly as a result). Whatever the truth, the Howard government moved almost immediately and dramatically to announce and implement its new 'Northern Territory Emergency Response' (NTER) on 21 June 2007, barely one week after the publication of *Little Children Are Sacred*. This response has been forever after known to the general public as "The Intervention". The atmosphere was very much as if a national emergency of military proportions had been declared, and indeed the Intervention's urgent despatch of both military and police personnel to help manage remote Aboriginal communities was reminiscent of Australia's recent military and peacekeeping interventions in East Timor or in some of the failing South Pacific nations such as Tonga and the Solomon Islands. Unfortunately, although both mainstream Australia and many Aboriginals agreed that incisive action was needed, it seems there was insufficient consultation with the actual remote communities affected before launching the Intervention. For many Aboriginals, this was yet another imposition of white authority, just like all the other ones in the past. Others pointed out that the admittedly dreadful conditions in their communities were not merely the fault of drunken irresponsible Aboriginals, but a direct consequence of decades of white neglect and contempt. There was deep resentment in some of the communities affected by the Intervention. It was not so much what was done that rankled, as the way it was done.

Things rolled at an amazing pace, with three pieces of major legislation passed in August 2007 specifically to cater for the Intervention, which in many ways was barely legal at its inception, and still questionable today in some areas. The new measures are estimated to have affected at least 500 Northern Territory Aboriginal communities, more than 45,000 individuals. And before long, versions of the same approach were being rolled out in Western Australia too.

The Intervention ostensibly was crafted primarily to protect Aboriginal children and has certainly paid attention to this with widespread health checks of Aboriginal children, covering about 66 per cent of all those eligible so far. Aboriginal communities, particularly the women, also welcomed its proscription or restriction in many communities of alcohol supplies, and of previously widespread pornographic materials. But the Intervention is also remarkable and controversial for several other seemingly less logical features of its remit:

- Because it targets a particular section of the Australian community distinguished by race, culture and colour, the Intervention has necessitated temporary suspension of existing anti-racial discrimination laws;
- It has used Federal Government powers to override the local authority of the Northern Territory Government to a large extent, throwing doubt on the exact nature of federalism and Federal-State relations;
- It has allowed the Federal Government to temporarily take over Aboriginal lands via five-year leases, thus breaking through the principle of Aboriginal ownership;
- It has quarantined welfare payments, releasing them only when recipients proved that they were using the money first to feed and care for their children, and that the children were attending school—this all comes under the heading of compulsory 'Income Management', which requires that 50 per cent of Centrelink (the social welfare agency) payments be allocated to food, clothing and education for a family's children.

All of this represented a quantum change in the approach to Aboriginal issues.

Since its election in November 2007, Kevin Rudd's new Labor government has continued the Intervention and maintained the policy almost intact, although it also commissioned an independent NTER Review Board in June 2008, to assess how well the Intervention was really working, resulting in a review report in October 2008. Significantly, the Review Board said, 'The single most valuable resource that the NTER has lacked from its inception is the positive, willing participation of the people it was intended to help. The most essential element in moving forward is for government to re-engage with the Aboriginal people of the Northern Territory. It is the considered opinion of the Review Board that there is a need to reset the relationship between Aboriginal people and the governments of Australia and the Northern Territory. The relationship must be recalibrated to the principle of racial equality and respect for the human rights of all Australian citizens.'

Nonetheless, positive feedback from Aboriginal women better able to manage their families without harassment from drunken males eager to filter off their welfare money, the support of some Aboriginal leaders such as Noel Pearson, and the general consensus in the wider community that 'at least something is being done', mean that aspects of the Intervention may be here to stay for a while yet. As Rudd, his successor Julia Gillard and others ahead might well say, "You got a better idea?"

TURNING OF THE TIDE

There was a palpable deterioration in the tone of the relationship between black and white Australia under John Howard's Liberal government from 1996. The biggest bone of contention was that powerful little word 'Sorry'. An apology was demanded by Aboriginal Australia particularly for the sufferings of the Stolen Generation, but also in general for all past suffering. A self-proclaimed warrior in the so-called 'History Wars' or 'Culture Wars', a war between Right and Left centred on how to interpret Australia's history and whether to be ashamed of some of Australia's past , Howard refused to apologise on behalf of white Australia for past injustices to black Australia. Apart from Howard, the chief proponent on the Right of the Culture Wars has been Keith Windschuttle, former journalist and now controversial historian, also the editor of the right-leaning Quadrant magazine (see his books *The Fabrication of Aboriginal History*, 2002 and *The White Australia Policy*, 2004). Howard and his camp argued that current generations could not be held responsible for the sins of their ancestors, and expressed his contempt for what he has called a 'black armband view of history'. He proclaimed war on what he saw as excessive 'political correctness.' Yet some 250,000 (overwhelmingly non-Aboriginal) showed their disagreement with Howard's line when they turned out for a National Reconciliation march across Sydney Harbour Bridge in May 2000. However, the 'S' word apparently had become so problematic for some whites at least that the declared annual 'National Sorry Day' reconciliation event on 26 May was for a short while renamed 'National Day of Healing', in 2005, in a bid to increase non-Aboriginal support.

But Kevin Rudd's Labor government, decisively handed power in the general election of November 2007, had understood that the 'Sorry' issue was becoming an absurd barrier to progress in tackling Aboriginal issues, a stick that almost every Aboriginal leader could use to beat white Australians with and a reason not to cooperate with even the most benign programmes. Rudd rapidly cut through all tape, red, white and black, and opened his first Parliament in February 2008 with 'The Apology'. It was an overwhelmingly emotional and historic moment, in fact much more than just a moment, with the usual Westminster-style ceremony of Canberra's Parliament now 'invaded' by the wildly colourful spectacle of traditional Aboriginal dancers, elders in kangaroo-skin cloaks, the clacking of rhythm sticks, the wailing tones of Aboriginal songs, as the community celebrated this significant rite of reconciliation. The feeling of history being made was palpable amid a silence you could cut with a knife as Prime Minister Rudd pronounced, in part:

"*To the Stolen Generations, I say the following: as Prime Minister of Australia, I am sorry. On behalf of the Government of Australia, I am sorry. On behalf of the Parliament of Australia, I am sorry. And I offer you this apology without qualification. We apologise for the hurt, the pain and suffering we, the parliament, have caused you by the laws that previous parliaments have enacted. We apologise for the indignity, the degradation and the humiliation these laws embodied. We offer this apology to the mothers, the fathers, the brothers, the sisters, the families and the communities whose lives were ripped apart by the actions of successive governments under successive parliaments. In making this apology, I would also like to speak personally to the members of the Stolen Generation and their families: to those here today, so many of you; to those listening across the nation—from Yuendumu, in the central west of the Northern Territory, to Yabara, in North Queensland, and to Pitjantjatjara in South Australia."*

He had gracefully glided over the issue of whether ordinary modern Australians should feel guilty about the actions of their forefathers, by appropriating the guilt solely for the Australian government and Parliament. He dismissed former critics of the Apology idea, saying, "This is not, as some would argue, a black-armband view of history; it is just the truth: the cold, confronting, uncomfortable truth." He positioned the Apology as simply the embodiment of a core Aussie value, i.e. the 'fair go' for all, and he pointed out that this was only a symbolic step on the way to more practical measures for closing the gaps between mainstream and Aboriginal Australia, albeit a crucial one. This was a pathbreaking speech, history in the making. For the full text of Prime Minister's Kevin Rudd's Historic Apology Motion in Parliament, visit: http://www.pm.gov.au/media/speech/2008/speech_0073.cfm

In many ways, Australia has breathed a huge sigh of collective relief over this decisive change in the landscape of white-Aboriginal relations. The debate on what to do after the Apology continues. Feisty Aboriginal commentator Noel Pearson, always ready to go out on a limb, had this thought-provoking comment on the Apology writing his regular column for *The Australian* newspaper in 2008:

'One of my misgivings about the Apology has been the belief that nothing good will come from viewing ourselves, and making our case on the basis of our status, as victims... We lose power when we adopt this psychology...My worry is that this Apology will sanction a view of history that cements a detrimental psychology of victimhood, rather than a stronger one of defiance, survival and agency.' But the Apology of course was not an ending, rather a beginning. In his Apology speech, the then Prime Minister Rudd also referred to "The Gap" that has become the focus of government policy under his successor Julia Gillard, and committed his government to "...A future where we harness the determination of all Australians, Indigenous and non-Indigenous, to close the gap that lies between us in life expectancy, educational achievement and economic opportunity."

There has been no recent advance on the idea of a long-overdue formal Treaty with Aboriginal Australia, nor (heaven forbid!) the idea of possible monetary compensation or damages to Aboriginal Australia for past wrongs. But the Prime Minister does now annually report on a constellation of *Closing the Gap* policies, some of which derive from the Intervention (which was on track to close down in mid-2012). Some major differences from the Intervention have been a gentler form of Income Management or guidance for remote communities (many of whom themselves said the idea was basically good), improved consultation with Aboriginal communities, and Labor's reinstatement of the Racial Discrimination Act 1975 in the Northern Territory, reversing the Act's controversial suspension during the Intervention proper. Current policy is based on the National Indigenous Reform Agreement endorsed by all State governments in 2008, while in the Northern Territory the new policy buzz-phrase is *Stronger Futures* rather than 'Intervention'. The Intervention's concern with tackling the widespread evils of alcohol and substance abuse, domestic violence, child abuse and too-easy access to pornography however remains. The overall goal though, is to close most of the life-chance gaps between Aboriginal and mainstream Australia within about a decade, i.e. by 2018. One of the most promising and effective initiatives has been the 280 separate corporate or institutional Reconciliation Action Plans, many of which have involved organisations and corporations offering apprenticeships and training to indigenous youth wanting to work. Government is also now moving towards recognition of the Aboriginals' special place in Australia's Constitution, which currently does not mention them at all. We can therefore soon expect the drama of Australia's first referendum on changes to the Constitution concerning the Aboriginals since 1967, when the text was amended to remove negatives against the Aboriginals, such as the provision *not* to count them in censuses of the population of Australia.

HOW AUSTRALIAN SOCIETY WORKS

CHAPTER 4

DID YOU KNOW IT'S ONLY SEVEN WEEKS TO WATTLE DAY?

'Democracy does not mean representative government
or manhood suffrage, or any other piece of machinery.
Democracy is a mental attitude. Democracy means a belief in
equality. It is based on the conviction that we are all blokes.'
—Sir Walter Murdoch, prominent Scots-born Western
Australian Academic, in his *Speaking Personally*, 1930

STRUCTURE AND FORM

To 'fit in' with Australian society, you first need to know how it is structured and how it works. It's important to understand that Australia's is a federal system, with a great deal of latitude for regional and state-based differences.

This huge continent is divided into six states and two territories: from west to east, Western Australia (capital, Perth); the Northern Territory (self-governing with an elected Legislative Assembly since 1978, capital, Darwin); South Australia (capital, Adelaide); Queensland (capital, Brisbane); New South Wales (capital, Sydney); Australian Capital Territory (home of the federal Parliament in the capital, Canberra); Victoria (capital, Melbourne); and Tasmania (an island state to the far south, capital, Hobart).

The Hutt River Principality

Not everyone has accepted the federation of Australia in 1901. In 1970, Western Australian farmer Leonard Casley announced his secession from the state of Western Australia over a matter of grain quotas. His 75 square-kilometre (29 square-mile) farm thus then became the independent nation Hutt River Province, with himself as Prince Leonard and his wife Princess Shirley, and a total of 20 inhabitants. This spot on the map has ever since issued its own passports (13,000 so far) and currency, and welcomed thousands of tourists every year. In 2006, Prince Leonard dropped the 'Province' tag to name his nation 'The Principality of Hutt River'.

(Continued on the next page)

(Continued from previous page)

Neither the Commonwealth of Australia nor the Western Australian State Government have been able to do much about Prince Leonard, since the Prince is quite a canny amateur lawyer. Prince Leonard is one of some 20 independent thinkers in Australia who have acted similarly. As reported by the *London Telegraph*, there's also His Imperial Majesty George II, once George Cruikshank, a Sydney sales manager, now Emperor of Atlantium, actually a one-bedroom apartment on the Sydney waterfront. Nearby, Prince Paul of Wy too seceded from his local council in November 2004, apparently after 11 years of argument over permission to build a driveway to his home. And this is not to mention the Gay and Lesbian Kingdom of the Coral Sea Islands, comprising some (uninhabited) islands off Queensland and touted as a final haven for gays and lesbians. It declared war on Australia in September 2004 following the government's refusal to recognise same-sex marriage

This is all in line with the English tradition of eccentricity of course.

But what it means is, there is room for all types in Australia and even if you are slightly nuts, you will fit in just fine.

DISSECTING DEMOCRACY
How Does It All Work?

The governmental system is that of a classic parliamentary democracy with full separation of executive and legislative powers, mixed with some elements from the USA. Australia was seen, and saw itself, in the 19th century very much as a repeat of the American experience.

A modification of this basically 'Westminster' system is the existence in Australia of a written Constitution dating from federation in 1901, a rigid instrument which the 'mother country', the UK, of course does not have.

Australia's Commonwealth Constitution, however, does not cover the area of civil and human rights in the way that the American one does. Chiefly, it outlines only broadly the system of national government and the relationship between the federal Commonwealth and the states. It does not even refer to the right to vote, nor to the exact structure of government and the cabinet. The Constitution is, however, supplemented by conventions which do spell out details and also control the theoretically extensive powers of the Governor-General.

Election Fever

For more on the history of democracy, see the story of the Eureka Stockade incident in 1854, (see Chapter 2: The Basics, page 45). Adult white males were given the vote for the first time in 1856, in South Australia. Elections take place every three years. Many observers have pointed out that any Australian government's capacity to implement policy effectively is severely hampered by its need constantly to keep an eye on the popular vote. The vote is not conducted on the first-past-the-post but rather on the preferential voting principle. This gives minority parties a better chance of making an impact on politics. Proportional representation is also adopted in the Senate elections, and in some states

Government, Government and More Government

The seat of the Federal Government is at Canberra, in Australian Capital Territory (ACT), which was created in 1911 solely for the purpose of housing government and Parliament. Some have called Australia 'over-governed'. The total number of Federal, State and local public servants in 2008 stood at about 1.7 million, or 16 per cent of the Australian workforce.

The System

Australians in the main are pretty happy with their system of government. When debates about whether or not to become a Republic raise their heads from time to time, a recurring theme is 'If it ain't broke, don't fix it!' So the Head of State still is Queen Elizabeth II of Great Britain, with Australia a valued member of the British Commonwealth, virtually Britain's reconstituted former Empire. The Queen's representative in the Australian Parliament is the Governor-General, appointed by the Queen in consultation with Australia's Prime Minister, and in theory she (the nation now has its very first female Governor-General, Quentin Bryce) can veto parliamentary legislation by not assenting to it. Famously, the GG once dismissed the Prime Minister and his Labor government (Gough Whitlam, in 1975).

(Continued on the next page)

(Continued from previous page)

He/she can summon and dissolve Parliament, dismiss ministers, is commander-in-chief of the armed forces and may appoint judges. An Executive Council advises the Governor-General of major decisions made at Cabinet level. The federal Constitution agreed upon in 1901 can only be changed via a national referendum.

The Australian government structure is a blend of Britain's Westminster model with some elements of American forms. As in Britain, there are two houses of Parliament: the lower, the House of Representatives, and the upper, the Senate. The House of Representatives is elected at general elections every three years; the Senate acts as a house of review or checks and balances on the lower house (rather like Britain's House of Lords), with the power to reject or amend proposed legislation, and the majority of senators from the various states are elected for six-year terms. Each State Government replicates federal structure to a great extent, including each having their own Governor to represent the Queen. Local governments operate at Shire or City Council level.

Voting in Australia is compulsory for those over 18, except for Aboriginals who may opt not to register on the electoral roll if they wish (but once they register, they must vote). One difference from the Westminster system is that voters must rank every candidate for a seat in their order of preference and if no candidate gets a majority vote, then the preference votes are distributed to reach a final 'verdict'. Australia was one of the world's first countries to grant suffrage to women, starting with South Australia in 1894, and extending to the whole nation in 1902.

THE FOURTH ESTATE

In any democracy, the media are important players, sometimes wild cards. The Australian press certainly ranks as wild, being one of the most aggressive in the world. And Australians are avid newspaper readers, as well as television watchers, spending more than 21 hours a week at the goggle box in 2007. More than two-thirds of Australians have two TV sets, and a third have three or more.

Unfortunately, their choice is somewhat restricted; there is not much light and shade, or depth, to the range of media available in Australia, partly because ownership is concentrated in a few hands—the principal owner is Richard Murdoch's News Corporation (News Limited), and the other power in the land is the John Fairfax Holdings group. The late Kerry Packer's Publishing and Broadcasting Limited (PBL) (owner of the Nine TV channel and the Australian Consolidated Press), now run by his son James Packer, has only recently moved out of traditional media (e.g. the former cornerstones of its empire, the Nine Network and Australian Consolidated Press (ACP) magazines with famous mastheads such as *Women's Weekly* and *Cleo*) in favour of digital and online media. The country press is dominated by Rural Press Limited, a Fairfax concern. The concentration of media ownership certainly runs counter to what should be found in a healthy democracy, and the trend has been intensifying since the relaxation by 2007 of laws limiting both foreign ownership and cross-media ownership. This means that a single investor can own both a broadcasting and a print medium simultaneously. Hence media magnate Kerry Stokes' Seven Network (Channel 7 TV) has quite recently been able virtually to take over and merge with West Australian Newspapers during 2011, creating Australia's largest media group.

A rough count gives two national dailies and 10 State dailies, 35 regional dailies, 470 regional and suburban papers, and 1,600 magazines, 30 of them with circulations of over 80,000. The only true national paper is *The Australian* with its *Weekend Australian*, although the *Australian Financial Review* comes close.

A casualty of these globalising times and the Internet, Australia's national news weekly, a PBL publication called *The Bulletin* and founded in 1880, is no more, since January 2008. In its early years, the magazine carried a masthead reading 'Australia for the White Man' but in its heyday, up to the 1990s, it was an influential and lively magazine along the lines of an *Australian Time* or *Newsweek*.

Interestingly, according to the independent international media monitoring group 'Reporters Without Borders', in

2011 Australia ranked only 30th in their list of 179 countries ranked according to their level of press freedom, behind New Zealand (13th). The concentration of media ownership is a factor in this, but the group also said that Aussie media had been subjected to criticism and investigation, and denied access to information.

The Small Screen and 'Wireless'

For 20 years up to 2007, there were laws to limit the extent to which print media moguls could also corner the broadcasting market, and foreign ownership of broadcasting was prohibited. All that changed in 2007. So Channels 9 and 10 now have majority foreign owners, and Channel 7 has a foreign co-owner. Foreign investment in media is still considered a sensitive matter however, and requires screening and prior approval by entities like the Foreign Investment Review Board and the Treasurer himself.

An umbrella authority, the Australian Communications and Media Authority (ACMA) is the overall regulator for broadcasting, Internet, radio- and tele-communications in Australia. It was formed by the amalgamation of the former Australian Broadcasting Authority and the Australian Communications Authority in July 2005.

There are 55 licensed commercial television services operating in Australia, including three national commercial television network, channels Seven (Seven Network), Nine (Nine Network) and Ten (Network Ten). There are also two public broadcasters—the long-established (1960) and publicly owned ad-free ABC (Australian Broadcasting Corporation), affectionately known as 'Auntie' to Australians; and the SBS (Special Broadcasting Service), which sadly has had to take advertising since the late 1990s. The increasingly frantic quest for the advertising dollar, leading for the first time to actual interruption of SBS programmes for advertising, in late 2006, has badly damaged SBS' original sense of direction. The SBS originally was slated as a multicultural and multilingual broadcaster but with a much more attractive menu than this description might imply (among other oddities, its multiculturalism seems to have given rise to a regular diet of 'naughty' foreign movies). SBS TV does however still broadcast in over 60 languages, more on its radio service. As time went on, the SBS TV charter became more broadly, the representation of a range of minority interests, from multiculturalism and eco-philosophy to gay culture. But public outcry at the increasing commercialisation and alleged dumbing-down of SBS has continued unabated till today; as a result there could be more changes ahead.

The government-funded National Indigenous Television (NIT) was added as a third public broadcaster in mid-2007; NIT programmes are produced in Sydney and broadcast via indigenous (Aboriginal) commercial broadcaster Imparja's satellite capacity via Alice Springs in the Northern Territory. WIN TV is prominent in rural districts, but this is in fact run by the Nine Network. In some areas, there is an additional not-for-profit community broadcasting station.

Digital television options have made great strides since digital's introduction in 2001 although initial uptake was slow and Australia is somewhat behind other countries in this area. There are also increasing choices for HD/High Definition television viewing. Each of the key broadcasters has more than one channel offering Analog, Standard Digital and also HD options. Hence, ABC now has three channels, including ABC 24, a continuous news feed featuring international contributions from the British BBC and also Al-Jazeera; SBS has two, while multiple commercial channels for Nine, Seven and Ten boost the total national free-to-air channels available to 15, excluding regional options. End-2013 is the deadline for complete switch-over from analog to digital.

Besides the free-to-air menu already detailed, there are satellite and cable pay television (Foxtel, or Austar in rural areas).

There are some 272 commercial radio stations. A rough-diamond style of democracy flourishes on radio, with a proliferation of phone-in, 'talk-back' shows. But the most international mindset and highest intellectual quality is probably to be found in a combination of ABC and ABC Radio National, while SBS Radio broadcasts weekly in 68 languages, more than any other radio network in the world.

In an unusual instance of media control, for Australia, the Australian Broadcasting Tribunal (now the Australian Broadcasting Authority) has since the 1970s stipulated an annual minimum quota of 55 per cent Australian programming between 6 am and midnight to be screened on commercial licensee television. Hence the growth of Australian soap operas like the now world-famous *Neighbours*, saga of the suburbs. These local content restrictions have survived even the potentially threatening Free Trade Agreement with the USA concluded in 2004, thanks to reservations claimed by Australia. The country's media scene is on the brink of change following the submission of a government-commissioned independent Convergence Review report in March 2012. This among other things may result in the Australian content quotas being extended all to the commercial TV stations' extra digital channels (currently quota-free), and more significantly, to the ABC and SBS (quota-free since their foundation) – however, in recognition of the SBS' special multicultural mission, the quota could be lowered to about 27.5 per cent for them.

Internet

It says much for Australia's seriousness of intent about communications technology that there is a Labor government Minister whose sole portfolio is Broadband, Communications and the Digital Economy. The goal is to become "a world-leading digital economy by 2020," as defined by putting Australia among the top five OECD countries in terms of the percentage of households connected to broadband at home. But there is plenty of catch-up to be done, as Australia's communications infrastructure still woefully lags behind that of some of its near neighbours and friends, featuring as it does, an ageing copper telecoms network. There are over 11 million active Internet subscribers in Australia, but that's not so impressive for a developed nation of more than 22 million people—in June 2011, out of the 34 OECD countries, Australia ranked 21st in terms of fixed broadband take-up. OECD statistics also confirm that Australia has fallen behind for fixed broadband download speeds, and that Australia is the fifth most expensive OECD country for broadband-users. The centrepiece of the current upgrade programme is the gradual rollout of the National Broadband Network (NBN) providing high-speed broadband to homes, mostly via optic fibre but also with some use of wireless and satellite technology. Australia is a huge country and delivery of services has to be piecemeal, district by district, sometimes to very remote locations. It's all happening at an apparently infuriatingly slow pace in the view of most eager would-be users, but gradually, it is coming. The initial rollout will certainly take us well into 2015 or later and the entire programme is slated for 10 years from its 2011 start-up.

MIND MY SPACE

It is a delicate task to balance freedom against the risk of that very freedom's invading other people's personal space.

Freedom entails freedom of speech whether you like what the other fellow is saying or not. And democracy is supposed to mean that you would die for his right to say it.

Democracy can be inconvenient. It means pressure groups, each lobbying the political process for their own self-interest—the wheat lobby, the wool lobby, the mining lobby, the environmentalist lobby, the feminist lobby, and so on. This tends to slow things down. Decisions take longer to implement. But it cuts both ways: it also means you get to have your say.

Freedom of the Personal Kind

Freedom may also mean that there is a bit more nudity and sex (both straight and gay) on television than you care for (try the notorious *Big Brother Uncut* on channel Ten, with amateur wannabes flaunting their all to the spy cameras in their 'reality TV' home), that someone has the right to open up a sex shop in your neighbourhood shopping centre, that the local pub has a lunchtime 'lingerie' strip show, and that scantily clad young people may be seen on the street kissing and holding hands. And for almost two decades, it has also been OK for the 'F...' word to be uttered on TV.

The open display of the human body and relative sexual freedom of Western-style societies like Australia is a particular problem for visitors from Asia and other traditional societies or religions.

A quick scan of the 'Personal' classified advertisement columns in several Australian newspapers will soon reveal the scope of the services available. You can pay to do it in bubble baths, with girls in suspenders, in groups big or small, with or without rubber and leather, to suffer 'discipline', just to watch, or even just to talk about it on the phone. Many of you will blush crimson at the visuals for similar wares advertised on late-night TV—it gets worse and worse after about 11:00 pm or so. In such a society, the old excuse for not being able to come over—'I'm sorry, I'm tied up right now'—might be only too literally true.

And so onward through the classifieds: Under 'F', a 'French Maid, Ooh La La.' Under 'H,' a 'Hot Housewife' or a 'Hispanic'. Under 'G,' things become decidedly 'Gay'. 'Guy seeks Guy, Chinese or any nationality,' reads one ad. There's 'Lesbian Lucy' too, while one 'Lola' offers to 'dress and make up inquisitive males.' There is some elegant G-for-Gigolo begging under 'G' too: 'Gent, 23. Is there a lady out there who can financially assist one honest young man in dire straits? Genuine ad.'

By no means are all these ads placed by professionals; there are quite a few amateurs, part-timers, one-off thrill-seekers, and those just looking for companionship, love and marriage, truly. In these days of Internet dating services, it's amazing how much of this type of activity still goes on in the conventional print and broadcasting media.

Look the Other Way

If such things disturb you, it is important to maintain your sense of balance by understanding that most Australians go about their daily lives without a second look at this underworld. They ignore such things, treating them like the wallpaper of life, quite unshocked and often uninterested too. So just take no notice of it—walk on! How you insulate your children from it, or teach them to deal with it, will be a challenge to your parenting, but that's a challenge you would have had to engage sooner or later anyway.

Australian attitudes to sex, violence and censorship are in any case ambivalent, reflecting the ongoing tug-of-war between the puritanism of the recent past and a more permissive present.

In general, the social premise is that non-violent erotica are a useful safety valve for normal human sexual emotions and fantasies. There is an elaborate system of film classification, to indicate films' content to the public: M or M(A) for Mature (15 and above), R for Restricted and PG for Parental Guidance, besides G for General and X for Adults-only. X-rated videos, for example, have been banned in most of Australia since 1984, except for the Australian Capital Territory (ACT), i.e. Canberra, and the Northern Territory. Otherwise sober Canberra is a major blue-movie mail-order supplier as a result. But this National Classification Scheme is likely to change soon, following the Australian Law Reform Commission's report lodged in February 2012. This seeks to standardise content classification across the nation, and across all media, whether online or otherwise.

HOW THEY THINK OF THEMSELVES

There are internal stereotypes about what is 'typical' of a 'Sydneysider', a 'Melburnian', a 'Taswegian' (Tasmanian), or a 'Sandgroper' (Western Australian), for example. The stereotypes are:

- Sydney: go-for-it dynamic, smart and young, pushy, fast
- Melbourne: stuffy, business-minded and worldly-wise, cultured and a bit pompous in the English style
- Tasmania: slow backwoodsman, introverted and inbred
- Canberra/Australian Capital Territory: boring monochrome melange of civil service, journalists and politicians with access to some beautiful landscapes
- Brisbane/Queensland: even brasher than Sydney, bordering on vulgar, redneck and somewhat uncivilised but fun- and sun-loving
- Adelaide/South Australia: slow and quiet, rather English reserved, quite cultured
- Perth/Western Australia: isolated and behind the times, small town, conservative, laid-back and complacent, grown fat on mineral wealth
- Northern Territory: pioneering frontier 'outback' society, a bit rough and tough but interestingly offbeat.

As ever with all stereotypes, where there is smoke, there is at least a little fire.

But overall, Australians do unite in a self-image that says Aussies are brave and tough, honest and without guile, anti-authoritarian and therefore democratic, egalitarian, loyal to their mates and willing to help others in crisis, keen on a 'fair go' or natural justice for all.

Your best bet when attempting to 'camouflage' yourself in Australia? Just be yourself—Australians hate play-acting, posing and insincerity.

JOINING THE CROWD

How difficult, or easy, do Australians make it for you to fit in with them? By and large, Australians on a face-to-face level are very accepting and will take you in as their 'mate' regardless of your ethnic origins, provided you can match a few of their most basic 'mateship' criteria. Among these criteria, paramount is your ability to speak English, even if you cannot actually produce 'Strine', the local patois. They may well prefer you if you enjoy an alcoholic beverage or two. They may prefer to avoid over-intellectual conversations and keep things light. Even better if you can discuss either cricket or 'footy' with some aplomb, but this is not essential.

Inviting them back to your home is appreciated. They will not be impressed with over-dressing, or showing off in any form at all, including spending lots of money, talking loudly and dominating the conversation. Criticisms of Australia, or negative comparisons with other nations, are completely taboo until you have been around a long, long time and hold an Aussie passport—but even then, think twice...

Differentiation may well appear not so much on the basis of ethnicity as on gender. You may have to sort out how you fit in Australian society in terms of your sex, and sexual orientation too. Australians still have quite a lot to sort out on this front. Family life, for instance, is very much in flux. One-fifth of Australian families with children under 15 years old are headed by a single parent. Divorces decreased by almost 10 per cent a year between 2002-'07 but in absolute terms they still numbered over 50,000 in 2010. In 2007, the average marriage broke up into separation within 8.9 years, but this was a big improvement on the 1990s. Perhaps divorces have fallen thanks to the increasing number of unmarried *de facto* relationships often substituted for marriage. Broken or single-parent families are no longer an 'alternative lifestyle'; they are becoming the norm. The agonies inflicted upon separating couples with children via the Family Court and the harsh impact of the controversial Child Support Agency structure on separated but still financially supporting fathers are a constant subject of national debate. There are far too many cases in the newspapers of traumatised divorcing or separated fathers kidnapping their kids during scheduled custody visits and then killing them. Watching these personal dramas play out (everybody has a friend involved in one story or another) makes it easy to understand why many young Australians choose not to marry; but even unmarried *de facto* partners under the same roof for more than a year may be subjected to legal considerations close to those applied to full marriages. Working men with non-working wives or partners (or vice versa) in particular need to understand that divorce or separation could lead to a 50:50 division of all their property, including their pension funds ('Super') and the family house, with ongoing close supervision and monitoring in terms of child support funding and child access or custody arrangements.

Same Sex, No Difference

If you come from a country where the idea of same-sex relationships can hardly be talked about openly in polite company, you will have to get used to a radically different environment in Australia. While gay -marriage has not been legalised (indeed the Marriage Act since 2004 has specifically defined marriage as 'the union of a man and a woman'), *de facto* same-sex couples now enjoy most of the same basic rights as heterosexual couples in key areas such as tax, social security, superannuation, health care, even child-support, following the passing of new laws in November 2008. The Australian government's position on this is clear, as stated on the Attorney General's website, 'The Australian Government believes that people are entitled to respect, dignity and the opportunity to participate in society and receive the protection of the law regardless of their sexuality.'

Men and Men, and Men and Women

If all you did was watch television in Australia, you might well come to the conclusion that the country was way ahead of the rest of the world in terms of men deferring to women, equality of rights, pay and opportunity for women, and the whole feminist caboodle. (On the other hand, those 'privileged' to watch the now thankfully defunct *Big Brother*, the 'reality TV' show that till 2008 beamed the private doings of a bunch of artificially hothoused 'house mates' right into your living room, may well have been appalled at the level of crudity and sexual harassment that goes on among even modern young men and women).

There are strident public-service advertising campaigns too warning against domestic violence that make you think it must be an everyday occurrence

Every other documentary on 'quality' free-to-air TV seems to be about something dreadful done to women and children by men—whether it be wife-battering, rape or incest. The concern demonstrated is so great, surely it must be practised in real daily life too?

Not necessarily. What you are really witnessing in the media is a sort of national self-flagellation in penance for the very real sins of the past and, it must be said, of the ongoing present. It is because things have been so bad that all the documentaries are necessary. In any case, it is by no means certain that the deep concern shown really extends very far outside of the sophisticated circle of television documentary producers and script-writers. Still, you should have heard the public outcry in 1994 when the somewhat bumbling now Foreign Minister Alexander Downer, then leader of the Liberal Party opposition, thought he would have some fun with a pun on the Liberal Party slogan 'Things That Matter' in an after-dinner speech, referring jocularly to wife-bashing husbands as 'Things That Batter.' Unsurprisingly, Downer lasted only nine months as Liberal leader.

Some extremely distasteful incidents seen in recent times

at an uncomfortably high level have further highlighted Australian males' innate unease with the female of the species. Many of them have involved male politicians' verbal or physical harassment of their female colleagues while under the influence of alcohol. The two episodes that got the gold medal for such behaviour in 2008 concerned the conduct of the now Minister for Transport, Housing & Emergency Services in the Liberal Government of Western Australia, Troy Buswell: first, he allegedly snapped open the bra of a Labor party staffer during a drunken party at the State Parliament House, and then on another occasion, he lifted the chair just vacated by a female fellow Liberal staffer and sniffed it in front of her and others, repeating this disgusting gesture several times.

But before we can understand how men relate with women in Australia, we must first understand how they relate with men.

Mateship and Machismo

So much has been written about this uniquely Australian phenomenon that it is difficult for me to know where to begin.

One of the first things the newcomer to Australia notices is that familiar, friendly form of address, for strangers and friends alike, 'Mate'. 'How are yer, mate?' or 'What can I do for yer, mate?'—these are all common currency. (Note that 'mate' is almost never used between men and women, or among women.)

This, however, is a mere casual greeting, albeit of symbolic significance. True mateship is an abstraction of almost mystical proportions. The term was first used by Australia's pioneer chronicler of the bush, Henry Lawson, who wrote his best material during the 1890s.

Mateship refers to that subtle brotherhood felt by men together, especially when they have had to work or fight together in harsh conditions or against great adversity. Rightly or wrongly,

> 'My mate is always a man. A female may be my sheila, my bird, my charley, my good sort, my hot-drop, my judy or my wife, but she is never 'my mate'.'
> —Donald McLean,
> in *The Roaring Days*, 1960

implicit in the concept is the idea that women can never share in this emotion (even if feminists would say that 'sisterhood' was the same thing for them). Indeed, traditionally, Australian discussions of manhood, manliness and mateship have made no reference at all to masculinity in relation to women. Women simply did not come into the picture.

The only problem with this concept in post-pioneer Australia is determining exactly what adversity it is that brings men together in mateship nowadays. One has a sneaking suspicion that 'the enemy' may in fact be women—especially wives—and the suburban stresses of home and family that they are seen to represent.

Mateship Über Alles

Mateship in Australia—the friendship of men with men—can override all other moralities. For example, the man who would 'dob in' (inform on) his drug-dealer mate to the police, would probably be considered to have committed a greater offence than the drug-dealer himself. Like the 'old-boy' networks believed to dominate business life in England, mateship is a system that works quietly behind the scenes of both business and politics in Australia. At its worst, it can breed simple corruption—'helping out a mate'.

Mateship has its highs and its lows. At its lowest, it can descend to brute displays of masculinity akin to gorillas beating their chests. As social commentator Donald Horne has put it, in such cases, 'Men stand around bars asserting their masculinity with such intensity that you half expect them to unzip their flies.'

On the other hand, Horne also characterises mateship as a noble 'ideology of fraternalism' permeating the nation. It means that Australians believe most other people are good fellows like themselves, 'mates'. Optimists all, they believe in the essential humanity of mankind—*man*kind unfortunately being the operative word.

Last word to a woman, though: Dr Carmen Lawrence, former premier of Western Australia, views mateship with benign contempt. She told journalists in 1990, "They're often extremely competitive and vicious, the so-called 'circles of mateship'. My observation is that many of the people who take part in these circles of mateship may in fact be grasping for comfort, in what would otherwise be a very hostile world. So I think we shouldn't take that away from them."

Men's Men

Hand in hand with mateship goes an almost unreasoning horror of homosexuals, tarred 'poofters' or 'queers' by macho Australia. There is a strong gay counter-culture, true, particularly in the great cities of the east, but mainstream 'matedom' vigorously avoids contact with it or, if forced into contact, bashes it, often literally. The suggestion that 'gays' of both sexes would address sex education classes in Western Australian schools in 2005 caused quite an uproar among parents.

As a result, Aussie males fear seeming too emotional—too female. Among the many Australian men who have, however, bravely resisted this neurosis has been former Prime Minister Bob Hawke

A reading of Robert Hughes' account of the early Australian colony, *The Fatal Shore*, yields convincing evidence that it is precisely because homosexuality was violently and sordidly practised in convict society (rather like any prison culture) that Australian men have ever since expended great energy in erasing the memory of those terrifying times.

himself, who won a reputation for crying in public. While it is uncertain what this did to his male vote, it must certainly have endeared him to his female voters. Generally speaking, this phobia is breaking down more as young Australia becomes more accepting of the 'New Age Man' phenomenon. An American-style taste for public *schmaltz* is rapidly taking hold in Australia.

Be aware that you could be misinterpreted if you are a male from cultures such as the Middle East or parts of Asia where it is common for men to be physically affectionate with each other, to embrace, hold hands in the street, and dance with each other. This is not so normal between Anglo-Australian men; you may be assessed as gay if you continue such customs in Australia. (No problem if you *are* gay, of course!)

Another no-no for males in Australia, sadly, is physical affection with children, of either sex. The paedophilia phobia is so rampant in Australia that such demonstrations almost always attract suspicion. If you are a teacher, or physical education instructor etc, keep the classroom door open, or have someone else with you, so that no false accusations of sexual misconduct can ever hit you. 'Don't touch,' is the best rule of thumb when dealing with kids.

On the other hand, Hawke's public admission of marital infidelity must have redressed the balance since it would have endeared him to Australian men ('He's human, just like us'), who probably secretly admired him for it, while it may not have pleased too many women.

On cooking, normally considered a woman's task in Australia, it is interesting to note how Australian men will take it on quite naturally when it comes to the great Australian barbecue party. There seems to be an unwritten law that it should be the husband who tends the sizzling meat—a kind of hunter-gatherer nostalgia referring to the caveman past?—while the wife may perhaps be pottering around with salads and the like.

The Other Side of Sydney

Try, if you will, to square this softer side with the image of a macho hairy-hunky Australia: Sydney is one of the world's great gay capitals and the annual Sydney Gay and Lesbian Mardi Gras extravaganza, dating back to 1978, has been Australia's highest-earning festival and tourist attraction, although in recent years it has turned a loss. Nonetheless, it's a huge crowd-puller. The 2012 parade saw more than 9,000 participants, headed up by pop (and gay) icon, singer Kylie Minogue, while spectators numbered close to 300,000. All the usual dressy (and undressed) sights were on show, from leather-clad 'Dykes-on-Bikes' to spangled drag Queens, lesbian nuns, body-builders, gays from the uniformed forces, anything goes; also, passionate political messages, most recently in favour of the movement's current Holy Grail, legal single-sex marriage.

Role-Swapping

In the past, periods of economic decline coupled with unemployment have in a way benefited the man-woman relationship in Australia, with part-time work and even job-sharing an ever more possible option for couples. Many more men than before are now willing to stay at home to be 'house husbands'. Not all of them accept this situation with good grace, however; there is still some stigma attached. But we may see more of this.

Sheilas

The scenes you have probably heard tell of, the parties where the men congregate on one side of the room or garden to discuss 'footy', the women on the other to discuss cooking, babies, or just possibly nowadays, feminist issues—they do still happen.

There is not much you can do about this, as a woman. You might very well find the women's conversations more interesting anyway. If you do decide to ignore the invisible line dividing the sexes and stick with the men, better be sure you can talk about what they want to talk about, and that might mean 'footy', cricket, politics or sex. Australian men are still not entirely comfortable with women.

The Subservient Asian Female?

It seems best as a woman in Australia wanting to get on with the men to play oneself down a bit. Take note of the thriving Asian 'mail-order bride' industry in Australia, or the proliferation of husbands saying, "Oh, we just met while I was on holiday in Thailand; there must be some reason the Australian male feels safer with what he believes (often wrongly) to be the more subservient, sweeter Asian female.

If you are a man trying to be a hit with Australian females, things look a lot easier for you. You need only display some of the common 'European' courtesies—offering to help carry shopping bags, opening doors, presenting flowers, etc.—and you will be viewed as totally adorable.

Convict Chattels

Another observer of the Australian female condition, Anne Summers, argued in her outstanding account of Australian myths about women, *Damned Whores and God's Police*, that the colonial experience had produced two Australian stereotypes of women—either as whores imported to service men's sexual needs, or as defenders of public morality, 'God's police'.

It seems certain that whether they were whores or not in their original state, many of the 24,000 women transported to Australia as convicts between 1788 and 1852 were indeed forced to resort to the profession, and if they did not, were raped repeatedly by male convicts anyway. Theirs, together with that of Aboriginal women, was a particularly brutalising experience.

Women convicts were exploited, beaten, enslaved and passed around or sold as mere chattels or objects of convenience. Yet for the most part, their crimes 'back home' had been little more than the pettiest of theft. Thus began the relationship of the sexes in Australia. Some say that this beginning has coloured the quality of the relationship ever since. Domestic violence incidents are carefully recorded for both genders in Australia and there is indeed some violence perpetrated by females towards their male partners. But suffice it to say that in 2005, an estimated 1.3 million women aged 18 years and above—that is, 17 per cent of all women of that age—had experienced partner violence at some time since they were 15. For indigenous, Aboriginal women, the incidence is at least three times higher, and often involves even more intense violence. One shocking statistic exemplifies the problem: a government report, *Women in Australia 2007*, states that in the State of Victoria, domestic violence is the leading contributor to death, disability and illness for women under 45 years of age. And just to put a hard business value on the problem, it is estimated that impacts arising from domestic violence cost business a staggering A$ 500 million a year.

Puritanism vs Paganism

Curiously, as with the homosexual past for men, this early trauma of pioneer Australia for a while produced a diametrically opposite reaction: a strong tradition of puritanism took root in Australia.

For long, the place of women was at home with the children, sex was a taboo subject and censorship of the arts was the norm in almost every state—such attitudes linger outside the main cities and in some states more than others, Western Australia, for example. Sex education did not reach state schools until the 1970s and still has not reached all schools.

The superficially permissive and sometimes outright pagan society that Australia seems to present to the visiting outsider is, in fact, constantly at loggerheads with this older tradition of puritanism, just as it is in a similarly pioneer society, that of the USA.

The austere moral values of the Roman Catholic Church that held sway over the descendants of the many original Irish-born convicts, as well as other Christian groups, have for long held sway in 'middle-Australia'. In fact, until very recently, as Donald Horne has pointed out, the average Australian lifestyle was downright killjoy: bars closed at six, liquor was not served with meals, Sundays were dead (Western Australia only got around to changing this in August 2012), betting was illegal, books were banned, and so on.

Fair Go for Women

There are exceptions to the generally strained atmosphere between Australian men and women, particularly in the larger cities. And there is slow and steady change. Certainly, in all the official and legalistic things that matter, Australia's treatment of women now is more than proper.

The Sex Discrimination Act of 1984 makes sex discrimination against the law, giving effect to Australia's obligations under the Convention on the Elimination of All Forms of Discrimination Against Women, and parts of International Labour Organisation Convention 156. And absolutely everybody is very 'full on' with their endorsements of the need to 'empower' women (which in a way is a bit of a put-down in itself since it implies that they are not already empowered).

This must be one of the very few countries in the world to have a federal post titled 'Sex Discrimination Commissioner' – held by woman lawyer Elizabeth Broadrick for a five-year term up to September 2012, successor to another woman, Pru Goward, (but presumably it would be discriminatory to reserve the job for women, right?).

Australian women have had the right to vote since the turn of the 19th century century (1895 in the state of South Australia, 1902 across Australia), earlier than in England, and the first female politician, Edith Cowan (after whom a Western Australian university has been named) was elected in Western Australia in 1921.

Equal Pay for Work of Equal Value

Ironically, it was male trade unionists' fear of cheap female labour that triggered agitation for equal pay during World War II. The equal pay principle was confirmed in 1972 but in fact, on average most Australian women still earn about 18 per cent less than men for the same work. If the Labor government stays in power after 2013 (a moot point, however), under the new Fair Work Act, the system will now shift, as evidenced by a 2012 Fair Work Australia ruling in favour of pay increases up to 45 per cent for community-work sector employees (social workers etc), on the grounds that the traditional female domination of this sector had depressed its wages disproportionately.

The 1970s saw many other reforms, such as the introduction of equal-opportunity legislation—classified ads in the media today often carry the banner 'We are an equal-opportunity employer' to underline the point—and a women's minimum wage, in 1974. It was in the decade of the 1970s, of course, that Australian feminism swept the world via Australian author Germaine Greer's controversial book *The Female Eunuch*, published in 1971.

Since the 1980s, there has been a boom in feminist discussions, fuelled by the mushrooming of women's studies courses in universities, colleges and even schools, as well as every conceivable feminist art form from women's cinema to women's theatre. Australia is certainly making up for lost time. But there are still serious examples of the gender gap to fix. For example, the Sex Discrimination Commissioner has felt moved in 2008 to launch a national survey on sexual harassment, after Australia's Human Rights and Equal Opportunity Commission (recently renamed simply 'The Australian Human Rights Commission') phone-poll found that 28 per cent of women report having experienced it in the workplace compared with only 7 per cent of men. And the Commissioner has also pointed out that 'Half of all women aged 45 to 59 have less than $ 8000 in retirement savings compared with $ 31,000 for men, and the average superannuation payout for women is a third of the payout for men. Women spend more time in unpaid work, particularly caring for children. They are also more likely to work part-time than men, leaving them with much less retirement savings. Right now, many women are living their final years in poverty.'

May 2011 saw new amendments to the Sex Discrimination Act that made it illegal for employers to discriminate against female employees on the basis of their family responsibilities, ranging from their need to take parental/maternity leave (which is mostly paid, since 2011), and their right to a job on returning from parental/maternity leave, to their protection from dismissal on getting pregnant or for practices such as breastfeeding etc. Sexual harassment laws were also tightened up. For more about the Commission's work, visit www.humanrights.gov.au

Obstacles, Real and Imagined

But many of the protection measures benevolently put in place by the early unionists now precisely stand in women's way: restrictions on what weights women may carry, for example, excluding them from many traditionally male occupations.

Increasingly, of course, automation is making such restrictions redundant anyway. But there are still many spheres of professional work also unbreached by women; the first woman judge was not appointed until the mid-1960s, for example.

Marriage and child-rearing have, until very recently, routinely meant the end of working life for most Australian women. As late as 1970, women were forced to resign from university service on marriage, and the public service limited the range of jobs they could hold. Things are still made difficult for married women teachers. Married women workers often turn out to be immigrants: about a quarter of the female workforce consists of migrant women, who feel a greater need to get ahead and make money.

As with the Aboriginals' struggle for equality, it is not the legal structures that cause problems for female emancipation. Quite the contrary. It is the underlying social climate.

There are still many effectively Men-Only pubs or bars. There may not be any signs saying 'Women, Keep Out'. They wouldn't be necessary anyway. You have only to step inside as a woman to 'feel' the invisible signs. Few women are interested in even trying to stick around. Many exclusive clubs have only recently thrown open their doors to women members—the Western Australian Club in Perth for example, did so only at the dawn of the 21st century, and had its first female President in 2003.

Australian women apparently are often willing participants in this atmosphere. A cursory perusal of publications like the one most read in Australia (2011 circulation 470,221, readership 2.3 million) the 79 year-old *Australian Women's Weekly* magazine (which is a monthly), reveals a predictable diet of British royals ("The sexy dresses that sent William running back to Kate", "Prince William traumatised by 'rottweiler' Camilla"), how-to-handle your husband/de facto boyfriend ('I was abused by my husband for over 20 years'), pudding recipes (in 2012, the search was on for the nation's "Sponge-cake Queen"), and celeb-floss ('Keith and Nicole (*that's Keith Urban and Nicole Kidman*): Home At Last'), etc, although nowadays these are likely to be spliced with slightly more thoughtful topics such as "I was nearly eaten by lions, now I'm a model" (about Sudanese-Australian models, refugees who've made it against the odds), "How I Survived the Tsunami in Phuket, 'Circumcision: To Cut or Not to Cut?', or 'Drugs and Your Child' etc. The trivial, sexsationalist, celebophiliac and British Royal Family-adoring tone of some national women's magazines is not unique in the Western world, however, besides the *Australian Women's Weekly* and *Women's Day* (circulation 372,146, readership 1.8 million), take a look at New Idea (circulation 305,159, readership 1.2 million) to see what I mean. However, the signs of the times are that they are changing, possibly for good: such magazines have been reporting significant drops in circulation even just over the one year of 2007–2008—10 per cent for *New Idea*, 12 per cent for the *Australian Women's Weekly* and *Cleo*, 18 per cent for *Cosmopolitan*, and further falls of around another 3 per cent a year during 2011.

For a really blistering look at Aussie women in middle-class suburbia, try to get a DVD of *Kath and Kim*, formerly an ABC TV, more recently a Channel 7 'soap' cum social commentary that mercilessly satirises the banal foibles of a materialistic, hedonistic, querulous mother-daughter duo, with wonderful comic side-dishes in the form of their husbands and best friends. It doesn't grab you straight away, has the same sort of subtlety of the British series *The Office*, so keep watching and let it grow on you. And the occasional portrayal of two snooty upmarket department store assistants, who are widely agreed to resemble a breed of woman working in the iconic Myers store, is pure genius.

Hair Talk

An interesting variation on this theme is the Great Australian Coiffure. For example, the average Australian woman-in-the-street has a predictably non-tall poppy hairstyle; usually middle-length and very tousled, the never-been-combed sheepdog look.

What this fairly typical Australian woman seems to be saying is, 'I'm feminine' (My hair's longish and kind of curly-cute, isn't it?), 'I'm not hard or cold' (Well, look how disorganised my hair is!) and 'I'm not a threat to you' (I can't be too much of a sex-siren or my hair would be longer,

wouldn't it?). ?). And above all, ' I'm not too successful, really.'
So, if you are a woman set on touching an Australian man's
heart, it might be wise to look a little daffy and tousled.
Excessive chic seems to be a turn-off, or at least may never
get you beyond the professional colleague stage.

As a man, be warned that although the base of Australian
society appears to be sexist in nature, any overt expression
of sexism, particularly in conversation, is now a no-no
in polite society, if women are present. If they are not,
probably anything goes. Neutral words like 'fore-person' (for
'foreman') are commonplace. And interestingly, note that in
some circumstances, opening doors for and offering seats to
women appears to have been classified by some feminists
as itself a form of sexism.

Role Models

The unease Australian women sense when struggling to
achieve their place in the sun is strange when you consider
the number of strong female models already enshrined in
Australian history, besides many new ones making their
mark right now. The single most powerful model of course
was the pioneer woman, who shared with her man the
unthinkable deprivations of life in the bush during the 19th
century and early 20th century. Only recently have several
studies concentrated on her story.

Women shine in many areas of Australian life, perhaps
none more than in the arts and culture. But they are noticeably
thin on the ground at the higher levels of corporate business.
Judging from a 2008 report commissioned by the Federal
Equal Opportunity for Women in the Workplace Agency,
the number of women in corporate executive management
has been declining since 2006, with women accounting for
only 10.7 per cent of management in 2008—a ratio trailing
behind the figures for the US, Britain, South Africa and New
Zealand. Only four of the 200 Australian companies surveyed
had a female Chief Executive Officer. At board level, there
were ten males to every woman.

In politics they seem to have an unhappy bent for self-
destructing, in recent times: there was for instance, the

former state premier of Western Australia and former Federal Minister of Health, Labor politician Dr Carmen Lawrence, who got involved in a nasty political honesty issue in WA from which she never really recovered, otherwise she had been touted as a possible Prime Minister; and then there was Cheryl Kernot, former leader of the Democrats party, who changed sides in 1997 to join the Australian Labor Party, with the possibility of the deputy premiership one day, but lost her seat in the 2001 election after a poor performance and a general demonstrable lack of fibre; and there was Senator Natasha Stott Despoja (pronounced 'Despoya'), also leader of the Democrats for just over a year 2001–2002, in 1995 the youngest woman ever elected to the Australian parliament (at 26 years old), who could not bring her party behind her own relatively left-wing policies. She left politics and Parliament in 2008.

But hope dawns. Labor Prime Minister Kevin Rudd's new government has certainly blazed a new trail in this area, with four women actually in his Cabinet, the most ever seen in Cabinet, and a total of seven women appointed Ministers: his impressive deputy, frequently in position as Acting Prime Minister while Rudd globe-trots, is Julia Gillard, while tripling up with the weighty ministerial portfolios of both Education and Industrial Relations; Penny Wong has the politically and globally key portfolio of Climate Change and Water; relative youngster Kate Ellis aptly holds the portfolio of Youth and Sport, at the age of 30; Nicola Roxon is Health and Ageing Minister; Jenny Macklin holds the Families, Housing, Community Services and Indigenous Affairs portfolio; in the Outer Ministry, Tanya Plibersek for Housing and the Status of Women, and Justine Eliot, Ageing; while former TV current affairs person, now Parliamentary Secretary Maxine McKew made history as a complete political newbie by toppling powerful incumbent Prime Minister John Howard from his parliamentary seat in the 2007 elections and is now in training for future ministerial duties.

Australian women have had more than their pioneer forebears for role models. There have been extraordinary women like Dame Roma Mitchell (1913–2000), for example, the former Governor of South Australia. She was thus the first woman to represent the Queen of England/Australia in this post, in Australia's 203 years of European settlement. Her 'firsts' were legion: in 1962, she was made Australia's first woman Queen's Counsel. Three years later, she became Australia's first woman Supreme Court judge, after which she was appointed the first female Acting Chief Justice. And of course today there is yet another such role model in the shape of Quentin Bryce, Australia's first female Governor General, the Queen's representative in Australia.

Australian women have also done well internationally in the entertainment and fashion worlds. Movie star Nicole Kidman is one example, another might be Perth-born super-model Gemma Ward, now resident in New York, and fellow model Miranda Kerr of New South Wales, also wife of Hollywood heartthrob, British actor Orlando Bloom.

Women have also excelled in the spheres of life most dear to Australian men: sport and the outdoors. They include Kay Cottee who in 1987 sailed solo round the world in 189 days, the first woman to do so, not to mention the youngest person ever to do the same unassisted in 2009-'10, 16 year-old Queenslander Jessica Watson. And of course, the Aboriginal gold-medallist runner at the Sydney Olympics in 2000, Kathy Freeman.

Another remarkable tale is told by Robyn Davidson in her book *Tracks* (1995), recounting her harrowing solo camel journey across 2,700 km (1,700 miles) of desert and scrub between Alice Springs and the Indian Ocean. Treks like Robyn Davidson's are probably just what it takes for women really to touch Australian men. Such experiences almost confer on them the status of honorary mates.

FREEDOM AND DEMOCRACY
You won't fit in well unless you have a strong belief in democracy and a healthy cynicism about authority and government.

Australia's hunger for freedom is hardly surprising in a nation that began its life in chains.

I am referring to white Australia here. Aboriginal

Australians have their own special need for, and definition of, freedom. Their definition is perhaps a more wide-ranging one too, since traditionally, even four walls and material possessions are a sort of prison for them. But the whites owe more of their psyche to Aboriginal beliefs than they realise. In a kind of osmosis between the races, the white Australian has imbibed some of the Aboriginal lust for freedom in the open under the stars.

Between 1788 and 1868, more than 160,000 white men, women and children declared criminals were transported as convicts from England to Australia, then a destination as remote, alien and terrifying as the moon today. No other nation in the world has ever been founded on such an experience.

These were the first white Australians. The bestiality of their lives in their new home is hard to describe and even harder to contemplate. I recommend a careful reading of Robert Hughes' epic account, *The Fatal Shore*. Still, it can be said that the convicts' ejection was in many ways preferable to a term rotting in an English jail. Again, Hughes' book gives a graphic account of exactly how horrible this would have been.

Despite the hardships of their initial landfall, many of the first Australians won their freedom within a short time and set out to make new lives in a new land. The Commander of the First Fleet in 1788, Captain Arthur Phillip, wanted Australia to be a free settlement and tried hard to release convicts onto the land, striving in many ways to relieve the convicts' misery.

But ever since 1788, Australians have consciously or subconsciously been concerned to remove from their lives what Hughes has called 'The Stain' of their convict past, studiously donning a camouflage of almost stultifying respectability for a while. Even in the 19th century, it was ill-mannered to use the term 'convict' in Australia; the euphemism 'government man' was preferred. This has changed in recent years to a sort of inverse snobbery where it is considered a proud pedigree to be able to trace one's genealogy to a convict ancestor.

It is in this convict context, however, that one can

begin to understand why any imposition of authority, any infringement of personal liberty, no matter how seemingly petty, will arouse Australian passions to fever pitch.

Don't Classify Me

Thus, it is almost impossible to determine with any certitude any Australian's true identity, so opposed is he to being a digit imprisoned in a computer data-bank, to being categorised in any way.

Notwithstanding our security-conscious era, post 9/11, the old tendency to take you at your word, bordering on naivety at times, does linger on in the everyday social and business life of Australia. It is a direct consequence of every man's respect for the privacy of every other man.

The government strove in vain during the 1980s to introduce the 'Australia Card', an identity card for every Australian, in the hope of controlling social welfare and tax abuses. But the average Australian saw this as the thinly disguised return of the convict's number tag, a sinister infringement of his freedom. No freedom is more treasured in Australia than the right to anonymity (they don't always think through the full implications of computerisation and the Internet). The outcry against the Australia Card was so loud that the government had to abandon its plan (but sneaked it in again by the back door with a compulsory Tax File Number system for all income-earners). Nowadays, the driving licence with a photo of the owner just about doubles for the dreaded identity card that Australians still fondly imagine they have escaped.

Another form of intrusion on privacy and freedom is the act of asking too many questions. In your efforts to get to know Australians, do not come on too inquisitive—What do you do? Are you married? How many children do you have? Where do you live? etc. are all considered normal questions in many other societies, but not in Australia. Excessive curiosity—'sticky-beaking'—especially at your first meeting, can make the Australian uncomfortable, and may cause him to retreat into a gruffly suspicious shell. Cool it.

Doing Your Own Thing

Freedom can be a lonely privilege. People who are used to more regimented, sheltered lifestyles, where relatives, governments, civic groups, neighbourhood groups, religious groups or whatever all combine to tell you what to do, when and how, often find that they miss this framework in urban Australia. (In the countryside, however, communities are still more intimately meshed.) Such newcomers find the sudden anonymity disorienting. Asians used to paternalistic governments and warmly interactive extended families particularly suffer from this syndrome.

In Australia, people largely leave you alone to get on with your own life, in whatever way you want to lead it. They do not interfere with you, which is pleasant; by the same token, this means you are on your own, mate. All too easily, by extension, it may seem they don't care about you. Yet on the other hand, any direct plea for help, or a greeting in the street, will always be met with a warm response.

Clearly, there are pros and cons to both ways of living. In any case, you can find support groups aplenty in Australia if you need them. Only in Australia, you have to make the effort to get in contact with them, not wait for them to arrive on your doorstep. Frequently in Australia, if you don't ask, you don't get. You are expected to stand on your own feet and fight for your rights, which fortunately, do exist.

Benign Neglect?

The area where the 'leave things alone' philosophy shows up clearest is in family life and child-rearing. Young Australians are noticeably freer and less disciplined than many other youngsters, offensively so in the eyes of Europeans and Asians particularly.

Here again, the Australian dislike for authority surfaces: parents stand for authority. Former Labor Prime Minister Bob Hawke's biographer, Blanche d'Alpuget, records that Hawke's own family was raised very much in this mould: 'Adult visitors were often shocked by the liberties in speech allowed to the children,' she says. 'Hawke was the obverse of an authoritarian father.'

Liberal parenting, and teaching styles at school too, do produce lively, creative and independent-minded—and opinionated—young people. An Asian migrant friend of mine used to a more dictatorial style of education said that for the first time he could remember, his children considered it a punishment if they were kept away from school, they enjoyed it so much in Australia.

But there are also scary incidents of major vandalism by schoolchildren, displaying that opposition to authority so typical of Australia. In one case in Western Australia, some teenage students simply went to their school at night and set fire to it. There are many other such stories. Dislocation of the family in post-industrial society is hardly a problem unique to Australia. In addition, economic hard times and the growth in single-parent families have made it genuinely difficult for Australian parents to supervise children properly. About a third of Australian children are born outside of a marriage, double the number recorded some 20 years ago.

Pockets of unemployment, and higher rates of youth unemployment (both likely to escalate in the current recession) have exacerbated the potential for the animal energies of young people to spill over into violence. All too often, children are on the streets with nothing to do. Theirs is not a desirable freedom.

At the worst end of this scenario are children actually living in poverty, although obviously definitions of 'poverty' can be both subjective and relative. A UNICEF report found in 2007 that Australia ranked 14th in the child poverty stakes within the OECD (Organisation for Economic Cooperation and Development) group of 30 rich nations. But Australia is also among only four countries (USA, Britain and Norway are the others) to have seen a reduction in child poverty between 1990 and 2005 (1.7 per cent). In 1990, the then Prime Minister Bob Hawke, Labor, notoriously—and erroneously—declared that by 1990 no Australian child would be living in poverty. The Australian Bureau of Statistics found in its 2006 Census that about 12,000 Australian children were homeless on Census night.

An equally worrying feature of youth culture in Australia that may possibly just be a reflection of trends throughout the Western world in the 21st century is an observable lack of sense of purpose or ambition. In an easy-come easy-go atmosphere where you can always take up university studies as a mature student (although that is psychologically harder to achieve than many realise), or just go to 'Tafe' (Technical and Further Education College, tailored both for vocational training and adult education, sometimes a stepping stone to university), in an environment where nobody seems to respect or put much premium on academic excellence anyway, and anyway, it's so hard to get a job, and besides, you'd rather work and get some money than waste time on studies, an alarming number of young people get into university but then proceed to drift, somewhere around the end of their first year. Often, they will take the next year off to work in some quite ordinary waged job, with the declared intention of returning to 'uni' but in reality, many never return, thus wasting their own, and their parents' time and money. Alternatively, they start to wander through an emporium of courses, picking and choosing, chopping and changing both major and minor subjects ('No, don't like law, too hard, think I'll try engineering instead'), desperately seeking what really suits them, but never quite settling, frequently not finishing their degrees as a result. And often accumulating a larger than necessary HECS-HELP (Higher Education Contribution Scheme-Higher Education Loan Programme) debt to the government along the way.

It's not as easy as it once was for youthful 'bludgers' to live off unemployment welfare, but it is all too easy for them to drop out into the twilight world of a substantial shifting workforce in underpaid temporary, casual, part-time or short-contract jobs.

If this happens to your children in Australia, as well it might under the general peer pressure of it looking like the norm, comfort yourself that you are not alone, and also be aware that an interesting minority of young workers is simply 'working to live' in jobs they do not like, while living their 'real' lives out of office hours—frequently, these are the artistic lives of dancers, writers and musicians. In few countries is it more true to say that a person is not defined by their work or job than in Australia.

On the other hand, you could take a leaf from the book of an Indian migrant mother I know who as soon as her live-in son announced that he would be joining several of his fellow students in taking the following year off uni studies to travel a bit and maybe work for money, said to him, "Fine, then you may as well pack your bags and get out right now, then your independence will be complete." The thought of having his support rug pulled abruptly pulled from under him so horrified the poor lad that it forced him to revise his plans; he went back to university and completed his studies on time, and proceeded to get a very good job. Interestingly, most of his mates who actually did take off never went back to their studies.

No Leaders Please, We're Australian

Crucial to the Australian concept of freedom, of course, is democracy. In its simplest form, this is seen as meaning 'Nobody is my boss.' Egalitarianism is another important pillar of the concept. Australians perversely enjoy cutting their leaders down to size to uphold this principle. Typical of the social atmosphere was the incident in 1991 when the then Prime Minister Bob Hawke was shown on television being interviewed in the back of his limousine. Unfortunately, he had neglected to strap up his seat-belt during the interview.

This point was certainly not lost on, nor tolerated by, the viewers, who promptly jammed the television channel switchboard with more than 1,000 complaints—why should Hawke consider himself above the common man when it came to the seat-belt law? (Australia was the first country in the world to make car seat-belts compulsory, in 1971.) Hawke's reaction was wise, and the only one possible in a robust democracy like Australia's: he said he was very sorry and asked the police to treat him like any other citizen. He was duly fined A$ 100 for his lapse.

In some societies, such public criticism would be unthinkable. But Australians were quite happy to put the matter out of their minds once justice had been done, the leader levelled. Besides, they prefer their leaders to be that way: ordinary men, capable of peccadillos. As Donald Horne has said, 'Australians do not crave great men.' Great men are 'tall poppy' material, asking to be scythed down.

Contempt for politicians and political processes is a reflex emotion for most Australians. In the average Australian's mind, politicians are just ordinary blokes like himself who have been 'put up there' with the sole purpose of 'delivering the goods' and serving the people. If at any time they should cease to deliver, begin to behave like masters or, heaven forbid, leaders, they should be summarily removed by the people who put them there. The scandals of corruption in Queensland and of economic mismanagement and influence-peddling in Western Australia, as well as allegations ranging from expenses-fiddling to sexual harassment inside Federal Parliament in recent times, have sharpened such attitudes.

The level of rudeness about, and to, politicians on television and in the media, for example, shocks most non-Australians, even the English and the Americans. 'It's a bit like watching soft porn,' said one migrant fresh from respectful Asia.

Fundamentally, it is a healthy attitude. Taken to extremes, it can make government close to impossible at times.

Teamwork is Australian

Here, pause a while to consider a paradox: the Australian soldier has long been saluted as an excellent fighting man. But isn't good soldiering founded on rigid discipline, hard training, hierarchy and unquestioning submission to officers' instructions? How then does the Australian soldier do it if the Australian character is inherently so rebellious?

The answer is of course that an Australian may be difficult to govern, but he responds better than most to those whom he admires and loves, and who stand beside him, rather than lead from the front. He is a team-worker. 'Mateship' reinforces this.

This principle could be extended to other spheres of life, in work and play. So do not too hastily write off Australian rebelliousness as being destructive to getting things done, nor as anathema to the collective good.

Another Way of Getting Things Done

The Australian way of doing things is eccentric and lateral rather than direct, apparently indisciplined, yet both creative and effective. And most important, humane. It is a way that works especially well for artistic endeavours and in the more arcane reaches of science—such as quantum or chaos theory and computer software-generation—which today are by definition anarchistic, as many Aussies are.

Get in Line

It used to be expected that male (less so, female) taxi passengers would sit in front next to the driver, flagging equality ('I'm nobody's chauffeur'). This is still good behaviour to adopt in Australia, but admittedly times are changing, following too many violent assaults on taxi-drivers, and also the proliferation of migrant taxi-drivers who know nothing of the Aussie ethos. (For women passengers, the dangers have increased: there have been recent cases of migrant drivers who have made unwanted advances, culturally unable to interpret appropriately the common sight of drunken half-naked females fresh from late-night parties).

However, you should always take your place in the queue, real or metaphorical, no matter who you are. Beggar or king, you wait your turn in Australia. There should be no privilege, no string-pulling to get ahead of your neighbour.

Well, that is the official Australian ethos, anyway. When practised, it is admirable. But it should be noted that in reality, there is quite a bit of influence-peddling going on behind the scenes, harmless 'mateship' though it may seem to its practitioners.

Yet another facet of this stance is the Australian's almost automatic sympathy for the underdog, 'the battler'. Similarly, we have already discussed in other chapters his ability to elevate failure into victory. These attitudes are the natural corollary of the anti-tall poppy syndrome.

You Pays Your Money and You Takes Your Choice

Freedom is a highly valued and generally very available commodity in Australia. The individual is expected to use maturity and judgement when shopping in this supermarket of choice. It's all up to you.

SOCIAL DO'S AND DON'TS

Fitting in includes understanding all those subtle social signals that remain secret and hidden within every culture until someone alerts you to them.

You will find the usual social rituals a bit more diverse in a multicultural society like Australia's than maybe they were at home. A wedding for example, could be the traditional white affair in church, but equally might be a much more free-form affair, say, in a park or on a boat, with a registered civil 'celebrant' not a priest to solemnise the marriage, maybe fancy dress and a wild rock band or whatever. It might even be a gay 'commitment ceremony' in the absence of legal marriage for same-sex couples. Try never to look surprised.

As I have said elsewhere, keep the conversation light and human at first, until you know people really well. Try not to ask them what they do for a job, certainly not what they earn, or what car they drive, or how much their house cost. Ask rather what they thought of the cricket score the other day, or even talk about the weather, a time-honoured stratagem borrowed from 'the Poms'.

Avoid temperature-raising topics like immigration, Iraq and Muslim terrorism, 9/11 or the Aboriginals. Do comment on their handsome home renovations and ask them how they did it. And their children, how are their schooling/uni studies/ first job going?—that's a safe topic the world over.

Deciding what to wear can be a bit of a challenge. Most Australians are religiously casual about their clothes for most events, avoiding anything more formal than a pair of shorts, but for a big dinner in a hotel, or a special dance, they will suddenly turn out in full 'tux' and ball gowns and stun you with their sequinned style. If in doubt, better ask in advance. For weddings and funerals, you can be sure there will be lots of hats and formal suits.

Don't be surprised by the many different ways that Australians may live their lives. Most Aussies don't even use the term 'alternative lifestyles' any more ('so last century') because these lifestyles have become so integrated with, and accepted by, a largely tolerant mainstream. So gay couples, single parents, lesbian parents (two 'mums'), organic farming communes... all these cause not even a lift of the eyebrow in Australia. Be ready for your sons and daughters to join in. Some may grumble and mumble about the 'irresponsibility' of such experimental family set-ups, but in essence, they will back off eventually, because everyone in Australia subscribes to a fundamental understanding that tolerance and non-discrimination are important if not crucial social virtues, besides being supported by a strong legal framework. Indeed, talking about a 'legal framework', one of Australia's most distinguished High Court judges,

Tips and Taboos

Don't

- Arrive late for dinner—while in some cultures (e.g. Mediterranean, Asian), it is more polite not to be too punctual, in Western societies like Australia, it is not.
- Overstay your welcome at a party, by hanging around too late (after midnight), especially not if it's a weekday night.
- Bring someone extra along for a sit-down dinner without consulting the hostess in advance—numbers and seating matter at western-style dinners, although for summer-weather barbecues and pool parties in the garden, there may not be such a problem.
- Bring your children with you for a sit-down dinner, at least not without consulting the hostess in advance; the Western style is not to have children around at formal dinners, or at best, to ensure they are 'seen and not heard'.
- Smoke in someone's home—go outside in the backyard to indulge this sin; you'll find everyone else there, doing the same thing.
- Arrive empty-handed for a dinner party or barbecue—

just recently retired from the Bench, Justice Michael Kirby, is openly gay and attends formal functions with his male partner Johan. (Ditto the Gillard Labor Government's Minister for Finance, Penny Wong, who is the openly lesbian parent of a baby girl, conceived via IVF by her partner Sophie). You may find that the organised secretary in your office is also a devotee of strange sequinned costumes and member of a drum-bashing samba group by night, while the clever young civil servant over there enjoys a nocturnal life as a febrile African-style dancer (both true-life examples, believe me). Never ever judge an Australian book by its cover.

the customary thing to bring is a bottle or cask of wine (not expensive in Australia), or a six-pack of beer, but sometimes an extra dessert or other food offering will do just as well.

- Bring expensive looking gifts for the host and hostess entertaining you at home; just something simple, whether it be flowers, wine or chocolates, will do—too much show may make them feel uncomfortable.

Do

- Ask your hostess what she is cooking and whether you can 'bring anything'; though she may not have asked in the beginning, you will probably find she leaps at the opportunity to ask you to bring a dessert or a salad to complement her meal.
- Help to clear the dirty dishes back to the kitchen at the end of a dinner party, and if there is no dish-washing machine in the house, offer to help wash up (because there will almost certainly be no maids around, barring the hostess); don't ever sit back waiting for them to be cleared—get up!

SETTLING IN

CHAPTER 5

'Australia will be strong only if it is open to immigration...
we have buried 'White Australia', and in its place have
raised a modern, diverse society... Australians should not
worry because other people want to come to our country.
The day to worry is when immigrants are no
longer attracted to our shores...'
—Global media magnate Rupert Murdoch, of News
Corporation—the Boyer Lectures (ABC), November 2008

BEING A MIGRANT

This chapter is not a detailed guide to the labyrinth of getting permission to migrate to Australia. It just gives a snapshot of what it is like to be a migrant, and what migration has meant to Australia.

Even if I wanted to give you a detailed 'how to do it' guide, I doubt I could. For a start, the rules of the immigration game change fairly often—signposts to change usually are imminent federal elections and economic upheaval, as well as international terrorist incidents. A perception that multiculturalism may be failing in other countries (as per the terrorist bombing of London's train stations in 2005) has put the government under some pressure to restrict immigration; however, the evidence is that to a large extent, Australia has successfully absorbed its migrant influx with far less accompanying social tension than many countries in Europe and in reality, the economic push factor of a too-small domestic market and population impels Australia to continue its migration programme—6.8 million people have migrated to Australia since 1945.

You can keep up with the policies via the government's Department of Immigration and Citizenship (DIAC) website www.immi.gov.au but you will need time and patience, because the site is quite an information maze! Always click on items titled 'What's New' or anything similar.

There are a host of useful booklets you can get from the Department either via the website, or by contacting them—

PO Box 25, Belconnen, ACT 2616, Australia, Tel: (02) 6264 1111 or enquiry line 131 881 (only from inside Australia), Fax: (02) 6225 6970.

The Labor Revolution

The Immigration scene in Australia ostensibly was revolutionised by Labor Prime Minister Kevin Rudd's election in November 2007. Gone are some of the former Liberal Howard government's most oppressive and wearisome ideas— among them the shameful principles of mandatory detention and restrictive Temporary Protection Visas for refugees and the so-called 'Pacific Solution' that outsourced refugee detention centres on paid contract to poor offshore island nations with economies in such trouble that any idea would be a good one—countries like Nauru in the South Pacific, the smallest island nation in the world. The whole immigration system is currently in flux, even more than it usually is (which it usually is—the most predictable factor being its unpredictability). But certain threads common to the Howard and the Rudd-Gillard regimes persist in the current immigration climate:

- Australia does want more people. Its labour force is contracting, partly due to ageing. Skilled migrants are essential to Australia's continued economic growth, across a wide range of skills, not just white-collar professionals (the list of desired occupations is updated annually). Under current global economic conditions, even though Australia has plenty of jobs, there will still be vigorous competition for them—an Australian immigration team marketing just 775 skilled jobs in Athens during October 2011 got 18,000 expressions of interest. Other Europeans are in that queue too, fleeing economic uncertainties and in some cases, collapse, among them large numbers of Irish workers.

- Australia does want to control carefully how many people it receives, what kind, from where, and by which entry method—the Labor government is still reserving its options on refugees, asylum seekers and 'boat people' and notably has not cancelled the Howard strategy of declaring certain offshore territories and islands (like Christmas Island in the Indian Ocean) 'not Australia' for immigration purposes.

However, the treatment of refugees is certainly more humane under current Labor government conditions.

- Somewhat immorally, while courting talent to come into the country, Australia on the other hand continues to charge as much as it possibly can while it is about it, making immigration and visa fees generally a nice little revenue earner. The visa costs are currently listed at the Department of Immigration & Citizenship website, go to *www.immi.gov.au/allforms/pdf/990i.pdf* Basic skilled migration visas will require at least A$8,000, plus some— every family member you bring will be costed individually and if, after forking out A$150-A$400 per head just to sit the tough IELTS or International English Language Testing System test that determines your English level, your or your dependents' English is not considered up to scratch, there will be additional charges. Add to all this the costs of medical clearance, police clearance, legal commissioner of oath certification fees for original documents, quite apart from actual moving costs when you have cleared all these hurdles. You really need to set aside quite a large lump sum to accomplish a full family migration.

- Australia now expects a higher level of commitment from migrants to 'Australian Values' and culture, particularly if they are to become citizens, and also a proven level of English language skills, albeit graded according to the nature of the job sought; these were demands articulated first by the Howard government but so far, also preserved and developed by the Labor government. Since October 2007, the majority of visa applicants have been required to sign an Australian Values Statement after reading the *Life in Australia* booklet handout. Typically, the Statement will spell out respect for Australia's laws, for freedom (of religion, speech etc) and democracy, the equality of men and women, the responsibilities of eventual citizenship etc. The backdrop to this has been repeated ideological (rarely physical) clashes pitting 'mainstream' Australian society against Islamic clerics operating within Australia, over issues like the equality of men and women, the nature of marriage and female sexuality, to name some of the more contentious issues. While stressing the core value of egalitarianism is necessary, there is of course a delicate balance to be achieved here when considering the equally core Aussie value of free speech for all, Muslims included.

- An important part of that commitment to Australian values is facility with the English language. The dreaded IELTS is something you, the wannabe migrant, should familiarise yourself with, as it may well prove to be your passport to residence.

An Overview Of Migration Streams and Some Specific Nasties

To migrate as a general migrant, you will need to score 65 points against certain criteria, and note, if you are aged 40-49 years old, you get 0 points! The migration visa programme sub-divides broadly into three different categories, although there are myriad arcane and bureaucratic sub-divisions, meandering highways and by-ways. When going into the DIAC website, don't click only on 'Migrants' but also on 'Workers', a category that you will find includes both the Skilled Professional and Business categories:

- Skilled Stream—including independents and those already sponsored by an employer. An interesting new addition in 2012, catering for Australia's acute skilled worker shortage, is the new fast-track section SkillSelect which allows you just to express your interest in working in Australia, and acts to find a matching Australian employer seeking your skills.
- Family Stream—for the reunion of spouses, *de facto* (unmarried) partners (whether heterosexual or homosexual), parents and children etc.
- Humanitarian Program—including Refugees.

And there is the Overseas Student Program for those studying at Australian colleges and universities. The numbers have fallen off somewhat since the 278,184 student visas granted in 2007-'08 but the inflow is improving again, covering about 195 source countries, with China (20 per cent) and India (14.4 per cent) in the lead. There are more generous provisions for students to work alongside their studies nowadays, and also arrangements for parents or guardians to accompany their student children on temporary visas. Go to http://www.studyinaustralia.gov.au for more information on these programmes.

Business

As with other visas, business visas are a complex matter. There are multiple options, including for short visits, but the most attractive options are various forms of Business Skills Visa. Certain "High-Calibre Business People" or direct investors may be treated preferentially if they satisfy certain criteria. However, do not ever move to buy an Australian business in the expectation that this will automatically bring you a visa; always obtain the visa first. The Australian government does not endorse any brokers attempting to sell you businesses, and does not run a list of businesses approved for migrant purchase.

Business migrants' business skills and capital are checked carefully. You will not get very far with your application if you do not already have proof of previous business ventures or skills. Most initial business visas, whether for a new business development or for investment in an existing business, are only provisional, but do offer a pathway to permanent residence within two to five years, and thereafter to citizenship later. But the business' success will be monitored in terms of criteria such as turnover, and how many Australians it employs etc. Be aware that failures under this system are commonplace and if you are not careful you may find yourself summarily shipped back home a few years and hundreds of thousands of dollars later. This is even more tragic if you have burned your boats back home, for instance by giving up a good job and selling your home, and by transferring your whole family, especially schooling children, into the Australian environment. There is however, an appeals process against visa cancellation. But the provisional business visa option requires enormous dedication and hard work to turn it into a success. Yet there are many such success stories around to learn from.

Australian Values

I understand:

- *Australian society values respect for the freedom and dignity of the individual, freedom of religion, commitment to the rule of law, parliamentary democracy, equality of men and women and a spirit of egalitarianism that embraces mutual respect, tolerance, fair play and compassion for those in need and pursuit of the public good.*
- *Australian society values equality of opportunity for individuals, regardless of their race, religion or ethnic background.*
- *The English language, as the national language, is an important unifying element of Australian society.*

I undertake to respect these values of Australian society during my stay in Australia and to obey the laws of Australia.

(extracted from the Australian Values Statement that visa applicants are required to sign).

Taking the Passport

There is less flexibility in the migration system these days—once upon a time, a smile and a nod could well win the day. But these days, mostly, 'the rules is the rules.' A new hurdle for would-be citizens has been the Citizenship Test, introduced in 2007 by the Howard government and retained by the Labor government, but revised in 2009.

Under new rules ushered in during 2007, to be eligible even to apply for citizenship, if you became a permanent resident on or after 1 July 2007, then you must have been legally resident in Australia for four years immediately before you can apply for citizenship. Of that four-year period, you will have to spend at least 12 months as a permanent resident, and during those four years you must not have been absent from Australia for more than 12 months, and also not more than three months just before you apply for citizenship. Once again, money kicks in: if you are a permanent resident already and generally eligible, the fee for your citizenship application is likely to be about A$260, with no extra charge for children under 16 applying on the same form with you. There is an appeals process available if you are refused citizenship.

Proving Yourself in the Citizenship Test

Once you have determined that you are eligible to apply for citizenship, you must take the Citizenship Test as well as submit your application (with some exceptions, such as if you are under 18 or over 60, physically disabled, or have an Australian parent). And hurrah, there is no extra fee for sitting the test which is covered by your main citizenship application fee. The pass rate for this test is a reassuring 98.9 per cent at first try (Skills Stream applicants). Unsurprisingly, the pass rate for applicants from the humanitarian visa category (including refugees), who are often linguistically and culturally disadvantaged, is only 86 per cent. But you can take the test as often as you like, until you achieve a pass, as many others do. There are also special arrangements for applicants with low literacy.

Your study primer before you sit the test should be *Australian Citizenship: Our Common Bond*, a DIAC publication available in book or DVD format and also downloadable online at the DIAC website. The 45-minute test is in English, is usually conducted on a computer, and consists of 20 multiple-choice questions. You will know on the spot whether or not you have passed the test. A 75 per cent mark (15 correct answers to 20 questions) is needed to pass.

You can do it. In 2010-'11, no fewer than 95,284 people from 185 different countries successfully took Australian citizenship. Oh, and by the way, your precious new Australian passport will cost you a cool A$233, and $117 per child. Always travel on it in and out of Australia, even if you have other passports.

What do we remember on Anzac Day

A) The arrival of the first free settlers from Great Britain

B) The landing of the First Fleet at Sydney Cove

C) The landing of the Australian and New Zealand Army Corps at Gallipoli, Turkey

You need to have done some reading up to answer questions like this practice question for the Citizenship Test.

Which of these is an example of freedom of speech?
A) People can peacefully protest against government decisions
B) Australians are free to not follow a religion
C) Men and women are treated equally in a court of law.

One of the trickier practice questions for the Citizenship Test, more like an intelligence or comprehension test than a test of knowledge.

You don't automatically lose your original citizenship and passport, so far as the Australians are concerned, when you take up Australian nationality; that will depend on the policies of your original country, not on Australia. And once Australian, you can still take yet another nationality later. But don't bank too heavily on the Australian government getting dual citizens like you out of any trouble in your country of origin.

Familiarisation Techniques

Would-be migrants would be well advised to read the Australian press for at least a year before they make their move. I myself subscribed to *The Weekend Australian* for a year before I migrated, and picked up the odd copy of my local *The West Australian* daily whenever I could find one. *The Age* of Melbourne and the *Australian Financial Review,* are also good backgrounders. But these days, you can learn even more on the Net.

Get a Feel for the Country First

It's a good idea too to have visited Australia before you decide to migrate there. This may sound like unnecessary advice, but not if my husband is anything to go by: a Singaporean-Indian, he was determined to migrate there without ever having set foot in the country.

Because he is black, I was just a wee bit nervous and insisted he travel across the country both with and without me first. This he did—and came back singing its praises even more loudly. So we filled in the forms and settled down to something like an 18-month wait before we got the good news. That was back in 1989. It can take longer.

You will find the DIAC's *Settlement Information* briefing at http://www.immi.gov.au/allforms/pdf/994i.pdf and also the *Beginning a Life in Australia* booklet (very thorough, highly recommended) at http://www.immi.gov.au/living-in-australia/settle-in-australia/beginning-life/_pdf/eng.pdf very useful starting points for your settlement. As the *Settlement Information* text wisely says, "The cost of living in Australia is high, compared to many other countries. It is essential that you think about how you will provide for yourself and your family for at least the first two years. Do not assume you will find a job quickly. The cost of relocating is high. There are significant costs involved in travelling to Australia, moving household goods and setting up a new home."

The Culture Gap

This section of the DIAC's Beginning a Life in Australia booklet is an amusing if also slightly disturbing guide to some of the 'cultural-gap' problems that dinky-di Aussies have to deal with among their newer migrant communities. The bit about "swearing in public" is a bit rich though—I hear swearing in public almost every minute of the day in Australia, and not much of it from migrants either!

Polite Behaviour

- Australians usually say "please" when asking for something and usually say "thank you" when someone helps or gives them something. Not saying please and thank you is seen as impolite.
- Australians usually say "excuse me" to get someone's attention and "sorry" when they accidentally bump into someone. Australians also say "excuse me" or "pardon me" when they burp in public or in someone's home.
- You should always try to be on time for meetings and other appointments. If you are going to be late, contact the person to let them know. This is very important for professional appointments (for example, an appointment with a doctor) as you could be charged money for being late or if you miss the appointment without letting the person know in advance. A person who is always late may be considered to be unreliable.

(Continued on the next page)

(Continued from previous page)

- If you receive a written invitation it may include the letters 'RSVP' with a date provided. This means that the person inviting you would like to know whether or not you will be attending. It is polite to confirm whether you will be attending by that date.
- Most Australians blow their noses into handkerchiefs or tissues, not onto the pavement. This is also true for spitting. Many people will also say "bless you" when you sneeze – this phrase has no religious intent.
- It is important to know that some behaviour is not only impolite but is also against the law. Examples of offensive behaviour include swearing and spitting in public, and urinating or defecating anywhere except in a public or private toilet...
- You may find some clothing styles confronting or offensive. For example, some women wear clothes that reveal a lot of their body. You should not judge people by the standards of your previous country. In Australia, no matter what a woman's style of dress might be, you should not interpret it to mean they have low morals or that they wish to attract men's interest.

You Can Take It With You

Frankly, it's hard to see why you would need to take almost anything into Australia as a migrant these days, barring only possessions that are unique to your country of origin, of strong sentimental value, or of genuine antique value, unless it be just because you fear the sheer hassle of shopping for everything all over again when you arrive. But reverting to the rules and regulations, what *can* you take into Australia as a migrant? There are generous concessions at your first landing: you can take almost anything that you have owned and used for the past 12 months, duty- and GST-free. This does not include your car (see the Fact Sheet at http://www.customs.gov.au/site/page4371.asp), the family pet (see http://www.daff.gov.au/aqis/cat-dogs), industrial machinery, or furs, however, for which there are special arrangements. And by the way, if you have a mobile phone from the US, it probably won't work in Australia anyway, and even iPads beyond #2 might not work so well, because of slow 4G rollout in Australia. Another tip: Australia's electrical plugs are virtually unique—three flat-pins in a triangular formation, with the two upper pins slightly slanting—so you will have to get ready to change the plugs on just about everything you have.

Either way, it's now or never if you want to take in a container-load or part-container load of items for your new life, there will be no second chance. Most of your documentation will be handled by your chosen freight-forwarding agent.

After this, you will have to travel as all Australians do, with a restricted allowance of duty-free overseas purchases that you can bring back to Australia (total value A$ 900 per head or A$ 450 for those under 18). Anything above the allowance must be declared with a supporting receipt proving the item's original sale value and tax already paid overseas (don't get too clever with creative under-invoicing, the customs officers aren't stupid!). Honesty is always the best policy; the duty payable is often quite low. Be careful too with dirty shoes from overseas and with illicitly copied computer software or movie DVDs. Forget the fantasy of smuggling in that odiferous cheese from Marseilles or your Singapore auntie's home-made curry powder, *never ever* try to import food without declaring it—and that includes aircraft food—(there are prohibitive penalties for this, try an A$ 220 on-the-spot fine, followed by potentially an A$ 66,000 fine or 10 years' jail). Ditto plant and animal materials, and items made of wood. Have a look at the informative Customs and Border Protection Service's Guide for Travellers at http://www.customs.gov.au/webdata/resources/files/KnowBeforeYouGoEnglishFeb2011WEB.pdf and also browse http://www.customs.gov.au/site/page4352.asp.

Toughing It Out

But don't get too smart by arranging for under-invoicing at a fantastic bargain-basement price; Australian Customs officers know very well what are the likely selling prices for most items, whether you are coming from Singapore or from London. Like Customs officers everywhere, they react pretty brutally if they discover you have been trying to take them for a ride.

Be careful too with illicitly-copied computer software: Australia strictly enforces copyright protection laws. (and that applies to pirated music and movie DVDs too).

Under Suspicion

Everyone has had at least one horror story with Australian Immigration/Customs officials. They can be toughies, although they come on initially with brighter smiles and more friendly chat than any of their counterparts worldwide. So relax. They will notice if you don't—and that could have 'negative outcomes' for you. Still, I shall not easily forget one unsmiling lady at Perth airport who had our entire luggage searched, apparently for drugs, just because we had travelled in and out of Malaysia once too often for her liking. Nor how she thrust her hands triumphantly into the tatty, torn silk lining of my suitcase—at last, a false bottom—flipped suspiciously through the pages of my notebooks, and even had my Indonesian wooden puppets' heads X-rayed for secret compartments.

On the other hand, both customs and immigration offices can be too laid-back, becoming fallible. Although emotionally scarred, we survived one of our migrant residence visas being accidentally cancelled at the airport (inspect your passport carefully to see what has been done before you leave the airport)—a frightening discovery made only just before our next flight.

On balance, though, a cool temper combined with a modest and pleasant demeanour will see you through. No showing off, please. One well-heeled Chinese visitor learned his lesson. Asked what he had come to Australia for, he facetiously replied, "To spend money." This was not a sensitive remark in the context of the Australian dislike for 'tall poppies', nor the average Customs officer's salary. Needless to say, they took him apart.

A MIGRANT NATION

Australia today is recognised as one of the most multicultural countries in the world, with approximately a quarter of the population having been born overseas, and closer to 40 per cent of the people with at least one parent born overseas. Australia is a country of 185 nations. Some Sydney suburbs are 42 per cent of non-English speaking origin. By 2056, the total population is projected to reach between 30.9 and 42.5

million people, given continued immigration. By the year 2010, say some studies, the Chinese-origin population of Australia alone could exceed one million. But the traditional countries, the United Kingdom and New Zealand, are still the leading sources of overseas-born residents of Australia, with China, India and Italy close runners-up, in that order, as of 2010.

MULTICULTURALISM—HANDLE WITH CARE

Beyond simple migration, Australia has further espoused multiculturalism within Australia. However, the word 'multiculturalism' itself went out of fashion during the conservative Howard government period and is less often heard these days, the flipside of a stronger emphasis on the importance of inculcating 'Australian Values.'

Multiculturalism is reckoned to cost the Federal and State Governments about A$ 514 million a year, or about A$ 30 for each Australian, revealed *The Australian* newspaper in its own 1991 investigation. These costs are incurred in a range of activities, from the Special Broadcasting Service (SBS) catering to minority culture, to ethnic language booklets on everything under the sun and English-as-a-second-language programmes.

This policy worries even some proponents of Asian migration, let alone conservatives concerned with preserving Australia's British or Anglo-Celtic heritage. They worry about 'ghetto-ism'. They fret slightly about the proliferation of ethnic clubs, and they froth at the mouth when migrants are discovered still promoting forced arranged marriages of under-age girls, or worse, continuing traditions of female genital mutilation inside Australia.

The upheavals of the late 1990s in Eastern Europe amply demonstrated the problem, as did the Gulf War of 1990–1991: émigré communities of Serbs, Bosnian and Croats in Australia avoided, or attacked, one another in tandem with the factions developing in what was Yugoslavia, while Romanian-Australians denounced the Ceausescu 'moles' in their midst after the Romanian revolutionaries had despatched their former dictator. Even today, rioting fans at sports events such as soccer matches, the Tennis Open in Melbourne, January 2009 (Serbs vs Bosnians), fracture along these lines.

Many migrants and refugees have, perhaps understandably, imported their domestic political and social problems into Australia. These nations within a nation have made many uneasy. This is an ongoing debate, as it is in some other countries too, such as Britain: should migrants be forced or persuaded into cultural integration? For instance, can Muslims be obliged to submit to Australian customs and laws?

Rubbing Shoulders with the World

As a migrant yourself, you may well find multiculturalism exciting. For the first time, you will find yourself side by side with exotic cultures you never dreamed of encountering before.

How, for instance, could my Sri Lankan engineer friend ever have guessed he would end up marrying a Colombian girl in Australia? Listening to the interplay of this family's three different accents when conversing together in English at their Australian dinner-table was something of a treat: his voice still heavily Indian-inflected, hers distinctly Spanish, and their little girl's, why Australian, of course.

You may have to be more careful than you were before. 'Irish jokes', or Sikh ones for that matter, may prove problematic in the wrong company. There are other potential social gaffes to avoid: you may find it next to impossible to mix your Serb and Croat friends from Yugoslavia, for example, and it would be most ill-advised to invite an Armenian and a Turk, or a Tamil and a Sinhalese, together for tea.

Yet multiculturalism is a furnace in which hitherto unheard-of new alliances may be forged: I think, for instance, of the Portugal Day hosted by the Portuguese Consul in Perth, which saw peoples of all the former Portuguese colonies come together in song, dance and festivity: from Indonesian Timor, from African Mozambique, from Latin American Brazil, from Goa in India, from Malacca in Malaysia and from Macau off China. And yet they were all Australians too.

Indeed, one's definition of an 'Australian' blurs somewhat when confronted with pedigrees like those of my friends. Former residents of Singapore, they now live in Perth. My girlfriend's mother was born in Shanghai and looks Chinese, but doesn't speak the language. (Her parents were

Australian officialdom tries very hard to be 'politically correct' when it comes to minority rights. Hence, this Australia postcard first ensures that the 'Postie' or post-person depicted is a woman and not the expected male, and second, also ensures that the mail she is carrying is addressed to a typical Australian, i.e. none other than Mrs Wong, presumably a Chinese-Australian.

Czech-Japanese on one side, Irish-Chinese on the other.) My girlfriend's father, on the other hand, was a Latvian who had fled his Baltic home-state during the Russian Revolution of 1917, to Shanghai via Siberia; in Shanghai, he had been adopted by a benevolent Iraqi-Jewish opium trader.

This couple got out of China in 1954, using the wife's part-Czech descent as a pretext for exit. And so to Singapore, where my ostensibly Singaporean, now Australian, girlfriend was born to them. She married a mixed Irish-Eurasian from Singapore. Should anyone be surprised that their little girl, dinki-di Aussie, has turned out fair and freckled of skin, with stunning red hair. That's as multicultural a make-up as you can get, but it's not such an unusual story for Australia.

Multiculturalism and the promotion of ethnic politics has led to ethnic lobbying. Former Malaysian-Chinese Dr Eric Tan, a prominent surgeon and community leader in Perth, has a shrewd idea of future directions. Himself an 'Asian-Australian' for 30 years now, he told me, "You can expect a trend towards the Chinese community entering Australian politics Australia-wide."

Perhaps a Chinese-Australian Prime Minister of Australia could even be on the cards one day. In 1990, Bill O'Chee of Queensland, then 24, was elected to the Australian Senate (for the National Party, straight from the rural heartlands). His grandfather was China-born but Irish-ised his name to 'O'Chee' to fob off Australian racism. Bill's mother is Irish, his father Chinese. He is no longer in politics, however. The idea of a non-white Australian Prime Minister got a lot closer to realisation with Labor Prime Minister Kevin Rudd's cabinet, announced at end-2007: this included Malaysian-born Chinese Penny Wong (from Sabah, eastern Malaysia) whose family brought her to Australian when she was eight years old. She now holds the powerful Ministry of Finance and Deregulation portfolio.

There are others: Hong Kong-born Michael Choi Wai-man, the first Chinese-Australian member of a state legislative assembly (2001 Queensland elections) and Queensland's Parliamentary Secretary for Trade and Multicultural Affairs, but defeated in the 2012 state elections; also Hong Lim, elected to Victoria's Legislative Assembly in 1996, and appointed Parliamentary Secretary to the Minister for Victorian Communities in 2002.

Making Things Different

"I want to tell the world that, despite some narrow-minded, uninformed and oversimplified comments from certain high-profile politicians, Australians are not racist and in fact are very fair-minded people... Multiculturalism has brought richness to Australia... Multiculturalism is not about taking one previous culture into this country lock, stock and barrel, it is about keeping the good and discarding those things that are perhaps incompatible... There are parts of my parents' culture that I would not want my children to learn because I know that they have no place in this country. But there are other parts of the Chinese culture that I want not only my children to learn, I would dearly like my fellow Australians to embrace them also, because they are simply good for our nation-building. Multiculturalism is about being the best of the best. I do not want Australia to be Asianised, whatever that word means. I do not want Australia to be Europeanised, whatever that word means. I definitely do not want Australia to be Americanised, and I know what that word means. I want Australia to develop her own culture and be the envy of the world because she has developed her culture from the best of the best."

—Michael Choi Wai-man, in his maiden speech as a new Member to the Queensland Legislative Assembly, 2001.

Integration Without Tears

You, as a migrant, should at least be sensitive to Australian concerns about multiculturalism. It is natural, and also helpful in the initial stages of migration, to turn to support organisations comprising your former compatriots. In every Australian city, you will find the right club for yourself: Greek, Italian, Austrian, Polish, Serb, Croat, Tamil, Malayalee, Sri Lankan, Timorese, Eurasian, Anglo-Indian, Singaporean or what-have-you.

But you would do well to make an effort to meet Australians by joining some of their activities too—from your street Neighbourhood Watch (crime-watch) committee, to the local church, the local heritage/history society, or a nature-walking group. Trouble is, you find that many of the 'Australians' around you prove to be migrants too. But even this discovery serves to make you feel more at home, less of an oddity.

Remember that Australia is remarkable for the ease with which you can strike up a conversation with a stranger. Don't be shy, speak up if you want to make friends, whether on the bus or when picking up the children from school along with other parents. This dictum applies especially to naturally conservative Asians. Remember that your accent may be as unfamiliar to older Australians as theirs is to you, so take it slowly and enunciate clearly. There will be some who don't feel comfortable with you, but many will respond kindly.

Remember too that elaborate structures are already in existence to help migrants: consult your local phone directory for contact with bodies like the Ethnic Communities Council or the Multicultural and Ethnic Affairs Commission. Ask them for advice, and the contacts for other migrant assistance centres. Australia is a country where there are myriad resources to help you, but you are expected to go looking for them—they are rarely handed to you on a platter. Ask and you shall receive.

As for general information, if you look up your phone directory listing for Recorded Information Services, or letter 'D' for 'Dial-It', you will be astounded at the range of things you can find out over the phone. Similarly, Australia excels in the prolific production of first-class information leaflets and brochures. A browsing session at your local library, Council and other local government offices, as well as hospitals, and medical and migrant resource centres, will harvest a sheaf of such literature.

Take an active interest in Australian politics and social issues by reading the local press; sample typical Australian activities, such as the local footy (Australian Rules football) or cricket matches. Watch television and listen to the radio; make a point of seeing the latest Australian movies and plays, art exhibitions and so on. This will help you converse with Australians on their own ground.

If, by any chance, your English is less than perfect (and not all migrants find it easy to recognise this simple fact—many Singaporeans, for example), work on it. When you detect misunderstandings, ask about them, find out what you did wrong. Remember, you are on somebody else's turf now, it's you who must adjust to them, not them to you. The language is absolutely crucial to your integration.

Lawyer Anthony Quahe (far right), is a former Singaporean migrant, now Managing Principal at Civic Legal firm in Perth, Western Australia. He's served in key local community posts, including Tourism Commissioner, Board Member for Eventscorp and Chairman of Celebrate Western Australia. Left to right, his daughters 21 year-old Ilona and 19 year-old Sasha, and his Hungarian-German wife Francisca.

Mum's the Word about Home

In the same box comes the problem of the 'Back home, we do it this way...' syndrome. Or the equally common 'I can't understand why Australia doesn't... what's the matter with them?' Avoid at all costs making public comparisons, particularly invidious ones, between your motherland and your newly adopted home, Australia. This goes down very badly with Australians. Put yourself in their place and this becomes very easy to understand. Also taboo—and many Asian migrants need to learn this—is talking about money and the cost of things (property, cars) all the time. Listen, Look and Learn—But Keep Quiet. Until you know people better, look for the common conversational ground found in children, sport, food, and as a last resort, the weather.

The Migrant Blues

No matter how gungho you have been initially about making a new life in Australia, there will come those moments when you feel depressed, alienated... You wonder if you have made a mistake. This applies to all—and I include those of Anglo-Celtic background, who may be all the more shocked to discover how 'foreign' Australia can be. How much more non-European migrants.

In many ways, the respectable, older middle-class migrant may suffer more, and more silently, from culture shock than a refugee. For refugees, there are all sorts of support and aid groups. For simple migrants—once you land, you're on your own, mate. The older you are, the harder it is. You will find that your young children, in contrast, take to it like a duck to water. I have noticed too that women often fare better than men. However, women's ability to adapt also depends on how much 'permission' they get from their men to go out and get things done (not always automatic in very traditional cultures, for example from Asia and the Middle East). The fact that all too often, Australia does indeed give women much greater opportunities to become independent, including individually delivered welfare cheques for child support etc, is the source of great conflict within traditional households from other cultures, where the man of the house cannot tolerate the spectacle of his women becoming self-sufficient. You must accept that it usually takes something like two or three years before you feel comfortable, and begin to 'fit'. Whatever you do, don't give up before you have given it a go for a couple of years. Believe that it will get better. Try to remember why you came to Australia in the first place, and hold fast to that thought. Statistics show that migrants usually quit within the first three years, but rarely later than that.

I'm Bored

Some new migrants simply get bored with Australia's relaxed ambience. With today's hyper-mobility, they can easily 'just do it,' move. Like this Singaporean friend of mine who wrote to me to explain why he was shipping out of Perth in Western Australia back to Singapore, after only just over five years— you can still see some internal conflict in his decision though:

I'm bored, altho' arguably mad... There's nothing here that interests me or that can leverage on my experience profitably enough. We miss the buzz of Asia and Singapore. We miss our friends and the food... In my fantasies, the ideal life would be to wake up every morning in my nice leafy (Australian) suburb, drive to Singapore to work, to eat, to shop, watch movies, and then drive back to Perth every day and have the river and beach there on the weekends... but we'll be back, when I'm more ready to slow down, but maybe in and out. This (Perth) is still a little corner of heaven. It'd be wonderful if we could have the best of both worlds... But we have grown so much more as individuals having lived here, especially the kids whom today would be very different had they not grown up here. They're still very grateful for the wonderful Australian childhood they have had.

Often, it is necessary to arrive with a passionate commitment, knowing that above all, you want to live in Australia. That must be the first premise. Then you adapt.

If you arrive believing that everything will be the same as back home—you will do the same work, have the same status and income and the same sorts of friends, and your children will continue to behave exactly the way they would have in your own culture—but just in a different physical setting, then you will fail as a migrant. I have seen many new arrivals pull out within a year because they couldn't make a big enough buck fast enough, or because they were puzzled by Australian bureaucracy and democratic rules that say you cannot just willy-nilly put a second storey on your house without your neighbours' consent, or you cannot develop a site because of heritage listing, or because of Aboriginal sacred-site rights, or just because their children were beginning to be a bit ruder and talk with a broad Aussie accent.

You must be prepared for big changes in your life. Very few migrants end up doing the same work in Australia as they did back home; teachers may drive a taxi, scientists open a restaurant. Many find that they 'lose status' in the terms set by their own culture and friends back home; but they need only to relax and realise that the status thing hardly figures in the Australian mind, to be happy. Yes, it's probably a waste of talent and skills, but that's how it has always been for migrants throughout the ages. If you have children, you can just look ahead and enjoy the new opportunities that they are certainly going to get in Australia.

But admittedly, it's the little things that get you down.

For those used to lively, noisy city streets and housing estates at night, it can be the lack of people, the silence of the dimly lit streets of suburbia. Many residential areas resemble menacing black holes at night: Australians seem to live mostly at the back of the house, turning off all the lights at the front as an economy measure, leaving a faceless and unwelcoming streetscape.

No more food-stalls or cafés in the street, unlike Singapore, Kuala Lumpur, Athens or Paris, except in the very heart of the city centre. Faced with steep restaurant prices and early closing times, you do more home entertaining than ever before. Not a soul on the streets; and it's not all that safe to walk the streets alone at night, either. And in the winter, well, you wouldn't want to.

Trials and Tribulations

An East European skilled professional worker in Australia and mother gives her take on the early stages of her experience, in a personal conversation with the author. Nonetheless, she still aspires to Permanent Residence:

Just my opinion, but multiculturalism here in Australia is only created by the presence of so many nations and cuisine, which economically is beneficial for the country, but Australia is not a true multicultural country like Canada for instance, which is truly working towards this direction. On the other hand, right now it is very difficult to migrate to Australia as a skilled individual, probably much more difficult than being a refugee. I myself started this process in 2009, before being sponsored by my company. I had to work for at least 18 months to write up all the career episodes required by the Australian professional body in charge of my industry, had to collate so much evidence from every place I had ever worked, and sit for the IELTS English exam... And all this was only to get the recognition of my professional qualifications necessary to allow me even to start rolling the ball for my PR application. The application would probably have taken another 24 months to get approval. All this is not easy when you are also handling a full-time job and child-care.

It is different for Canada's migration process and as a result, more skilled migrants enter Canada than Australia, at least in terms of East European migrants. When I visited Canada, I was amazed to note how many different languages are used in TV shows or newspapers there, and how much the Canadian government praised the multicultural features of the country and encouraged migrants to preserve each of their national identities. I was in a small town, where everyone noticed I'm a foreigner, and they would speak with me very slowly so I would understand. I was never told, as I am in Australia, that I speak "East European English", and if I wanted to find out how things really worked, I was never pushed away, on the contrary the reaction was positive and I was asked to make further suggestions to improve the process.

Beaten, you retreat behind the four walls of your home like the rest of Australia. Having read the over-active local press for the latest, often horrific, crime stories, you fearfully lock up the house and barricade your bedroom door with chairs for good measure.

Can't Stand the Quiet

A Singaporean Malay friend in Perth bought a plot of land and decided to build his own house on it. When I looked at his plans, I exclaimed, "But why have you chosen to live so close to a highway?"

"It's the silence," he said. "I just can't stand it. I just have to have more noise, else I get lonely." Some call it peaceful, others lonely.

Unfortunately, the fear of crime is to some extent justified. It was only yesterday that Perth-dwellers still left their doors and windows open all the time, and never locked their cars, but alas, no more.

I got a burglar alarm and paid a monthly fee to connect it to a monitoring station that would call the police if it went off. I would recommend a dog too if you have the time to maintain one, as well as metal grille-reinforcements to windows and doors.

But you soon learn which places to avoid at which times, how to protect yourself, and the fear eventually recedes into the background as you become more street-wise.

TRANSPORTATION

If you have never driven before, which was the case with me, thanks to tiny Singapore's excellent public transportation and punitive car costs, those four walls of home quickly become a cosy cage. One crucial element in entering Australian society can often be whether or not you can drive a car. If you can't, the result may be extreme isolation. Mum, your favourite nanny, is no longer just around the corner; your best friend no longer just a phone call away. The buses and trains run infrequently on weekends and at night—and anyway nobody with their head screwed on would want to loiter long at a lonely bus-stop by night.

You need to tackle this issue very early on. I know this, because it was my problem too when I first arrived in Australia. One of the keys to happiness in Australia is having a driving licence: don't leave without it. (If you hold one already, you can drive on it for the first three months in Australia—but in Western Australia and Tasmania, that means three months from the date you are granted permanent residence, not from your arrival date). Then, after three months, you will still need to pass a 'Driver Knowledge Test', a practical driving test and an eyesight test. If you don't have an existing licence, then you will need to pass the Knowledge test before you can get a Learner's Permit which will enable you even to learn to drive. In Australia, mostly anyone over 18 can drive a car, although some states set the benchmark lower. State rules differ but generally there is usually a Learner L-plate stage, and then an approximately two-year Provisional or P-plate stage for all new drivers. In between, there may still be a 'Hazard Perception Test' to test basic overtaking and turning skills etc. There are also often special rules and restrictions for younger drivers —e.g. young P-platers may also have to clock up at least 25 hours' proven driving under adult supervision. You should check with your local authorities, which will differ from state to state—for example, in New South Wales, you talk to the Roads and Traffic Authority, whereas in Western Australia, you talk to the Department of Planning and Infrastructure. Total cost of all your tests and permits, except for the licence itself, around A$ 120

Buying a car in Australia is pretty much a breeze: there are plenty of choices, including a lively second-hand market

Driving on the streets of Sydney can be a different experience especially if you come from a more urbanised city or if you are used to driving on the right.

featuring quality cars at bargain prices. Maintaining the car is also affordable, although you need to shop around a bit when choosing a garage to service your car—car yards are notoriously predatory and often downright tricky. And remember, Australians don't really care whether you run a smart car or not; on the whole, they don't measure your worth that way.

While driving is the key to freedom in Australia, on the other hand, you need to understand that driving a car in Australia is very different from driving back home, especially if your experience is limited to a very urban context. Americans and Europeans have to deal with driving on the left in Australia. In the cities, be aware first that drink-driving laws are strictly enforced, so don't do it—in Western Australia, for instance, the limit for alcohol in the blood is 0.05 g per 100 ml (zero for all novice drivers, such as P-platers, bus- and taxi-drivers etc), and while a first offence at this level will attract a fine of A$ 250 up to A$ 500, as well as driving Demerit points, the penalties escalate for second offences, and also for first offences at 0.08 g per 100 ml, with removal of your driving licence for at least three months likely. Most groups of people going out for the night either negotiate for one of them to remain sober and be the driver for the night, or else arrange taxis if they are going to drink.

Seat belts are compulsory and driving while using a mobile phone is illegal.

If you are used to a free-wheeling situation (as in many Asian cities) where you can zig zag among lanes almost at will, please re-train yourself to the safer and more courteous procedure of signalling your intentions before you change lanes, as most Australian drivers do. Learn to be patient while polite Australian drivers slow down in front of you to allow an elderly person, or indeed any pedestrian, to cross the road, even when not at a pedestrian or zebra crossing. Generally, learn to exercise plenty of patience and consideration.

In town and in most built-up areas, a speed limit of 60 kmph is the norm, sometimes dropping to 50 kmph in suburban streets, or 40 kmph in zones around schools. Outside of the cities, and indeed on many freeways inside cities, speed limits can be as high as 110 kmph. Handling speeds like this on winding country roads—sometimes only partially surfaced—and even more so, at night on only partially lit roads (you will find road lighting generally dimmer than what you are used to), can take some skill. Quite a number of visiting Asian drivers have come to a bad end on Western Australian country roads, for example, and it has often seemed that unfamiliar speeds might have been a factor in many of these accidents.

Australians are used to distance in their daily lives, so may think nothing of driving a couple of hundred miles to visit a friend. Be ready for this, and if you are not used to this idea, take care with the risk of fatigue on long journeys up roads that seem to stretch for ever into the horizon.

The Cost of Four Wheels

As everywhere, the affordability of running a car in Australia depends on globally volatile petrol prices: in 2012, roughly 145.8 Australian cents per litre. Watch out for fuel-guzzlers if you intend to drive long-distance and outback.

- **The Car**
  Perhaps A$ 8,000 or less for a five-year old second-hand Japanese or Korean standard, to around A$ 15,000 for brand-new one, or upwards of A$ 30,000–A$ 50,000 for luxury models, 4WD and the like.
- **Your Licence**
  About A$116 for a five-year licence (concessions for Seniors etc).
- **Licence Registration and Third Party Insurance**
  (from government/police—known in Strine as 'Reggo'). About A$ 561 for 12 months in a standard vehicle used for both business/family purposes.

Another, more unfamiliar, hazard in the countryside is large wild animals, such as kangaroos or buffaloes. As a rookie, it is best simply not to try to drive at night at all, since kangaroos start to move around from twilight into the early morning; believe me, a collision with an angry adult kangaroo about 1.8 m (6 ft) tall, can cause an accident that will kill you, especially if the animal crashes through your windscreen into the car. It seems that 'roos' are in some way attracted to car lights, or dazzled and confused by them, so this event is a distinct possibility.

Often, the roads go for set distances without any provision for overtaking lanes, which appear only sporadically, signed in advance. When stuck behind a big vehicle, you should take advantage of these opportunities.

- **Royal Automobile Club (RAC) Membership & Insurance**
  Membership is optional, but you could regret not having it when you leave your lights on and burn out the battery, or lock yourself out in some lonely spot —A$ 89 Standard metro area help; A$ 139 Classic for more perks and further afield. RAC are not the only car insurers, but for example, basic insurance with an Excess of A$ 450 costs about A$ 500 a year, payable in phased direct-debit instalments (more costly for under 24 year-olds)
- **Annual Service in a Garage:**
  It all depends on how many kilometres your car has done. A simple check-up with oil-change might be only A$ 150, but a more elaborate one could head for A$ 500.

More information: *http://rac.com.au/* and individual State-government traffic authority sites.

By day or by night, outside of the city, you may also be confronted with enormous 'road trains'—lorries towing joined, articulated containers or trailers stretching quite some length behind them, sometimes 50 m (165 ft)—steaming along the main freight roads, across the vastness that is Australia. You have to learn to pull off on the shoulder and let them pass, or when and how to overtake them safely (they will often help you by flashing their right indicators to say that you can go), or they may make your life a misery; absolutely no point, dangerous too, in 'having an argument' with a road train. Apart from these juggernauts, you can also drive for hours in Australia without seeing a soul, so huge is the land and so small the population. This combined with a general inadequacy of mobile phone signals in the countryside means that you must be very self sufficient—have your own spare tyres and wheel jack (and know how to change a wheel) for instance, carry water, oil, maybe even a safe container of some extra petrol, ropes, spades, refrigerated boxes with food and water, and never move without good maps. Petrol stations may be few and far between once you 'go bush.' If long-distance driving is going to be your thing in Australia, having a GPS (Global Positioning System) facility built into your car is never a bad idea, likewise some kind of radio- or satellite-phone system (about A$200 for a fortnight's hire).

With outback driving, you need to be careful. Every year there are stories about unwary visitors who have become stranded in remote areas for lack of a spare part in a breakdown, even because they run out of fuel, or get bogged in sand or floods, and who quite simply die as a result , either because they are not found in time and have insufficient food and water, or because they try to walk for help, get lost and find themselves in some of the world's most inhospitable country. Never leave your vehicle in such a case—air search crews will find you so much more easily if there is a vehicle to spot, and the vehicle may offer some shelter from extreme weather. Always inform national park rangers or policemen when you are driving into the interior about your planned route and return date. Listen to the locals and acquire their know-how. Don't do silly things like camp close to pretty creeks —there are very large crocodiles around who are smart enough to stalk you and observe your habits for several days before they strike—and don't swim in un-patrolled ocean bays where you know nothing about the tides and currents, let alone the resident jellyfish and sharks.

Saved by EPIRB

One British tourist recently stranded for three days in the remote Kimberley region of the north-west, after getting bogged in a marshy area near the coast, was saved just as he was running out of food and water because he had an Emergency Position Indicating Radio Beacon (EPIRB), which he set off. The beacon's digitally coded international distress signal alerted the Australian Search and Rescue Services far away in Canberra, who asked the Coastwatch unit to get a rescue helicopter out to him. You can buy an EPIRB for around A$ 300–A$ 500, and you can also hire one for maybe around A$ 100 a week.

Other Transport

There are transport systems other than the car in the city centres of Australia and some of them very good ones—there are trains, trams in Melbourne, and often networks of free buses within the city, such as the 'CAT' bus system in Perth and Fremantle, Western Australia. If you are travelling a regular route every day to work, you can often buy a cut-price season pass or 'multi-rider' ticket which just deducts cash once inserted into a special reader machine on the buses; a convenient, cheap and fast way of moving around that is often valid for both buses and trains. In Sydney, Perth and other places, there are also ferries crossing rivers and harbours.

MORE BUMMERS

For those accustomed to 24-hour shopping—as many Asians are— it takes some getting used to that shopping hours tend to vary wildly from state to state, and place to place, the legacy of archaic but still recent restrictions on night and weekend shopping, most visible in Perth, Western Australia. This situation is now relaxing even in Perth, and there's a livelier scene anyway in the big cities of the eastern states. In Perth, you can rely on the big supermarkets, Woolworth's and Coles, as well as IGA, and also family-run Italian, Middle

Eastern and Mediterranean small businesses. Yet again, you learn to adapt if you keep looking at that brilliant blue sky, reflect on your freedoms and savour the pleasures of life in the backyard with your family and friends.

Some migrants, especially Asians, are uncomfortable with the degree of freedom and free speech they find in Australia. They feel bombarded by brutal frankness, harassed by the sight of nudity and sex on television and in the cinema. In a way, they miss the firm framework of stricter rules and the soothing absence of moral choice. They are used to governments making decisions for them, like proxy parents. But suddenly, nobody cares what they do. So they feel uncared for—freedom too can create culture shock.

Another 'bummer', to use an Australian phrase, is the Australian pace of work, much slower than say, a Singaporean, a Hongkonger or an American might be used to. One former executive with a multinational corporation, whom I know resigned in frustration from a civil service job, told me, "I was going crazy, just twiddling my thumbs doing nothing all day. I had finished my work!" Needless to say, she wasn't very popular with her laid-back Aussie colleagues. Another rule—don't show off by working too hard if you want to be loved. Or work hard, but disguise it somehow.

Similarly, if you get too proactive at work and bounce around with queries and suggestions for new ideas, backing them up with lots of email too, you will find you start to get the cold shoulder. The Australian workplace seemingly just doesn't have room for this kind of initiative, energy and involvement. Your colleagues and bosses will simply feel threatened—and fatigued—by it. Better keep quiet, move slowly, and smile supportively at all times.

More serious is the discovery on arrival, too late, that your professional qualifications are not valid in Australia. This is a very common problem, so do check carefully what you need to do to re-qualify for work in Australia, well before you arrive. Otherwise you will join the growing band of doctors, teachers and engineers running takeaway food shops or struggling on student study grants.

THE DOLLAR

"The Aussie" as the TV business pundits call it, is a periodically volatile currency, one of the top five heaviest traded in the world, and pins its fortunes very much to the value of primary-produce commodities of the sort that China loves to gobble up —it is therefore also levered more than a little on the fortunes of the China's own economy. Since 2009, thanks to an amazingly healthy banking system, relatively high interest rates, internal stability, enmeshing with successful Asian economies and Australia's comparative immunity from the Global Financial Crisis, the Aussie has been riding high, regularly surpassing parity with the US 'greenback' dollar. At the time of writing however, with interest rates dropping, it looks softer for the immediate future, hovering just below parity.

The Australian currency is decimal, featuring some attractive plasticised notes (yes, you can wash them by mistake in the laundry and they come out just fine!) and some of the world's clunkiest silver coins, such as the enormous wavy-edge 50-cent coin. Inexplicably, of the two gold coins available, the A$ 2 coin is smaller than the A$1 dollar coin. Entrance to charity events and the like is often by 'gold-coin donation', meaning you can give either A$ 1 or A$ 2.

The banking system has been under fire in recent times because of an array of transaction charges, duties and taxes generally considered rather unfair. They can certainly add up. The big names are the Commonwealth Bank of Australia, the Australia and New Zealand Banking Group (ANZ), Westpac Banking Corporation and the National Australia Bank (NAB).

Opening a bank account is fairly easy. Within the first six weeks after you have landed in Australia, the only identity you will need to present is either your driving licence or your passport. Don't delay, it will get more complicated later. If you have interest-earning deposits, you will also need to cite your Tax File Number to reduce the tax payable on interest earned. Do check on the necessary arrangements for using Internet banking and linking all your accounts so that you have full freedom to bank online. If you are in the habit of moving large sums of money around among bank accounts, particularly from overseas accounts into Australia, be aware that transactions of A$ 10,000 or more have to be reported specially by your bank, and so could attract government interest; by the same token, you are obliged to declare cash in any currency amounting to A$ 10,000 or more if you are carrying it in or out of Australia. More info from the Australian Bankers' Association Inc at *www.bankers.asn.au*

Take advantage of credit cards supplied by the banks that offer you frequent flyer points on airlines; compare carefully the relative interest charges for credit cards, personal loans, overdrafts, home loans and car loans before you decide which way to go.

Banks are open from about 9:30 am till 4:00 pm and on Saturday mornings too, an improvement made only in recent times.

KEEPING IN TOUCH

Telecommunications in Australia is in a bit of a mess at the moment, to be frank, with the original core supplier, the once government-owned, Telstra now privatised since 2006 (the 17 per cent still in government hands has been invested in the 'Future Fund' set up to meet public sector superannuation or pension needs). The wholesaling at present involves Telstra selling fixed-line capacity to its rivals, such as Optus and Vodafone; thus, it is...obliged to charge you for services. Telstra's profit for 2010-'11 was just over A$3.2 billion, lower than in the past, but not bad at all. The big push now is to improve services to remote areas in the bush and outback, and the long-overdue rollout of the eagerly awaited A$36-billion National Broadband Network, in favour of which Telstra is already committed to hand over to government its entire antique fixed-line infrastructure. Broadband should be complete nation-wide by 2020. You can get a full briefing on the strategy in place via www.nbn.gov.au and http://www.nbn.gov.au/files/2011/05/National_Digital_Economy_Strategy.pdf.

While other nations, including small Asian nations like Singapore, were already speeding along the Internet highway and getting their entire populations totally wired, in June 2011, Australia ranked only 21st of the 34 Organisation for

Economic Cooperation and Development countries (OECD) for fixed-broadband take-up. As of September 2011, OECD statistics also showed Australia to be way down the rankings for download speeds and cable speeds, and 13th slowest for DSL speeds. On top of this, Australia is the fifth most expensive OECD country for low speed, low data capacity broadband plans. A new dawn is coming, but for the moment, you still need to check on the availability, level and quality of broadband Internet access in the area where you intend to live.

You can opt to place your tele-custom with a multiplicity of operators—Optus (actually largely Singapore-owned), Telstra, Vodafone, Virgin and iinet, to name only a few—but for the moment at least, the fellow charging for line installation and rental will still be the giant Telstra. A typical monthly line rental charge is around A$ 27. Trends reveal that Telstra's fixed-line business is however collapsing, as many younger communicators opt for their mobiles as their only phone instrument. There is full portability for mobile numbers, so you can switch operators as often as you like.

The telecoms environment is highly competitive so you can shop around quite a bit. There are many Internet/email providers but among the best known are iinet (sic, no caps, double 'i') and Telstra's BigPond.

HEALTH

For your first two years as a permanent resident of Australia, you will not be able to access the national Medicare health and welfare net. But eventually, you will find that you are well protected, though the majority of Australians now also opt to pay for extra private health insurance as well (big names, Medibank, HBF). Note that there is an actual tax penalty (1 % of assessable income) on high income-earners (above A$80,000) who do not take private health insurance. Most Australians who take private insurance are rewarded with a 30 per cent government rebate (means-tested) on the premium, 35 per cent or more if you are over 65. But many Australians are still dropping out of private insurance because it is expensive. What private cover essentially does for you is ensure that non life-threatening or 'elective surgery' (but still painful if left undone, for example, a knee replacement or kidney stone removal) will be done promptly, at the hospital and by the surgeon of your choice. On the public Medicare system, you may join a long waiting list and have fewer choices. Private insurance also somewhat cushions the largely unprotected area of health-care in Australia: dental care, which has become extremely expensive. There are signs that a government 'Denticare' scheme may emerge to mitigate this situation over the next few years, but meanwhile, dental costs.

You can sign up for different insurance plans, with special extensions for dentistry, podiatry, sometimes even homeopathic and chiropractor services.

You need also to be aware of the Pharmaceutical Benefits Scheme (PBS) under which government subsidises the costs of prescriptions for the eligible, such as pensioners, the disabled and other consumers with special needs or exceptionally high consumption of drugs, who are holders of the national Medicare card. This also applies even to overseas visitors from countries with which Australia has a Reciprocal Health Care Agreement: Italy, New Zealand, the Republic of Ireland, Finland, Malta, the Netherlands, Sweden, Norway and the United Kingdom. So if you are in the eligible category and are just holidaying in Australia, you may still be able to get your prescription medicines delivered at a subsidised price. You will need to show your passport to the pharmacist, or you can contact Medicare (http://www.medicareaustralia.gov.au/) and get a Reciprocal Health Care Agreement Card to prove your eligibility.

There are both private and public hospitals, all offering high-quality services, although treatment in the city centres may well be preferable to treatment in remote rural hospitals—the figures for cancer survival in country areas, for example, have given cause for alarm and suggest that services are not adequate in the bush. If you have private health insurance, you are more likely to be able to choose exactly where you are treated. It's a good idea to consult your general practitioner or family doctor first before deciding on a specialist, as his or her referral to a specialist may make the difference in how much money you can save on the process. You also need to check with your private health insurance fund whether the doctor or specialist you have been referred to is registered with the fund so that you can get as much as possible of the fees paid back in your pocket.

SHOPPING AROUND

Most of Australia, except for the liberally deregulated states of Victoria, Tasmania, and territories of ACT (Canberra etc) and the Northern Territory (Darwin etc), is still struggling to emerge from the retailing Dark Ages, with myriad restrictions on trading hours emanating from a potent mix of causes and emotions ranging from long-gone reverence for the Sabbath, fear of competition, fear that families (how many of those are left anyway?) will break up if not kept at home together with nothing else to do, fear of strange working hours, and simple fear of change. Generally speaking, shops open from about 9.00 am and as discussed elsewhere in this book, cannot always be relied upon to open till late at night or on Sundays. Most major cities, including even Perth now, are rapidly improving on this score, but out of the main centres, and also in Queensland, you may encounter other, more bewildering, scenarios. Just don't take anything for granted, check it out in advance. For Sunday or holiday trading, look out for the really big supermarkets in some cases, or else very small family-run, or migrant-run, 'delis' (from 'delicatessen', but many of these shops are very far from true delicatessens!), and neighbourhood corner shops, nearly always.

Do not look for alcohol in supermarkets either! You will need instead a separate 'bottle shop' (which also may not be open on Sundays).

There's plenty of choice for shopping around in Australia, from fancy department stores to shops specialising in second-hand 'pre-loved' gear, often channelling their proceeds to charities, and both covered and open markets, including non-commercial neighbourhood 'swap markets'—even some of the suburban and rural church fêtes and agricultural fairs can be an excellent place to shop, especially for items like crafts

One of the glories of clothes shopping in Australia for we 'mature ladies' is that there are quite enormous sizes available, up to size 22 or 24 (when the average is more like a 12 or 14), so if you are a European living in Asia and sick of schoolgirl sizes, Australia is the place to shop.

and home-made jams or other local produce. For fresh food and value for money, seek out your local 'grower's market'; many such markets are run by Italian or Asian immigrants and offer a wide range of foods as a result. Every Australian city however has its own network of 'Oriental' stores, and the beauty is, they stock everything from Sri Lankan to Korean ingredients, all in one place. Generally, it's a good idea to seek out speciality stores rather than visiting only the big chain stores (David Jones, Myers, Aherns, Target, K-Mart, Woolworths and so on), if you want real choice and quality. Fixed weekend markets—of the type seen in Fremantle, Subiaco and Kalamunda in Western Australia—are good fun, offering plenty of life and colour, as well as good buys across a wide range of goods, from bakery to furry koala toys and sheepskin-lined boots. The community markets where you, too, can turn up with your car and sell things out of the boot, can offer surprising bargains.

You will find clothing stock sharply seasonal; it is very difficult to buy summer clothes in winter and vice versa, which is a bit of a pain if you are going overseas to another climate. On the other hand, if you can get into the end-of-season sales, you can pick up whatever you want at rock bottom prices.

If you are looking for 'Australiana' as gifts, try to look for it in reputable large stores, rather than tacky little souvenir stalls festooned with koalas and rude teeshirts. There are tasteful things you can choose, from macadamia chocolates and good wine, to unusual items like the version of Italian panforte cake made by the only Benedictine monastic community in Australia, at New Norcia in Western Australia (available in some mainstream stores, such as David Jones), or the fun novelties and environmentally-aware items stocked in millionaire Dick Smith's chain of Australian Geographic shops.

Remember the GST
Whatever you are buying, remember to check whether the 10 per cent GST (Goods and Service Tax) has been included in the listed price, because it will be, in the end.

Generally speaking, bargaining is not appreciated in Australia, except perhaps in simple open markets; however, you will frequently come across kind souls who will round prices down for you if you have struck up a friendly relationship with them.

AWFUL THINGS THAT COULD HAPPEN

You learn the hard way about certain basics of Australian life: if you forget to leave the rubbish bin out on the kerb for emptying on the appointed day (usually once a week only), too bad. After the third visit in a week from a door-to-door canvasser for charity, you learn to say 'No,' or ask them to send a letter instead. Thank goodness, the public nuisance of tele-marketers that specialise in phoning you to promote home security systems or insurance just as you are making the evening meal has now abated—thanks to the Do Not Call Register Act of 2006, you can register your phone numbers to flag officially that you are not willing to receive such calls (although many charities, political parties and educational institutions are exempt from the requirements of this Act)—for more on this, go to https://www.donotcall.gov.au/

You thought that swimming pool in the back garden a great idea, but now you find it costs a bomb to maintain in tip-top condition, the local Council has passed a rule on regular pool inspections (charging you an inspection fee for good measure) and any pools considered too accessible to children (your own or other people's) must be surrounded by an ugly isolation fence that will cost the earth to install.

You are terrified of your first winter after many years of living in the tropics, so you order three tonnes of firewood in advance and then spend the next three backbreaking days wheel-barrowing it from where the suppliers have dumped it, to your woodshed.

When you get more localised, the same happens with a huge Everest of wood-chip mulch in your driveway that you want to spread over your garden to protect native plants from soil and water loss in the summer. (Don't listen to the urban legend that goes, "Native plants don't need any care or watering," it's not quite accurate!).

Yes, all this has happened to me and my spouse. We kept

the mulch but got rid of the swimming pool, creating raised vegetable beds and a native flower garden instead. As for the firewood, we switched to piped natural gas, slightly more environmentally friendly.

CHILDREN CHANGE

Luckily, however, I am not a parent. Migrant parents get upset when their children show signs of assimilating too well.

More serious identity problems may surface later. All that a migrant parent can do is be ready for these when they come, and perhaps just try to live with them.

Cutting the Apron Strings

Singaporean friends of mine were typically protective Asian parents: they were driving their young son to and from school every day. But the boy soon asserted his new identity, demanding the same independence as his Australian schoolmates, who were all left to cycle to school by themselves. He didn't want to be seen as a sissy. Road safety is one issue here, but even Australian parents are now also agonising about 'stranger danger.' These parents gave way.

Although such parents invariably will assure you that they migrated 'for the sake of the children', paradoxically they are filled with dread at the thought that their offspring may become loud, boorish and rebellious, or generally fall victim to sex, drugs and rock 'n' roll, as it were. Some kids do indeed react against their own background. That is a natural part of their adjustment process and must be accepted as such. The first symptom of mutation is the child's changing accent.

I witnessed an extreme teenage reaction to Malaysian roots. Gathering together for a home-cooked curry, the adults sat down with gusto to whack the goodies in time-honoured Malaysian fashion: with their fingers. When the family's daughter arrived home with her Australian friends, loud expressions of disgust were heard from her. The adults understandably told her to get lost. From the girl's point of view, she had been shamed before Aussie mates by her parents' primitive table manners, quite unacceptable to an Australian.

Yet I have also seen the Australian children of first-generation migrants cheering for their parents' motherland's soccer team in matches against Australian teams. So you never can tell …

Australian education in democracy and rights can make a parent's life perilous indeed. My Eurasian lawyer friend from Singapore got his comeuppance when he discovered that his Australian-born teenage daughter had reported him to the local Human Rights and Equal Opportunity Commission for giving her a typical Asian 'tight slap' over some minor cheek the day before. She should have reported him to the local welfare authorities; but the incident did give him some pause for thought about brats' rights as he prepared his defence … Seriously though, physical discipline of your child has become close to a capital crime in Australia, and is frowned on by both the law and the government, so don't even tap your child when in public at least.

Admirable environmental education in Australian schools can also produce annoying little home preachers, demanding you buy only dolphin-friendly, ozone-friendly and recycled-paper products.

Going to School

Surprisingly, school in Australia is not compulsory after the age of 15 (although there are moves to raise this age), but it is free. There are four terms and their exact timing varies state by state, but roughly speaking they are:

- Term 1   February–April
- Term 2   May–June
- Term 3   August–September
- Term 4   October–mid-December

As with the world of work too, everything comes to a grinding halt over the December–January summer holiday period, although Australian families are showing increasing interest in private tuition and extra coaching during holidays, and outside of school hours—mainly as a reaction to the pressure from highly competitive migrant parents, chiefly from Asia.

Children in very remote outback areas study at the 'School of the Air', with homework arriving by mail, and instruction via two-way radios, as well as the Internet.

> **Public Schools**
>
> For the British especially to note, 'public schools' in Australia are not elite institutions—they are the government schools open to all (free of charge), and unfortunately, often very far from elite. The other system comprises high-fee private schools, including independent and community or religion-based schools (the Jewish school, Roman Catholic schools etc). Note, if on a temporary visa, you may have to pay fees even for public schools.

Many parents are beguiled by Australia's charming attitude to early education, which is unpressurised and emphasises creativity, individual expression and so on, giving the child a lot of freedom, well, to be a child. This contrasts favourably with pressure-cooker environments in Asia, for example, where even streaming of children may be common at primary-leaving age. However, things suddenly toughen up towards the tertiary entrance examination level (pre-University), reached in Year 12, usually at the age of 17 (a bit too young to be a school-leaver, in many observers' opinions). The pace starts to heat up some time after Year 10, through Year 11.

The tertiary entrance exam goes by several different names across the states (in WA it is the West Australian Certificate of Education, for example) but a rose by any other name would be just as thorny—it's a demanding test and if your child is not academic by nature, it's better not to push him or her through it. It is possible also to stretch the tertiary exam preparation year into two years, on request. For non-academic children, and for the many who—at any age—decide to repeat or sit their tertiary entrance exam outside school, there is always the excellent Technical and Further Education (TAFE) college network, which also offers good vocational training courses. TAFE courses can also be a stepping stone to university courses, especially useful for late developers.

The score that emerges from the tertiary entrance exam, which determines your child's university admission status, is the ATAR, a national standard Australian Tertiary Admission Rank (except not in Queensland). This tells you how the student stands in relation to their current Year 12 cohort. An ATAR of 80 per cent means the student is equal to or better than 80 per cent of the total Year 12 population. Just as an interesting observation, it has to be said that in the Western Australian announcement of the elite who had achieved scores over 99 per cent, it was observable that a disproportionate number were of non-Anglo descent, judging simply by their names.

The tertiary entrance exam is one good reason you should not wait until your children are already in their mid-teens to migrate; many children switching from a different system too late really flounder at tertiary entrance level in Australia. Often their chief difficulty is a change of mindset: if they have come from a system where learning the facts off by heart is enough, they will have a hard time learning that the Australian exam system values opinion, judgement, intellectualising and analysis more than knowledge of the facts. They will find, for instance that English Literature is analysed more in terms of gender, race, politics and prejudice, than in terms of the elegance of the language, or the nature of structure, character and plot. 'English' on the other hand is not so much about the use of language, more about analysing and critiquing anything that qualifies as a 'text', from advertising jingles through pop songs to movie scripts. Children who have migrated before their teens grow with the system and by the time they get to tertiary entrance level, are well accustomed to these ways of thinking.

During the tertiary entrance exam year, Year 12, the student will be assessed during the entire year, with project scores during the year contributing to his or her final results— hence the pressure is on for the whole year, not just on the examination day. Another thing to remember is that marks in a class or year are usually averaged out, so that if your child has the highest mark in the class but everybody else is closer to another, lower, level, then his or her marks will likely be brought down to match the average more closely. Or up. True!

You should note that despite ongoing discussions towards a long-awaited National Curriculum, there is no coherence among the differing education systems from state to state and if you attempt to sort them out by yourself, for instance by using websites, you will go plain crazy with the complexity of it all. It is a labyrinthine mess, incomprehensible to most people of good sense. Your best recourse is the government Education Department of whichever state you are going to live in—ask them for information, arrange to go and see them.

As a parent, you need to maintain vigilance and watch over how your child is really doing at school. Despite allegedly being a 'first-world' nation with a quality education system, the shocking fact is that, as of 2006, approximately half of Australians were judged by an Australian Bureau of Statistics (ABS) Adult Literacy and Life Skills Survey to lack the literacy and numeracy skills necessary to meet the complex demands of everyday life and work—by that, the Bureau means even very basic skills such as reading newspapers, using bus timetables, counting, understanding health advice and solving simple problems. Another survey in 2010, the National Workforce Literacy Project conducted by the Australian Industry Group, found that about three quarters of employers report that their businesses are materially and adversely impacted by the low levels of literacy and numeracy they encounter in their workforce at various levels, from labourers and apprentices through to managers.

No wonder that government is now talking loudly about 'Building the Education Revolution' and ostensibly is committed to widespread education reform. One of its most unpopular measures (chiefly with teachers) has been the *MySchool* website (http://www.myschool.edu.au/) meant to assist parents with selecting the high-performing school (out of 10,000 listed schools) most likely to give their children a head start. This venture has caused uproar to the effect that it creates a 'scoreboard' for schools, encouraging schools to worry more about their ranking than actually educating those who most need help. But in fact, it's a very useful and informative site even for the wider community in general.

Fortunately for parents, the government is also monitoring children's literacy regularly as part of the data collection for *MySchool*— your child, if in Years 3, 5, 7 or 9, will probably have to sit a 'NAPLAN" test (National Assessment Program—Literacy and Numeracy) as part of this process. For more information on NAPLAN, see www.naplan.edu.au.

'Uni'

Going to 'uni' or university frankly is not respected as the privilege it is by the current generation of Australian students, but perhaps that is also a worldwide phenomenon. Many Australian kids do not even bother to try to go there. A worryingly large number drop out (about 20 per cent of Australian students, in their first year, only half as many international students), or else 'shop around' their university, changing courses every so often and never really achieving anything, just chalking up scattered 'units' of education. The number of students who quit in the second year, ostensibly to go to work and earn some money 'for a while', but who for one reason or another never go back, is striking, and depressing. You will need to keep a careful watch on your child if you want him or her to resist the peer pressure of seeing plenty of examples like this around on campus. I think the problem is partly attributable to the inherent immaturity of 17 year-olds fresh out of Year 12. In other words, they are too young to settle down to a university routine as yet. Employment also is not guaranteed just because you have a degree; most graduates wait months to a year before they find a job, or a job that uses their degree. So the reward for a degree seems more distant than it did to the 'baby-boomer' generation, or even to 'Generation X' for that matter. Even more tempting is the mining boom that has beset the Australian economy for the past few years, offering astoundingly high wages to strong youngsters who can tolerate tough conditions in the far north, just for simple technical jobs, or driving a truck.

I myself think it is a good plan to pre-empt this desire to quit university mid-stream by encouraging your 17-year-old youngster to go see the world, or even just Australia, for a year, do some voluntary service overseas, or within Australia, to get it all out

Shy Asians and others need to understand that in Australia debate is considered desirable, so expressing yourself publicly is no shame and expressing views that are different from your teacher's is not a problem, rather it is expected of you, especially at university.

of their system before they enter university. That way, there is some hope they will by then appreciate all the opportunities they have in Australia compared with other countries, and will want to use their chance to its fullest. (However, I should declare my inexpertise here—I am not a parent).

If you have been in Australia as a resident for just over two years (104 weeks), and are undertaking full-time studies, you can benefit from the government's Youth Allowance subsidy (16-24 year-olds) or Austudy (25 years old and above). There is a still a Student Contribution to be paid by you, but if you cannot manage this, you can borrow the sum needed from government and arrange to pay it back progressively via the HECS-HELP scheme, when you have started working and earning a salary. So to that extent, university education does not come free.

But once you are into choosing your university, there is another useful government website to help you choose from among Australia's 39 public universities: *http://www.myuniversity.gov.au/*

ON THE POSITIVE SIDE

It would be negligent not to warn you of the migrant blues. But there is a brighter side, some of which I hope will emerge in other sections of this book. Among the plus points are the exhilarating experience of freedom, space, and that special bright light that the Australian climate and geography produce. Enlightened attitudes to medicine, to education and to the environment abound. There is an easy friendliness on the streets, possibly the world's most genuine attempt at a truly equal society, and the peacefulness of daily life—and real, wild democracy. There is the excitement of a vast, largely wild land.

You may decide you like it all so much that you want to become an Australian citizen. Check on your own country's rules about dual citizenship (allowing it or not allowing it) before you take the plunge.

You are eligible to apply if you have spent at least 12 months as a Permanent Resident of Australia immediately before making your application, and providing you did not leave the country for more than 90 days during that 12 months. Additionally, you must have had four years total lawful residence in Australia (including the 12 months as a PR) and during those four years, your absences from the country must not total more than 12 months. Depending on your individual case, there may be other circumstances that will affect or aid your application. Have a look at the website www.citizenship.gov.au/ Your confirmation of citizenship letter may follow your application quite quickly. The ceremony at which you receive your Certificate of Australian Citizenship, necessary before you can get an Australian passport (without which you cannot safely leave and re-enter Australia once you are an Australian national), could be a few more weeks.

Here is one new citizen's account of the modest ceremony at which he received his citizenship, in Perth, Western Australia:

'We all trooped off to the Mayor's office, me and my two witnesses (you are not allowed more than two). On the seats in this room upstairs was a small package with our name tags on and a leaflet explaining our rights and duties as citizens. Altogether, our group of new citizens numbered 30.

'The Mayor's deputy made a speech and then they called us up in groups of about four or five to recite the oath of allegiance to Queen Elizabeth II (that probably won't go on much longer) and the country. … The Mayor shook our hands and gave us our certs, and also a little badge with the Aussie flag on it for us to wear. Then we posed with the Mayor for a photo if we wished, holding up our certs.

The Citizen's Pledge

This is the pledge recited at the citizenship ceremony for newly naturalised citizens. Note that the oath of allegiance to the Queen is no longer required.

'From this time forward, under God*,
I pledge my loyalty to Australia and its people,
whose Democratic beliefs I share,
whose rights and liberties I respect,
and whose laws I will uphold and obey.'

The irony is, Australian-born citizens never have to pledge anything to anyone!

*those who wish may affirm their loyalty without a reference to God.

'Our local councillor made a speech: he said wasn't it wonderful how the Aussie World Cup soccer team was almost all migrant and how migrants introduced soccer and in such a short time took Australia to world standard, etc. Then we had some beers or sherry and what the Aussies call 'finger food' (otherwise known as 'bites', '*dim sum*' in Cantonese or '*makan kecil*' in Malay), and we all sang 'Advance Australia Fair', and then went home.'

My own citizenship ceremony was rather rushed, because I asked for an individual date owing to a need to travel on business. But I enjoyed the fun it all provided to my neighbours, an Aboriginal family, whom I invited along as witnesses.

HOMES AND GARDENS

A detached house set on at least a quarter-acre garden (a tenth of a hectare), with about six rooms, is central to the Australian definition of happiness. 'The first suburban nation', Donald Horne has called his own country, in his seminal psycho-analysis of Australia, *The Lucky Country*, of 1964, a classic to which all subsequent studies owe a debt, including this one.

Certainly, an Australian's home is his castle. A home of your own is the Great Australian Dream.

Impossible Dream?

Unfortunately, that dream has been punctured over recent decades, as house purchase prices and bank-loan interest rates have soared in tandem over the past two decades. While interest rates are lower now, they are not as low as in the rest of the developed countries that are experiencing recession, which Australia is not. Australian housing still ranks as some of the world's most unaffordable, with rentals also climbing sky-high, particularly in economic 'hot-spots' like Western Australia, where the mining boom is distorting most of the economy. Many young Australian couples are now unable to contemplate buying their own home. To Australians, this upset has seemed akin to an infringement of their human rights. This is a key election issue every three years. All across the nation, resentment hangs in the air like smoke over a

Author Ilsa Sharp (back, second left, holding the citizenship certificate) on the proud day she received her Australian citizenship, in 2002, from the City of Canning offices in Western Australia (Canning official on far left), with her Singapore-born husband Siva Choy (far right) and her favourite Aboriginal neighbour, Stephanie Eades, with two of her three children, Wayne (centre front) and Courtney (front right) as her witnesses.

barbie; the government struggles constantly to meet its people's expectations of affordable homeownership. If you have been able comfortably to buy your Australian house outright, do not flaunt the fact.

Still, something like 70 per cent of Australians are homeowners, a pretty high rate in world terms. Public housing has become the mark of virtual welfare cases—broken families or families otherwise in crisis, single mothers, the unemployed, refugees, Aboriginals and so on—and the housing provided, albeit low-cost, is often only minimally maintained.

Land Hunger

The quarter-acre fixation is also being re-examined, by thoughtful town-planners in particular. How much longer can Australian cities spread outwards in massive suburban sprawls, as can already be seen in Melbourne and Sydney and as is happening apace in Perth?

Not only does the Australian homeowner expect to own a fair amount of land, but he also expects literally to sit on it.

Apartment living, even medium-rise, is only just beginning to occur as an option to most Australians, and the vast majority abhor high-rise homes. One of the most striking characteristics of the Australian city is its low skyline, except perhaps in the very heart of the central business district, where skyscrapers are considered reasonably appropriate for work—but not for home.

I personally find this a much more human way of living. With the population so small in such a huge land, one can sympathise with the Australian's instinctive insouciance about using up land. However, it must be admitted that a widely spread population makes the planning, administration and servicing of cities very difficult indeed. The provision of sewerage, roads, transport and a host of other infrastructure and services becomes a costly problem. Suburban sprawl is not acceptable either to environmentalists eager to protect wild Australia.

It seems most likely then that residential areas within a certain radius of Australian city centres will no longer be able to corner quarter-acre blocks for each housing unit in the future. Noises in this direction have already been made by various city authorities; 'high-density housing', a phrase which would have caused an uproar only a couple of decades ago, is now an Australian planner's buzz-word. An influx of Asian and American investors, more used to apartment-block living, has also fuelled the building of high-rise residential blocks. But many ordinary folk now end up in small single-storey concretised 'units' on sub-divided quarter-acre plots with little backyard and no garden.

The Great Australian Dream is steadily receding to the outer suburbs and the outback countryside itself. But you can rely on the Australian homeowner to fight this 'reform' all the way. He feels as strongly about holding land as some Americans do about the right to own a gun, or the English about the importance of pet dogs.

Australian Style

The vast majority of Australian homes are single-storey, what are known as 'bungalows' in some parts of Asia, and each home is gloriously individual. It is still extremely unusual in Australia, I am glad to say, to be confronted with serried ranks

Homes of the wealthy overlook Sydney Harbour's north side.

of exactly identical estate homes looking as though they came out of the same plaster mould, off a factory conveyor belt, of the sort now common in many other parts of the world.

Very much in vogue, at a price, are historic, or even imitation, 'Federation' homes, harking back to a colonial architectural style popular at the turn of the century: these charming buildings usually feature porches and verandahs supported by pillars and elaborately lacy wrought-iron work, among other things. Other recognisably Australian housing styles are the neo-classical and Spanish designs of Mediterranean origin, 'weatherboard' wooden cottages, and the 'Queenslander', a largely timbered tropical exotic set high above ground level, usually with open verandahs.

The 'Greenie' movement is taking some designs closer to Nature, so timber and stone, or mixtures of the two, can also be seen. A most attractive, but not cheap, 'back to Nature' option is rammed earth, very popular in southern Western Australia, which produces a marvellously smooth caramel-brown surface. It's a strong material and naturally well insulated. Cheaper are baked mud-bricks, but it's an exhausting labour of love to construct a home of these.

In the older homes, all kinds of antique fixtures may be found. Like the wood-fired cooker I found in my 1950s home, on the edge of metropolitan Perth, when I moved in, in 1989. It was perfect for baking bread, and ingeniously linked up to the water piping to provide hot water, and a constant source of warmth, but eventually I tired of it and passed it on to a couple living in more rural parts, where such cookers are still found.

On the Ground

One of Australia's greatest attractions is surely the fact that it is still possible to acquire large chunks of wild land, and also to own a home on the ground for a reasonable price. Many a homeowner buys his land and then designs and builds his own house. A whole industry is geared to helping him do this, once planning permissions have been cleared with the authorities. There are catalogues of ready-made doors, windows, roofing, tiling, you name it.

Usually, you call in a professional to lay the foundations at least. After that, you could build it stick by stick yourself if you really wish. But most people use professional builders under their personal supervision. Be aware though that Australians dine out regularly on their horror stories of negative encounters with irresponsible or outright crooked builders. You must monitor your building project closely and do your own homework so that you understand what is going on.

When buying land, you need to have good advice and to be aware of all sorts of pitfalls. You may well find that you are not allowed to keep your land vacant of a building for more than a set period of time, say, about two years. There may also be requirements that you fence the land, which could be expensive, and there will certainly be strict rules about maintaining fire-breaks and burning back the land every so often.

You could also find that although you own the land, you do not own the soil beneath it, as the government may have reserved mining rights. This could put you in a sticky position if gold or iron ore is found beneath your house. Do also research your water supply and fire risks. Beware of the allure of a coastal, seaside property: state governments are starting to penalise, or even forcibly move, those who wilfully confront future climate change-driven sea-level rises and possible tsunamis, and insurance companies are not so benign about the risk either.

As in any other country, you need to study planning programmes for the area where you are buying: will your beautiful wilderness be a new town in a few years' time? The extraordinary and virtually unplanned growth of outpost mining towns in recent years is a case in point; many of these have developed no sense of community owing to the number of 'fly in fly out' mining workers, and few social amenities, making them tough places to live in.

These are but a handful of the most common problems with land ownership. Tread carefully. For all these and other important considerations, such as taxation, please do refer to a professional consultant.

Shop Around

Any day, the newspapers are chock-a-block with house-sale ads. In Perth, I found that it was an accepted Sunday leisure activity to tour the various homes up for sale and open for viewing, sometimes just for fun, sometimes to update one's understanding of the market. These are not display homes, but real people's homes up for sale—the owners just have to go out for the day while a pack of strangers tramp through their home.

Most Australian home sales are done through a real estate agent, followed by a 'settlement agent' or lawyer who actually sees all the various, final payments through. The real estate agent will be sitting around in the house open for viewing (complete with all the occupants' furnishings). While Australian agents are no more honest than any others, I have found them pleasantly un-pushy, in that they rarely speak unless spoken to.

Here's the drum, as the Australians say, the latest on property, at the time of writing...

Taking Perth in Western Australia as an example (but don't ever forget, there are enormous differences, state by state, among Australia's property markets; generally speaking, the east, especially Sydney, is always the most expensive area).

As William F Shire, Director of Australian Business

& Property Services in Perth, says, "Prior to this boom period [in 1989], an average four-bedroom, two-bathroom brick-and-tile house could be bought for approximately A$ 72,000." In 2008, this kind of property had already more than quintupled. In suburbs close to the city centre, there is very little below A$ 500,000 nowadays.

Another Australian, Peter M Brown, Associate Professor at the National University of Singapore's School of Building and Estate Management, who is hung about with qualifications much like a Christmas tree with lights (including being a Fellow of the Australian and New Zealand Institutes of Valuers), apparently has got the Australian real estate cycle all figured out. It follows an eight-year boom-bust pattern, he says. There have been property price peaks in 1973, 1981 and 1989, and then again at the turn of the 20th century, so this looks about right—say a ten-year cycle then, all other factors being equal. Which means right now, we are on an upturn again.

Buy Now

When to buy? Well, you could wait for a peak to decline. But quite honestly, if you are not speculating and are prepared to sit on your property a while, you probably cannot lose, whatever time you buy. But it's always worthwhile keeping an ear out for what might happen in the next federal, and state, Budget. And in general, it's a good plan to buy in winter when the market is much quieter. Australian property owners who want to sell always try to capitalise on the euphoria that spring or summer sunshine stimulates in buyers confronted with nice fresh winter-watered gardens crammed with flowers.

How and What to Buy

First, do be aware that buying an Australian property does not in any way enhance your chances of securing permanent residence or citizenship. And if you enter on a temporary residence/business visa that later fails, you will have to sell whatever property you have bought in the interim.

For your first information on what's available, the local newspaper's real estate section and local real estate magazines are a good start. About a year before you move, get friends in Australia to send you pages of the newspaper, cruise around Internet sites, and generally do your homework. Make up your mind what exactly it is that you want—how many bedrooms, bathrooms, a big yard or a small one, a swimming pool or not—and what will be the best location for you in terms of proximity to schools, work and so on. Take the occasional flight into Australia and look around a bit just to familiarise yourself. Buying sight unseen does happen— especially with cashed-up investors, as has been the case in Singapore at certain travelling real estate exhibitions—but it can be a foolish and unnecessary risk. One real estate agent friend of mine has told me that the average agent's commission for property sales at such exhibitions is easily upwards of A$5,000, so exhibitions and their costs can often become part of the buyer's cost.

The FIRB

Visitors and non-residents can only buy brand new properties, or buy an old property and demolish it to build a new house or a building that is at least a 50 per cent renewal of the old building— but to buy an old property, you need Foreign Investment Review Board (FIRB) approval, which is usually available within about 28 days. Or you can buy land for building but must build on it within 24 months of buying it. For commercial properties, the FIRB is likely to approve any non-resident if the purchase involves a shop or hotel. Go to http://www.firb.gov.au/ for more information.

The vast majority of property available in Australia will be freehold, a concept of complete ownership that is commonly referred to as 'fee simple'. 'Green title', you should note, means your title is complete, you can do anything with the property. That will not be the case with a shared 'strata title' however—there will be other owners to consult.

If you want to develop the site as, say, a 'duplex', i.e. with two smaller home-units on it, be aware that there will be rules on what size the block must be to do this, particularly about the width of the frontage and the amount of spare land available for creating full access at the sides (for cars, emergency vehicles like fire trucks etc). And rules restricting height too.

In some areas, there may be restrictions like 'R' (Residential only) coding that will dictate what you can do with the property; be sure to consult the local Council about such rules, as well as special issues like heritage areas. Your real estate agent, however, is legally required to divulge such issues to you in advance. Other issues may be Council plans to take land for the widening of roads ('road resumption'), in effect compulsory acquisition but usually compensated with the market value plus 10 per cent.

What kind of Australian house is a good buy then, in capital gains terms when you sell? (There is no capital gains tax for the sale of a 'first home' or principal home).

When you buy an established property, you buy it as is—it must be in the same condition in three months' time as on the day you agreed to buy it. So it's the vendor's responsibility to ensure that the condition remains the same. But if the water heater is not working when you buy it and you didn't check it then, you cannot complain if it is not working when you move in. On the other hand, if the reverse is true, you can complain when you move in.

Here, the experts recommend purchases of brick-and-tile (brick walls, tiled roofs) homes (around A$500,000 upwards, more in Sydney and other eastern states centres), and careful attention to location—not more than 15 km (9.3 miles) from the city centre, with easy access to the nearest freeway, to schools, shops, parks and bus routes, and so on. Get to know the local geography and understand details like, in Western Australia, the fact that nobody actually lives in 'Perth', since Perth is only the city centre; people live in a suburb with its own name, like Bentley, Victoria Park, Mirrabooka or Mount Lawley. Be careful when ads say '5 mins from the city'— which city? It could be the city centre of a satellite city like Rockingham, well outside Perth, not Perth city itself. Don't be like one would-be migrant calling me from India, who thought we were going to be close neighbours simply because my address is just off Albany Highway and she was going to live in Albany town—Albany is in Western Australia's deep south-west, on the southern coast, and more than 400km (250 miles) from Perth, where I am.

'Brick-and-tile' as opposed to what, you may ask?

Many older Australian homes are built of 'weatherboard'—overlapping timber planks—or of 'fibro', compressed-wood fibreboard, or even metals like zinc or anodised aluminium. In the case of metals, particularly, there will probably be an asbestos insulation layer under the metal cladding. In many old buildings, roofs are either of zinc or other metals, or also of asbestos. The weatherboard styles often have a pretty, old-fashioned and traditionally Australian look about them, but brick-and-tile immediately confers greater prestige, something you have to consider in terms of resale value.

There is also a psychological problem with asbestos owing to a prolonged health scare about asbestosis in Australia. Loose asbestos fibres certainly are not great for your health and intensive exposure to asbestos, in the industrial, manufacturing context, has been proven dangerous, even fatal. But there really is not much hard evidence about how dangerous it is just to live in a house with asbestos insulation. However, in view of fairly hysterical public perceptions in Australia at the moment, asbestos is probably something a home buyer should worry about, again in terms of resale value if nothing else.

Fenced or walled gardens are the insignia of the wealthy, successful 'tall poppy' but many suburbs pleasantly exhibit the more trusting look of open, unfenced front gardens. Speaking of which, don't be beguiled by most Aussies' claim to live in a totally classless society: certain suburbs are 'smarter' than others; check your chosen suburb's reputation and crime figures before you buy. Among the things that can lower your house value, sadly, is the existence of too much public housing (provided by your state government's Housing Department), as well as rental properties, in your street, or worse, right next door to you.

Older Australian properties will not necessarily have more than one bathroom and may have the toilet separate, even distant, from the main bathroom, nor will they have ensuite bathrooms, so if these are important for you, you need to check carefully on this.

Most properties will be sold fittings included—fittings such as carpets, window and light fittings, perhaps even with cooker, washing machine, air conditioners and fans. Be clear about this before you buy, and check that what has been promised is indeed in place before you take possession.

GETTING STARTED

You'll probably start your property hunt with a real estate agent. Make sure he/she is a member of a proper professional association with certification—in WA, this would be REIWA, the Real Estate Institute of Western Australia.

Beware of loans taken outside Australia, as they may attract a 10 per cent Australian withholding tax. In Australia, you can go to a bank or a finance broker and mostly, a 10 per cent deposit is expected when your offer is accepted, although this is sometimes negotiable. The deposit is fully refundable if the finance is not approved or if the sale does not go through for any reason that is not the buyer's fault. If you, the buyer, just change your mind, the owner can re-offer the propery on the market and sue you for the difference he has lost, with costs.

Help for First-home Owners

If you are legally resident and meet all the eligibility criteria (go to www.firsthome.gov.au for more information) you can probably get the Federal Government's A$ 7,000 'First Home-Owner Grant', providing the house value that you are buying or building is below A$ 750,000 and in certain defined locations, and providing you have never owned residential property in Australia before. You must move into the property within the first 12 months of ownership and live in it as your 'principal residence' (i.e. at least six consecutive months' residence in a year), and you cannot rent it out. There are stamp-duty concessions for first home-buyers too, differing from state to state; in Western Australia for example, up to a A$ 500,000 property value, there is no stamp duty (on an established home), but above that value, the duty kicks in at A$ 22.51 per A$ 100 extra.

Making an Offer

If you like the house and the market is currently busy, then don't fall into a tedious bargaining process, just offer the stated price, or you may lose the place during the delay. But in some circumstances, you may wish to make a lower offer. Always remember that the real estate agent selling the property is acting for the seller-owner, not for you the buyer. If you have cash in hand, you are in a very good position to knock the price down, but if there are long-winded procedures to endure, moving money around banks etc, then you can expect the vendor to exact the full price as originally stated. Even when you make an offer, you can still hedge it around with conditions, such as 'subject to checking for termites', or 'subject to the structure being checked for wiring and plumbing', or even 'subject to property being cleared of all rubbish.' If you have certain considerations before you can raise the money, you can say things like ' subject to me selling my boat' or 'subject to me getting my accident insurance settlement.' You can also state in your offer that you would like to take over some of the furniture that you have seen in the house, or the pot plants or whatever.

Settlement

The 'settlement' system is unique to Western Australia—in Sydney or Melbourne, you can use lawyers to handle your property purchase (as with conveyancing lawyers in Singapore, for example), but the upside is, WA's settlement system is cheaper than using lawyers. You can't progress a property purchase or sale in WA without a settlement agent. Make sure you choose one that is registered with the Settlement Agents Supervisory Board. The settlement agent then does all the legal paperwork for you, liaises with your bank and organises the stamp duty, which on an A$ 500,000 property would be nearly A$ 18,000. You'll also need to budget for the settlement agent's fees, about A$ 1,600 on an A$ 500,000 property, as well as a Mortgage Registration fee of about A$ 160, and a Land Transfer Fee of about A$ 250. Amongst the paperwork the agent will handle for you will be items like the settlement of your share of rates and taxes or utility bills outstanding on a property you are selling.

Make a point of stating in your offer that all plumbing, electricity and water must be working at settlement time—this will force the vendor to ensure any repairs needed are done before you pay up. You can also make your offer subject to structural inspection—this must then be done within about seven days, at your own cost, probably about A$ 500 upwards. Once you have made an offer on the place, this is a sort of legal contract, but only truly binding once your offer has been formally accepted by the owner. He or she has the option of accepting or rejecting your offer, or making a counter-offer to you, in terms of price, terms, conditions or settlement dates.

You can refuse to settle until all the items you want fixed are indeed fixed, although you cannot actually withdraw from the promise to purchase. Or else, you can deduct the cost of fixing the items needing repair from your final purchase price. Your offer will state the final settlement date and finance terms.

What if you have a complaint against your real estate agent? The Real Estate Practices Act has set up the Real Estate and Business Agents Supervisory Board to take care of such incidents. You can complain to the Board, or to your nearest Consumer Protection/Fair Trading unit, under the Trade Practices Act.

And what about cutting agents out of the process altogether? You may see private sales advertised, with no agent involved. This is not necessarily cheaper from the buyer's point of view; it is the seller who is saving money, not you. The property could still be overpriced or agents may not have wanted to handle it for some reason—an ominous sign for you too.

Even if the price is good in a private sale, there is now little or no protection for you as the buyer. Since the owner is not a member of any formal real estate agents' professional association and your only recourse with any complaint will be in the civil courts. In contrast, when the agent belongs to a professional association, a complaint to that association threatens him or her with loss of his licence. And from your point of view, any agent belonging to a formal association will have professional indemnity insurance and professional liability insurance to cover against complaints such as yours, so there is the possibility of quite speedy compensation for you. So private sales are not as attractive as they might seem at first glance.

HANDYMAN MANIA

Because the home is such an important possession, Australians spend an awful lot of time 'doing things around the house' (when not tinkering with the car). In fact, they are forever renovating, rebuilding or extending. It is estimated they will be spending something like A$ 25.5 billion annually on combined Do-It-Yourself (DIY) and home renovation projects by 2016. See Fiona Allon's book *Renovation Nation*, University of New South Wales Press 2008. Some social commentators say that the home renovation obsession has only intensified in the years following the 9/11 terrorist disaster in New York of 2001, and the ongoing Global Financial Crisis: the Australian response to such insecurities has been, individually, we can't do much to change the state of the world, but we can at least change the tiles in the bathroom. The typical Australian, the commentators surmise, is turning inwards, his back to the world, facing into his own backyard.

So, if you want to be a real Australian, you should always have at least one room of your house in total chaos when visitors call on you: 'Oh, we're just renovating the lounge/bathroom/kitchen.' The wreckage of broken timber, drilling dust and stripped wallpaper should be strewn over the floor. The man of the house (yes, they're still traditional that way in Australia) should be glimpsed, paint-roller, electric saw or wallpaper-steamer in hand, slaving away in his filthy dungarees, or, more likely, shorts.

Alternatively, the whole house, including the tea-set crockery, could be coated in a fine film of red wood dust—'We only just finished hand-polishing the wood floors.' Or there could be a curious odour—'The pest men just came to spray for termites.' All these constitute a perfectly normal state of affairs in any Australian home at any one time.

DIY is Dinky-di

If you are in any doubt about my telling the truth in this matter, just take a look at the *Yellow Pages* phone-book for

What to Check Before Making an Offer

Having identified your property, follow a few more steps to check things out before you make an offer:

- Check on add-on structures in the back garden—sheds, studios and 'sleep-overs' or 'granny cottages' and double-check whether they have all had Council building permission or not.

- Be sure to check on whether the fencing on the property reflects the actual boundaries of the block of land that you are buying, and whether any neighbours have intruded beyond their boundaries into your site.

- Check on how much the local property rates are—an average locality might be around A$ 600 a year.

- Check there is sewerage already laid and connected, make sure old leach drains (covered drains) and septic tanks have been decommissioned, otherwise this may have to be done later—and septic tanks will need emptying every five years.

- Check whether piped gas has been laid; you may have to pay for it later.

- If there is a swimming pool, check whether you will inherit a useful automatic pool-cleaner machine, whether it is a self-chlorinating salt-water pool (a good idea) and whether local regulations require pool fencing; if there is no pool, check that it is a clean-fill site—sometimes, people simply bury a pool rather than remove it (expensive), which will be a problem for future site development.

- If there is a well-planted garden, consider whether you really want to maintain a full garden, or how much it would cost you to pay someone else to do it; take note that beautiful green-turf lawns guzzle expensive water in the summer, and check on the local Council's probable water restrictions in summer to see whether you can really maintain that lawn; native plant gardens are easier on water consumption, but still need some, and also need regular re-mulching every couple of years.

What to Check Before Making an Offer

- Check on whether there is a built-in burglar alarm system, monitored or otherwise, and check the quality of all security locks on doors and windows.
- Check that the house is insulated.
- Check whether there is a cooling system in place for the summer—evaporative air conditioning (water circulating over wood chips) is both economic and environmentally friendly, and quite efficient, with the plus over traditional air conditioning that you need to keep the windows open not shut when operating it.
- Check whether there is a heating system for the water, such as a solar heater unit on the roof—these are very efficient and economical considering the amount of sunshine Australia enjoys.
- Be sure you know how old the house is. You might like to check when it was last roofed. If it's raised on stumps, you will want to check when it was last 're-stumped', i.e. physically lifted and re-stabilised on a new footing. Both these issues have confronted us in our house in Perth—the roof had to be replaced within five years of moving in. But if you are buying more for the land value than the building value and intend either to sell or develop soon, these issues may not bother you so much.
- You can expect—and demand—that full treatment of the house for preventing termite damage has recently been done, if there are any timber structures at all.
- Check out the neighbours and the neighbourhood, ask Australians about your chosen suburb's reputation. If there is public housing next door, or a high crime rate in the area, you may wish to reconsider.
- Visit the area and the house if possible without your real estate agent, and at different times of the day and night, to get a real feel for it.
- If high-speed broadband and the Internet matter to you, check whether they are available in the area you have chosen; you would be surprised at how commonly 'black holes' in broadband supply manifest themselves even in apparently metropolitan areas.

any city in Australia and see how many 'DIY' (Do It Yourself) centres you can count.

I guarantee they will take up several pages.

DIY is a massive industry in Australia, partly because the cost of labour makes hiring contractors prohibitive, but also because it is the approved, macho way of 'doing things around the house'. It's part of the 'pioneer, frontier syndrome' that infects every Australian mind. A visit to any major DIY emporia reveals vast warehouses stacked with every conceivable thingamajig to do every conceivable practical thing from building your own greenhouse to mending a leaky tap. My husband says it's Heaven; others have more mixed feelings.

Most Australian homes have a workshed in the garden, crammed full of tools for this and that, paint tins and so on (most men, like my husband, have long ago lost track of what is in there, and so have to keep buying new things anyway because they can't find the old ones they already have somewhere in the shed). And garden tools. Sometimes home brewing equipment too. The 'Men and their Sheds' culture is not an Aussie urban myth, it's for real. Sadly, it must be said, sometimes it is difficult to appreciate what has been achieved by all this toil, when gazing at the ill-matching but all equally awful wallpaper and carpets in many Australian homes.

On the other hand, there is a certain vitality in Australian home décor. Often, in younger and more educated households, the furnishings will reflect the new multicultural society in which Australians now live, as well as a consciousness of Asian neighbours—Italian touches, Aboriginal artefacts, vases bought in Singapore, batik paintings from Indonesia and so on, stone statues from Bali and 'water features', tinkly little fountains, from somewhere in South-east Asia or Japan.

Some Real Estate Jargon

When you scan the Australian classified ads for house-sales, there may well be some abbreviations which are a mystery to you. Following are a few examples—for the rest, consult an Australian friend or real estate agent.

- **Backyard**

  A general term for the patio plus garden, poolside area, and everything else at the back of the house that is related to the outdoor life that is so central to the Australian lifestyle.

- **Bgp**

  Below-ground pool. A much better sort of swimming pool than the above-ground sort, this is a properly sunken pool.

- **Blt in robes**

  Built-in wardrobes.

- **Bore**

  A deep well driven into the ground to tap deep aquifers or ground water, and equipped with a pump to bring it up. This is an important plus for homes with gardens and reticulated watering systems, not least because it saves on the cost of what is sometimes called 'scheme water', or the the more expensive treated drinking water supplied by local authorities for delivery to your household taps.

- **Brick veneer**

  Simulated brick facing for houses, used as a disguise over inner walls of other materials such as asbestos or aluminium.

- **Dbt**

  Double brick-and-tile, a better quality, better insulated version of simple brick-and-tile.

- **Games room or Family room**

  A large living room where the family congregates, usually separate from the dining room, and often also separate from a front lounge room or what sometimes may still, in old fashioned parlance, be called 'the front parlour,' a kind of guest reception room away from the more private family areas.

(Continued on the next page)

(Continued from previous page)

- **Harbour glimpses**
  Common in Sydney, this half-promise means that if you stand on a stool, or if you are about 2 m (8 ft) tall, you can, by squinting through the bathroom window, spot a small part of the spectacular harbour view.

- **Retic**
  This refers to 'reticulation', the below-ground piping that pumps bore water up through automatic sprinklers to water your garden. Increasingly, severe water restrictions are limiting when and how much you can use this anyway. And it's expensive to lay from scratch. Many gardeners are turning to more economical, slower drip-feeding reticulation using above-ground tubing.

- **Weatherboard**
  These are the old wooden cottages of 1950s Australia and earlier, with overlapping planks of wood, very commonly seen in Perth, Western Australia. Today they are charming heritage properties. Though often poky inside, they characteristically sit on a 'quarter-acre' block of land and have a cottage-like look, with curlicued wooden ornamentation on pillared front verandahs.

GARDEN GNOMES

The garden is the other Australian obsession, very much part of the British heritage. Older Australians (39 per cent of gardeners anyway) illustrate the origins of this heritage beautifully, as they lovingly tend look-alike English country-cottage gardens full of roses, chrysanthemums and dahlias, with verdant lawns tediously kept alive by a wasteful water-sprinkler system ('retic') using bore water from beneath the soil.

Australian grass, such as it is (you will soon become familiar with the menace of everything from buffalo-grass to couch- and kikuyu-grass, among various undesirable grasses), is not meant to be green and lush, particularly in the summer. The natural state of an Australian lawn is dry, brown and sparse. I gave lawns up and mulched mine over with wood-chip! But in many upmarket suburbs, over-conservative councils may insist you maintain neatly clipped turf lawns on all frontages.

Such English-style gardens are of course quite ridiculous in a largely arid ecology. The 'soils' in Perth, for example, consist almost entirely of sand.

Among the foreign plants which do seem to do well in Australia are those which come from a very similar setting, in South Africa. Thankfully, recent decades have seen the growth of a 'Native Gardens' movement (about 23 per cent of styles chosen) which encourages the cultivation of indigenous Australian species. These 'natives' include the Eucalypts (gums), the Acacias (wattles), and the colourful Grevilleas, Bottlebrush, Banksias and Kangaroo Paws and so on. They are much more sensible choices than roses since they demand less attention and waste less water: native plants are geared to manage with very little water—but not *no* water, as many beginners fondly imagine.

This great change signifies that at last, the white Australian is coming to terms with his real environment, the Australian ecology, and breaking away from the English motherland of the past.

Here are a few things you need to know about native gardens that are quite different from European temperate or Asian tropical gardens:

- Native plants do *not* like highly nutritious phosphorous and nitrogen-rich fertilisers and manures—they are adapted to much less rich diets; use only a designated special native-plant slow-release fertiliser and don't place it too close to the plant's roots.

- You may still have to water some native plants in the hot dry summer and also during their first year when they are still young, but it is better to water infrequently and deeply than to water frequently but too shallow—if you do the latter, the roots will spread all over the surface with only fragile grasp and eventually the plant will just fall over; you need to encourage the plant to drive its naturally deep tap roots way down into the soil, seeking out water. Generally speaking, you need to water native plants only at the height of summer, and even then, not much. Many natives need water but also dislike 'wet feet', preferring good drainage, so sometimes it's a good plan to place them on a slope, mound or embankment.

- Once planted, a native plant will dislike any further moves, as its root systems hate to be disturbed.
- Many native plants need full sun if they are to produce good crops of flowers, but not all of them; study the local species well, read books, identify your local native plant specialist nurseries and visit them often, asking for advice when needed.
- Planting time is in late autumn to winter, with most flowering plants achieving their full glory in spring and early summer.
- If you don't mulch, mostly your garden just won't work for you. Try a wood-chip mulch to give it a nice bushland look, but take care not to pile the mulch high and too close around the stems of plants and trees, as this can encourage moisture accumulation and fungal rots; leave a circle of non-mulched area just around the base of the plant;

Gardening is an Australian obsession. The author has adopted this national hobby and is seen here displaying the carrot harvest from her own suburban vegetable garden. *Picture by Siva Choy.*

Banksias, which come in a diverse range of species, are an iconic group of Australian flowers, related to the South African proteas.

- In areas like coastal Western Australia, much of which has only sand for soil, water runs off or seeps through too quickly, so you may need to use a soil-wetting agent to help soils retain the water you apply, or water granules in your pots and baskets; if you see the soil surface crusting in pots and baskets so that the water just runs off and never penetrates to the plant's roots, apply a simple dilution of dish-washing liquid and water to loosen up the soil structure—it won't harm the plant.

Putting on a Front

Whatever the character of their gardens, you will see them on weekends, all the gardeners toiling long and hard at weeding, digging, pruning, mulching (using woodchips, newspapers, grass clippings, even pebbles) and mowing their lawns.

Businesses providing services such as 'garden bags', delivered empty and collected full of garden rubbish at regular intervals, are thriving. So are lawn-cutting and tree-pruning services, for the lazy.

Interestingly, it is always the *front* garden above all that is so lovingly tended. Traditionally, the back garden, or 'backyard', has two areas, the smart entertaining area around the patio and pool, and a discreet bit you can hardly see, usually around the garden shed, that is a much messier, more utilitarian place, where the washing is hung out, the dogs and cats hang out, handyman activities take place, and a vegetable patch might be cultivated for cheap, fresh food.

The front garden is the image the householder wishes to present to the world; the Australian cares about what his neighbours, and passers-by, might think of him, in terms of middle-class decency.

THE FAMILY DOG

Australians have inherited the British love of pets, particularly dogs. Take a look at any public park over the weekend and see how many dogs you can spot being walked; you are bound to see an amazing number, and variety.

If you are settling into Australia and want a dog, you should take a look at typically Australian dogs, most of them stemming from sheep- or cattle-mustering breeds. Breeds include the Blue-heeler and the Kelpie. The smooth-haired Kelpie is a cattle-dog that derives from the border collie. But remember, they need a lot of space and a lot of walking; energetic dogs, they will probably chase anything around, including your neighbour's cat, and should never be let out of your garden unaccompanied.

Also typically Australian are the Australian Silky, a long-haired toy dog, and the Kangaroo Dog, a greyhound-Scottish deerhound cross once used to fight off kangaroos and dingos (wild dogs).

Be responsible and keep your dog on a leash in parks, or at least supervise it carefully, and bring a plastic bag to pick up dog-poo and put it in the bins (would you want your children sitting in poo on their Sunday picnic in the park?). Don't take dogs into wildlife reserve areas at all. In the suburbs, be respectful of your neighbours and don't let the dog run wild; if it's always barking, consider some training to find out how you could control this better.

FRONT-ROOM FORMALITY

A strange thing about the Australian suburbs is the deathly quiet, and darkness, of the streets at night. This is partly because the seasonal weather does not always encourage people to be out on the streets, as you might expect in Mediterranean or tropical Asian settings, and partly because the level of urban crime (or at least the *perception* of the level) does not encourage it either.

But it is also because in truly traditional Australian home designs (this is beginning to change now), the front room is never in use and therefore never lit up. 'The front room', also known as the lounge-room, plays much the same role as the parlour did—and still does in some North-country parts—in England. It is a starched, tidy, formal room for 'serious' socialising only—a visit from the local priest perhaps, the police, the family lawyers, the doctor or prospective in-laws. It is not really meant to be lived in.

The underlying idea, of course, is that most visitors are (a) unexpected and (b) unwelcome, so they should be contained at the front of the house and got rid of from there. Australians are paradoxical in that, although they are very friendly on the surface, they in fact have a highly developed concept of privacy.

Real life takes place at the back of the house, in and around the kitchen, in the larger 'family room' and, in the summer, in the backyard, on the patio or verandah as well as the decking around the barbie (barbecue pit) and perhaps also in and around the swimming pool.

Kitchens are often open-design, allowing for maximum social interaction. A great deal of social life takes place in the kitchen. It is rare to be invited to a sit-down dinner in a separate dining room. More likely, you will find yourself milling around the kitchen talking to the lady of the house cooking at the stove, snacking from a mobile buffet, or standing in the garden around the barbie pit.

LOO LORE

Another odd thing about Australian houses from the non-Australian point of view is the bathroom and 'loo' (john,

WC, toilet, lavatory, little room) disposition. Only the newer houses will have more than one loo. Older and rural homes might even have the loo in a separate shed in the yard—the 'dunny' of Aussie folklore. Writing in *The West Australian* in 1993, Pam Casellas remarked, 'We grew up with good bladders, us country kids, because we were too scared to venture out to the lav in the middle of the night.'

Very few homes have loos in the bathroom itself (the place where you shower or bath)—they are usually separate. So do not ask for the 'bathroom' nor to 'wash your hands', if what you really want is to relieve yourself, as you will probably find yourself facing only a hand-basin and a towel-rail. You will have to be more specific and ask either for the 'toilet' or the 'loo'.

I am pleased to say that the more sophisticated homes are improving on this lamentable situation by installing more than one loo, and also incorporating loos with the shower-room in some rare instances. Despite the British tradition of taking a bath in a tub, or 'long bath' as some call it, most Australians opt for showers in preference, by the way.

Other Rooms

Bedrooms and the master bathroom, if there is one, are designed to be out of the way of visitors and it is expected that they should be treated as strictly private areas, although a proud new owner may perhaps offer you a tour of the entire house

THE BARBIE

Some have called this 'the high altar' in the ritual of outdoor living. The outdoors area of the home is very clearly a male domain, controlled by the man of the house. As mentioned earlier, the hunter-male cooks the 'primitive' meal of raw meat burned on charcoal. Visiting females should not attempt to interfere. Outdoors settings are the ideal environment for the naturally sociable and easy-going Australian to mingle without formality.

The barbie party is the Australian's safe route to nostalgia about life in the bush, brewing tea in a billy over a campfire.

The same macho psychology pushes suburban Australians to wear cattle-driver 'cowboy' hats, display huge 'roo bars' on the front of their cars (for fending off kangaroos crossing the roads) or to purchase impressive 4WD (four-wheel drive) vehicles, meant for heavy bush-driving, when in fact they hardly ever go bush (making them a complete menace on ordinary suburban roads, where drivers behind these monsters can never see past them).

VISITING

There is certainly more visiting without a prior appointment in Australia than there would be in England. All the same, you have to be careful about your timing.

In Asia of course, and many Mediterranean countries too, the problem simply would not arise: the family would naturally invite their friend to share the evening meal with them. But this kind of familiarity does not come easily to Australians, so do not expect it; instead, leave at the unspoken but appointed time, i.e. by about 5pm latest. Neither is it as automatic to Australians to offer visitors a drink on arrival as it is in some cultures, particularly Asian cultures.

If you come from a society where home-help or servants are easily available, pause to remember that this is not the norm in Australia. It would therefore be a good idea to offer to help clear the table and to wash up. The offer may be refused, but it will certainly be appreciated.

TROUBLESHOOTING CHECKLIST

Here is a random and by no means exhaustive checklist of potential problem areas.

Swimming Pool

'Just what I always dreamed of, my own backyard pool!' you may sigh as you move into your new Australian home. All pool-owners quickly learn how costly and troublesome it is to maintain a pool in proper condition. You will be forever measuring the chlorine level, the pH level, the alkaline-acid ratio, tipping in great sacks of salt (for salt-water chlorinators), repairing pumps and filters, and so on. Once your children

Cooking up a storm at an outdoor barbecue.

grow up and leave home, you may well start wondering why you are bothering.

Pool maintenance is a serious matter in the scorching Australian summer—the hotter it gets, the more likely a badly maintained pool may breed bacteria, the sort that cause potentially fatal meningitis in children, for example. The chemicals necessary to maintain balance in your pool are costly. So budget carefully before rushing for one.

Pool Problems

Take note of our salutary lesson when we accidentally emptied our pool. We had turned the pump onto 'Backwash' to clean out the filter, which entails draining some water out of the pool. We then went to bed and forgot about it. Next morning, hey presto, no pool! Well, no water anyway.

We decided this was a blessing in disguise since the swimming season had just ended and winter was on its way, and thought nothing further of it until someone wiser remarked that he hoped our pool was not fibreglass. Yes it was, we told him.

In that case, said he, better get it filled straightaway, as the sides would probably buckle under the pressure of soil subsidence around the pool during heavy winter rains. Sure enough, when we anxiously inspected our pool, there was a distinct bulge on one side. That meant hosing in about 30,000 litres of water as quickly as possible—and the consequent water bill.

Today, we are sans pool—it got too expensive, too time-consuming, definitely environmentally unfriendly in the context of Australia's serious water shortages, and we hated the idea of newly compulsory perimeter fencing, for its visual ugliness. It cost us an arm and a leg to take out and fill in, but now we have a spacious four-bed veggie garden, fruit trees, flowering plants, and no pool maintenance costs.

Trees

For those who have previously lived in city apartments, it may be quite marvellous to find you have trees in your Australian garden, perhaps fruit trees as well. But be aware that all trees, and especially fruit trees, need special care.

The iconic Aussie gum trees (eucalypts) are highly inflammable. Nature built them that way. Conquer your romanticism about the traditional Australian landscape, think instead about building a living firebreak around your home by not planting gums too close to the building—perhaps not closer than 150 metres away. Plant fire- retardant and low-growing species instead (e.g. Cape Lilac, the native Lilly-Pilly, Oaks, Willows, deciduous or sub-tropical trees, or fruit trees. But also, don't plant truly invasive exotic weeds). Prune dead wood regularly, keep the ground clear of loose leaf litter and twigs, all 'fuel' for a fire. Study this issue (try the book *Green Living Spaces: A Guide to Landscaping with Fire Retardant Trees*...by Christine Sharp and Rofry Balingup, published in Balingup, Western Australia by Small Tree Farm, 1994, if you can find it—and visit http://www.smalltreefarm.com.au/).

Some species, such as the paperbarks (Melaleucas) may have acid foliage which renders all the soil beneath their canopy bald of grass. Some may be poisonous if children attempt to eat them. Others (like lemon trees) may detest exposure to strong winds. Some unique Australian ones, like the iconic Blackboy (aka Grass Tree, aka Balga, aka Zanthorrea sp.), may need to be set on fire every so often, not to mention the huge area they need for their extensive root system. Besides which, plants like the Balga or the orange-flowered West Australian 'Christmas Tree' (*Nuytsia floribunda*) grow at tortoise pace, so you need either to plant a fairly mature one (not always easy to transplant) or be patient and plant for posterity.

Wattles look great, with their gorgeous yellow blossom, but don't plant them close to the house or drains, as their root system will one day invade and destabilise the building or the drainage system.

Bottlebrush also look wonderful with their drooping red blooms, but they promote hay fever and asthma, with high-pollen counts a common problem in the Australian spring.

You will have to choose between organic pacifism or chemical warfare on your garden pests. Fruit flies are a terrible pest of stone-fruit trees: try festooning tins of Vegemite-and-water solution to trap them organically. Snails will joyfully drown in a saucer of beer. Bag your fruit against parrots. Consult your local gardening societies.

With other plants, you have to watch out for snails and slugs—guess what, a small saucer full of beer embedded in the ground next to your plant will attract snails, who will joyfully drown in the amber fluid

Wooden Houses

Termites, or white ants as they are more commonly called in Australia, are a problem, but so are the chemicals used to spray against them. Spraying every 5–10 years may be necessary, especially if you have an older home with weatherboard and timber floors. Discuss the options with your chosen pest control company after they have assessed your termite risk (Inspection fee, about A$ 180). If you don't

0The Blackboy of Western Australia.

undertake an annual re-inspection, you will lose the cost benefits of the five-year warranty that the pest company usually offers after treatment. The treatment itself is likely to cost A$ 1,000 upwards but instalment payments are possible. Nowadays the chemicals used are less toxic than in the past. Do your research, and shop around. Oh, and while we are on this subject, watch out for 'treated' fencing sold in DIY stores that may have been termite-proofed by arsenic—placed next to your veggie plots, this could leach into your veggies. On the other hand, untreated fencing might be vulnerable to termite attack. Be careful how much loose wood you stack around the garden: it will be like candy to termites, drawing them to your home.

Creepy-crawlies

Spiders stand out in this category, with some 2,000 species identified in Australia. Some Australian spiders commonly found in the garden and the house are a lot more dangerous than anything you are likely to have experienced before.

In the eastern states, there is the Funnel-web, named after the silken tube it builds at its burrow entrance, one of the world's deadliest spiders—the antidote must be administered almost immediately after the bite to be effective.

In the west, there is the Red-back (related to the Black Widow), a small glossy black spider with a red patch on its abdomen, brightest in females, which are also the more dangerous—again, an antivenin is available, however. The Red-back loves to hide in places like the top of fences, inside letter boxes and on the handles of gardening tools among other places. This spider's bite has been known to kill. The least it will do is hurt—a lot—and put you temporarily in hospital.

Flies

Your image of elegant luncheon parties on your patio on sunny Sunday afternoons could be marred by a common Australian pest, the fly. There are about 7,000 species in the country.

In rural areas, the flies are notorious for their persistence, and their tendency to sit anywhere moist, including your nose, eyes, ears and mouth. Hence the famous 'Australian salute', the constant rhythmic flicking of the hand across the face to keep the flies away. You will find this gesture comes very naturally indeed. Politicians can be seen doing it all the time on telly, as they pose in the searing outback to show that they are in touch with 'the ground.'

Houses are suitably equipped with extra mesh-and-metal fly-screen doors besides the usual doors, as well as window fly-screens. If you want to enjoy peace in your own home, and if you want to stay popular with your Australian hosts, remember

Beware of the Red-back spider; its bite can be fatal.

always to close the fly-screens, leaving the normal doors and windows open for good ventilation during the summer. And keep your own fly-screens in good repair, free of holes.

Burglary

House-breaking is definitely a risk in Australia, with drug-taking and youth unemployment among the causative factors. If you are alert and careful, you should be able to protect yourself. A dog is a good idea. So is a burglar alarm, although most security installations will set you back a few thousand dollars.

The sort of alarm system that links up to a monitoring and patrol system that can alert the police as well, is probably the best, and will cost you about A$ 400 a year to maintain; a loud alarm bell might possibly scare a would-be burglar off, but it wouldn't necessarily get help to you quickly without such a monitoring system (and be aware too that there is a general public outcry in Australia at the moment about the slow police response to emergency phone calls). Alarms that use sensor beams to detect movement across rooms are quite effective. Make sure you have a 'panic button' activating the alarm and a working telephone near your bed for emergencies. Alarm systems that can generate their own battery power should the mains power in the house be cut off are also a good idea.

Now plaster the house with the stickers provided by your security service, announcing that 'This house is protected by X Monitored Alarms' (even if it isn't).

Leave lights on and radios or televisions playing when you go out. (Cent-conscious dinky-di Australians never leave lights on, though.) Sensor-lighting systems that switch on in response to movement are also a good idea, to light up the front drive when you drive your car back home, or to light up the garden suddenly if an intruder climbs over the back fence.

Lock up properly at night and when you go out. Fix metal-grille screens on windows and make sure fly-screens are also reinforced with metal. Never answer the front door without ensuring the second, fly-screen, door is locked; as an extra precaution, use a peephole to view who is calling before opening either door.

Get a house-sitter rather than leave the house empty when you go on holidays. Note that in car-oriented Australia, a car in the driveway usually indicates someone is home. No car means it may be OK to break in. About the car—don't rush out to stop an intruder stealing your car from the driveway. Throw him the car-keys from your window, trust your insurance, and be glad you are still safe.

Charity Canvassers

The newcomer is at first intrigued, later astounded, and finally infuriated by the number of people who come to the front door collecting for charities. This is a great Australian nuisance.

Many of these people are professional, paid collectors and while many may need the job, it is very difficult to sort out who is genuine and who may be just operating a neat little scam. The best tactic is probably to ask them to write to you instead, so you can decide at your leisure whether you want to donate, how much and to which charities. Don't feel bad, just send them away. There are just a few groups I rarely send off without some money—'The Salvos' as the Salvation Army is often called in Australia, and sometimes the Red Cross too. They do tremendous work across the board with the poor and disadvantaged (of which there are a surprising number in Australia).They will often announce a door-knock campaign well in advance, in advertisements or newspaper announcements, so you can always know when to be ready for them. (We won't get into the other door-knockers here—the religious type, usually Christian. I usually greet them with a firm "Sorry, this is a Hindu household" and close the door on them. You could try various permutations of this or simply, "Go away, we don't believe in God.")

Fire

You must always be aware of the very great danger that fires pose in Australia, especially during the summer, when everything is tinder-dry. Keep an eye on the daily television announcements for the level of Fire Hazard and obey instructions on whether or not it is safe to light fires (including barbecues), at home, in the park or camping in the countryside. Check with your local city council on rules (legally enforced) about firebreaks on your land. In many suburban areas, it is illegal all year round to burn off rubbish, leaves etc., so it would be best to check with your Council whether and when you can do this.

You may always have dreamed of a country home surrounded by tall trees, but think hard before you act on your dream—every summer brings terrifying days of walls of fire and fireballs hurtling through the skies, right into the suburbs, let alone the country, leaping from tree to tree faster than you can imagine. Thousands of volunteer fire-fighters regularly demonstrate Australia's gutsy civil spirit, but countless homes are regularly lost, with such scenes repeated all over the country.

How to protect yourself if it happens? First, leave the area, abandon your house, *but early*, never at the last moment, that will be too late—when the flames are upon you, it's marginally better to stay put inside the house than to run. Out there in the firestorm itself, you could die of radiation or smoke inhalation. You can almost never out-run a fire. (Equally, even the swimming pool may not be a safe retreat if you have your head above water breathing the smoke, or if the water heats up.) Preventive measures include making firebreaks, removing all dead twigs and debris on your land, clearing gutters of leaves, plugging all holes, including down-pipes, and sealing windows, hosing down your property and the land to drenching point, not just before the fire comes, but for days before. And of course, get rid of all inflammable items such as tins of paint or firewood and heating oil supplies.

Rubbish Disposal

We had come from tropical Asia and so were quite taken aback at first to discover that refuse collection did not take place daily. If you forget to wheel your bin out onto your front kerb on the designated night for emptying the next day, too bad—you wait for another week.

Most suburbs have two or three separate bins—one for real rubbish and wet kitchen waste etc. (if you haven't yet got wise to composting) and perhaps some light 'green waste' from the garden (not huge tree branches though); one recycling bin for paper and cardboard; and one other recycling bin for plastics and aluminium cans. (In some places there will be only one recycling bin, however.)

At regular intervals, your Council will inform you of the dates for its 'Verge Junk Collection Service' and you can chuck

Recycling bins for bottles at a local supemarket.

out on your verge the equivalent of one car trailer-load of household junk ranging from old fridges to broken furniture, but not construction waste such as bricks and cement rubble. Another regular collection will be for 'Prunings'—this is the time to get your trees lopped and place all the big branches on the verge for the Council to take away. Another useful thing is to remember that most Australians are avid recyclers and bargain-hunters, so if you just put something unwanted out on your verge at any time, ten to one it will be snapped up by some junk hunter cruising by in their car. Which is kind of handy.

Mail Boxes

Your motorcycle-borne 'postie' (postman) will probably zip past at great speed on the pavement at the front of your house. The idea is that you should have a mail box out on the pavement at the front of the house so he can drop the letters in as he passes. He will not expect to get off his bike and walk up to your front door to deliver, although you might get that favour from the newspaper delivery man. If you don't want sheaves and sheaves of junk mail flapping about in your mail box, put up a sign saying 'No Junk Mail' and that will likely be respected; my husband on the other hand says that he loves the junk mail and it helps him make informed decisions on where to buy the cheapest hand-saw, cutest tool-kit for a Christmas gift etc., while I have girlfriends who instantly rush out to Target or Myers stores the minute they see a brochure saying '50 per cent off all knickers and bras.' These flyers certainly are good guides to all the 'Specials' at the supermarkets.

And some poor soul does make a living delivering the junk mail to your mail box every week, rain or shine.

Heating

If you are not used to winter, remember that the idyllic Australian summers in the garden do not go on forever and you will need to keep warm, eventually. The most economical and environmentally acceptable way of doing so is to wear good woollen clothes, especially under-vests, hats and socks, and sleep under a heavy feather 'doona' as the Australians call the duvet or continental quilt.

The winters are generally not very severe—in Perth, for example, winter night temperatures only rarely fall below 5°C (41°F), daytime rarely below 15°C (59°F)—although Melbourne and Tasmania are another story in this respect.

Depending on where you are in Australia, you may feel you need heating, particularly to provide hot water. The 'sunburnt country', Australia, is the ideal country for solar heating and power generation. Many homes already have it. You should certainly consider installing it. It's cheap, efficient, and there are even schemes for you to sell surplus power back to the state grid.

There is enormous romance, of course, in a flickering log fire of a cold winter night. But you should consider what you are burning: Australia's native forests—such as the jarrah trees of the south-west—are precious environmental resources, which should not really be allowed to go up in smoke. Besides which such fires cause air pollution.

However, you can ask for 'mill ends'—the waste chips and blocks left over from processing at furniture and plywood factories—which are cheaper and somewhat more environmentally acceptable. 'Mallee roots' are another choice, although they too are part of the unique Australian ecology, being eucalypts.

A better path might be to use kerosene oil, a fuel resource with which Australia is richly stocked, as with liquid petroleum gas (LPG) for cooking and so on. But of course, every heating fuel comes with some environmental cost or other. Natural gas is the newest option and very much the way to go in terms of affordability, cleanness and efficiency; once you have laid down the capital investment necessary for the gas-fires themselves, the gas supply is relatively cheap.

Cooling

The Australian summer will take some newcomers aback, reaching temperatures of 40°C and above at its height. It is a dry heat, and the sun comes at you out of a dazzling clear blue sky.

We installed an evaporative air-cooling system in our home, much nicer than conventional air conditioning, and vastly

Take note of our backbreaking experience when wood suppliers delivered 3 tonnes of firewood outside our gate, in the public back lane, while we were out. We had to cart the whole lot into the woodshed—this took us three days!

cheaper to run. One attraction with this system is that you actually have to leave windows and doors open to make it work well, instead of being hermetically sealed into the house, as you are with traditional refrigerated air conditioning. Air passes over recycling running water which cools it.

You can deal with temperatures up to about 35°C degrees or so with an evaporative cooler but as it heads towards 40°C, things get tougher. Evaporative systems also add humidity. This is great when the Aussie summer is traditionally dry, but we have noticed that in these days of climate change, they are becoming increasingly humid, which makes the added humidity of the evaporative cooler a lot less attractive. However, this is usually only a problem for isolated periods of a couple of days at a time at most.

Antique Furniture

If you have brought precious antique wooden furniture to Australia, beware of the dry summers I have mentioned. Most timbers will eventually crack and split as a result. The safest policy is to give your furniture an annual oil rubdown (linseed oil is one option).

TUCKER

CHAPTER 6

'We're happy little Vegemites, as bright as bright can be,
We all enjoy our Vegemite for breakfast, lunch and tea.
Our Mummy says we're growing stronger every single week.'
—Advertising ditty of the 1950s

NOTHING DIVIDES OPINION QUITE LIKE FOOD—'tucker' is the Aussie word for it. Different strokes for different folks… And perhaps in no other area have Australians changed more radically or more rapidly than in the kitchen over the past couple of decades. Post-war migration, first the Italians and Greeks (go to Melbourne for their cuisine), followed by the Lebanese and other Middle-Easterners, then latterly of the Chinese, Indians and Vietnamese, has transformed Australian eating and cooking habits. We now wait bated breath for the inevitable influences from Africa that must now be in the pipeline. It's probably best summed up by a recent item on the menu of one South-east Asian restaurant in Western Australia (which called itself in good Aussie fashion, 'The Tucker Room'), announced as 'Chook Masala' (i.e. Chicken Masala curry).

Overall, Australian cuisine has traditionally followed in the lamentable footsteps of its English counterpart. Despite England being my own birthplace, I really hesitate to call it a 'cuisine' at all.

Time was, 'food' in Australia meant a roast joint of beef or lamb—or cheaper meat items such as tripe, offal ('fry') or salt-meat—with potatoes and over-boiled greens (they thought them safer this way in the old days), followed by a treacly pudding with custard. Dairy foods were also important staples.

The Australian, his country being a beef and lamb-producer, consumed meat in prodigious quantities and, like the English, was often overweight. (Well, still is actually—

more than half of adult Australians are overweight or obese, likely to reach 80 per cent by 2020). This gastronomic 'culture' still survives in Australia outside of the major cities and in suburban heartlands—French and Chinese gourmets, you have been warned—but the cosmopolitan minority is expanding its influence steadily.

The turn of the 20th into the 21st century also saw the rise of what is known as 'Modern Australian' cuisine, an eclectic and innovative style drawing on multiculturalism, 'fusion food' that is fast acquiring a unique Australian identity. You can get everything from lemongrass to couscous in Aussie markets nowadays, and chefs are going to town with some of the world's freshest, purest ingredients.

As an example of the style, cited in *The Weekend Australian* paper, 1997, from the Paramount restaurant in Sydney, try Duck Pie with Shitake Mushroom Sauce and Ginger Glaze— 'Everyone identifies with a pie—the term is Australian, the taste is Chinese, the appearance is French,' says chef Christine Manfield. Nowadays you are quite likely to encounter prawns, kangaroo and papaya in the same dish. It's an enormously exciting new scene, and, combined with the 'Bush Tucker' movement (*see later in this chapter*), it's anyone's guess where it will ultimately go.

Recommendations

To get a feel for the finer points of traditional Australian cooking, do consult Shirley Constantine's excellent *Traditional Australian Cooking*, which is more than just a cookbook; it's a readable social history too. There are some good basic recipes, too, in Margaret Nicholson's *The Little Aussie Fact Book*. The original Country Women's Association of Australia classic handbooks are a treat too if you can find a copy—Penguin re-issued their *Country classics: a collection of 500 classic recipes* in 2007.

THE ASIAN INVASION

Wandering around historic Fremantle, Perth's twin port-town, not long ago, I spotted an odd item on a traditional Aussie fish-and-chips shop blackboard menu, reading, 'DIM SIM'.

"Wozzat, mite?" I enquired amiably of the proprietor in my newly acquired super-casual Aussie vernacular.

"Ere 'tis, luv," replied he, indicating a squat little item somewhat like a half-spring roll, a pastry case stuffed with veggies and minced meat of some sort. It was priced at about US$ 0.60.

"Nao fanks, mite," quoth I, quailing, recalling with nostalgia the infinite variety that the classic Cantonese Chinese snacks-buffet, *dim sum*, usually offers. (*Dim sum* or *dian xin* is a range of small steamed and fried snacks eaten for lunch or breakfast from mobile buffet trolleys.)

But this was just another example of Asian migrants' subtle subversion of Australian cuisine. Or, to look at it another way, it was an example of Asian cuisine absorbed and mutated within Australian cuisine. Tough to tell who is dominating whom when it comes to 'Dim Sim', Australian-style. It works both ways—it's common to see Western dishes like 'potato wedges and sour cream' appearing on Asian menus, in a desperate attempt to keep the children quiet while the parents slurp their noodles.

You wouldn't have seen this sign at a Perth fresh market a decade or so ago: the availability, and sale value, of Chicken's Feet, not on most dinky-di Australian menus, is a sure indicator of the Asian (Chinese) presence in Australia. *Picture by Ilsa Sharp.*

No Need to Bring Your Own

Anyone who's ever flown into Perth airport on one of those ghastly flights that get in at almost 3:00 am will be familiar with the sight of Asian visitors and returning residents arguing their way past Customs officials with bags of spices and unattractive-looking dried foods, from squid to waxed duck.

Grave Concern

There are all sorts of stories, apocryphal and otherwise, about Australian Customs' reactions to some of the foodstuffs that Asian migrants typically try either to import legally or to smuggle through when they land in Australia. A food-related story that I particularly like concerns that traditional essential in the Asian kitchen, the often massive, heavy granite slab that Indian housewives, especially, use as a base for pounding or roller-grinding the fresh spice pastes that are the foundation of good curries.

"What's this, then?" cried one Aussie Customs officer at the airport on being confronted with one such slab, a particularly large specimen (an ammi for those South Indians among you). "Oh, it's just for grinding," said the timid Indian lady lugging this heavyweight piece of hand baggage. After further suspicious exploration of the stone, almost as mysterious to them as the mystic obelisk in the cult sci-fi movie *2001: A Space Odyssey*, the Customs officers gave up and let it go. As the ammi's relieved though puzzled owner left their desk, one officer turned to the other and said, "These Asians, now they're even bringing in their own tombstones!"

Australia understandably has to police imported food and agricultural items sternly to protect its own agriculture against foreign pests and diseases still foreign to its own continental island environment. But I don't know why these would-be gastronomic smugglers persist in running the gauntlet of Customs when Australia is fast producing the goods for them on the spot.

Take my own Perth suburb, for example. Within 10 minutes' drive in any direction are two 'Oriental' provisions stores stocking everything from Chinese *wok* (frying pans) and chilli powder to fresh Indian *roti canai* (bread; Sundays only) and crisp Indian-style *samosa* snacks (pastry triangles stuffed with meat and vegetable), and two 'international food centres' featuring stalls offering Indian and Chinese favourites—besides the Italian, Lebanese and Greek dishes

A food centre that has a variety of cuisines from different countries, attracting customers from different ethnic backgrounds.

which have long been Australian standards. There are also at least four Indian food suppliers and one Indonesian emporium of food. A drive just a bit further away, maybe 20 minutes or so, will open up the options even wider.

At one of these food centres, white faces are in a distinct minority, the southern-Chinese Hokkien dialect of Singapore and Malaysia is spoken, several characters are to be seen slopping about in thongs (flip-flop rubber sandals), shorts and singlets, and the *char kway teow* (a sort of fried fettucine) could comfortably compete with the Chinese original back home in Malaysia.

It's not just the food centres that have gone Asian, either. Any Australian city restaurant area will feature at least a Cantonese- and a Peking-style Chinese restaurant, a Lebanese falafels-and-kebabs café, a Malaysian *satay* (barbecued kebabs) joint, an Indonesian *nasi goreng* (fried rice) restaurant, a Thai seafood spot, besides a Vietnamese restaurant, a Japanese sushi and tempura stall, and an Indian curry house.

Unfortunately, you have to shop around quite energetically to identify the ones serving the real thing, because many Asian restaurateurs have adversely tailored their cuisine to Australian taste.

Even the fish-and-chip shops have mutated. Increasingly now, these typically Australian establishments are being taken over by Asian migrants. Few of them offer only good old fish and chips lathered in batter and salt and served in brown-paper packets (more traditionally, they should be newspaper). Nowadays they also serve *calamari*, or batter-fried squid, a borrowing from Greece, Chinese-style spring rolls, Indian *samosa*, and other alien imports. Health freaks can also get their fish grilled rather than fried.

Memories of Days Gone By
By the way, if by some chance you have never experienced the great British working-class tradition of batter-fried fish and potato chips served up in paper packets, liberally doused in salt, pepper and vinegar, you must go through with it at least once in Australia. After years in Asia, visits to the Australian fish-and-chip shops brought back my childhood and student years in northern England, scoffing the sizzling, calorific stuff from newspaper as I walked along cold wintry streets at night. Very nostalgic.

Asian DIY in the Kitchen

Some pioneers have been busying themselves for many years to make all this come about. One such is Charmaine Solomon, nee Poulier, one of Australia's best-known Asian residents, a Sri Lankan-born 'burgher' or Eurasian by origin. She has lived in Australia for more than 50 years. If you are an Asian migrant to Australia, afraid you will no longer be able to eat your traditional food, either because you will no longer have a servant to do it for you or because you fear Australia will not have the ingredients, take heart from Charmaine Solomon's work, showcased in her more than 40 cookbooks, almost every one of them an ambassador for Asian food to Australians. The most famous, back in 1976, was her groundbreaking *The Complete Asian Cookbook (one million copies sold worldwide)*. Her goal has always been to prove that good Asian cooking can come out of a Western-style kitchen, and she has amply succeeded. Her books have been vital to the task of preserving Asian heritage among second or third-generation Australian-Asians.

In this book, too, it is revealed, for instance, that Australians refer to snow-peas but Americans talk about sugar-peas or *mange-tout*, while green and red peppers may be described as capsicums, sweet peppers or bell peppers, depending on where you are from. *The Complete Asian Cookbook* also lists Australia-based suppliers of Asian ingredients and foodstuffs. Here again is a sign of the times; in 1976, Charmaine could list only one shop stocking Chinese goods in Perth, and none selling Indonesian, Malaysian, Indian or Sri Lankan goods. They are all over Perth now. What isn't in the shops is growing in people's gardens—all the Asian herbs, *lengkuas*, *pandan*, *daun kesom*, *serai*, the lot. They got past Customs somehow.

KITCHEN CELEBRITIES

Once upon a quite recent time, few Aussies would know a bunch of bok choy from spinach, and most would certainly avoid garlic, chilli and coriander like the plague. If they affected to love food at all, then it had to be French 'haute cuisine' or marginally, perhaps Mediterranean. Nowadays, it's seemingly impossible to sate the Australian hunger for exotic foods linked to exotic places, preferably in Asia, although Aussie foodies often are mere 'armchair gourmets' from the comfort of their living room, in front of the telly. On SBS and ABC television in particular, you will be presented with an endless parade of celebrity chefs and food presenters, many of them on the road in foreign parts. Supplanting the great Aussie names of the past—Stephanie Alexander (*The Cook's Companion*) Maggie Beer and Margaret Fulton (*Maggie's Harvest and The Margaret Fulton Cookbook*), and Western Australia's very own Ian Parmenter (*Consuming Passions*) – today's celebrity food presenters range from Maeve O'Meara with her engaging Food Safari programmes and tours and the 'simplicity queen' Donna Hay (*Off The Shelf and Modern Classics*), to a host of Asian-Australians such as the earnestly bespectacled, fifth-generation Australian-Chinese Kylie Kwong (*Simple Chinese Cooking*), lively multicultural chef Peter Kuruvita (English-born of a Sri Lankan father and Austrian mother, and both Sri Lankan- and Australian-raised— *Serendip: My Sri Lankan Journey*), and one-time 'boat-person' refugee from Vietnam, Luke Nguyen.

Hand in hand with such cross-cultural maestros, Australian chefs have come up with a distinctive 'Modern Australian' style in the kitchen: a delicate fusion of East and West, including chilli and garlic, with a strong affection for fresh seafood, and 'surprise' local ingredients ranging from wattle seeds and lemon myrtle to freshwater 'yabbies' (crayfish) and 'Moreton Bay bugs' (small lobsters).

CUTLERY

There is one very odd thing about Australian eating habits, especially when it comes to consuming Asian food. I can understand a general reluctance to tackle eating instruments as esoteric as chopsticks, or as alien as one's own pinkies (connoisseurs of Indian and Malay food, however, always prefer to use their hands, as the natives do).

But it does seem really benighted to try to eat curry or fried rice with a *knife and fork*, as most Australians do. The less uptight Australians do at least relax with just a fork. But why, oh why, is there a hidden taboo against eating it with a spoon and fork, as sensible South-east Asians themselves do nowadays?

Apparently, for Australians, it is somehow not nice to use spoons for anything other than soups or desserts, but nobody has ever explained to me why this is so. Even long-term Asian residents in Australia have given it up as a losing battle and are to be seen stabbing away with forks instead. Logically then, the American custom of cutting food into small pieces and then picking it up with a fork should be quite acceptable in Australia.

Mine and Yours

For Asians in particular, the 'my dish' syndrome evinced by Australians will seem quite remarkable. Each diner has his own plate of food in a typical Western-style Australian meal. If a Western-style meal is served at home, care should be taken that food is available in multiples of the number of guests (six carrots for three guests, for example, i.e. two each), as the guests are likely to feel more comfortable if they can actually count how many pieces they are 'supposed' to take for themselves. It is all very precise.

This kind of thing can occur even at Asian restaurants in Australia, where some Australians will order for themselves one plate of noodles or one plate of fried rice, rather than ordering several dishes to put in the centre of the table to share, as Asians would. Call it individualism, selfishness or meanness if you like, but you will have to go with the flow.

Allied with this situation is the 'my drink' phenomenon. In Asian societies, the bottle of whisky, brandy or whatever will be plonked on the table for everyone to help themselves as they wish. In Western societies like Australia, the host will ask you whether you want a drink, serve you a carefully measured measure and wait until you seem to need another one before asking if you do, and then refilling your glass. Appalling as this may seem to some Asians, again, just learn to live with it.

QUICK FIX

Unfortunately, one of the less welcome post-war food imports has been 'fast food'. Australians eat far too many 'takeaway' meals, from fish-and-chip cafés as well as from 'Chinese takeaways'—estimated at four to five times a week. They rank fourth in the world, after the US, Canada and UK, for fast food consumption in terms of dollars spent per capita in a year (US$ 363 in 2006), and 40 per cent of the money they spend on eating out goes to fast food. The national expenditure on fast foods of all kinds is projected to total about A$ 37 billion for 2011, ranking Australia as the 11th biggest spending fast-food consumer in the world. In the mid-1990s, it was revealed that more than 8 per cent of the Australian family food budget went on snack or 'junk' foods. It obviously does not make them happy: a 1996 survey found that Australians had a guiltier conscience about what they ate than any other nationality.

Perhaps not surprisingly, some experts reckon the situation is rapidly heading towards as much as 80 per cent of the population being obese by about 2020. The situation is even more alarming when it comes to children: a quarter are now considered obese, whereas 20 years ago, the statistic was only 10 per cent. As in other countries, long hours at the TV and computer monitor are part of the reason—and, on top of that, Australia has the greatest amount of junk food ads per hour of television of any country in the world, including the US and the UK. About one third of the TV ads screened during kids' viewing times are for food or drink. Medical surveys reveal that of these, about 99 per cent are for junk food: burgers, chips, soft drinks and sweets.

The Fat File

- More than half (61 per cent) of the Australian adult population (over 18 year-olds) is overweight or obese (2007-'08).

- About 20–25 per cent of Australian children are overweight or obese, with the proportion fast increasing, particularly since the mid-1980s—a trend which reflects international patterns.

- Obesity rates are even higher for men (68 per cent) than for women (55 per cent), for the elderly (75 per cent of the 65-74 age group), and also for those living in remote and regional areas.

- The Australian National Health and Medical Research Council (NHMRC) recommends at least two serves of fruit and five serves of vegetables per day. The 2007 National Health Survey showed that 54.4 per cent of adults (over 16) ate the minimum two serves of fruit daily, while only 10.7 per cent ate the recommended five serves of vegetables daily—although this represented a substantial improvement on the 1997 figures.

- The financial burden associated with obesity in Australia is estimated to be A$ 37.7 billion in 2010, factoring in everything from health-care costs to losses in economic productivity.

- Outside of school hours, only 63 per cent of children aged 5–14 years participated in organised sport in 2006.

—Australian government figures

However, a vocal health-food lobby, backed by an array of official government programmes, particularly in schools, is fighting back. Despite campaigns to limit junk food ads on television during children's programmes, however, the Australian Communications and Media Authority has ruled so far that a cause-and-effect relationship cannot truly be established between junk food advertising and childhood obesity.

THE AUSTRALIAN SHOPPING BASKET

Within the past 15 years, the fondly remembered era of the milkman (the 'milko') and his daily doorstep delivery has disappeared from the suburbs of Australia. The phone directory reveals a host of 'Dial-a-Meal' services and there are endless pizza deliveries on call, but most Australians do the bulk of their shopping in supermarkets and at the many fresh fruit-and-veg markets, especially the wholesale growers' markets, very much in the American style: they load up their big cars with a week's supplies, wheeling their laden supermarket trolleys out to the car across the huge car park, and store many things in deep-freezers. (The trolleys, by the way, are in some areas obtainable only through a coin-slot machine which consumers, say, an A$ 1 coin deposit, refundable when you return the trolley).

Hurry Up, The Shops Are Closing!

Australia's shopping/retail trading hours are in transition, although in most eastern-states metropolitan areas you can expect pretty much the same liberated night- and weekend- shopping hours that you are probably used to back home. But because each state has been slowly adjusting laws of differing levels of antiquity and conservatism, there is a very uneven picture nation-wide; your shopping patterns will depend very much on where exactly you are. Western Australia has only just freed up Sunday shopping in its metropolitan districts in mid-2012, after years of patchwork nonsense that nobody could work out for themselves; there is still plenty of opposition in WA to the more liberal new laws—on the grounds that longer working hours will destroy family life, the bigger department stores will kill small business, maybe the Sabbath was a good idea, etc etc. A 2005 referendum on whether or not to reform WA shopping hours actually drew a resounding and astonishing 'No' vote of about 60 per cent. But younger people, tourists, migrants, big business and tourism industry officials have prevailed in the end.

The Australian family diet includes essentials like eggs, meat and vegetables and old Anglo favourites like custard powder, pickled onions and canned baked beans (oh dear), but also betrays European influences—Polony sausage, pizza, pasta and tomato paste. A major item in the shopping trolley is dairy, e.g. milk at a high 103 litres (181 pints) per person per year, and cheese at 12.7 kilograms (28 pounds) per person.

Consumption figures from the Australian Bureau of Statistics show that Australians are upping their veggie intake but still don't eat enough of them for good health, and they certainly haven't abandoned meat. Their consumption of their top choice, beef, stood at 33 kilograms (73 pounds) per person in 2010–11, and total domestic Australian spending on beef amounted to A$ 6.7 billion, according to the key producer organisation Meat and Livestock Australia.

Trial by Yeast

The shopping list would not be Australian if it lacked one particular item—I refer of course to 'Vegemite'.

Vegemite is the trade name devised back in the 1920s for a bread spread that describes itself as 'concentrated yeast extract'. It is the Australian equivalent of Britain's Marmite but different. Indeed, Vegemite was created specifically to compete with Marmite. It was launched in 1923 as 'Parwill' but then changed its name to Vegemite.

Vegemite offers the same kind of test for whether you have integrated with mainstream society as that posed by warm beer in Britain for wannabe Brits or by the odiferous durian fruit in South-east Asia. This thick dark brown goo usually comes in a small glass jar with distinctive yellow and red labelling and packaging. The strongest impression left by its taste is, well—salt. With yeasty undertones, naturally.

Vegemite is considered quintessentially Australian. If you don't like it or don't eat it, your Australian-ness is open to question. But take heart, some Australians don't.

The ingredients are listed on the packaging as: yeast extract, salt, mineral salt (508), malt extract (from barley), natural colour (150d), preservative 220, vegetable extract, and the vitamins thiamine, riboflavin, niacin and folate. The numbers are the official food additive codes. The label further points out that five grammes of Vegemite gives you half your daily allowance of Vitamin B1, riboflavin and niacin. I personally can recommend the stuff as a piquant backdrop to a robustly-flavoured Australian Cheddar cheese sandwich,

The Great Australian Meat Pie—this photo was first used to publicise the opening of 'The Jolly Pieman' store in Mirrabooka, Western Australia.

topped with a layer of watercress or fresh sunflower sprouts. Go for it.

The Meat Pie

Least attractive of all is the unofficial 'national dish', the Great Australian Meat Pie—meat and vegetables in a pastry shell— it's an individually sized mini-pie that we are talking about, not one big one that you cut up into pieces and share at the table. The Aussie meat pie can be eaten at a meal but is also used as a snack that you can eat on the run. A particularly dreadful version of this is the 'Adelaide floater' which features the said pie, with peas, awash in a gooey gravy soup.

As columnist Buzz Kennedy has said in *The Weekend Australian*, 'Meat pies are not meant to be healthy. They are meant to be squidgy and dribbling with gravy thickened with white flour and eaten in great chomps.'

All part of the Australian gastronomic experience, but definitely an 'acquired taste'. On average, it seems your average Aussie may be eating about 12 of these pies every year.

Other Australiana

There are many other Australian endemics when it comes to food. Take 'puftaloons', for example, increasingly rare nowadays. ('I haven't seen a puftaloon for 40 years,' complained one reader not long ago, in a Western Australian newspaper, 'but I suppose that my body, nowadays conditioned to forever seeking low-cholesterol tucker, would not allow me anywhere near one.')

This is a fried-dough scone that rises high and fluffy during frying, eaten smothered in treacle or honey, rather like waffles. Puftaloons have been recorded as far back as 1853 – some older Americans may recognise them as 'puff-ballooners'. They were used to fill families up when times were hard and meat was short.

What's a Choko?

The Choko fruit, seen by Australians as a quintessentially Aussie 'vegetable' but in fact a South American vine-fruit akin to gourds or pumpkins, has long been the poor man's all-purpose survival food and hence has won itself a reputation for being boring. It took me a long time even to notice the insignificant little grey-green ridged grenade-shaped thing, and even then it seemed very alien. Whatever does one do with it? Actually, it's a versatile staple in anything from soups and stir-fries to curries and salads. Give it a try.

Still beloved household names today, despite most of them now being under foreign ownership, are Arnott's biscuits, Jaffas (spherical choc-orange sweets) and Minties, the mint 'lollies' (sweets, candies) wrapped in green and white paper with red writing on it. Chewiness, say Aussie aficionados, is the factor that elevates the Mintie above the 'Pommy' Minto or Polo Mint. A traditional Australian children's party game is the 'Mintie Hunt', where a trail of clues laid outdoors leads to the treasure-trove of Minties.

Among the snacks you will find at venues such as the fish-and-chips shop are sure to be 'Chiko Rolls'—crisp-fried semi-cylindrical pastries stuffed with corn, potato and gravy, nearly as Australian as Vegemite. Similarly Australian are Anzac Biscuits, substantial constructions of rolled oats, syrup and coconut, named after the Aussie soldier boys who gratefully received them at the Gallipoli warfront in parcels from home during World War 1 (see Chapter 2, *The Basics,* in *A Sense of Nation*).

Food traditions dating back to the days of the bushman are Billy Tea—tea brewed in a metal mug or can of boiling water over a campfire—and another camp-food, Damper, a heavy unleavened wheat bread baked in hot ashes, which could 'damp' your hunger.

FRUIT

Most fruit grown in Australia today has foreign origins. This is revealed more clearly nowadays, since the successful campaigning of several consumer movements to ensure that all fresh food in Australia is labelled with its country, and preferably also its Australian state, of origin. Australian consumers increasingly want to support their local farmers. There are also a few racists and political activists who want to boycott foreign food whether for its own sake or in order to send a political message about one thing or another.

What some of you may know as a 'papaya' is a 'paw-paw' in Australia and along with bananas, pineapples, avocados and mangos, is common in the tropical regions of the north, mainly in Queensland. Citrus fruit and apples are the most abundantly produced—apples from Tasmania are particularly famous and the Granny Smith apple variety was first developed from a Tasmanian seed. The zappy, crisp 'Pink Lady' branded apple first developed during the 1970s in Western Australia, derived from the Cripps Pink apple variety, is also a legend at home and abroad, in England and beyond.

There are some spectacular stone-fruit to be had in season—nectarines, peaches and apricots among them. And there are also home-grown berries such as strawberries and raspberries. And what a luxury it is to be able to gorge on cheap Australian-grown avocadoes.

DINING OUT

The single most alien aspect of Australian dining and wining is the BYO phenomenon. The acronym stands for Bring Your Own (Booze/Grog). Few restaurants are licensed to sell liquor, but most will let you bring your own. You will have a pretty miserable time if you forget this custom, only to find yourself without wine to go with your special dinner. So the routine preliminary to dining out is nearly always to visit the bottle-shop first. With BYO, you get your choice of wine, no restaurateur's mark-up, and mostly, no corkage charge either—but at any licensed eatery that also allows BYO, you probably will have to pay corkage (even for the wildly popular modern screw cap bottles), whether per head or per bottle, so do ask about this in advance, as the rates vary widely.

No Drinks Only

Note that it is often impossible to order just a drink, such as a glass of wine, as in many areas the law insists that all alcohol in restaurants must be served together with food.

Australian restaurants usually close fairly early (in traditional homes, 'tea', i.e. dinner, is eaten as early as 6:00 pm). Tipping is rarely necessary. Water is just as rarely offered unless specifically requested.

You will find Australian portions extremely generous. The nation eats heartily, mostly scorning the inadequacies of 'nouvelle cuisine' with all those fancy white spaces on the plate. Some of the best-value meals are those found in pubs, but the ubiquitous Asian/international food-centre stalls also offer very attractive options.

SHOUTS AND SPLITS

The custom of 'shouting' rounds of drink in the 'pub' (anything from a bar to a hotel is a 'pub' in Australia), taking turns, is entrenched and woe is he (less often she) who forgets it. Remember that Australians are not too well off nowadays, so pull your financial weight at the bar. On the other hand, they are proud as well, so offering to pay more than your

The pub bar is important to social life.

share of shouts could also be taken amiss.

Pride really comes to the fore when the bill for a restaurant meal is delivered. The Australian is pathologically opposed to carrying a whole dinner tab, and equally opposed to letting anybody else carry it for him. If you are a man dating a woman, be warned that there is a distinct suggestion you may be angling to bed her pretty soon if you go so far as to pay for her meal. Play safe and offer to 'go Dutch', as the English saying has it—that is, unless you are trying to tell her something.

Asians, and some southern Europeans too, find this particularly difficult to cope with; they are used to immense shows of generosity, hosting whole dinner parties, on the quiet understanding of course, that the others will owe them a debt in turn when the time comes, some time later.

But it is precisely the unspoken indebtedness that the fiercely independent Aussie dislikes about this system. An Australian married to an Asian woman had encountered this embarrassment many times and he explained it to me thus: "We feel our independence has been compromised when somebody pays the whole bill. It's kind of throwing your weight around, showing your power. And when they do that, you haven't any choice in the matter; the next time around, you will have to do it, but you haven't any choice about it."

So when in doubt, always split the bill.

TRADITIONAL FARE

Conventional or traditional Australian cuisine divides into two streams: classic Continental European cum cordon bleu, and good old Australian tucker.

It is possible to eat quality European food in Australia, however, sometimes in the most surprising places, in regional locations well outside of the big cities. This is true as you travel through the rural farming and vineyard countryside of south-western Western Australia, for instance, in areas around Margaret River and Pemberton, right down to Albany on the far south coast. Ask around and you will find many 'best-kept' secrets in most Australian states.

Old Favourites

In an attempt to characterise traditional Australian food as compared with any other, one newspaper writer came up with the word 'gutsy'. We have already discussed some of the more hardcore dishes in the genre.

Setting aside the old 'meat and two vegs' formula, however, the strongest item on any truly Australian menu would have to be seafood and fish dishes. Prawns and 'yabbies', or small freshwater crayfish, are delicious. The Barramundi fish, the John Dory and the Dhu fish are among many great Australian epicurean experiences. Be aware however, Australian fish stocks are being fished out, as elsewhere in the world, so seafood prices are really rising now. Mud crabs are well worth the effort, oysters world-famous.

More puzzling may be the mention of 'Bugs' on the menu. These are a small seafood item, allied to lobsters, some from tropical Moreton Bay, others from the southern Balmain region.

A tolerable introduction to traditional Anglo-Saxon fare is probably the Yorkshire Pudding. At its crispy, piping-hot best, this is a delicious batter pudding consisting of egg, milk and flour baked in dripping served as an accompaniment to the main dish. Another tasty standard is Steak and Kidney Pudding. Reflecting the increasingly cosmopolitan flavour of Australian cuisine, however, such dishes are no longer as easy to find on Australian restaurant menus as they once were. Look for them in the smaller cafés perhaps.

The salad is growing in popularity and variety on Australian menus and Australia's abundant fresh vegetables and fruit make it an ideal option. Asians not used to so much raw food may find it all a bit alarming, but it is indisputably healthy. By the way, you will find it extremely difficult to avoid beetroot, that violently purple vegetable. Australians love it (I loathed it at first, but I am beginning to come round, a bit like my experience with Asia's durian fruit which I now adore).

Outdoor barbecues are a favoured setting for most Australian food. The ultimate Aussie of his day (pre-Steve Irwin era) was Paul Hogan (he of *Crocodile Dundee* fame) and he made the catchphrase 'Toss a Shrimp on the Barbie' ring around the world in the bicentennial year of 1988. A favourite way of raising money for good causes, or attracting customers to a shop, is a 'Sausage Sizzle' or 'BBQ' tempting

Sausage sizzle at a Perth garden centre.

passers-by with the wafting aroma of 'snags' (sausages) and lamb chops charring on the barbie.

And Now for Afters

Australian desserts, cakes and puddings—'afters'—are quite unique. Perhaps the best known are the Pavlova dessert and the Lamington cake. Both of these are delicious.

The Pavlova, it is claimed, was created at Fremantle's Esplanade Hotel in Western Australia for the prima ballerina Anna Pavlova, when she toured Australia in 1935. It's a mouth-melting froth of meringue, whipped cream and fresh fruit.

Lamingtons, probably a Queensland invention in the early 1900s and named after 19th century Queensland governor, Baron Lamington, are small sponge blocks layered with raspberry jam, covered with thin chocolate icing, like a skin, and then rolled in desiccated coconut. Really yum!

Other more traditional English puddings personally make me cry, remembering my schoolhood in austere post-war northern England, made miserable in gastronomic terms by the gagging effort of desperately trying to shovel down monumental stodge like Suet Pudding, Golden Syrup Dumplings, Bread and Butter Pudding, or Steamed Jam Pudding, afloat in dreaded yucky-yellow custard...

CHRISTMAS

No matter if the sun is high in a bright blue sky and the temperature well over 40°C (104°F), many Australians will still have their Christmas Day lunch very much in the traditional English mode, complete with turkey, stuffing and 'Christmas pud' (more archaically known as 'Plum Duff').

There are some concessions to Australia's 'reversed' seasons. Ice-cream cake does sometimes replace or supplement the Christmas pudding, for example. (They say that in the 19th century gold-rush days, miners would put gold nuggets in the Christmas pudding instead of the traditional sixpence coins). But increasingly, the old ways are being set aside in favour of more trendy versions of Christmas lunch or dinner, with creative salads and light Asian fusion food predominating.

Suggested menus in the daily press sometimes even propose a curry as a way of getting rid of Christmas leftovers. Curry in most Australian households has always been used as more of a disguise for leftovers than considered as an art in itself.

The more sensible option is to perform the 'Christmas in July' charade, thus reserving all the heavy festive-season food for the Aussie winter.

ABOUT TEA

"They can't even make a decent cup of tea over here," a disgruntled migrant Sikh once told me. He leaned over the table with confidential mien, "I mean, it's like dishwater!" He snorted his contempt, pausing only to swill down some of his own dubious brew of sugared milk laced with coffee.

Such criticism would shock Australians if they heard it. They reckon they know about tea. After all, they take after their English forefathers when it comes to tea: they are addicts. Or so goes the stereotype. But in fact, it's generally agreed that Australia today is switching to coffee and cafe culture at a rapid rate, particularly among the young. While Australia might still brew up about half a kilogram (18 ounces) of tea per person per year, coffee sales will hit A$ 800 million in 2013 (excluding takeaway drinks), compared with only about A$ 473 million spent on tea. Coffee products consumption is slated for 23.4 million kilograms (about 23,000 tons), as opposed to 16.5 million kilograms (over 16,000 tons) of tea products. Australia only ranks about 55th in the global annual per capita tea-consumption stakes, compared with the United Kingdom at 7th place. It's been a big shift.

Indians like my Sikh friend, of course, are used to a stiff brew of fine tea-dust cooked up for some considerable time, with the milk and sugar, as well as some spices, already in the drink. Whereas the Australian will add the milk and sugar in the cup, whether before or after pouring the briefly-brewed tea.

Once again, do not forget that an invitation to 'tea' is in fact an invitation to the evening meal, a tradition deriving from old-fashioned north-country England.

BUSH TUCKER

When the first whites arrived in Australia, they took no notice at all of whatever it was the Aboriginals were eating, nor did they even attempt to farm the land for the first five years or so. They simply imported all their food. At times, they well nigh starved on account of this stupidity, or worse, almost killed themselves.

Once, seeing that the Aboriginals ate the roasted seeds of the *Zamia* cycad (an ancient, primitive palm-like tree), the white settlers did likewise. But because they had not observed carefully enough, they died from the potent poisons contained in the seeds. The Aboriginals had learned how to soak and prepare the seeds for consumption, removing toxins, for many weeks prior to cooking.

Over the past decade, there has been a growing realisation that the Aboriginals knew, still know in some cases, how to live off the land, and that this 'bush tucker' can be quite good for the health. It was certainly better for Aboriginal health than the whites' imported flour, sugar and alcohol. Take a food like Billygoat Plums. They have the highest concentration of Vitamin C of any food in the world, as much in a single plum as in a dozen oranges.

Needless to say, knowledge of bush tucker could be the key to survival if you were unfortunate enough to get lost in the outback.

It is estimated that there may be 30,000 types of bush tucker. Perhaps only about 30 or 40 of them have been introduced to urban Australia so far. The first moves are now being made towards mass production and processing of some of these traditional foods, which already appear on the menus of chic restaurants in the eastern states. If you visit an Australian bookshop, you will surely encounter perhaps half a dozen or more major books on bush tucker.

This back-to-nature movement got an immense kick-start from a television series in 1990 titled *Bush Tucker Man* and hosted by Les Hiddens, an army major who is an expert on edible plants from the survival-skills point of view.

Buffalo, kangaroo (raised on farms, not taken from the wild, they say), camel and crocodile hardly qualify as bush tucker any more, so commonplace have they become. Camel meat is turning up in the Australian meat pie, as is kangaroo. Crocodile, like kangaroo and emu, is considered a particularly healthy meat, being low in fat and cholesterol, with a chicken-like texture and a flavour much like veal.

Aboriginal women have traditionally been the gatherers of tubers and roots, such as yams and ground orchids, in particular, hence the woven or wooden collecting trays, 'coolamons', and 'dillybags' they often carry around with them.

There are grass seeds and ferns which can be eaten, also many fruits and berries. The blue-black Davidson's Plum of the rainforest makes a delicious, sourish jam, for example.

Aboriginals in their natural state also eat wildlife, of course, such as the Goanna, a monitor lizard, reputed to be pleasantly edible if a little gamey, and the fatty Mutton Bird (short-tailed shearwater) of the south-eastern coast. Goanna is another example of the healthy lean meat available in the bush.

In some areas, Aboriginals also nibble on live green ants—the green comes from chlorophyll in the plants eaten by the ants and the ants as a result have an attractively tangy taste, rather like lemon juice (Yes, I've tried it). One imagines it would take an awful lot of these to make any nutritional impact or to affect energy levels, however.

Gourmet Grubs

And then there is the Witchetty Grub. The Aboriginals' consumption of these fat maggot-like creatures, live and raw, has acquired a horrid fascination for outsiders, thanks to Aussie tour guides' propensity for macho demonstrations.

Witchetty grubs are in fact insect larvae, usually of wood-boring moths. You do not have to eat them raw (when they taste creamy and squashy—you bite off their heads first); they can be cooked in hot ashes, which renders them something like underdone pork crackling. I have tried it both ways myself. Just for the experience.

The grubs, no doubt a fair source of protein, are now appearing on the smartest of menus. They are even available from gourmet supermarkets in tinned soup form (from Vic Cherikoff Food Services, http://www.cherikoff.net/shop/). Chef Diane Holuigue once told *The Australian Magazine* how she served this up to a Florida dinner party in the USA, 'fluffed into cappucino-like consistency and dredged with wattle seed'.

Vic Cherikoff pioneered the integration of Australian bush foods and Aboriginal delicacies into mainstream cooking, as seen in his books *The Bushfood Handbook*, *Uniquely Australian* and *Dining Downunder*. The impact of his work can be seen in the rest of Diane Holuigue's Australiana menu, which included crocodile macadamia brochettes with bush tomato chutney; prawns fried in coconut with curried mayonnaise; quail and emu ham salad, among other more conventional items, such as Australian lamb. (Macadamia nuts, by the way, are another fine Australian native food, unfortunately known to some people abroad as 'Hawaiian nuts', since they were first commercially grown on Hawaii, but originally came from Queensland.)

Another of Diane's efforts produced baby Wattle-seed Blini topped with cress, smoked emu, handmade agnolotti filled with Yabbie Mousseline, and baby Barramundi fish wrapped in the bark of the paperbark tree (the wrapping, she says, imparts a 'delicate earthy taste' to the food), served with Kakadu plum sauce.

The list of exotica is seemingly endless: the Quandong and Boab fruits, Lemon Myrtle, Lilli-Pilli berries, Warragal greens, Bunya nuts, the Bogong Moth, Black Nightshade, Lemon-aspen Lemon Curd and Wattle-seed everything...

A great treat awaits the world when bush tucker at last hits international gourmet circles, as it surely will one day.

GOURMET SURPRISES

Several foods usually thought of as Continental European icons are now produced in Australia to very high quality. Some key examples would be Greek-style feta cheese, olives and olive oil and most extraordinary of all, truffles. Farming of the high-value truffle (using dogs, not pigs, to sniff out the harvest) began in Tasmania in the 1990s. Now there are experimental truffle farms dotted all over in Australia, notably most recently appearing in Western Australia too—the current approximately 800 kilograms (almost one ton) annual national harvest is predicted to rise to 5 up to 10 tonnes by 2013 even without any additional farmers coming onto the scene.

On the olives front, production, branding and marketing are all already very mature and Australian supermarkets now showcase a wide range of Australian-made olive oils, all very tasty indeed. Australia now produces easily 5,000 tonnes of olive oil annually, and exports about half of that.

GROG

We spent a lot of time tramping supermarkets puzzling over where on earth the beer and wine could be, before we cottoned on to the Australian system which has separate 'bottle-shops' (what the British call 'the off-licence') to sell alcohol. If you're feeling lazy, there are plenty of drive-in bottle-shops, allowing you to order and collect through your car window.

Traditionally, Australia has been a beer-drinking nation, and it still holds a place among the world's top 10 beer-drinking nations. But annually, the Aussie today is only knocking back about 83 litres (146 pints) of the stuff, compared with the 1980s when he would have gargled 125 litres (220 pints). As a result, Australia now barely scrapes into the world's top 10 beer-drinking nations, sitting at eighth place in 2010, behind top beer-drinker, the Czech Republic, as well as Ireland (3rd) and Poland (7th). This is a steep fall from number three in the world, Australia's ranking in the early 1990s. Wine is the culprit, wine-sipping is shooting up, now standing at about 25 litres (41 pints) of wine per person by 2011, compared with less than three litres (five pints) in the late 1930s. Australia ranks about the 11th biggest consumer in the world (but well behind the biggest, France, at a whopping 49.6 litres or 87 pints in 2008). In terms of wine production volume, Australia ranks seventh in the world (2008).

Nonetheless, there is a host of beers to choose from, brewed by five major companies: Foster's lager from Victoria is best known abroad, but there are many others, such as Castlemaine's XXXX (Four-ex) from Queensland, VB (Victoria Bitter), Carlton, and Western Australia's Swan Lager, Emu Bitter and Redback (named after the spider), among others— and the very latest cold-filtered beers, such as Carlton Cold, or Tooheys' Hahn Ice, or interesting new boutique beers such as Little Creatures.

The bottle shop, an Aussie institution.

Americans should be warned that the alcohol content in Australian beers is far higher than what they are used to—it is higher than in most British beers too, often over 4 per cent of volume. Some pubs offer in-house brews with extremely high levels (try a Fremantle 'Dog-Bolter', over 5 per cent alcohol). And of course, Australian beer is always drunk ice-cold, hence the importance of the 'esky' or insulated freezer box on trips to the beach or into the bush.

Alcohol has always been an Australian social problem, but it's getting worse, and binge drinking among young people (including school-leaver teenagers) is a big worry. In 2008, about 40 per cent of Australians over 18 were drinking at a measurably risky or high-risk level, and the trend was upwards. The strong possibility of encountering drunks or drink-drivers is one reason my husband and I prefer not to be out and about on weekend nights in Australia's major cities. But drink-driving is rigorously policed, with random checks on all roads, and it can lose you your licence.

Many Australian pubs feature a 'do-it-yourself' breathalyser affixed to the wall, which will tell you whether you are over your limit or not; permitted alcohol limits vary from state to state. It is the custom in all responsible groups of friends, or among husbands and wives, to decide before going out for the night who will remain sober and within the alcohol limits in order to be the driver when the time comes to go home.

A variety of low-alcohol 'light' beers is now available to help moderate drinkers stay within the rules. If you are a woman, remember that female physiology is such that it takes fewer drinks to push your alcohol readings up than for a man.

THE GRAPEVINE

The availability, affordability and high quality of Australian wines are among many good reasons for living in Australia. Nowadays, wine-lovers outside of Australia too have a very good idea of the quality of Australian wines; gone are the days, thankfully, when the country was judged solely on its then outrageous invention, the cardboard-cask wine. Wine exports, at about 700 million litres in 2008, are booming, as are domestic sales (about 464 million litres or a million gallons during 2010-'11), but Australian wine-growers are eyeing a distinct upward trend towards higher consumption of imported foreign wines, now accounting for around seven per cent of Australia's wine consumption, with some discomfort.

A clear indication of the quality of Australian wine is the fact that some of the domestic industry is now in the hands of French investors (names like Bollinger and Veuve Cliquot), with the Japanese also emerging as important players.

Although the big names—Wyndham Estate, Wolf Blass, Seppelt, Hardy Bros, Penfolds, Orlando, Lindemans and the like—dominate the market, there are also regional stars like Western Australia's Leeuwin Estate or Vasse Felix in Margaret River, besides many small independent 'boutique' vineyards, challenging the would-be connoisseur with one-off gems. I myself have much enjoyed bottles from the Cullen's, Fermoy Estate and Moss Wood vineyards, among others in Western Australia.

Note that Australian wines, largely for obvious legal reasons, are named after the grape variety used, e.g. Shiraz, rather than a European counterpart based on location, such as Bordeaux or Beaujolais.

In Vino Veritas

Since the start of the 21st century, Australian wine-lovers have been delighted to find themselves in the midst of a wine glut, making it possible to get excellent wines for just A$ 10-12 a bottle. The 'clean-skins' phenomenon—unbranded bottles of wine stating only the region of provenance and grape type used—has become trendy and canny clean-skin buyers can now walk off with a premium vineyard bottle at a mere A$ 7. This is the result of top vineyards' desperation to clear surplus stock and keep their best bottle prices up. Their loss, our gain. But clean-skins can also be a rip-off, take care.

Australia has 60 wine regions, the major wine-growing states being Western Australia, New South Wales, Victoria and South Australia; the Northern Territory for example, has only one winery.

In Western Australia, you'd best opt for the Margaret River (south-west) and Swan Valley (close to Perth) regions, with newbie southern districts like Pemberton, Mount Barker and Denmark coming along nicely. The state produces superb Cabernet Sauvignon and Merlot reds, as well as tasty Sauvignon Blanc and Semillon whites, also quite respectable Verdelho.

If you are a Chardonnay-buff, stick to the eastern states' wines. An interesting oddity is WA's oldest inland winery (1870s), Coorinja (5914 Toodyay Road, Tel: (08) 9574 2280), outside the country town of Toodyay (a nice stop en route for the fascinating historic Benedictine monastery town of New Norcia, a couple of hours' drive from Perth, noted for its olive cultivation, home-baked bread and cakes, Spanish architecture, pioneer museum and religious art collection), where you can pick up excellent sherries, ports and other fortified wines (try liqueur Shiraz) for bargain basement prices.

Victoria offers rarer fortified styles such as Muscat, in the Rutherglen region, and fine Chardonnay (white) as well as Pinot Noir (red) in the Yarra Valley.

In South Australia are found the famous German-style whites of the Barossa Valley, and other famous regions such as Coonawarra, Clare Valley and McLaren Vale, rich in reds. The jewel among the New South Wales regions is the Hunter Valley, with its exceptional Chardonnay and Shiraz (red).

Red Red Wine

What to try? First, be aware that the only wine that Australian vineyards do not seem to be very good at is champagne (which they are not allowed by the French to call champagne, so look for 'sparkling wine' instead); Australia is still a big importer of the original French champagne. But the Australian version (look for the Pinot Noir-Chardonnay grape blend to get that 'real' champagne taste) is getting better by the minute. Delightful diversions are the pink sparklers often based on Pinot Noir or Shiraz grapes.

A distinctive feature of Australian wines is experimentation with blends of grapes. They are often fruity and soft, easier for novices to enjoy than some French wines. As a very crude guideline, you will probably like Hunter Valley reds (New South Wales) as well as Coonawarra reds (South Australia), Barossa Valley whites (South Australia) as well as Cabernet Sauvignon ('Cab Sav' in Strine) or Merlot from Margaret River (Western Australia) and Chardonnay whites from almost anywhere in the eastern states. The Cabernet Sauvignon-Merlot red blend is particularly in fashion at the moment. The Sauvignon Blanc-Semillon blend is a lovely sparkly white.

Pinot Noir refers to the red grape of Burgundy, best from the cooler areas of Victoria state—it produces a wonderfully light red wine. Shiraz, is another attractive, sometimes tangy, red, particularly when matured in American oak barrels.

> Trivia: in Australia, suave well-heeled left-wingers who frequent big-city boulevard cafes and conduct political debate over a glass of wine are often referred to contemptuously by their right-wing adversaries as 'Chardonnay socialists.'.

The aristocrat among Aussie wines, and the dearest (a cool A$200-A$400 per bottle upwards, depending on the vintage) indisputably is the famous Penfold's Grange Hermitage, a South Australian shiraz, born in the 1950s. It's a collectible, and an investment wine.

A word in your ear about sweet wines ('late harvest' etc), especially if you are Asian (i.e. fond of sweet wines): serious wine-drinking countries like Australia mostly serve sweet wines with ice-cream and desserts, not the main meal!

If you have come from the tropics, you will find it a real joy, after wisely avoiding red wine for years (in the tropics it sends you to sleep in the heat of the afternoon and/or gives you a headache, is too expensive, travels badly and tastes so-so), to sample good red wine once again in an Australian winter. Cheers!

THE PHILISTINE SLANDER

CHAPTER 7

GOANNA + ICE CREAMS
BY BRUCE POLLACK

HOW MUCH FOR A SMALL ONE?

'I was carried by mother Wititj,
I am a Rainbow child, mm mm...'
—Blind Aboriginal singer Geoffrey Gurrumul Yunupingu's
lyrics carry deep cultural references. Here his song
'Djarimirri' recalls the links between his people, the Gumatj
nation of the north-east (Arnhem Land), and their Spirit
Ancestor the Rainbow Python. Australia's arts similarly derive
from the confluence of a wild land, white settlement
and Aboriginal Dreamtime stories.

"AUSTRALIA? IT'S A CULTURAL DESERT!" snorted one of my acquaintances when I told her I had a home in Australia.

Only the very ignorant—perhaps also the blind and deaf—could possibly support such a slander about Australia. Especially with reference to any time after the 1960s. Even before that, there is a case for saying much was going on that the outside world simply did not know about. But the personal commitment to the arts of the 1970s Labor Prime Minister Gough Whitlam did act as an important catalyst to artistic activity.

One of the most stimulating things about the Australian artistic tradition is that, like the continent's ecology, it has often had to evolve in isolation, generating its own forms. At times, that has also been a problem, but more often, distance from the world's more acclaimed artistic centres has been a plus for Australia in terms of achieving a truly singular artistic identity.

Whether the home audience—Australians themselves—always appreciates or understands its own compatriots' artistic achievements is another issue. This is possibly because very few Australian artistic works really address or empathise with ordinary Australian lives as they are today—in a word, urban middle-class. Instead there has been a romantic obsession with the land, the environment and the past in which pioneer Australians battled with Nature to create their present. You can still see this at play in Australian director Sue Brooks' excellent 2003 movie *Japanese Story* starring Australian actress Toni Collette alongside Japan's Gotaro Tsunashima, a bicultural love story with a sting in its tail, set against the backdrop of the Australian wilderness, as you can too in Baz Luhrmann's blockbuster epic *Australia*, released in late 2008.

In recent years, concerns like the environment, feminism and Aboriginal rights, as well as a strong stream of political satire, have been influential themes right across the board of the Australian arts. Development of the arts has been somewhat constrained since the 1990s, however, by the realities first of a national economic downturn, and then of a slightly less generous government.

Despite all that, these days, Australia is stuffed with its own domiciled talent. The generation of Aussie 'expat' artists and writers that once routinely departed for foreign shores, especially London (names like Germaine Greer, Clive James, Barry Humphries and John Pilger), there to snipe at their own homeland, is gradually fading today. It has been replaced by a confident, 'cultural-cringe' free new generation that seeks (and often finds) its fortunes in America, or else forges creative partnerships with US production houses (Aussie film director George Miller's animated penguin saga *Happy Feet Two* was an example in 2011). This is a sensible strategic response to globalised competition in the arts. But increasingly, Australian performers and artists can hold their heads high on the international stage, where they already enjoy a considerable reputation for professionalism and also distinctive, innovative individualism.

Some of the liveliest and richest Australian artistic endeavour can be seen 'on the fringe' or at the community-neighbourhood level, perhaps not as well publicised as the more formal events. You must seek it out for yourself; it is there, tucked away in obscure corners. Like Western Australia's open secret, American-born 'Lucky Oceans', genial host of ABC Radio National's influential *The Planet* programme, but also an internationally acclaimed pedal steel guitarist and well-known for his zydeco-style band

Children from Goollelal Primary School in Kinsgley, Western Australia, dress up in vibrant costumes and have a parade on the streets.

The Zydecats. Look out for his gigs, often around the port town of Fremantle just outside Perth.

On the Australian art scene, small very often means even more beautiful—like the exquisite performance of one of Gilbert and Sullivan's ultra-British, Victorian-era operettas that I stumbled upon one evening in a quiet suburb of Perth, or the laid-back exhibition by young artists in a converted Fremantle warehouse, against the backdrop of Moroccan and Malay drummers, or the Caribbean reggae gig in a Perth pub, or the bouncing Seychellois folk music another evening, the blues musicians in the bars of Fremantle, or...

There is no shortage of cultural things to do, see, hear and experience in Australia—all this in Perth, supposedly a backwater that isn't anywhere near the centre of all that is going on.

STILL PICTURES

The ancient and sacred tradition of Aboriginal art has already been dealt with in Chapter 3: The People (pages 125–127). It has taken a long time for this school of art to influence the work of white Australian artists; there was no sign of real interchange until after World War II. A turning point was the comprehensive exhibition of Aboriginal art displayed at the Australian National Gallery in 1989, seven years after the Gallery's foundation. Today, the understanding and the actual practice of Aboriginal art has expanded far beyond the 'dot paintings', 'X-ray' styles and bark or rock paintings that rightly first impressed white society, to include much more sophisticated and contemporary styles and materials, including new skills such as sculpture, weaving and Indonesian-style wax-resist *batik* fabric art. In 2005, a life-size reed-woven 4WD jeep sculpture produced by the women of a remote Aboriginal community caused quite a sensation with its innovative, witty style.

Painters of the 1850s gold rush at last abandoned earlier colonial artists' picturesque, Eurocentric distortions of the Australian landscape and began to record truly Australian scenes—painters like S T Gill on the goldfields or Tom Roberts on the Australian landscape and lifestyle.

The Australian art world remained for the most part resolutely conservative right through the 1920s and 1930s, taking only slight notice of the revolutions of impressionism, cubism, surrealism and so on, abroad. The social-realist depiction of immigrant and working-class suffering favoured by a group of artists led by Noel Counihan and Josi Bergner during the 1950s somehow seemed more 'Australian'.

One expatriate Australian artist who is particularly well known overseas is Sir Sidney Nolan (1917–1992). He developed a number of styles—abstract before World War II, more topic-oriented after the war, with famous works on Australian historical episodes, such as the WWI debacle at Gallipoli, bush-ranger Ned Kelly, and the ill-fated Burke and Wills expedition.

Charming mural on a wall in the Western Australian Wheat Belt town of Carnamah. It shows the typical farmer taking a break from a hard day's work, with his typical working farm dogs by his side.

For the period immediately following World War II, names that leap to mind include Albert Namatjira (1902–1959), the Aboriginal watercolourist from Central Australia who switched with ease to European styles and techniques; Donald Friend, who lived and worked in Bali in 1967–80, producing complex, sensual works until he died in Australia in 1989; and Sir Russell Drysdale (1912–1981), whose landscapes dwelled on the harsh Australian terrain, on outback lifestyles and the Aboriginal people.

American avant-garde thinking began to influence Australian artists as the 1960s moved into the 1970s. However, there are several men-unto-themselves, like neo-expressionist Peter Booth, who specialises in the frightening, the doom-laden and the bizarre. Women artists have also begun to play a bigger role in cultural life in recent years.

It is interesting to note that the latent puritanism in Australian society could surface in the art world as late as 1982, when New South Wales police raided a Sydney gallery to seize Juan Davila's work, *Stupid as a Painter*, for being 'sexually explicit'. However, the painting was later returned to the gallery. In more recent years, controversy has tended to centre more on artistic works considered by some to be offensive to Christians, as with the exhibition by American photographer Andres Serrano at the National Gallery of Victoria in 1997 that included the image *Piss Christ* depicting a crucifix submerged in urine; the exhibition was quickly closed down.

Australia's current extreme fear and loathing of paedophilia provoked another censorship incident in 2008, when art photographer Bill Henson was taken to task, and investigated by police, for exhibiting photos of nude children as young as 12, and also adolescent teenagers. Even the then Prime Minister Kevin Rudd was moved to call them 'revolting'. Such incidents are all the more bemusing in a country that feels free enough to indulge in quirky and outrageous stage entertainments like *Puppetry of the Penis,* pioneered in 1997 by comedians Simon Morley and David Friend and featured in Mike Molloy's documentary film of 2000, *Tackle Happy.* The fun contortions that Morley and Friend manage to contrive with their own personal 'tackle' is perhaps best left to your imagination for the time being.

Australian art today is vibrant and diverse, with a distinct character of its own and a much more realistic appreciation of the country's natural environment. From the funky graphics of designer Ken Done to the sometimes tortured explorations of Brett Whiteley (died 1992), Australian art has found its place on the international scene. And let us not forget that the most iconic Aussie expat of them all, the multi-talented Rolf Harris, now in England, donned his artist's beret-hat in 2005 to serve the throne when Queen Elizabeth II of England consented to let him produce a formal portrait of Her Majesty (also Queen of Australia, remember) for her 80th birthday celebrations.

Biggest 'Chook Raffle' of Them All

The Archibald Prize for portraiture is Australia's oldest, best-known and most controversy-stalked visual arts award. Its judgements are always eagerly awaited and debated by the arts world. This coveted prize offers the winner A$75,000 cash and a guaranteed national profile. Final judgement is delivered by the Trustees of the Art Gallery of New South Wales. It all started in 1921 with a bequest from Jules Francois Archibald, the editor of Australia's current affairs weekly *The Bulletin*, setting up the prize for the best portrait of a distinguished Australian produced over the past year by an artist resident in 'Australasia'. To make things more democratic, a 'People's Award' category was introduced in 1988—the gap between the expert judges' and the popular vote for the prize is often instructive.

In 2008, whereas the main prize went to Sydney artist Del Kathryn Barton for her self-portrait with her young son, the People's Prize went to Vincent Fantauzzo's arresting portrait of 28 year-old Australian film-star Heath Ledger, completed during the shooting of his compelling performance as 'The Joker' in the 'Batman' movie The Dark Knight, only weeks before Ledger's death in New York, apparently from a mistaken medications overdose while under stress.

In 1991, yet another prize category was created, the 'Packing Room Prize', where the behind-the-scenes workers who unpack and hang the Archibald entries, vote for their choice. This one is always awarded a couple of days before the Archibald Prize proper.

Sir William Dobell's much disputed win in 1943 gained the prize somewhat negative publicity when the subject of Dobell's painting, fellow artist Joshua Smith, took offence, and a lawsuit, against Dobell on the grounds that his work was not a portrait but a caricature. Smith lost the case, thus pushing the boundaries of what kind of art could be considered for the prize.

Just for the record, the 2012 prize went to veteran artist Tim Storrier's bizarre (alleged) self-portrait (without a face) *The Histrionic Wayfarer*, inspired by 16th-century painter Hieronymus Bosch. While Storrier remarked wryly that his win would make him "the most unpopular artist in the country – with other artists," the 2005 winner, John Olsen, once described the Archibald as a "chook raffle," a dismissive term for a parochial, small-time Australian neighbourhood fund-raising event that raffles chickens, cooked or otherwise.

Tales of Two Cities

Melbourne and Sydney are old rivals and perhaps in no area more than the arts. Goldrush wealth in the 1850s made Victoria rich, hence the rise of its capital city Melbourne as a major cultural centre, well endowed with wealthy merchant patrons of the arts.

Melbourne established the country's first public art gallery, the National Gallery of Victoria, in 1861. Since the

Located on Bennelong Point, the Sydney Opera House was officially opened by Queen Elizabeth II on 20 October 1973.

mid-1990s, this gallery has been housed in two buildings at separate locations, one housing important Australian works, the other an impressive array of acquired European and international art.

The Art Gallery of New South Wales, founded in 1875, is housed in what was supposed to be a 'temporary' building back in 1895 and also features a good collection of colonial Australian art.

Perth too has its own extensive Art Gallery of Western Australia, founded in 1895, housing an important indigenous art collection, and also collections focused on design and graphic arts, as well as Western Australian art.

Australian painting got a big boost with the opening of the Australian National Gallery in Canberra in 1982, late though this was for such an institution to emerge for the first time. The ANG was quite recently handsomely extended.

MOVING PICTURES

There were Australian films made before World War II, some of them very good, but for the purpose of this book, what happened after the war is probably most interesting.

The Australian cinema virtually slumbered after the

war, until the Labor government of Gough Whitlam set up the Australian Film Development Corporation, later the Australian Film Commission (AFC), in 1970. The AFC created the government's own film-making unit, Film Australia, and also funded other films. Naturally, this immediately stimulated a new rush of cinematic creativity. One of the most active participants was Phillip Adams, also known today as a newspaper columnist and advertising guru. Since then, Australian film-makers and directors have won an undoubted place in world cinema with their unique style.

Among the giants of the Australian industry are names like:

- Bruce Beresford—*The Getting of Wisdom* (1977), *Breaker Morant* (1980), *Driving Miss Daisy* (1990), *Black Robe* (1991) set in indigenous Canada, *Paradise Road (1997),* and *Mao's Last Dancer* (2009)
- Fred Schepisi—*The Chant of Jimmie Blacksmith* (1978), *Evil Angels* (1988), *Six Degrees of Separation* (1993), *and The Eye of the Storm* (2011), an outstanding dramatisation of novelist Patrick White's portrayal of a dysfunctional family
- George Miller – *Max Max trilogy* (1979-1985), *The Witches of Eastwick* (1987), *Lorenzo's Oil* (1992), *Babe* (1995), and *Happy Feet* (2006)
- Gillian Armstrong—*My Brilliant Career* (1978), *The Last Days of Chez Nous* (1992), *Oscar and Lucinda* (1997), *Charlotte Gray* (2001), and *Love, Lust and Lies* (2009), Part 5 of a life-long documentary on three women's evolving lives
- Peter Weir—*Picnic at Hanging Rock* (1975), *Gallipoli* (1981), *The Year of Living Dangerously* (1982—an interesting exposition of the Australian interface with Indonesia at a turbulent time), *Fearless* (1993), *Dead Poets Society* (1989), *The Truman Show* (1998) and *Master and Commander* (2003)
- Phillip Noyce—*Patriot Games* (1992), *Rabbit-Proof Fence* (2002), *The Quiet American* (2002), and *Catch a Fire* (2006)
- Rolf de Heer—*Bad Boy Bubby* (1993), *The Tracker* (2004) and *Ten Canoes* (2006)

Weir, Schepisi, Beresford and Noyce have all long since removed themselves to the USA, where the substantial expat

Aussie film-maker and movie star community is often tagged 'the Gum-Leaf Mafia'.

Many of the more interesting of these films, from the point of view of the non-Australian, are those which deal with the Australian landscape and Australian history or issues. I would rate *Picnic at Hanging Rock, Gallipoli, The Chant of Jimmie Blacksmith, Rabbit-Proof Fence, The Tracker* (these last three all indictments of white attitudes to Aboriginals), *Japanese Story, The Dish* and *The Castle* (see below), and *Kenny* (compelling porta-loo humour) pretty highly as paths to understanding the Australian psyche. Unmissable too are Rolf de Heer's *Ten Canoes* fable, narrated and acted by Aboriginals in their own language, and Aboriginal director Warwick Thornton's heart-rending début *Samson and Delilah* (2009).

Early Australian cinema was somewhat slow-moving, melancholic even, and this tradition has survived into the 1990s with contributions like Gillian Armstrong's wistful dissection of a failing marriage, *The Last Days of Chez Nous*, and *The Sum of Us* by Geoff Burton and Kevin Dowling, a moving examination of a father's reconciliation with his son's homosexuality.

But more typical of the 1990s crop were literally punchy works like *Romper Stomper*, a brutal stare at street warfare between Vietnamese gangs and white skinheads in a Melbourne suburb, and delightful comedies such as Baz Luhrmann's bitter-sweet *Strictly Ballroom* starring twinkletoes heart-throb Paul Mercurio, the romantic (straight) *Muriel's Wedding* (featuring the then newbie, now big star, Toni Collette, looking incredibly different – plump and naïve – from her current US TV role in *United States of Tara*), the glamorous (gay) *Priscilla, Queen of the Desert*, and the farcical *The Castle*, depicting a very ordinary family's battle to stop their home being compulsorily acquired. Following the trail blazed across the world and in the USA by *Crocodile Dundee* in 1986, starring archetypal bushman Paul Hogan, George Miller and Chris Noonan's animatronics triumph *Babe,* and Scott Hicks' *Shine* about mentally-ill Western-Australian concert pianist David Helfgott (played by Geoffrey Rush) won international accolades and box-office returns in the

1990s. Rush has gone on to play magnificently in *Elizabeth* and *Shakespeare in Love* (both in 1998), *The Tailor of Panama* (2001), *Pirates of the Caribbean: The Curse of the Black Pearl* (2003),*The Life and Death of Peter Sellers* (2004), and *The Eye of the Storm* (2011).

New-Zealand-born Australian woman director Jane Campion took the coveted Palme d'Or best-film award with her dark drama *The Piano* at the Cannes Film Festival in 1993, and continues such quality, as in *Portrait of a Lady* (1997) and *Bright Star* (2009).

Notable Australian film actors not already mentioned include Judy Davis, Rachel Griffiths, Sam Neill, Jack Thompson, Hugo Weaving, Hugh Jackman and the late lamented Heath Ledger. And does anyone remember that the swashbuckling Errol Flynn, darling of the 1930s, was in fact a Tasmanian-Australian? Another bright Australian star, Cate Blanchett, has proved her talent in *Oscar and Lucinda* and *Elizabeth*, also playing the iconic Katharine Hepburn in director Martin Scorsese's 2004 movie *The Aviator* and almost incredibly, playing Bob Dylan in *I'm Not There* (2007), followed by a stellar performance alongside Brad Pitt in *The Curious Case of Benjamin Button* (2008).

Aussies are big in Hollywood these days. Oscar-winners include Judy Davis (*A Passage to Indian, The Eye of the Storm*), Nicole Kidman (*Eyes Wide Shut, Moulin Rouge, Australia, The Hours*), Russell Crowe, Geoffrey Rush, Mel Gibson (he of *Max Max* way back and more recently in 2004, *The Passion of the Christ*), Toni Collette, Jacki Weaver, and the late Heath Ledger. Crowe, though personally temperamental by all accounts, is a stunningly versatile actor, shining in diverse roles through L.A. *Confidential* (1997), *The Insider* (1999), *Gladiator* (2000), *A Beautiful Mind* (2001), *Master and Commander* (2003), *American Gangster* (2007) and *Body of Lies* (2008).

Australian movie-makers' quirky style has continued in the 21st century, with delicious contributions such as *The Dish* (2001), about Australia's contribution to America's 1969 moon-walk via a satellite dish in a boondocks place called Parkes, and the fantasy extravaganza, Baz Luhrmann's *Moulin Rouge* (2001). There has also been the murderous but very clever *Chopper* (2000), the interior tale of a notorious Australian criminal, starring Australian Eric Bana, now well established internationally (*Troy* 2004, *Munich* 2005, *Romulus, My Father* 2007). Another strong Aussie film was *Lantana* (2001), featuring Anthony Lapaglia (besides Geoffrey Rush). More recently, Kriv Stenders' *Red Dog* (2011), the quirky true story of an Aussie dog who became a hero in the tough north-western mining region of Western Australia, and also the much harder-edged crime drama, David Michôd's *Animal Kingdom* (2010) – the latter winning stellar Australian actress Jacki Weaver long overdue awards and acclaim, while also showcasing once again the outstanding talent of Australian actors Guy Pearce and Joel Edgerton. At the end of 2011, Julia Leigh's erotic *Sleeping Beauty* also caused critical waves internationally, including at the Cannes Film Festival.

Australians in Hollywood

Here's a selection from Screen Australia's top 10 Australian movies in terms of how many times they were viewed by Australians in 2011, via all media (e.g. DVDs).

Australia (2008) – Baz Luhrmann's epic Darwin-centred romantic drama combined with WWII and Aboriginal history, starring Nicole Kidman and Hugh Jackman.

Mao's Last Dancer (2009) – Bruce Beresford's adaptation of Chinese ballet-dancer Li Cunxin's autobiography (he's now an Australian stockbroker), with Chi Cao, principal dancer at the Birmingham Royal Ballet, UK, in the lead role.

Charlie & Boots (2009) – Dean Murphy's road cum father-son movie set in rugged northern Australia and featuring the ageing Paul Hogan (dad) with Shane Jacobson.

(Continued on the next page)

> *(Continued from previous page)*
>
> *Bran Nu Dae* (2010) – Aboriginal director Rachel Perkins' lively road movie based on Jimmy Chi's musical about Aboriginal life in 1960s Western Australia; a star-studded cast includes Geoffrey Rush, Ernie Dingo, Magda Szubanski, Ningali Lawford and Jessica Mauboy.
>
> *The Black Balloon* (2009) – Elissa Down's much acclaimed study of a young boy's journey in coping with his autistic elder brother, starring Toni Collette, Rhys Wakefield and Luke Ford.
>
> *Mrs Carey's Concert* (2011) – probably the most successful documentary film ever in Australia, the true story of a dedicated music teacher's determination to get her 1,200 girls to performance standard for a concert at the fabled Sydney Opera House. Directed by Bob Connolly and Sophie Raymond.

As part of a worldwide trend, Australia too has made its contribution to the popular 'diaspora genre' of films that tell the story of migrants' up-and-down experiences in their adopted countries: try Eric Bana's tender performance in *Romulus My Father* (2007), about European migrants farming in Victoria state during the early 1960s; Macao-born Tony Ayres' semi-autobiographical *Home Song Stories* (2007) starring the luminous Joan Chen as a desperate former Shanghai nightclub singer fallen on hard times and trying to bring up her children in 1970s Australia; the much less arty but fun *The Wog Boy* (could such a title survive in any other country?) of 2000, written by Nick Giannopoulos about the lives and loves of his fellow Australian-born Mediterranean types (mostly Greek); *Footy Legends* (2006), a happy movie along the lines of the UK's *Bend It Like Beckham*, that tells of Luc Vu, a Vietnamese Australian from Sydney, who is obsessed with the Australian footy game and risks all to win a sporting competition; *Looking for Alibrandi* (2000), a chronicle of a young Australian-Italian girl's struggle against her parents' clinging family and foreign mores. A new offering in this genre during 2011 was Pauline Chan's 33 *Postcards*, a pioneer co-production between Australia and China. It explores a cross-cultural relationship between an orphaned Chinese teenager played by Zhu Lin and her Australian sponsor (Guy Pearce), who turns out to be in prison.

A documentary also worth seeking out on DVD is *A Sense of Place* (2007), a short account of four very different Vietnamese who have made Australia their home for the past 30 years. The same goes for *Race for the Beach* (2007) about the remarkable Mecca Laa Laa, Australia's first female Muslim lifesaver on the beaches of Cronulla, New South Wales. SBS Television in particular has produced many fascinating documentaries likes these on the stories of countless first and second-generation settlers.

A really fun—and sometimes tasteless—bit of viewing is *Not Quite Hollywood* (2008), a candid documentary ('doco' in true Strine) collation of some the worst 'Ozexploitation' stereotype movies of the 1970s. It's an embarrassing survey of some quite bad movies, but it says something interesting about Australia's most cinematically naïve era. Also a genuine giggle is the *Cane Toads* doco (1988), a tragi-comic exploration of the invasion of alien Hawaiian sugar cane toads in northern Australia now threatening native biodiversity.

Sadly, Australian audiences still have to be won over to Australian productions. Under the umbrella government agency Screen Australia, formed in 2008, enhanced funding and tax incentives are at last stimulating activity in the domestic movie industry. But in real terms, home-grown movies cornered only A$42.9 million of a total A$1-billion box-office take in Australia during 2011. In 2008, had it not been for Luhrmann's much-hyped film *Australia*, not even 1 per cent of cinema tickets sold in Australia would have been for an Australian film.

THESPIAN THINGS
In theatre as in other arts, government support in the past has been a stimulus, specifically the establishment in 1975 (another Whitlam creation) of a government-funded statutory authority, the Australia Council for the Arts.

Aboriginal theatre and dance are thriving, although most of the recent action in the indigenous performing arts seems centred on the cinema and also quality television drama. An established name in Aboriginal dance is Bangarra Dance Theatre, founded in Sydney in 1989—you'll have to be very quick off the mark to beat the queue for their tickets when they are in town. The name Jack Davis towers above all others in this niche, his *Sugar* of 1985 and *In Our Town* (1990) both still standards on countless theatre companies' repertoires. Davis, a Western Australian Aboriginal from the Noongar people of the south-west, died in 2000 at the age of 83. Western Australia continues a tradition of indigenous theatre, notably through the Yirra Yaakin Noongar Theatre group established since 1993.

Australia's most productive, best-known playwright now is David Williamson, with plays like *The Removalists* (1971), *Don's Party* (1973), *Travelling North* (1980) and *Influence* (2005—a shot at Australia's often right-wing rabble-rousing 'shock-jock' journalist and radio hosts). With a backlist of more than 35 plays now, he is among the few Australian artists to examine average middle-class Australian life. Other Australian theatre standards are Louis Nowra's *Cosi* (1992), exploring a stage production by mental hospital patients, and *Cloudstreet* (1998), Nick Enright and Justin Monjo's five-hour adaptation from the classic Tim Winton novel set in Perth, besides musician Jimmy Chi's energetic musical *Bran Nu Dae*.

One of the richest and most successful of all Australian live-stage acts, going strong for years now, is a children's show staged by the amiable four-man group The Wiggles, on the road now for a full 21 years. Their well-crafted and cheeringly innocent onstage idiocies, complete with lovable characters like Dorothy Dinosaur, are a global hit with tiny tots, and their parents. And the show has made these hard-working blokes rich, at mega-star level, with an estimated combined annual income of around A\$50 million. They have sold 23 million DVDs and seven million CDs since 1991. But a generational handover is underway right now. In 2013, only one of the current Wiggles will remain. New faces, including a woman, Emma Watkins, will pick up the Wiggles baton.

THE BOX

Television has also fostered Australian theatre, partly through its attempts to comply with rulings that set a minimum quota for Australian-origin television drama (although the big television story of the late 1990s was the rise of quality programming on the so-called 'ethnic' channel, SBS, now as much respected as the ABC). The ABC's recent well-crafted drama series such as the suburban saga *The Slap* (based on Christos Tsiolkas' bestselling novel) and the mouth-wateringly elegant *Miss Fisher's Murder Mysteries* have signalled big changes in audiences and in Australian society, with more sophisticated staging and acting, strong plots and diverse, often multicultural, characterisation, not to speak of top-notch acting by stars like Jonathan LaPaglia, Alex Dimitriades and Essie Davis (Miss Fisher).

As in other countries, however, much of today's television is toxic to real theatre, struggling to compete with a barrage of 'lifestyle' programmes, from the ABC's *Gardening Australia* (now hosted by the hairy community-hugger, 'Costa') to a host of quality imports from England, or *Better Homes and Gardens* on Network Seven etc, as well as dancing-talent contest shows like *So You Think You can Dance, Australia*. And worse still, the internationally franchised pestilence of countless 'reality TV' shows pops up everywhere. No room for actors there.

Home-grown soap operas like *Neighbours* (yes, it's still running, on Channel Eleven, heading for 7,000 episodes since its début in 1985) have always been hits. This series was the theatrical cradle of global star Kylie Minogue in her role as 'Charlene' during the 1980s, and has been watched by more than 15 million British viewers too. Aussie sitcoms and comedy shows are often excellent but for some reason always burn themselves out quickly, more on the *Fawlty Towers* model than the *Seinfeld* one, so you have to catch them while you can. One quintessentially Australian gem has been *Kath and Kim* (premiered 2002), a scary recital of all that is most mundane and banal in Australian suburban life, set in the fictional Fountain Lakes estate. Since it isn't on TV nowadays, go get the DVDs or whatever; it will be worth it for the deep probe into Australian manners and mores that the series offers. This is the natural, and in some ways more subtle yet more relaxed and comfortable, heir to Barry Humphries' acerbic observations of 'Moonee Ponds' (see below).

The Artistic Bottom Line

In 2001–2002, the Australian production of cultural goods and services was valued at almost A\$ 48 billion. Australian Bureau of Statistics figures for 2007 show that arts and leisure employ more than 3.5 million Australians, including more than 700,000 virtually full-time workers.

—Figures from the Australian Bureau of Statistics

CABARET AND COMEDY

Australian performers seem particularly adept at cabaret comedy and satire, both of which translate well to the small screen. But in recent years, there has been far less comedic material around in the arts than there used to be, with the new focus now much more on 'serious' drama. Could it be that as Australia has matured into an international player on the global board game, she has begun to grow up and lose her sense of humour?

King of the field—or should one say, Queen?—has been Barry Humphries, but his generation, one that made its début in the 1950s and'60s, is now in the twilight zone and his most iconic, putatively immortal, creation has very recently announced retirement from the stage: 'Dame Edna Everage' (Everage = Average, geddit?) has been perceived by the Australian public as an entirely real person. Journalists interview her straight, no mention of Barry Humphries. You need to know this, or else you may swallow Dame Edna, the 'housewife megastar', hook, line and sinker, without ever realising you have been experiencing satire, in drag. In her huge horned specs, the Dame is reminiscent of old English pantomime dames, given to addressing her fans as 'Possums.' She has written her autobiography, *My Gorgeous Life*.

Humphries also created a cluster of other unattractive personae, including the vile 'Ocker' Aussie cartoon-strip character Barry McKenzie, who popularised 'Strine' in Britain, the buck-toothed, improperly behaved Australian diplomat Sir Leslie Paterson, and the quietly tragic but boring resident of some Melbourne suburb, Sandy Stone, who would appear in his dressing gown and bedroom slippers to spout his ignorant and racist views.

Other well-known names like Paul Hogan have also reached their 'use-by' date. Popular in the eastern states and on TV has been acerbic game-show host and satirist Paul McDermott of the popular *Good News Week* on Network Ten, a younger generation but still old news.

Probably the most impressive new celebrity and heir to the Australian comedic tradition is musical satirist Western Australian Tim Minchin, whose leprechaun-like appearance on stage, with his wildly tousled locks, deep dark eye make-up and usually bare feet, can be mesmerising. Born in 1975, this innovative performer has made waves from Melbourne and as far afield as the Edinburgh Festival Fringe with his iconoclastic explorations of everything from sex, drugs and rock n' roll to religion (he is a card-carrying atheist). He now bases in London, so if you get a chance to see him on tour in Australia, you should take it.

Even more one of a kind are the confronting topics addressed by two very special comedians, cerebral palsy victim and comedian 'Steady Eddy', and Vietnamese former 'boat person' refugee Hung Le

There has also been the phenomenon of 'Mary G', a kind of Aboriginal Dame Edna, played by Mark bin Bakar, a Broome-based Aboriginal celebrity already carrying many 'gongs' (awards) such as the West Australian of the Year title for 2007, making him a front-runner nominee for the Australian of the Year title in 2008. His Malay-sounding name betrays the mixed-race heritage of many Broome Aboriginals. His alter ego Mary G aka 'Queen of the Kimberley' has been described as a "straight-talking, wise-cracking Aboriginal matriarch" by West Australian writer Belle Taylor. In the 1980s, he was the creator-founder of

Abmusic, a Perth-based institution that fosters Aboriginal musicians, first starting it in his own house—it now runs out of the historic Clontarf College grounds near Curtin University. In 1992 he also created 'Stompen Ground', a key Aboriginal music festival. His Mary G character, who has been seen on national SBS TV, is notable not just for her raw humour but also for the 'message' she conveys to indigenous youth—stay away from drugs and alcohol, look after your money. Apparently, the Aboriginal elders just love this entertaining support for their own drive to put indigenous youngsters on the right path.

Ethnic humour such as that purveyed by Vietnamese Hung Le is now as common as it is in other western societies dealing with migrant and minority issues these days. An excellent contribution from SBS TV in 2008 was the pathbreaking *Salam Cafe*, featuring Australian Muslims themselves the funny, sad and ludicrous aspects of being an Aussie Muslim. This excellent and almost painfully hilarious show is no longer onscreen but there are plenty of references to it on YouTube, so go check—try for instance 'Working with Muslims' at http://www.youtube.com/watch?v = GCWBrMPZtH0

However, it has to be said that far too much Aussie humour is based on very rude four-letter words and raw sexual vulgarity. At its best though, it pushes the boundaries in a creative way.

You can make a study of the Australian sense of humour just by watching the TV ads, some of which are quite hilarious and utterly unlike ads you will see anywhere else. A 2005 ad for Carlton beer, has for Carlton beer, has an epic-scale cast of hundreds rushing around impressive open spaces to form a huge image of a human being drinking beer that can be seen clearly from the air—the operatically chanted captions for this ad run something like "This is a big ad... a very big ad... and expensive too... it's a bloody big ad... it had bloody well better sell some beer..." etc. Uncomfortably though, many Australian feature 'blokey' themes along the lines of 'Nothing can compare with a good beer—including sex, my

Another Aussie wit who made his name largely overseas is the urbane Clive James, well known to British television viewers.

wife/my girlfriend' etc, which kind of tells you something... Still other ads simply embarrass with their attempts at humour via stereotypical portrayals, for example of Chinese (slanty eyes, buck teeth) when marketing pre-mix packets of Fried Noodles, or Indians (funny accents, turbans) when it's sachets of Rogan Josh.

FANCY FOOTWORK

Ballet has always—quite wrongly, of course—been derided by philistines as a 'sissy' art. In this context, it is intriguing that 'macho' Australia should have excelled in this very art form. There are something like 2,500 ballet schools in the country now.

The great dancer Sir Robert Helpmann, active in the 1920s–1930s, was Australian. Other great Australian dancers include Marilyn Jones (most active in the 1950s), Meryl Tankard of the Australian Dance Theatre, Paul Mercurio (known for his role in *Strictly Ballroom*) of the Sydney Dance Company and Lisa Bolte of The Australian Ballet (founded in 1962 with the eminent Dame Peggy Van Praagh as its first director, thereafter well-shepherded by Maina Gielgud, from 1983-1986). Artistic Director since 2001 is David McAllister. The 'AB' enjoys an international reputation for excellence, staging some 200 shows a year at home and abroad.

MUSIC
The Serious Stuff

Opera Australia is Australia's largest performing arts organisation but heavily dependent on government subsidies, at about A\$20 million a year. It was established in Sydney as the Australian Elizabethan Theatre Trust, but was recreated in 1996 as it is today. The opening of the magnificent Sydney Opera House in 1973 has ever since given the company a proper home, and boosted the art. An interesting development since 1996 has been the development of the company's *Oz Opera* arm dedicated to taking opera on the road, to the Australian people, no matter how remote their location. Lyndon Terracini

Time to Change

Opera Australia's Artistic Director Lyndon Terracini, himself a baritone opera singer, showed a deep understanding of where the Australian arts have to go, and in many cases already are going, in the new age, in his 2011 Peggy Glanville-Hicks Address, Sydney, extracted below:

I noticed recently in our extremely successful production of La Boheme... that when we had an African-American soprano and a Korean tenor singing the leading roles, we had more audience members from those ethnic communities than we usually see in the theatre...We are in real danger of creating an elitist arts community and an audience that is not representative of contemporary Australia... Our food culture has voraciously embraced the changing demographic, and consequently some of the most innovative eating in the world can be found in Sydney and Melbourne... It's a hybrid of extraordinary eating experiences, so why haven't we, as creative artists in music and theatre in particular, replicated the success of our creative culinary colleagues? Why are we so protective of our meat and three veg that we refuse to consider the extraordinary tastes of Asia? ...

We expect to see English or American acting styles represented on our stages, and when we don't see that from ethnically diverse artists we complain about over- or poor acting. This is because we want to see a Korean singer, for example, acting like a European, or an American. In fact what was extremely interesting in the Opera Australia production of *La Boheme* recently was that the artist to whom I'm referring responded emotionally (particularly at Mimi's death), the way a Korean man would respond. We from Anglo/European stock may not like that acting style and emotional response, but when you watch Asian cinema you will see a very different style of acting – an Asian style – and Asian audiences connect strongly to it because it reflects the way they are conditioned to respond. We need to consider the performance styles we employ and the way we attempt to communicate artistically with a changing audience.

Australia's favourite animal, the koala. Today, the greatest threat facing the lovable koala is the loss of its natural habitat. It is believed that there are only about 50,000–80,000 koalas remaining in Australia.

Australia is home to many majestic beaches, and the white, sandy coastlines are well loved by both tourists and locals alike.

Australia has a lively cafe and pub culture. Here friends and families enjoy an evening meal and drinks at a restaurant at Circular Quay, Sydney.

The Melbourne Cup is Australia's most important annual horse race and one of the most popular spectator events in the country. Melbourne Cup fever takes over the city on this public holiday and attendees arrive decked out in their most fashionable and stunning outfits.

FREET STATION

NA

RM

RAIN FOR

ST ALBANS
LINE

PLATFORM 5

NEXT TRAIN FOR

BROADMEADOWS
LINE

PLATFORM 5

NEXT TRAIN FOR

UPFIELD
LINE

PLATFORM 5

NEXT TRAIN FOR

WERRIE
LINE

PLATFORM

NEXT

Customer Servic

Flinders Street Station is among Melbourne's most recognisable
landmarks and is the hub of Melbourne's transport system.
The station is also a popular meeting place, usually under the
row of clocks above the main entrance, which indicate the
departure time of the next train on each line.

Australian Lebanese-Muslim girl life-saver Mecca Laa Laa proudly shows off her Australian-designed cover-all Islamic 'Burqini' swim costume on a Sydney beach.

Australia has produced more than her share of world-class operatic singers, with sopranos Dame Nellie Melba (1861-1931) and Dame Joan Sutherland (1926-2010) among the most famous, and new names like Aboriginal singer Deborah Cheetham rising fast.

Among composers, another Sutherland, Margaret (died 1984), stands out for her Australian-themed classical compositions. Percy Grainger of *Country Garden* fame is another well-known name (see the movie Passion for an account of his bizarre private life). Other cherished names include internationally rated classical guitarist John Williams. Each of Australia's six states has its own resident symphony orchestra, nurtured to quite a high standard. And classical music lovers can tune into ABC Radio's Classic FM station all day long for wall-to-wall music.

The Other Stuff

You must have heard of the Bee Gees and the Easy Beats. Perhaps also of INXS, Men At Work, Midnight Oil, Little River Band, AC/DC, Air Supply and The Black Sorrows. Almost certainly of Olivia Newton-John and Kylie Minogue (a whole crop of Kylies is growing all over Australia, thanks to her). And what better illustration of the Aussie sense of humour than Bjorn Again, the Abba look-alike-sound-alike that started in Melbourne in 1988? They are all Australian pop bands and singers of course. Men At Work are to be commended in particular for having given the world the song 'Down Under', containing the immortal words:

'I said, "Do you speak my language?"
He just smiled and gave me a Vegemite sandwich.'

Among other groups that have been rated highly, either inside Australia or beyond, are Midnight Oil (now defunct since gangling lead singer Peter Garrett went into Labor politics and became Minister for School Education, Early Childhood and Youth), Regurgitator, Savage Garden (split in 2001), Silverchair (still big), Mental as Anything, Powderfinger and The Screaming Jets. On the rock and pop solo vocalist scene, Jimmy Barnes and John Farnham go on forever, seemingly indestructible monuments.

The white-Aboriginal fusion band Gondwanaland is excellent but seems relatively cerebral compared with the raw energy of Yothu Yindi, straight from the Aboriginal heartland of Arnhem Land, a band sprung from among the Yolngu people, demonstrating a stunning blend of traditional sound and Western technology. Listen to their song 'Treaty' on their *Tribal Voice* album, 'Super Highway' on the album *Bercuta*, and get their latest, sixth, album *Garma*. Much of their genius derives from the vision of schoolteacher and lead singer Mandawuy Yunupingu, voted 1992 'Australian of the Year', and the first Aboriginal from Arnhem Land to achieve a tertiary degree.

Kylie Minogue needs no introduction. From her sweet girl-next-door image in the *Neighbours* soapie, she has morphed into a sexy icon (adopted as a mascot by Gay-dom), but still retains something essentially fresh and Aussie about her when she fronts up for personal interviews.

Aussie singers such as Kate Ceberano, Delta Goodrem and Natalie Imbruglia are also visible on the international radar, and Malaysian-born Guy Sebastian, winner of the first *Australian Idol* contest in 2003, has also carved himself a solid reputation. Songwriter and singer Paul Kelly is a national icon.

But there is no doubt that the latest singing sensation from Australia is the sweet-voiced blind Aboriginal Geoffrey Gurrumul Yunupingu, a self-taught musician who nevertheless served an apprenticeship with Yothu Yindi before going solo. His moving friendship with his white producer Michael Hohnen, creative director of Skinny Fish Music, is clearly one of the founts of his creative genius. Yunupingu's tech-free acoustic guitar work (played left-handed) and his haunting voice, often combined with Western classical support instruments, have been hailed as a unique cultural bridge between settler and indigenous Australia. Former musician and now Minister Peter Garrett told *The Weekend Australian* in 2008, that Yunupingu's song 'Djarimiiri' was 'chock full of soul and melody, unadorned by technological fetishism', no exaggeration. Yunupingu's compositions are soaked in his cultural background in remote Arnhem Land, sung in his own language, and yet have a musical form that speaks to a diversity of audiences. His debut album *Gurrumul* of February 2008 was an instant, award-winning hit. By late 2010, Australian sales were well over 200,000, with increasing worldwide interest attracting a global market. Following the Australian government's first official apology to Aboriginal Australians for past wrongs, in 2007, Gurummul's work is a signpost to exciting contributions ahead from Aboriginal artists, witness singer Jessica Mauboy already emerging from the wings.

Somewhat dated—but still going strong—and undeniably Australian, is Rolf Harris of 'Tie Me Kangaroo Down, Sport' fame (1960s). ('Play your didgeridoo, Blue,' it went.) Another Aussie singer who left her mark on the international scene in a Germaine-Greer sort of way is Helen Reddy, known internationally for her song 'I Am Woman'. For a glimpse of the future, spot the winners on Channel 9 TV's *The Voice* reality talent contest.

In bars, pubs and restaurants, you will find surprisingly good new groups cutting their teeth. You have to know your way around the scene to find them from one day to the next, however, for Australian bands rarely sit on long-stay contracts at the same venue. They move from spot to spot very frequently.

Be warned, showmanship of the sequins-and-lamé kind is not really part of the Australian performance style (except during Gay and Lesbian Mardi Gras of course). Many a time, a nondescript band in the most unremarkable everyday gear will shuffle onstage, mumble a few inaudible words of introduction, perform brilliantly, then shrug, take a swig of beer and amble off. Only later do you discover by chance that this was one of Australia's top groups. That kind of understatement is very Australian: remember the tall poppy syndrome?

Bushed
Australian folk music is of great interest for its historic roots stretching back into Celtic, especially Irish, and English

traditions, including old Victorian sea shanties. The early bush ballads are like libraries of memories about early pioneer life, on the goldfields and the cattle ranges, in the mines and in the outback deserts. Songs like that old favourite, 'Click Go The Shears', for example.

Australian themes have also been converted into the American country-and-western style, which is very popular in rural areas and among the Aboriginals in particular. Among the most famous songs in this genre are 'A Pub With No Beer' by Gordon Parsons (based on a poem by Queenslander Dan Sheehan) and another ode to beer and mateship, 'Duncan', both recorded by Australia's Slim Dusty, in 1958 and in 1980 respectively. (Slim Dusty, born David Gordon Kilpatrick, himself remains an Aussie icon even after his much lamented passing in 2003 at the age of 76, still working even then, on his 106th recording album.)

If you see a 'bush-dance' advertised, do go to sample the down-to-earth fun; among other things, you may catch sight of strange bush-band instruments like the 'lager-phone', constructed of beer-bottle caps. Among the better-known bush bands are the traditionalist Bushwackers and the more political Redgum, also the Mucky Duck Bush Band of Western Australia, while big-name singers include John Williamson and Eric Bogle. Two of Bogle's protest songs are 'And The Band Played Waltzing Matilda' (anti-war) and 'I Hate Wogs' (anti-racism).

Beer-less in Oz

'It's lonesome away from your kindred and all
By the camp fire at night where the wild dingoes call,
But there's nothing so lonesome, so morbid or drear
Than to stand in a bar of a pub with no beer.'

— First verse of Gordon Parsons' 'A Pub With No Beer',
recorded as an Oz-country hit by the legendary Slim Dusty.

Bush Balladeers

Closely allied with the country and folk music movements is the literary tradition of the folk poets of the past, chief among

Street musicians serenade passers-by with a variety of tunes.

them Henry Lawson (1867–1922), C J Dennis (1876–1938), hailed as 'Laureate of the Larrikin' and bush balladeer 'Banjo' Paterson (1864–1941). The bush poetry movement is very democratic and to some extent, every Australian is a potential bush poet. The tradition of homespun bush poetry is still strong and you may hear Aussies spontaneously break into verse over a campfire, or you may be able to attend specially arranged bush poetry events where wannabe poets will turn up to perform in the literary equivalent of a karaoke contest. Learn more at the Australian Bush Poets' Association website http://www.abpa.org.au/

THE LITERARY TRADITION

Just as Screen Australia has stimulated growth in the cinema, so the Literature Board of the Australia Council for the Arts, set up in 1973, has promoted Australian writing. Achievements in this field have been considerable, attracting world attention in some cases.

One of the greatest early novels was based on convict life, although published well after the days of transportation—*His Natural Life* by Marcus Clarke, 1874. The bush poets of the late 19th century represented a breakaway from English traditions, in search of a more Australian identity. Backing this trend energetically was the national news-and-views weekly magazine *Bulletin*, founded in 1880 but sadly deceased in 2008.

The novel gained strength from the 1920s onward, with major contributions like *Coonardoo* (1929) by Susannah Prichard, a novel of cattle-station life in the far north-west which, for the first time in Australia, dared to touch on black-white sexual relationships, and *Capricornia* (1938) on a similar theme, by Xavier Herbert. Herbert's very long *Poor Fellow My Country* (1975) is also well regarded.

A giant has been Patrick White (1912–1990), who won the Nobel Prize for Literature in 1973, the first Australian ever to do so, for his *The Eye of the Storm*. One reviewer, Greg Sheridan, however, wrote recently that reading White's work, *Riders in the Chariot*, was a 'dread and dire duty that hangs over every Australian'. I myself tend to fall into the Sheridan camp.

Today's giants of the Australian literary scene are probably the ocean-obsessed Tim Winton of Western Australia, Peter Carey (one of only two authors to win the Booker Prize twice) and Bryce Courtenay. Winton's *Cloudstreet* (1991) is possibly his defining work, but there are also *The Riders* (1995), *Dirt Music* (2001) and *Breath* (2008), and quite a stable of children's books too. Winton has won the Miles Franklin Award three times and been shortlisted for the Booker Prize twice.

Peter Carey, a former advertising copywriter, produced his Booker Prize winner *Oscar and Lucinda* in 1988. His other Booker winner, *True History of the Kelly Gang* (2000) is a superb introduction to Australia's folk history centering on the Robin Hood-like figure of Irish-Australian bandit Ned Kelly, written entirely in the authentic Irish working class voice of Kelly himself, missing punctuation and all.

Bryce Courtenay, like Carey, was also an advertising man before he wrote his first novel *The Power of One* at the late age of 55. Now he's more than 11 books away from that, with the best known titles including *April Fool's Day, Tommo & Hawk,* and *Jessica*.

Ex-priest Thomas Keneally is another Australian literary name to conjure with. *Bring Larks and Heroes* (1967) and *The Chant of Jimmie Blacksmith* (1972), also a film, are among his best-known titles, and his 1982 title *Schindler's Ark* (the book of the movie, so to speak, 1993) is world-famous. His *An Angel in Australia* (2002), set in 1942, addresses a recurring theme, Irish-Australian Roman Catholicism.

Murray Bail's 1998 award-winning *Eucalyptus* is a must-read, with a strongly Australian setting.

Other notable contributions have been the short stories of David Malouf (try *An Imaginary Life*—1978). Malouf's *Remembering Babylon* (1993), set in 19th century Australia, with the extraordinary story of a white boy brought up by Aboriginals struggling to return to his own culture, is also considered a classic text.

Gigantic success came to Colleen McCulloch with her 1997 epic blockbuster novel *The Thorn Birds*, an Irish-Australian saga. Nor should we forget Nevil Shute, a Briton who migrated to Australia in 1950, and his famous Aussie boy-meets-Pommie girl romance *A Town Like Alice* (1950). Other classic Australian writers are Miles Franklin, Robert Drewe, Elizabeth Jolley and Judith Wright. Theirs is a distinctly Australian voice.

In poetry, the World War II poems of Kenneth Slessor, who died in 1971, and the passion of Aboriginal poet Kath Walker ('Oodgeroo Noonuccal', died 1993), stand out. High school students are also regularly exhorted to absorb the down-to-basics morality of poet Bruce Dawe (still with us), and also strong on the curricula are poets Gwen Harwood and Judith Wright.

On the non-fiction front, there is the massive six-volume *History of Australia* (1962–1987) by the late Manning Clark. This, read in conjunction with Geoffrey Blainey's *The Tyranny of Distance* (1966—on how Australia's geographical isolation shaped the country's history) and Robert Hughes' moving account of the early convict years, *Fatal Shore* (1987), makes for a near-perfect Australian history lesson. I have mentioned Donald Horne's important study of Australian society, *The Lucky Country* (1964), before and must do so again.

As with movies and other art forms, the impact of migrant Australia is now being felt in literature too. There are many examples, but try the fascinatingly diverse anthology of diaspora essays by Asian Australians, *Growing up in Australia* (2008) edited by Melbourne-born Alice Pung (of Cambodian descent), and Pung's own memoir *Her Father's Daughter* (2011), as well as Australia-raised, Vietnam-born Nam Le's short-story collection *The Boat* (2008) (he's now Fiction Editor for the *Harvard Review* in the USA), and former Eurasian Singaporean Simone Lazaroo's excellent novels, *The World Waiting To Be Made* (2000), *The Australian Fiancé* (2001) and *The Travel Writer* (2006).

Where to Get Your Books

To browse physical books, besides your well appointed local library and its online book-loan reservations service (excellent!), you will find many independent niche or boutique bookshops – even discount supermarkets like Big W, Kmart and Target sell books (cheaply). But the big 'bricks-and-mortar' bookseller names like Dymocks (surviving) and Angus & Robertson (its 160 stores put into administration in 2011 along with Borders) are in trouble. In these online shopping days, you can of course just as easily write to New York or London to get what you want, with the Australian dollar not vastly below (and sometimes above) par with the US dollar; outfits like the Book Depository in England are offering free shipment to Australia. The booksellers' dire plight is of their own making to some extent since there has been a degree of protectionism, even price-fixing, in Australia that has rendered imported books about 35 per cent more expensive for Australians than for readers in other countries if they are sold in Australia, with even paperback prices running around A$25. It's all about parallel-import restrictions and copyright laws, but I won't go into the detail here. You can read about the parallel import issue on the Australian Government's Productivity Commission website at *http://www.pc.gov.au/projects/study/books/report* , the report itself *at http://www.pc.gov.au/__data/assets/pdf_file/0004/90265/books.pdf* and about copyright law reform at *http://www.pc.gov.au/projects/study/books* The Federal Government rejected the Productivity Commission's 2009 report recommending a relaxation of the system.

BRICKS AND MORTAR

Finally, a word about architecture. Australian architects have excelled more in small-scale, detailed works, and especially in the area of heritage conservation. Only gold-mining and wool-industry money brought a degree of pomposity into public buildings, around the mid-19th century.

Among the more monumental buildings are the Queen Victoria Building in Sydney (foundation stone laid in 1893, officially opened in 1898), the National Art Gallery in Canberra, which has touches of the style set by the famous Swiss architect Le Corbusier, the Victorian Arts Centre in Melbourne, and of course, the Sydney Opera House. The Opera House, opened in 1973, is the work of a Danish architect, Joern Utzon, although finally completed by Australian Peter Hall amid some controversy; it cost A$ 100 million. When Utzon handed over the project to Hall in 1966, according to the *Sydney Morning Herald*, he told him, "You're a brave man, but I don't think you can do it."

Canberra in particular has been an architects' playground, as a planned city from the beginning, a fact which gives it something of an artificial look and feeling.

The Maritime Museum of Fremantle in Western Australia, designed by Cox Howlett & Bailey Woodland is a maritime delight, built right into a working port with ships docking right outside the windows. It's likely that WA will produce other striking buildings very shortly, considering that the state is now flush with mining-boom cash.

As noted elsewhere in this book, low-rise sprawl provoked by the bungalow on a quarter-acre block is characteristic of Australian cities. Australian nostalgia surfaces often with the use of rustic features and materials, from exposed brickwork to timber and rammed earth. Revivalist features such as stained-glass windows and panels, wrought-iron 'lace-work', ornamented porticos and verandahs, and elaborate ceiling mouldings, are also much favoured. The climate has also made possible the wholesale import of many Californian, Mediterranean and tropical Asian styles.

In recent times, architects have directed their attention to issues of energy conservation, recycling and so on.

Heritage conservation is a particularly active field, with a very wide-ranging brief, including Aboriginal sacred sites and rock-art treasures.

National trust bodies have existed since 1945, but the real catalyst was the establishment of the Australian Heritage Commission in 1975. Australia's conservation work in areas like Sydney's Rocks, and parts of Adelaide, as well as Fremantle, Perth's port city, to name only three examples, has won world renown. On the other hand, the destruction of old Perth in the 1970s and 1980s has also been quite remarkable.

STREET-WISE CULTURE

Culture, of course, does not reside solely in books, plays or impressive buildings. It can be found in a people's lifestyle. Australians remain some of the most hedonistic of any people, reflecting the many hours of sunshine that they are blessed with every year. In a way, the enjoyment of life is, for them, a serious matter that they regard almost as a cultural heritage. You will find Australian culture at the many festivals and carnivals that Australians just love to create, almost at the drop of a hat, whether at the school and neighbourhood level, or at the State or national level.

There will always be locally made handicrafts and amateur artworks to view and buy, always some local band comprising cheerful volunteers, people selling things at the market, others cooking—civil society at street level is healthy, vigorously 'DIY' and completely spontaneous. Key opportunities for such grassroots culture are of course the various public opportunities, so you would be well advised to get out and about on such days, always supposing that you have not taken the alternative Australian lifestyle option, the much loved backyard barbecue party with good mates. Note, though, that some holidays vary from state to state, which can be a bit confusing; for example, the Queen's Birthday holiday is the second Monday of June everywhere in Australia except Western Australia, where it is 6 October (Don't ask me why!) They don't call Australia 'The Land of the Long Weekend' for nothing—most public holidays are skilfully engineered to fall on a Monday. Watch out too, for the time-zone differences between the states, and for the slight shift in these caused by daylight saving every year.

Yet another way to indulge in cultural 'interface' with fellow Australians it to get out on the road and maybe join the 'grey nomads' as the armies of retirees determined to 'see Australia before we die' are called—the endless highway ribbons of the wild north and central interior are dotted with the 4WD vehicles and caravans belonging to this 'tribe' and Australia's well-organised camping sites and parklands, as well as the many roadhouses, are abuzz with these Australians getting to know each other. This traditional ritual of 'going walkabout' or rather, 'driveabout' to get to know each other and the land is also a central part of Australian culture. It's hard to resist the suspicion that it was the naturally nomadic Aboriginals who first gave white Australians this very good idea.

Sydney's old Queen Victoria Building was restored as a shopping arcade by Asian investment.

Barwill House (also known as Wilhelmsen House) in Fremantle, Western Australia, is just one of the buildings in the Heritage Grants Programme. Comprehensive conservation plans are underway to see to its restoration and preservation.

Australia's vibrant street-life is showcased at weekends, at fairs and markets; this 'statue' posing on the sidewalk in Fremantle, Western Australia's port city, is in fact a live actor painted up to look like a sculpture and shocking passers-by as he springs to life every so often.

THE ART OF LEISURE

The tradition of home-based arts and crafts is still quite strong in Australia and those who want to take up hobbies other than the ubiquitous gardening craze that inhabits every Australian suburb, may well opt for something artistic. Every community centre and adult education college is replete with offerings of courses in everything from woodcarving and ceramics to stained-glass work and block printing, often at very affordable prices or even free of charge. Consult your local TAFE college or university adult extension course list.

Other hobbies that Australia is well suited to include many outdoors options such as bush-walking, bird-watching, horse-riding, rafting or rowing. Or you might fancy a tango or salsa class, ballroom dancing or belly-dancing (there's an awful lot of the latter!). Whatever, when you get really good at it, you can go back and pass it on, become a teacher yourself.

A Selection of Public Holidays and Special Dates

* all holidays falling over a weekend will attract a further holiday on the following Monday; refer to Tourism Australia's website for a full list of official public holidays, state by state, http://www.oztourism. com.au/public_holidays.htm

January

1	New Year's Day
26	Australia Day
	Festival of Sydney

January–February Festival of Perth

March

1st Monday	Labour Day, Western Australia
2nd Monday	Labour Day, Victoria, and Moomba Parade
2nd Monday	Labour Day, Australian Capital Territory (ACT)
	Canberra Day Festival
	Adelaide Festival of the Arts (even-numbered years)

April

	Easter holiday—from Good Friday until the following Monday, or Tuesday in some states
at Easter	Clare Valley Wine Festival, South Australia
	Barossa Valley Vintage Festival (odd-numbered years)
25	Anzac Day

May

1st Monday	Labour Day, Queensland
	May Day Holiday, Northern Territory

June

1st Monday	Western Australia Day (formerly 'Foundation Day')
2nd Monday	Queen's Birthday (except Western Australia)
	Brisbane Festival of Creative Arts
	Darwin Beer Can Regatta, Northern Territory

(Continued from previous page)

August

1	Wattle Day (not all states)
1st Monday	New South Wales Bank Holiday
	Broome Shinju Matsuri Festival (multicultural), Western Australia
1st Monday	Henley-on-Todd Regatta, Alice Springs (yacht race on the dry bed of Todd River)

September

29	Queen's Birthday, Western Australia (2014)
30	Queen's Birthday, Western Australia (2013)*

* both dates are Mondays; the Governor-General can shift the dates for this holiday as wished.

October

1st Monday	Labour Day, New South Wales, ACT & South Australia
2nd weekend	'Spring in the Valley' Wine Festival—Perth

(Continued from previous page)

November

1st Tuesday	Melbourne Cup Day, Victoria (nation closes down)
11	Remembrance Day*

* commemorates the end of World War I and honours the war dead

December

25	Christmas Day
26	Boxing Day (in South Australia, called the Proclamation Day holiday)
28	South Australia Proclamation Day)
	Sydney-Hobart and Melbourne-Hobart yacht races/Tasmanian Fiesta (start)
	Hobart-Salamanca Arts Festival, Tasmania

SPEAKING STRINE

'To employ more than the most limited of vocabularies is not only ostentatious but anti-democratic. If the teachers are half right, little has changed since I attended primary school in the 1940s, when to show an interest in words was to damn yourself as some sort of deviant. As a wimp, or worse.'
—Columnist Phillip Adams in *The Weekend Australian*, 27 July 1991, on the Australian attitude to words

AN ENGLISH-SPEAKING COUNTRY?

Nothing distinguishes the Australian more sharply from the average Anglo-Saxon than his very special brand of English.

Many English-speaking newcomers to the country make the awful mistake of imagining that operating there will be a breeze because 'They speak English there, don't they?' Well, not quite. Like English in other former colonial outposts, from the West Indies to South Africa and Zimbabwe, from India to Singapore and Malaysia, the language has mutated in Australia's desert soils.

The extraordinary thing is that many of the central features of Australian English were well in place by the late 19th century, hiving off from the mother tongue very soon after the original convicts' and settlers' arrival in Australia. The language of a rebellious subculture.

Unfortunately, the lingo is extremely hard for the outsider to penetrate, or to imitate, (for practice, try saying 'Australia' the Strine way—'Orst-rai-ya', or else recite 'in moi aoun toime' for 'in my own time'—but these are not scientifically phonetic spellings, needless to say). If you are a new migrant, you may gain comfort (or despair, depending on your point of view) from the certain knowledge that your children will be fluent 'Strine' speakers within months of setting foot on Australian soil. ('Strine' is an approximation of how the word 'Australian' sounds, coming out of an Australian's mouth.) It's definitely catching.

So no point in giving you a formal pronunciation guide now—a forced attempt at speaking like the locals can sound quite awful and few Aussies will be taken in by it. When in doubt, better just be yourself. The chances are though, that the accent will just naturally 'grow' on you until one day, your Mum, your Dad and your best friends back home, all say, "Hey! What happened? Your accent has completely changed!" You won't even have noticed and this news will come as a shock to you.

There is still an older generation of Australians, particularly the more educated ones, that was brought up to speak 'English English', but this cohort is fast dwindling. There are also some distinctly well-moderated, gentler accents to be found among educated and well-travelled Australians and some Cabinet ministers, especially in the eastern states, in major cities such as Sydney, Melbourne and Adelaide.

Although the trend is definitely for a more earthy Australian accent to take over the airwaves, out of a sense of increasing national pride, there are still quite a few such moderated accents to be heard on 'Auntie', the Australian Broadcasting Corporation's radio programmes.

There are some wonderful insights into the oddities of Australian English to be found in Lonely Planet's pocket guide, *Australian Language & Culture,* October 1994/March 2007.

A headline from *The West Australian* newspaper. A 'rort' is sharp practice of some sort, a scam, dirty dealing or cheating, and 'fixing' or 'rigging', especially in business and financial matters. 'Rorting the system' is a frequently used phrase referring to 'bludgers' who take advantage of, say, welfare assistance payments etc.

No Plums Please, We're Australian

Generally speaking, though, you will be considered suspect and a bit 'up yourself' (an obscene but commonly heard reference to er, 'having your head up your own arse'; 'wanker' is another frequently heard insult of the same breeding, referring to masturbation) if your English comes with too 'plummy' an accent. ('Plummy' refers to the over-careful speech you would produce if you had a plum in your mouth.)

Not only does the majority of the nation favour 'Ozspeak' but there is now also a subgroup of youngsters whose dialect of choice is sarcastically alluded to by older journalists as 'Wayne-speak', this term being a reference to the 'in' names for Australian children of the Generation X vintage, such as Wayne (or Jason; female version, Kylie), rather than the good old Bruce (or Jan). (There was also a brief hippy interlude during the 1960s, which produced Amber, Jasmine, Jade and Sky for some.)

Much of Wayne-speak is plain old lousy pronunciation, rather than just dialect English. Examples are *heighth* for height and *esculator* for escalator, as noted by journalist Deborah Bogle in an article for *The Australian Magazine*. In the same category can be bagged the increasing tendency to pronounce 't' as 'd', thus, *qwordah* for quarter and *wordah* for water. Overlaid on this is the growing impact of American English. As for Generation Y Aussies, it really is, like, quite difficult for an English-born native English speaker to, like, understand much of what your average Australian 20-year-old says, like it's really bizarre? Americanisms are definitely commonplace in Aussie 'teen dialect'. They speak, nay mumble, very quickly, with no clear articulation, and slur and blur all the consonants and syllables together. But never mind, for as the youngster in question would surely say, using a newish Americanism that has virtually eclipsed the old "No worries" among their generation, "It's all good." Perhaps I'm just displaying an international generation gap!

Today or To Die?

True-blue Australian English differs from the 'mother tongue' both in terms of its accent and in terms of its vocabulary. The accent is best gauged from old jokes which run thus…

Wounded soldier to nurse in Australian hospital: "Have I come here to die?"

Nurse: "Now, love, yer came 'ere yesterdie!"

And a punning headline in *The West Australian* newspaper, 30 April 1993, would not have been possible were it not for the Aussie accent: referring to Princess Diana of England, the newspaper headlined 'Diana—Princess of Wiles' (should have been Princess of Wales, for those of you who do not already know).

... and the national form of greeting, 'G'day, mate!' (not common currency between the sexes or among women, it should be noted), which could be transcribed roughly as 'Gerdie, mite!' And my two migrant friends desperately looking for Hay Street would have been better understood if they had said 'High Street' like everybody else in Australia.

Be very careful whom you label an Australian on first hearing. It is difficult for the beginner to tell an Australian accent from a New Zealand one, but New Zealanders do not like to be taken for Australians, not one bit (the feeling is mutual). As a general guideline, Australians open their mouths wider, while New Zealanders are said to speak through their clenched teeth and semi-closed lips. Typically, a New Zealander will say 'yis' for 'yes', and 'fush n' chups' for 'fish and chips', somewhat like the Scots' accent.

The contortions that Australians can perform with diphthongs are a marvel to the ear. Often they are extended to double-diphthongs, to the point that a simple 'no' may well become more like 'nah-oh-oo-u'. For reasons I do not quite understand myself—probably sexist ones—the essentially nasal accent sits particularly uneasily with the female voice, which in Australia also seems to be higher-pitched than it would be in most of Western Europe (although not so much higher than is common among Asian females).

A commentator in the 1940s once surmised that the Australian accent was attributable to a permanent inflammation of the nose, due to the excessive pollen to be found in the air. It's true that it can sound extraordinarily nasal. For a good sample of this, tune in to the inexplicably popular blonde newscaster Sandra Sully on Channel 10 TV,

Dorothy dixers to rule, cries Labor

BEN RUSE
CANBERRA

The Government would field 66 fewer questions from the Opposition and minor parties after using its new Senate majority to change the rules for Senate question time, Labor claimed yesterday.

The Opposition is outraged by the changes, which will allow ministers to answer more soft questions from their own backbenchers, but the Government says they simply reflect the new make-up of the Senate.

Traditionally, the question roster has been worked out co-operatively between all Senate parties. Labor is angry that the Government did not discuss its changes with other parties.

Labor says the Government intends to use its control of the

already raised concerns that the Government will dominate Senate committees and prevent them from investigating issues that may embarrass the Government.

Under the new rules, out of every 14 questions, Government

'It was a farce when we were in Government, and a farce now.'

ALP SENATOR CHRIS EVANS

senators will get six, Labor will get six and senators from other parties will get two. Previously, Labor was able to ask seven, the Government four and the minor parties three. This gives Government senators, who now control the Senate, fewer questions per head than the

Liberal Senate leader Robert Hill said the changes were fair because they were based on the number of senators each party had and that Labor should not be contractions.

Questions from Government backbenchers to Government ministers are known as dorothy dixers, after a newspaper advice columnist who was suspected of writing both the questions and the answers in her columns.

Although the questions are supposed to be asked without notice, generally ministers have a prepared answer which makes fun of the Opposition.

Labor's Senate leader Chris Evans admitted the truth yesterday when he said of dorothy di

Another headline from *The West Australian* newspaper. What's this? 'Dorothy Dix' was an American newspaper columnist in the 1950s who ran an agony aunt column in which many suspected she just made up the Q and A to suit her own purposes. In Australia, this memory has set in aspic and the term 'Dorothy Dixer' has now come to mean a completely pre-planned, unspontaneous 'planted' or 'fixed' question with a pre-prepared 'fixed' answer, usually in Parliament, by politicians.

who has been lampooned in comedy shows as 'Sandra Sultry' for her husky voice delivered firmly via the nose. Australian vocal delivery is most often slow and rather flat by outsiders' standards, without great light and shade contrasts, tending to a monotone in some cases. An Australian is capable of saying something extraordinarily interesting and lively in such a low-key manner that you may not notice he has said anything out of the way at all. It's a style of speech uniquely suited to deadpan humour. "Bought the supermarket, 'av yer, luv?" might be the typical comment as you stagger to the checkout counter with a trolley laden to the top with goodies for the party you are holding tonight.

Ups and Downs

For this reason alone, never mind the accent, you need to concentrate on what Australians are saying (try hard not to fall asleep), in case you miss something. Since the Australian also has a penchant for terse understatement, the risk of misunderstanding is great.

Here is a guide on how you should converse with an Australian. Loud, assertive delivery will not go down well. Lower your voice and flatten it like his, erase all excitement or emotion, and you should be able to get your point across without too much offence. There is one interesting exception to this rule: the infectious Australian habit of lifting the voice at the end of the sentence as if asking a question or seeking your approval/understanding, although I have noticed that this is happening less often nowadays.

'And it was raining, really hard' (on 'hard', the voice goes sharply up as if '?' were there and '… you know what I mean?' were tacked on the end), 'but we had no umbrellas…' (up again on 'umbrellas'… 'you know what I mean?').

This verbal tic can be infuriating to the novice but it will insidiously creep into your own voice over time, sure as the sun shines. And when you think about it, it is really quite a friendly habit, this constant seeking of others' involvement in the conversation.

One aspect of Australian speech that breaks the 'don't get excited' rule is the 'full on' (another Australianism) argument. Australian arguments can get very loud and very public—often on the street—and will be laced with violent expletives of all kinds. More of this later.

Antique Hangovers

Some Australian English is, in fact, more original and 'pure' than the version spoken in Mother England today. Many Australian words were long ago discarded in England. Australians, as a rule, betray an innate conservatism by clinging on to old forms and idioms, while at the same time creating new ones. This makes Australian English quite a rich, 'dense' language.

You have to look back to white Australia's roots in 19th-century, Cockney London and Ireland to understand this. Quite apart from the accent (which some academics however say originated not in London but was home-grown in Australia), how else can you explain the extraordinary survival of Cockney rhyming slang in everyday Australian speech? It even gets printed in the daily newspapers as a matter of course—like the photo caption I once came across, reading

'Mr So-and-So on the dog and bone'. This photo showed Mr So-and-So using the telephone.

I might have passed this by and thought nothing of it, had not a young Aussie friend remarked to me over a coffee, "So you're all on your Al Capone, then?" when I said my husband was away. That of course translated as 'So you're all on your own, then?'

I must mention here, however, that at least one reputable dictionary lists 'Al Capone' as the rhyming slang for telephone (and not 'dog and bone'), but 'Pat Malone' as the rhyming slang for 'alone', so I am not quite sure where this leaves us. But the examples I have cited have come from my first-hand experience.

Rhyming SMS

The old cockney rhyming slang is alive and well even in the era of SMS or 'texting'. I was present at the Perth end when two older generation Aussies in Melbourne texted their grandson in Perth, about to attend his younger sister's 21st birthday party, with this message for his mobile:

'What time's the gay and hearty?
Don't get elephant trunk!'

Get it? Translation: 'What time is the party? Don't get drunk!'

Thinking Little

An Australian idiosyncrasy is the strange obsession with reducing any word possible to its diminutive form. (Such words are known as 'hypocorisms' to academics but we could call them 'hypos' here.) This, too, is quite a catching disease for newcomers. Hence 'postie' refers to the postman, 'U-ie' for a motorist's U-turn, 'barbie' for barbecue, 'vegie' or 'veggie' for vegetable, prezzie for present, Chrissie for Christmas. You even get 'firie' for a fireman, and 'tantie' for a tantrum.

Other words are shortened with an '-o' at the end: 'reffo' for refugee, 'Freo' for the port of Fremantle in Western Australia, 'reggo' (soft 'g') for car registration, 'journo' for journalist, 'muso' for musician, and so on. The 'o' suffix more usually applies to people than things—for example, a 'veggo' (soft 'g') is a vegetarian, whereas a 'veggie meal' is a vegetable or vegetarian meal.

An official campaign card for Australia Post, mailed out to all households in Western Australia, promoting safety for postmen using the typically Strine abbreviation 'Postie' for postman.

Conversation Smoothers

Then, of course, there are the famous Australian catchphrases: 'No worries' and 'She'll be right,' epitomising the nation's fabled plucky optimism and laid-back style. These are by no means clichés and are still in common use, although 'Not a problem', 'Too easy' and 'It's all good' seem to be gaining ground. 'She'll be apples' (from the rhyming slang 'apples and spice' for 'nice'?) belongs to the same family of phrases but increasingly is seen as archaic. You are more likely to hear the simpler 'She'll be right.'

However, it must be said that the trials of economic hard times have of late strained even the most sanguine of Aussies and such phrases increasingly have a hollow ring to them, belying the desperation beneath. It's all part of the macho Aussie psyche, which delights in showing personal cool when challenged by an adverse situation or a person, ranging from a wall of flame in a bushfire through economic disaster to breaking a leg.

Another, fairly newly arrived, phrase in this conversation-lubricating category is 'There you go'. This crops up all over the place and if you use it skilfully, it will help you blend into the Australian background nicely. When a shop assistant totting up your bill tells you, "That'll be 20 dollars then," you should reply pleasantly as you hand over the cash to her, "There you go!"

The Americanised pleasantry 'Have a nice (or good) day' is rampant, but the equally common Aussie version is still strong, simply 'Have a good one!', without specifying exactly one what. When the weekend is imminent, it is also almost mandatory to greet others with the friendly query, 'Got anything planned for the weekend then?', not so much out of rude curiosity, but more as a kindly hope that they are going to have a good time. You will find many check-out girls and boys in the supermarket asking you this apparently personal question of a Friday or Saturday. Don't be alarmed. Give them a general (and genial) answer, along the lines of "Yeah, planning to visit the rellies (relatives) and then do a bit of gardening!" You are not supposed to tell too much truth: "I'll be attending my best friend's funeral actually" would be too much information.

'Just Popping into Manchester'

The way Australians have clung to very old language is yet another illustration of their innate conservatism and strongly traditionalist urges. We have seen how 19th century forms from East End London have survived in modern Australian English. Here's another example of this modern usage of 'linguistic fossils' in daily Australian life: the newcomer may at first be mystified by the word 'Manchester' to be seen on signs in many Australian department stores and over many shop windows. This refers back to the late 19th century, when the industrial town of Manchester in north-eastern England was the world's greatest centre of textiles and cotton manufacturing, exporting to the farthest corners of the British Empire, including Australia. Although Manchester's pre-eminence in the cotton trade had declined even before World War II, still, since the early 1900s at least, 'Manchester' in Australia has referred to all household linens, bedding, towels and cottons. You can quite confidently ask a shop assistant in a big Australian store like Myers 'Which way to the Manchester department, please?' and expect an immediate response.

The *Australian National Dictionary* cites an article in a 1983 issue of Australia's now defunct national weekly *The Bulletin* which tells the comic tale of an Australian customer shopping in London who asks the shop assistant in the dress department to hold on to her purchase while she just 'goes over to Manchester,' assuring her 'I'll be back in a while.' The baffled English assistant points out to her that Manchester is really quite a long way from London. 'Only Australian shoppers buy their sheets and pillowcases from the 'Manchester department,' smiled *The Bulletin*.

THE ART OF ABUSE

When it comes to insults, the Australian suddenly springs to life and abandons his laid-backness with a vengeance. In general, Australians are quite free with abuse and obscenities, swearing liberally, so you need to discount this as much as possible.

If you should happen to become the butt of Aussie artistry in this department, try to take it all with a smile and a pinch of salt. Do not take it to heart. There is more bark than bite in it all. In Australia, you must always be a sport. Better still, once you have got the hang of things, give back as good as you get—it's expected, and accepted.

Australian English is particularly rich in invective (especially the obscene sexual variety), easily matching close rivals, such as Cantonese, for example. Four-letter swear words are used like punctuations by the man-in-the-street and even by politicians in Parliament. 'Bloody' hardly raises an Australian eyebrow. There is much worse to come.

If you come from a genteel background, it's best you prepare yourself for this and train yourself not to hear it. There will be no avoiding it. (The most painful experience is when your children start picking it up.) Relegate it to wallpaper status, for that is all it really is—wallpaper. Those 'bad' words have lost their violence and their meaning in Australian English, through over-frequent use.

'Bastard' is one word that leads to great misunderstanding. Learn that in Australia, more often than not, it is used affectionately, very rarely as an insult. Only when it is applied to a 'Pommy', an Englishman, is it really meant to hurt. (There are many other terms of racist abuse, but I deal with these in another chapter). Beware of using the word affectionately too early in a relationship; it must be reserved for fairly close friends or longstanding workmates, and normally is used only among men, not across the genders. If you are visibly, physically foreign—Asian, for instance—you will need to take your time using such language, as some Australians will find you difficult to 'read' and will wonder whether you might mean these words literally.

Paradoxically, however, until quite recently such words as 'Fuck' were still considered fundamentally taboo in Australia, as elsewhere. It was only in 1985 that the Western Australian police charged the Sydney comedian Rodney Rude with obscenity for using the word to excess onstage (once every 3 minutes, during a 90-minute show). Western Australia has been one of the last bastions of a once uniformly puritanical Australian culture, yet this case was dismissed in the end with the following rationale, to quote *The West Australian* newspaper of 22 April 1986: "Used in combination with the word 'off', the offending word was vulgar and quite impolite, but well understood and not necessarily obscene. The word's primary meaning was 'to copulate' but more often than not it was used simply as a strong expletive, and repeated use had tended to lessen the impact."

The word has become common currency, on the streets and in the arts. In fact the 'F' word was deemed no longer offensive by an Australian magistrate in 1999 when in Dubbo, New South Wales, he dismissed charges against a man who allegedly told a police officer to 'Fuck off'. The same trend is discernible for other borderline obscenities: in 2000, the Supreme Court of Victoria amazingly ruled that it was not contempt of court for a riled solicitor to call the sitting judge a 'wanker', since "The matter must be judged by contemporary Australian standards. It may be offensive, but it is not contempt of court, for a person to describe a judge as a wanker." Yet a survey by AustraliaSCAN in 2001 found that 69 per cent of Australians still believed sexually explicit language on TV was unacceptable, a statistic 10 per cent up on a 1997 finding.

Punchy Politicians

The master of Australian invective without sole recourse to swear words is generally agreed to have been the former ALP Prime Minister, Paul Keating. He would berate his political opponents in public as 'Boxhead', 'Pig', 'Clown', 'Sleazebag' and so on. To a vociferous leftwing delegate at the New South Wales state ALP conference in 1982, he remarked, "You could talk under wet cement."

To sum up, the standard Australian attitude to excessive politeness is that it is anathema in a truly democratic society. Being able to call a spade a bloody spade is a

Another former Labor Prime Minister, Bob Hawke, is also well known for once turning aside from the irritating heckling of an old-age pensioner to remark *sotto voce*, "Silly old bugger!" The remark unfortunately was overheard by the entire nation, courtesy of TV and radio.

politically important Australian freedom. With leaders like these using lingo like this, the man-in-the-street needs little further encouragement. After an upbringing soaked in English hypocrisy and a young adulthood saturated with Asian evasiveness, I personally have found this trait refreshing, once you get over the initial shock.

The simile is a dynamic living form. Of very recent coinage is one I myself heard: 'Yeah, he's as busy as a bricklayer in Baghdad!' Then there is 'He's as camp as a row of circus tents!' referring to a person's gay tendencies. 'This idea hasn't got a snowflake's chance in hell!' is a popular one right now. More on the scatological side is 'That's not worth a fart in a hurricane.'

MIS-SPEAK

Differences in vocabulary can sometimes lead to hilarious misunderstandings, or embarrassing double entendres. Take, for example, the experience of my Malaysian-Eurasian friend, a fresh migrant to Australia. Invited by some new Australian friends to their dinner party, she asked politely if she should bring anything along and was at first puzzled by their response: "Yes, bring along a plate, will you?" Poor things, she thought, they must be a bit short of crockery, and so she took along practically her entire dinner service, only to discover that a 'plate' referred to a dish of cooked food. This was what is known elsewhere as a 'pot-luck' dinner, where each guest brings a contribution of food, a very common variation on the 'Bring Your Own' or BYO theme in Australian life.

And then there was my other Malaysian friend, a timid new migrant in his early teens. He had made arrangements to meet someone on a particular street and so he was loitering there quite peaceably at the appointed time until he noticed a large sign which said, 'No Standing At Any Time'. Panicked, he proceeded to pace up and down wildly in the belief that so long as he kept moving, he would not be arrested.

But this was in fact a traffic sign, which in other countries would probably have read something like 'No Parking' or 'No Waiting'.

Pity the Macedonian refugee lady who went on her first visit to an Australian doctor's clinic. At the end of her consultation with the doctor, the doctor bid her a warm farewell, saying "See you later then." The Macedonian woman sat down in the waiting room—and waited, and waited and waited, until the very last patient had left and the doctor emerged from his room with a puzzled look: "Goodness, what are you doing here still, is anything the matter?" he asked her. "No", said she, "but you said you would want to see me later, so I am waiting to see what it is that you want." The doctor laughed heartily. "See you later" is just an Aussie way of saying "*Au revoir*, see you again some time." Heaven knows what the poor woman would have done with another version of this phrase, "Catchya!", for "Catch you later."

In the same vein, Australians have concocted some extraordinary and often ingeniously insulting similes, making hyperbole a typically Australian vehicle. "Three old ladies dressed like Queen Elizabeth II in floral prints and sensible shoes tell me they think their premier Bob Hawke is as "shady as a rat with a parasol"," reported Singaporean journalist Chai Kim Wah in the *Sunday Times* of Singapore, 26 November 1989.

The Tender Tea-Trap

The classic in this genre is, of course, the Australian 'tea'. The worst case scenario is that you, an English or Asian migrant, have invited your Australian friend round for tea. The Australian will wait around hopefully—and hungrily—for a long time before he or she realises that 'tea' is just tea, and very little more.

For an Australian, tea is the full evening meal, known to most other cultures as 'dinner'. Beware of 'The Tea Trap'—it still catches out many a foreign visitor!

Subcultures as well as communities within multicultural Australia have spawned their own lexicons. The surfing subculture is one example: when they refer to 'a Margaret' in Western Australia, they mean a big wave of the type found around the popular surfing beaches of Margaret River in south-western Australia.

A Beer is a Beer is a Beer?

Besides the macro-differences between Australian English in general and other 'Englishes,' there are also interstate micro-differences to be considered.

You can see this particularly with measures of beer. 'Grog' in Australia is known as 'Jimmy' in 'Tazzie' or Tasmania, whereas it would be a 'Stubby' anywhere else (a small bottle holding 375 ml). A Western Australian 'Middy' measure brings you 7 oz, but 10 oz in New South Wales. And so on, ad nauseam. A pint, thank goodness, is just that.

In New South Wales, you may don a 'cozzie' (i.e. costume) to swim, but in Queensland it would be 'togs', and in Western Australia, 'bathers.' There is plenty more like this.

Budgies are Black

Influences from ancient Aboriginal cultures, not to mention many newer migrant minority ones, have further complicated Australian vocabulary. Northern, north-western and central Australia are the heartlands for these original tongues.

The Aboriginals once boasted some 250 separate languages, Australia-wide, but less than half of these are still alive today, although there is a movement to revive them. Many Aboriginal words, particularly place-names and words referring to wildlife or natural phenomena, have entered white Australian English: 'wombat', 'kangaroo' and 'budgerigar', for example.

SPELLING BEE DAMNED?

The language is of course evolving, like any other living language. But that does not seem to be sufficient excuse for the sheer volume of misspellings on show in Australia.

I was charmed by the offer of 'Lovely Cheeries' outside a grocery shop and intrigued by the display of 'Laces and Brades' at a drapery shop. It was fascinating to learn in a leading television and entertainment magazine that a certain popular TV compère has a beautiful 'Frency Penny' tree in his garden, but surely, this must have been a Frangipani?

Semi-literate shop signs and the like could perhaps be excused in the context of a multicultural nation full of 'NESBs' (Non-English Speaking Background persons). But what really is disturbing is the fact that very few official letters escape serious spelling mistakes. I have remarked elsewhere on the surprisingly high levels of functional and actual illiteracy among Australians, especially the younger ones. Views on why this has happened range from cursing a liberal education philosophy encouraging 'self-expression' over actual reading, writing and spelling or berating negligent parents, to citing the admitted fact that groups suffering from extreme social disadvantage, such as Aboriginals, are more at risk and are pulling down the national statistics – some 40 per cent of indigenous teenagers are well below most functional literacy benchmarks.

Add to this, uncertainty throughout the country as to whether to adopt English or American spelling and the whole situation spells, as it were, confusion. Even the ruling party of the 1980s–1990s, the ALP, spells itself the Australian Labor Party, rather than using the English 'Labour'. That would be OK if the nation used consistent American spelling, but it does not; it mixes the two forms almost at random—as just one example, you will find English 'colour' not American 'color' is fine, but the norm is American 'program' not the English 'programme'.

JOKE FOR DEMOCRACY

Language, of course, is the foundation of any nation's sense of humour. And Australia's humour is special indeed. It is considered a sacred cow of sorts.

Significantly, when certain states decided in 1989 to legislate against public incitement of racial hatred, racial jokes were specifically excluded from the list of offences that could be penalised under the new laws, particularly if they were performed as an entertainment, on stage. It is an article of faith in Australia that everybody must be able to take a joke. The freedom to pull tails, tweak noses and generally satirise all comers is considered fundamental to democracy. Probably the most internationally known of Australia's satirists is Barry Humphries, who has dissected Australian society far more cruelly than any outsider.

A great deal of non-satirical Australian humour is outrageous in some way, whether salacious or sacrilegious. There is almost

Australian gardeners exhibit the Australian sense of humour with their garden signage – here's a collection from around Perth. *Pictures by Ilsa Sharp.*

nothing you cannot make fun of, from cripples to Christ on the Cross. Nothing is sacred, except the right to poke fun itself.

But there are still a few hidden boundaries, it seems, as the popular ABC TV comedy team The Chasers discovered to their cost in 2009 when they did a skit centring on the idea of a terminally ill child going to one of those 'last wish' foundations that make such kids' dreams come true. The team has never recovered from the uproar and outrage this caused, and is no longer seen regularly on ABC.

Australian humour, when it's not just plain bawdy (which it often is) is above all as dry as the country itself, always understated, and if possible, mumbled out of the corner of the mouth. Listen carefully—there are some gems around.

YOUR VERBAL CAMOUFLAGE
Finally, a word of advice to those trying to acquire Australian camouflage: do not rush in too enthusiastically greeting everyone 'G'day, mate!' This phrase is so quintessentially Australian that if you don't have a 'full-on' accent, you cannot really pull it off.

A useful greeting, more easily adopted by foreigners than 'G'day,' is 'How're yer going?' (frequently followed by the rhetorical 'Orright?'). On the other hand, the phrase 'No worries' is quickly and effortlessly adopted by most new arrivals, with some success. Also, the casual dropping here and there of single words, such as 'reggo' (car licence registration), 'dag' (an apparel-challenged individual) or phrases such as 'Good on yer!' (to indicate approval) can be achieved quite naturally.

BODY LANGUAGE

Like a lot of Westerners, Aussies don't like you to intrude on their body space too much—don't get too close to them when you are talking to them.

You will observe a version of this respect for private space both in supermarket and other types of queues, and particularly in the queue to use an ATM banking machine on the street. The Australian will stand well away from the person actually being served at the counter, or using the ATM. Of course there are security reasons for this—not intimidating the person doing the banking with the fear that you might be about to snatch their cash, and not leaning over their shoulder to see what their PIN is, for example—but this innate respect for personal space is another factor behind this behaviour. It is not considered good manners to crowd up against the people in front of you in a queue.

A less attractive form of non-verbal communication you may encounter, particularly as a driver on Australian roads, is 'the finger'—it is unfortunately quite common to have a motorist overtake you or draw up alongside gesticulating and 'giving you the finger' in an obscene gesture to indicate their disgust at something you may or may not have done. Even more alarming, in such cases, the gesticulating driver may as well be a woman as a man. The only thing to do is to ignore it, keep your windows and doors locked and shut, and drive on calmly.

WORKING IN AUSTRALIA

CHAPTER 9

"We have to turn around our deteriorating performance in productivity. Without that, there is no sustainable improvement in our living standards. We can't just rely on being a quarry for Asia and the rest of the world generating the kind of society that we've become accustomed to."
—Charles Macek, a respected director on the board of major Australian company Wesfarmers, on excessive red tape and the failure to create a seamless national economy across State borders, in *The Australian* in February 2012

THE LEISURE ETHIC
Work and Play

Australians today are very far away from that lazy, laid-back stereotype that some outsiders still wrongly ascribe to them. They are working quite hard. The legal maximum working hours is now set at 38 hours a week under the 'Fair Work' system, but then there is overtime of course. For example, in 2010, average weekly working hours for full-time male employees in Australia settled around 41 hours (closer to 36 hours for women); the proportion of workers reporting 41-50 hours of work a week has sat at about 13 per cent for three decades now, while those reporting over 50 hours of work has come down from nearly 20 per cent in 1999 to just 15 per cent in 2010.

The major banks' attempt in 2012 (since withdrawn) to extend normal opening hours into Saturday afternoon and Sunday may be a signpost to the future: traditionally, employers have had to pay 'penalty rate' bonus payments to any workers that they oblige to work at "unsociable hours', such as over weekends. But if such hours are redefined in law as 'normal' working hours, then the penalty rates may be under threat. Not very likely under a Labor government, but possible under the Liberals.

5The Australian Council of Trade Unions (ACTU), representing the workers, ran a *Working Australia Census* in 2011 that reported stress, insecurity and lack of confidence in their employers among workers. It found that 73 per cent were regularly contacted about their jobs outside of working hours (a big no-no in Australia), and 61 per cent were working more hours than they were paid for.

There is a constant national debate, also playing out at the micro level inside most workplaces, about 'Family-Work Balance' or 'Life-Work Balance' and while the achievement of this ideal is a mantra for all parties involved, few seem able actually to achieve it.

In many ways, the world of work in Australia is split sharply into two separate worlds: the stressed environment of the conventional full-time worker and the drifting, insecure world of the casualised part-timer, representing some 60 per cent of the workforce.

Why does being able to buy more stuff make up for husbands and wives being able to see less of each other, having less time with the kids, having a lot more trouble getting together with your friends, and having your day off when everyone else is at school or working? Why is this an attractive future? Why should our elected representatives reorganise our economy in ways that suit business and promote consumption, but do so at the expense of employees' private lives?

Writing in the online *WAToday*, April 2012, business and finance journalist Ross Gittins expresses in a nutshell the strong reservations many Australians have about a 24/7 economy, in retail or elsewhere. One man's economic flexibility is another's decline in the quality of life.

With unemployment around a manageable 5 per cent and a mining boom spreading prosperity and new jobs, the Aussie worker and his family should have very little to complain about, right? Wrong. You will hear a lot of 'whingeing'. Australia's 'Patchwork Economy' (it has also variously been labelled a 'Two-Speed' or a 'Three-Speed' economy) has produced uneven benefits and a generalised sense of insecurity. Manufacturing and retail are in trouble and certainly not hiring. Agriculture is afflicted by a combination of natural disasters and creeping climate change. Unemployed or under-employed workers in the east cannot figure out how to move their families out west (and sell their homes maybe?) to the jobs in the mining heartland of Western Australia, where the outback mining towns are so difficult to live in that most choose to leave their families in Perth, where rentals are sky-high. Hence, there is a chronic skilled labour shortage in the mining areas. But the proposal in 2012 for WA to import just 1,700 foreign workers as a part-solution provoked uproar, and rank xenophobia, among the labour unions. Meanwhile, the employers say the cost of doing business in Australia is just rising and rising. And underlying all this is the simple maxim, 'It's all about China, stupid!' If anything happens to provoke a slowdown in China, Australia's prime customer, then the Australian economic balloon could deflate very quickly. Australia's economy is in troubling transition, and the workers know it. But you betcha, they still want their weekends.

As Australia's veteran national analyst, writer Donald Horne, has said of his compatriots, "To some they seem lazy. They are not really lazy but they don't always take their jobs seriously."

Slowing Down

Once you have learned to calm down your New York, Singapore, Hong Kong or Tokyo mindset, you can get used to Australia's 'leisure ethic'. After all, there is a lot to be said for being able to spend more quality time with your family over the weekend. And for being able to develop social life, hobbies or further studies in the evenings. And for watching your blood pressure slowly drop, thus prolonging your life.

The Australian leisure ethic (as opposed to the work ethic) cuts two ways. While other people may not always want to work for or with you, it also means you may not have to work so hard yourself.

It seems more than possible that Australians have got this one right, especially when you watch the rest of the developed world struggling with the problem of excess leisure time in this automated, information technology age. Indeed, one of the underlying reasons for apparent 'laziness' in Australia, and for some of the unemployment or underemployment as well, is increasing computerisation and automation, replacing human labour, as is the case in many affluent post-industrial countries today.

Other times besides weekends when you might as well go whistle in the wind as get some action on the work front, are Christmas–New Year, with the wind-down starting fairly early in December, and the Great Exodus at the Easter holiday, in early April. Oh, and Melbourne Cup Day too (first Tuesday of November)—forget it for the few hours before, during and after this great horse race, plus the bibulous lunch that often ensues, whether to cry about lost bets or celebrate winnings. Well, make that the whole day, actually. Businessmen, take note. Employees, don't be an outsider, pitch in for your office Sweep bet, study the form and be one of the crowd.

Appearances Can Be Deceptive

Australian workers are deceptive. They often look and sound extremely slow and casual. But in the majority of cases, they turn out to be meticulous workers, and nearly always specialists in their field.

You will rarely get that 'I don't know how it works, I only sell the things' style sadly found in many other countries. They really like to discuss their equipment and explain it to you. They will always service it and repair it, unlike the 'escape artists' often encountered elsewhere. If achieving this quality means slowing things down a bit, personally I still prefer it as a work attitude to the 'wham bang thank you ma'am' type of deal which leaves you with not the faintest idea of how to handle whatever it is that has just been delivered.

Perhaps that is one of the reasons the Australian worker costs so much more than others. But remember, costly workers means that you too are rewarded handsomely if you choose a so-called 'menial' or manual occupation—Australia has justifiably been called 'a working-man's paradise'.

The cost may be one reason you will get fewer workers on a job than you might see, say, in Asia, where labour costs are low. When my husband and I packed up our goods and chattels in Singapore, our apartment was swarming with at least six men looking very busy indeed, creating much sound and fury. It all looked very impressive.

When our huge 20-foot container arrived at our new home in Perth, there were only two Aussies to unload it. We helped a bit, of course (that is the sort of thing you are quietly expected to do in Australia, anyway), but they would have done fine without us.

Now which of the two teams could be called the more hardworking, more efficient, or more productive, I wonder?

Keep It Friendly, Mate

By 'casual', I mean that Australian workers expect you to be friendly. If you want to develop a productive relationship with an Aussie worker, make sure you offer him a cup of tea and a chat. You will be amazed at how much time (often, it's really his boss' time, but that doesn't seem to matter) he has to sit down with you. He will be quite happy to tell you his life story. And that can be quite fascinating sometimes, especially if you are new to the country.

If you come from a country used to a more formal relationship between client and contractor, or between boss and employee, you would be well advised to adapt to Australia's more chatty, egalitarian mode as quickly as possible. Too much of an 'I'm the boss' or 'I'm paying you, aren't I?' type of attitude, or too formal a demeanour could well provoke hostility, or at best, only minimal co-operation. The job might not be done as well.

There is one particular category of worker that you have to look out for a bit: the secretary/personal assistant/receptionist person, usually a woman. Because there is an underlying thread in Australian society of 'I'm not your servant, I am a proud worker earning an honest crust, and besides I know what I am doing, I am in charge', this person may often seem offhand and rude on the phone, or even in person, if you come from a culture used to a more fawning style of service. Some of them are over-anxious to prove that their role is not to serve but is actually sort of pseudo-executive and please go away, they are busy with important things. Don't lose your cool and don't be rude. But also, don't be fazed, just remain calm and be firm, insist on getting from them whatever you think is your due.

Tall Poppies

One of the reasons an Australian worker will sometimes look and sound much less competent or professional than in fact he really is, is the ingrained Australian fear of appearing too 'uppity'. This fear often prevents him from competing effectively and from demonstrating his maximum potential.

The Australian does not want to appear too good at what he or she does, lest this in some way offend or put down other people around him or her. Worse, to truly excel might put him or her in the category 'Tall Poppy'—and tall poppies exist only to be cut down.

Western societies are quite used to airings of this problem in the context of women's relationships with men: the phenomenon of intelligent women working hard at the 'dumb blonde' masquerade lest they be put on the shelf by insecure men, is well known in feminist circles. But a whole nation working hard to appear dumb?

You better believe it. But then again, you better not believe it—because, as I have said, appearances are deceptive.

Remember, you too must play the game if you are to get on with Australians. If you are working hard, try not to show it or talk about it. If you are successful or intelligent, hide it, or at least actively play it down. If you have money, look as poor as possible (besides, flashing it too much is only an advertisement that you may have some to spare and therefore available to steal).

The Tall Poppy Syndrome in Australia has been described by some observers as 'the psychology of envy'. Eminent academics such as psychologist Professor Norman Feather of Australia's Flinders University in 1989, and historian W K Hancock back in 1930, have noted this strong trait in the Australian character.

It is the Tall Poppy Syndrome that most sharply separates Australian psychology from that of the Americans, for whom individualistic achievement in contrast is almost a religion. In America, you aspire to achieve the same heights as some rags-to-riches role model, 'the American Dream'; in Australia, you grudge him/her their success and aim to bring them down to your own level. Some say it's a trait inherited from the English.

Don't Judge This Book by Its Cover

One of the manifestations of the anti-tall poppy school of thought is sloppy dress. This is quite rife in Australia. Viewed benevolently, it looks pleasantly unpretentious, undemanding of others too. But a lot of the time, it just looks, well—sloppy.

In men, it takes the form of shorts for everything—often unpleasantly short and tight ones, too, in the case of older adults. In women, just poorly co-ordinated wardrobes. In both sexes, tatty jeans, and above all, the ubiquitous 'thongs', aka Japanese slippers, flip-flops, rubber sandals, etc.

Setting aside the fact that many Australians truly are strapped for cash, a factor likely to limit one's ability to run a snazzy wardrobe, considering the price of clothing in Australia, the real reason for this lack of attention to personal appearance is the strong desire not to stand out, and above all, never to look at all well off. In short, not to threaten others.

This makes it very easy to dress in Australia, since the trick really is either to un-dress or to down-dress, depending on the time of day. But it makes it very hard to dress up—with the notable exception of the 'special ball' or dinner dance type of event, in which case absolutely everybody dresses to the nines, the women uniformly clad in very ritzy full-length ball gowns.

In immaculate European countries like Austria, I have observed chic ladies in the supermarket, beautifully turned out; never in Australia, where the supermarket is a grossorium of 'who cares, I just got up, and anyway this is only the local supermarket' levels of dress.

This anti-couture culture does mean that nobody can be classified by the way they dress or look. If you come from a country where dress really matters, particularly when negotiating business deals, try to throw your prejudices out of the window when in Australia.

Sickies, Overtime and Wages

Australian work attitudes are in transition right now, as a result of 'down-sizing' and a realisation that globalisation means business. It used to be commonplace for younger workers in particular to save on the job, then leave work for a year or two to travel the world, fully confident that they would be able to step straight into a job on their return. The young still do it—but most workers nowadays are a lot less confident, and rightly so. Many adults even avoid taking leave now, in case they return to find their job gone. Others stick to holidays in Australia and keep a watchful eye on the workplace. Although most Australian full-time workers are entitled to 20 days' paid annual leave (compared with 30 in France, 25 in some Scandinavian countries), in 2010, the South Australia-Western Australian governments' *Australian Work and Life Index* report found that 30 per cent of workers said they were too busy to take leave, and in all, 60 per cent were stockpiling leave for one reason or another and not taking holidays.

For many (around half a million people), the only occupation they will have for some time is regular visits to the job centre (Centrelink agency), looking for work or to register for unemployment benefits, currently on the 'Newstart Allowance' (dole)—applications for this benefit happily have declined slightly by about two per cent between 2011 and 2012. But among those still at work, certain old habits still die hard. For one thing, the 'sickie' is commonplace. This refers to the institution of declaring yourself sick for the day when in fact you just do not much feel like going to work, or it would be handy to extend a holiday long weekend even longer (the President of Toyota Motor Corporation Australia estimated a 30 per cent absenteeism rate in the form of 'sickies' at his Australian (Victoria) factory every long weekend). So if you don't 'use up' your sickies within the year, you're a bit of 'a mug' (stupid), since they represent potential extra leave you cannot get any other way than by declaring yourself unfit to work. This is a situation that the Liberal government under Prime Minister John Howard was trying to stamp out within the terms of unpopular new industrial relations laws ('Work Choices') that eventually cost the Liberals government at the end of 2007. The figures show that workers do indeed take close to all their 10 days' annual sick leave, and the trend is rising to record levels. One professional survey, the Direct Health Solutions Absence Survey of 2010, estimated a cost to the Australian economy of A$ 30 billion a year, or three per cent of Gross Domestic Product, with 15 per cent of employers believing that more than half the sick days taken were faked.

A completely new variation on this theme in 2005 was the phenomenon of 'blue flu' (originally an American term), in which workers suddenly report sick en masse, thus paralysing worksites. This is a disguised strike, designed to circumvent tougher laws these days against 'wildcat' strikes. It's still a rare occurrence in Australia, but surfaced with a vengeance in Western Australia's construction industry during 2005.

Workplace relations are still somewhat in flux as the Labor government first elected in 2007 moves to consolidate the implementation of its new Fair Work Act of 2009 and the new Fair Work Australia system (see *www.fwa.gov.au*) which has also put in place the Office of the Fair Work Ombudsman (see *www.fairwork.gov.au*). The Fair Work industrial relations system now covers the nation, except for Western Australia, the only state that has not bought into it.

Fundamentally, this new regime overturned previous Liberal government attempts to remove collective enterprise bargaining by grouped company workers or labour unions in favour of individual worker-employer negotiated work contracts, and also reversed Liberal attempts to remove unfair dismissal claims by sacked employees that would have made it easier for employers to fire their staff pretty much at will. The system also now works on agreed wage brackets or ranges for specific occupations, called "Modern Awards." Fair Work Australia also rules regularly on the prescribed national minimum wage level. As of mid-2012, this was ruled to be A$ 606.40 per week, or A$ 15.96 per hour, with extra loading for those disadvantaged by casual work.

Hence the key features of the Fair Work system are:

- a set of 10 minimum National Employment Standards (NES)
- 'modern awards' that apply nationally for specific industries and occupations
- a national minimum wage order (where it applies)
- enterprise bargaining
- protection from unfair dismissal.

Fair Work's 10 National Employment Standards (NES)*

- Maximum weekly hours of work—38 hours per week, plus reasonable additional hours. (*Author's note: beyond these hours, you are looking at higher overtime pay, or else 'time in lieu', i.e. extra time off in exchange for the overtime*).
- Requests for flexible working arrangements—an entitlement allowing parents or carers of a child under school age, or of a child under 18 with a disability, to request a change in working arrangements to assist with the care of the child.
- Parental leave and related entitlements—up to 12 months unpaid leave per employee, plus a right to request an additional 12 months unpaid leave, plus other forms of maternity, paternity and adoption related leave.
- Annual leave—four weeks paid leave per year, plus an additional week for certain shift workers.
- Personal/carer's leave and compassionate leave—10 days paid personal/carer's leave, two days unpaid carer's leave as required, and two days compassionate leave (unpaid for casuals) as required (*Author's note: this includes the concept of 'sick leave', although the NES do not clearly state this!*).
- Community service leave—unpaid leave for voluntary emergency activities and leave for jury service, with an entitlement to be paid for up to 10 days for jury service.
- Long service leave—a transitional entitlement for employees as outlined in an applicable pre-modernised award, pending the development of a uniform national long service leave standard.

- Public holidays—a paid day off on a public holiday, except where reasonably requested to work. (*Author's note: employees have the right to refuse to work on public holidays*).
- Notice of termination and redundancy pay—up to five weeks notice of termination and up to 16 weeks' severance pay on redundancy, both based on length of service.
- Provision of a Fair Work Information Statement—must be provided by employers to all new employees, and contains information about the NES, modern awards, agreement-making, the right to freedom of association, termination of employment, individual flexibility arrangements, union rights of entry, transfer of business, and the respective roles of Fair Work Australia and the Fair Work Ombudsman.

* Author's note: Specific enterprise agreements in individual workplaces may permit deviations from some of these standards.

One potentially high cost to the employer is payment for overtime work, which comes on top of already relatively high wages—the Australian Bureau of Statistics recorded average weekly ordinary time earnings for full-time adult employees in 2012 as about A$ 1,345 a week, i.e. without overtime, and on a rising trend.

Depending on your particular workplace agreement, there are other commonly encountered additional costs for employers, or goodies for workers, according to your point of view: paid holiday leave ('leave loading'), and long service leave (usually three to six months, available after ten years' continuous employment in the same job) are two of the key items.

The concept of a legal right to long service leave is uniquely Australian, a throw-back to colonial days when officers needed time to travel back 'home' from the colonies to England. Since then it has been seen as a just reward for faithful service, a useful means of preventing labour turnover, and an opportunity for workers to 'recharge their batteries' that is also beneficial to the employer in terms of getting full value out of his/her employees.

To some extent, the accumulation of these 'perks' for employees is one of the reasons that the Australian workforce is now significantly 'casualised', with around 64 per cent in some form of casual, part-time or short-contract employment (30 per cent in plain part-time work, with more women than men part-timing). Protection for such workers' conditions is far less structured than it is for those in conventional full-time employment, hence part-time workers are much cheaper for employers to run. The result is that a large part of the Australian workforce is underemployed and also financially insecure.

Back to Work!

The Budget in 2012 for the first time undermined single parents' entitlements by ruling that once theirv child turns eight years old, they will be taken off their special welfare allowances and put onto the 'Newstart' allowance (which at about A$ 529.80 a fortnight will reduce their fortnightly allowance income by about A$ 118)—this of course is the 'dole' and brings with it the responsibility to actively seek a job. The ruling means that single parents will no longer be able to stay at home and live off welfare indefinitely. The government's intention is to get as many people into the workforce as possible.

The Dignity of Labour

Australian workers won their basic rights very early, and have defended them vigorously ever since—but again, times are changing. The eight-hour day was secured by striking stonemasons in 1855, the basic minimum wage in 1907, and the 40-hour week in 1946. The world's first legislation providing for paid sick leave and paid long-service leave was enacted in the state of New South Wales in 1951.

Australians are particularly hot on matters of industrial/occupational safety and health, and 'duty of care' issues, to a degree that may take some more cavalier outsiders aback. Would-be employers are strongly advised to research this issue carefully, as there are set procedures to follow, and heavy penalties to pay for failure to observe the Occupational Health and Safety Act.

Without going into the detailed pros and cons, enormous fusses have been made in recent years about allegedly debilitating 'Repetitive Strain Injury' or 'RSI', incurred through repeated restricted movements of the hand and arm in particular—such as those made by high-speed typists and computer-keyboard operators—about workers in contact with asbestos (many of Australia's older homes are insulated and roofed with asbestos), and about the health dangers or otherwise of extended work at Visual Display Units (VDUs) such as computer monitor screens.

SERVICE, CIVILITY AND SERVILITY

As already mentioned, the Australian style of service can be a problem, depending on where you are coming from. Possibly another hangover from the tribulations of a convict past and of the triumphant shaking off of those fetters, is the average Australian's determination never again to bow his head to any man, to serve no one—but to his credit, neither does he particularly wish to be served. Nothing embarrasses and confuses your average Australian, a natural socialist, more than being presented with a servant, as happens to him when travelling in Asia, for example. He simply doesn't know what to do with one.

Service industries like tourism do have a hard time in Australia. It is not that Australian workers are rude—far from it —but they are offhand, casual and familiar if you compare them with, say, the best available in the European capitals, or in many Asian capitals for that matter. To put it another way, they do not crawl. To put it the earthy Australian way, they do not 'brown-nose' (an unpleasant reference to being so much of an 'arse-licker' that you get a brown nose).

Columnist Ruth Ostrow once surveyed poor hotel and restaurant service, remarking, "To be unable to serve is a testimony of our ever-present national insecurity complex." And a 2011 consumer service industry survey found that two-thirds of Australians felt service standards had declined sharply over the past five years, with young retail workers a particular issue. Well, what did I already say about the risks of a casualised workforce? Some of these younger workers

One of the glories of the Australian system is that the tip is still considered demeaning by most Australian workers—although admittedly, increasing tourism, migration and the pressures of recession are now all combining to create some cracks in that façade. But traditionally, the tip is seen as the thin end of the wedge towards making excuses for low wages; a man should be paid what he is worth in the form of a decent wage, no more, no less. No tips please, we're Australian.

are also poorly paid, and virtually untrained. Australian employers need to invest more in professional development; but with a here-today, gone-tomorrow workforce, would you?

On the other hand, I surely cannot be the only person who has enjoyed the straight, eye-to-eye equality assumed by all Australian service personnel, and the candour that goes with it: the waiter who warns that you may not enjoy your order as 'it's not so fresh today', why don't you try something else?

EVERYBODY OUT!

The bad old days for 'the Great Australian Strike' were epitomised by 1974 when an horrendous 6.3 million working days were lost to industrial action. Since 1991, when 1.5 million working days were lost, the trend has been downwards, and the Australian worker's legendary propensity to strike has been no more than that, legend. This has coincided with increasing prosperity and low unemployment, but also with stronger legal restrictions on when and whether a strike can be considered legal or not. In other words, if you can't legally strike, you tend not to strike. But it has to be said that industrial disputes have shown an upward tick since 2010. The context for this may well be more unevenly spread prosperity in a 'patchwork economy,' and greater insecurity. Most of the disputes occurred in transport sectors – from ports to airports to buses and trains, in community service industries and health, or in education, not so much in the heavy manufacturing and engineering industries, or even in the notoriously fractious construction industry.

Under the new Fair Work industrial relations regime that barely kicked in during 2010, Fair Work Australia can stop strikes in their tracks, if they threaten significant economic damage, or lives, for example, as indeed happened in October 2011 in relation to the infamous Qantas airline industrial dispute that culminated in a management lockout and grounding of the airline's entire fleet (this forced the two parties into conciliation discussions and possible arbitration by Fair Work). Fair Work also requires labour unions to seek a Fair Work order for a protected, secret ballot among workers to authorise their proposed industrial action. That said, strikes and lockouts (management locking out employees) together doubled in 2011 to score a quarter of a million lost working days. Some are saying that the new Fair Work system encourages strike action.

To look at the history of the industrial relations scene in Australia, it is useful to start with the signing of the so-called 'Accord' (the Prices and Incomes Accord) between the Australian Labor Party and the Australian Council of Trade Unions (ACTU) in 1983, an agreement that muted industrial relations problems somewhat, what with Labor in power until 1996, and the legendary Bob Hawke, a former ACTU president, prime minister for much of that time. Relations between the labour movement and the Labor Party traditionally have been close, although the unions have become increasingly uncomfortable with right-wing dominance of party policy in recent years. The unions have often shown their muscle over purely political, even foreign-policy issues, for example, against Japanese aggression in China during the 1930s, against Australian involvement in the Vietnam War in 1965, against foreign sailors' working conditions, and against Indonesian action in East Timor in more recent years. Even the Labor government saw the need to modernise the union movement: in 1987, it moved to restructure and rationalise the movement with the objective of reducing the number of unions from 215 (1987)—only nine of which were truly, numerically, powerful—to about 20 by the turn of the 20th century, by means of amalgamating some of the smaller unions.

Under Liberal Prime Minister John Howard, from 1996-2007, there were even more concerted and persistent attacks on the old Labor orthodoxy that favoured the power of the labour unions. But a more right-of-centre Labor party has also done its own damage. The traditional idea of fixed 'Awards' —benchmark payment rates for various industries, set by a tripartite pact among government, employers and labour unions—has survived under the Labor government since 2007, as has some form of collective bargaining, but alongside a diversity of more flexible and enterprise-specific formats, as well as new restrictions on union activity. The strength of the unions has steadily declined. partly as a result (although they still wield perhaps disproportionate political power): union membership dropped by 20 per cent during the 1980s, to less than 40 per cent of the workforce, and again during the 1990s, to the point where on average, the unionised percentage is only just 18 per cent now (2011). Revelations during 2012 of malpractice within certain unions is thought likely to provoke a further slide. The most strongly unionised sectors today are teaching, nursing and the public service. .

Caution, All Kiwis and Wannabe New Zealanders

New Zealanders used to get a cushy 'special relationship' type deal in Australia, on an automatically obtained 'Special Category Visa' (SCV) which automatically made them an Australian resident, with full access to social security and welfare. This was a convenient 'backdoor entry' too for migrants who failed in their application to move to Australia but succeeded with New Zealand. No longer.

The Australian Government changed this situation in 2001. New Zealanders can still live and work indefinitely in Australia but now they are not classified as Australian residents. They need to apply to become a citizen or permanent resident, and, like other new arrivals, wait for two years, before they can access social security.

HANDOUT HEARTBREAK

Australia is fundamentally a welfare society. But unemployment benefits—'the dole', recently metamorphosed into the 'Newstart' allowance—are nowhere near as easy to get nowadays as they used to be, particularly if you are young and strong enough to work. There is now a strong drive to reduce welfare dependency across the board. But despite a fairly low unemployment rate of around five per cent, the number of long-term (more than 12 months) unsuccessful job-seekers on Newstart welfare payments numbered just under 349,000 in February 2012, a steep increase on previous years; the total on Newstart was almost 575,000 people.

The ongoing restructuring of Australia's economy and labour market is already having real impact on the handout psychology of the dole.

Even the disabled are subjected to closer scrutiny these days, with a government policy declared in 2002 that anybody deemed fit to work 15 hours or more a week would automatically be moved from the Disability Support Pension (DSP) welfare grant to the Newstart allowance, meaning that they would only be supported by welfare pending finding a job, if they have been assessed capable of some work. Previously, the cut-off level had been set at 30 hours a week. (However, since 2012, DSP recipients are now allowed to receive a part-pension even if they actually work 30 hours a week). Eligibility for the DSP is also dependent on means and asset-testing. Total DSP recipients stood at over 800,000 by 2012, slated to cost the nation close to A\$ 15 billion for the 2012–13 Budget year. Numbers have been growing faster than for the DSP than for any other form of welfare support programme but this may be natural in an ageing population like Australia's. But some observers feel that the DSP figures hide further unemployment or under-employment statistics. The idea now is to focus more on what the disabled can do than on what they cannot do.

The 2012–13 Budget scoped a total cost of A\$ 131.6 billion for all welfare and social security combined.

For all the inside information on the Australian welfare scene, go to Centrelink's website http://www.centrelink.gov.au

Australia's relatively high rates of income tax (for many people, between 32 and 37 per cent) cover not only social security but also include a Medicare levy for the provision of almost-free medical care; your doctor bills the government ('bulk-billing') and you pay your share later, or if he bills you for the total amount, you then claim a partial rebate from the government. This perhaps over-generous system, like the unions, is suffering nibbling erosion at present as the government struggles to prevent its costly abuse by the public. It is virtually compulsory now to pay for private health insurance cover—financial disincentives against not taking private cover include an extra penalty levy on your insurance premium if you decide to take up private insurance only after the age of 30. If you delay taking private cover until the age of 40, you will pay 20 per cent more than someone who has held that cover since more than 10 years ago. Among the big names offering such coverage are 'HBF', and Medibank. The advantage of private cover for the consumer is assured medical attention when you want it (there is a long queue for non-emergency surgery under the Medicare system in public hospitals), with your choice of hospital and surgeon, but the disadvantage is, of course, the high premium to be paid and the frequent discovery of an awkward 'gap' between your coverage and the cost of your treatment, a gap which you largely have to cover with your own money. Needless to say, Medicare still takes care of emergencies immediately, whether a person has private coverage or not. In other words, a private health subscriber still has the option to choose public health—Medicare—when admitted to hospital suddenly, as an emergency, provided he/she understands that they may not get a plush bed or ward immediately. But they will still get excellent care under the public system.

Medicine prescription charges are high, but the Pharmaceutical Benefits Scheme (PBS) available to all residents with a Medicare card provides a subsidy on all PBS-listed medicines and drugs. You are only liable for A$ 35.40 of the cost of your prescription medicine, with the rest paid by the government; if you have a concession card, as for pensioners and the disabled, your co-payment will be only A$ 5.80.

But when the moan goes up about decent taxpayers forking out for layabouts on the dole ('dole-bludgers') or for fake 'sickies', as it often does, my thoughts go to two mercy cases I have encountered. One was my girlfriend whose little girl was born four months prematurely, with cerebral palsy which prevented her from walking properly. In the other case, another girlfriend's daughter, aged about eight, was quite suddenly diagnosed with a hole in her heart. Both stories had a happy ending, largely thanks to the Medicare welfare system. I was paying for it as a tax-payer, but why wouldn't I ?

YOUR PARTNER IN BUSINESS

The Australian businessman is strangely schizoid: superficially pally but really quite cagey, seemingly mild and undriven but in fact capable of unbridled aggression, apparently egalitarian and incorrupt but actually a lot more 'flexible' than that would imply, casual and relaxed on the surface but deep down, quite tense. Once again, avoid judging the book by its cover.

The best way to break the ice is to share a beer together at the pub, to talk about sport, or to meet at a barbie party and talk about anything but work.

The fundamentally anti-intellectual stance of the average Australian sometimes affects business too. People get things done in a makeshift, nonchalant 'She'll be right' fashion, without reference to any real expertise, whether published or in the person of a flesh-and-blood expert.

Getting To Know You...
The phenomenon of the use of the familiar first name, and a general reticence about handing out business cards, means that it is entirely possible to exit from even a business meeting in Australia, certainly from a social gathering, still not knowing the full names of anybody present, even less what their titles, functions or phone numbers are. You may have to impose yourself fairly aggressively on your business associates if you really want their details, by making the first move yourself. But be aware that you risk being thought of as a bit 'pushy.'

Be prepared, too, for the familiarity of official and business letters from complete strangers addressing you as 'Dear Bill' or 'Dear Susan', etc. Australia has never liked honorific titles of any kind and now it seems, even 'Mr', 'Mrs', 'Ms' and 'Miss' have been cast aside forever. And you can call your boss 'Bill' or 'Susan' to their face too. It's all part of the national egalitarian ethos, although one does doubt that these people would write to their Prime Minister in quite the same tone. I could be wrong, though. This is Australia. Certainly, at cocktail parties I myself have witnessed people bounding up to State ministers with a cheerful, "Hello, Judy, how yer goin'?" Asians in particular will be horrified by this.

But, reverting to letters, you will have been very lucky indeed to get any kind of letter at all. Australians are notoriously reluctant to write or to answer letters. Email response may be somewhat better, but, like the Americans, Australians respond better to phone calls, and also to faxes.

KEEPING UP APPEARANCES
Overall, dress standards in Australian offices are relaxed but conservative, if that makes any sense. You shouldn't dress to the

nines, and women don't really need make-up, but on the other hand, men in suits and ties and women in long-skirted dress-suits are favoured. Boring black and grey are omnipresent. The younger generation seems oblivious to this hidden code, however, especially in recent times of low unemployment and easy job-seeking. You may well be amazed – or possibly, if you are male, pleasantly entertained – at the level of inappropriate dress among young female office workers: secretaries' cleavages 'letting it all hang out', pierced navels and tightly sheathed butts all clearly on show, you name it. And note that it's quite common for workers to arrive at work by bicycle in full cycling gear, helmet and all, but they will always go to the office social club changing rooms or gym to change into something formal before starting work. It all depends on your industry, really, as well as local weather conditions, and generally speaking, standards in the eastern states capitals like Sydney and Melbourne are more international, more 'hip-chic' than in far-flung parts like Western Australia or the Northern Territory. Public relations and media are, as elsewhere, notoriously eccentric. But the public sector is pretty stiff.

EARNING A CRUST

It has never been altogether clear whether or not Australians really *want* to make money.

To take one example from everyday life, I once bought some black olives at a supermarket delicatessen counter in Australia. After the woman serving had weighed and priced them, she then said, "Would you like some of the juice-stuff they're in as well?" Why not, said I. "Oh yes, I always ask that *after* I've weighed them," the woman told me, "because you'd be surprised how much the juice adds to the weight, and to the price." So I got my 'olives-juice' free, as an extra.

I marvelled at this. A shopkeeper almost anywhere else would have weighed the whole lot and charged for it all. After all, if you want juice, you should pay for it, right?

Then there was the barman on a Saturday night who said lackadaisically that he'd run out of half of his printed wine list the night before and he was 'just coming to terms with how much his stock had run down'. I said nothing, but thought,

Some Do's and Don'ts in the Office

Don't

- Turn down an invitation to go out for lunch, a drink, or to view the Melbourne Cup, least of all while saying, 'Sorry, I've got too much work to do.' You'll get a name as an unfriendly workaholic bore and too ambitious by half, a bit of a threat.
- Treat secretaries, personal assistants or tea-ladies (if any) etc. as anything other than valued equals and intelligent comrades fully participating in the tasks of your office—that would be very un-Australian.
- Express too many new ideas about good new things to do or ways to change established procedures in the office, until about a year after you arrive—take things slowly, and quietly.
- Call up co-workers about work issues after 5:00 pm, or at weekends or when they are on holiday—urgency no excuse!
- (As a male) Touch female workers, even in an affectionate platonic way, offer elaborate compliments on their looks or dress, or make off-colour jokes in their presence—sexism and harrassment charges lurk around the corner!

Do

- Observe whether there is a roster for stocking the office fridge or making tea etc., and offer to participate accordingly.
- Stop by the water dispenser, or while making coffee in the kitchen, for a quick but light chat with your co-workers, on the lines of 'So how was your weekend?', or 'Has your kid got better now?' Or better still, 'Mate, did you see that footy score on Saturday!?'.
- Join office sports teams and leisure clubs.

is this any way to do business? Why not move heaven and earth next day to restock the bar? Don't ask.

In another incident, a shopkeeper who was regularly selling out of a particularly popular fruit juice blend told his customers he doubted he would be stocking it much more. Why not? "Oh, I don't really like it, myself," he explained. Any self-respecting Asian businessman would have filled his store wall to wall with the stuff.

This blunted economic drive and general lack of apology for it, is part of the country's charm, but also of its economic downfall.

When I enquired about the cost of hiring a computer from a company specialising in such hire, the reply came that it would be A$ 20 a day, or A$ 600 a month, which of course amounted to the same thing. Yet normal business practice would surely be to entice the customer into a longer hire period by charging *less* per day for a longer-term contract. This would benefit both the hire-firm and the customer. This simple way of making more money apparently had not occurred to the rather literal management of this particular company.

> 'Why do business with a country where "She'll be right" means she'll be wrong and the delivery will be late as well? Why bother to believe a country whose national catch-cry "No worries" really translates into "We've stuffed it up again"?'
> —Journalist John Hamilton, in Western Australia's *Daily News*, 27 December 1989

Another endearing feature of this syndrome is the Australian shopkeeper's willingness to send you up the road to his competitors, where, he blithely tells you, they will have just what you are looking for and maybe cheaper, too. Or the waiter's whispered advice that "the fish isn't that good today, I wouldn't if I were you." Of course, this also has a lot to do with the extreme mobility of the Australian workforce, and the prevalence of part-time and casual work—few workers are one place long enough to develop loyalty to their employers.

Clearly, the desire to make money, or at least, to make profit, is consciously or subconsciously considered an evil reserved for 'tall poppies', those shooting comets so successful that their only way forward is down in most Australians' opinion.

Just Dig It Up

Australia has been able to afford such complacency in the past because it is so rich in natural resources—bauxite, iron ore, zinc, uranium, oil, gas, coal, lead and gold among them. For a long time, Australia has been 'The Lucky Country'. All you had to do to stay wealthy was go dig something else up. Linkage with England provided a ready market for Australian wool, lamb, beef and wheat. And a past pattern of government protectionism further sheltered Australian business from the real world.

Among the realities are the very small size of the Australian domestic market and the high freight costs of reaching all-Australia—the 'tyranny of distance'. A report once pointed out that Heinz UK could export canned baked beans to Perth more cheaply than its Australian counterpart could get them to the Western Australian capital from its plant in the Victorian capital of Melbourne. And I have long wondered why I can get fresh eastern-states Australian cherries in Singapore for about A$ 8 a kilo while in Western Australia I would have to pay A$ 15 or much more.

Australian businessmen have found it hard to keep up with a fast-changing world—the increasing self-sufficiency of the European community (including Australia's traditional business partner, England), for example, the impact of synthetics, as well as increased cotton production, on wool, and competition from almost every direction, especially from low-cost Asia, notably China.

There is little doubt about the quality of Australian products. But nowadays, hunting Australian retail outlets for anything not made in China is like looking for a needle in a haystack. The Achilles heel of Australian business has always been marketing.

The fatal combination of almost unbridled consumerist materialism in the prosperous 1950s and 1960s (often based on credit), and complacency about primary produce and protected industries, sowed the seeds of Australia's miseries in the 1980s and beyond.

A Cautionary Tale

Take wool as a case study of how things can go wrong. It was once said that the Australian economy rode on the back of the sheep. But the national sheep flock declined by an estimated 23 million head or 21 per cent in the six years between 2001 and 2007, from 111 million head to an estimated 88 million (now about 72 million head). The value of wool production fell by about half a billion Australian dollars between 2001-2007. Long lasting drought conditions over the decade of the 21st century have been one factor, making maintenance of big flocks just too expensive and the climate change ahead does not bode well for the industry.

In 1990–1991, the 70,000 'woolgrowers' of the Australian wool industry, which supplied something like 70 per cent of the world's wool, learned a hard lesson: their market crashed, leaving them with debts of A\$ 2.6 billion in hand, 4.5 million bales of wool stockpiled and about 20 million of their 166 million sheep shot, because suddenly they were not even worth the food they were eating.

As Jacqueline Huie of the Australian Graduate School of Management at the University of New South Wales told *The Australian* in 1991, 'If you take your eyes off what your customers want, it is at your peril. We took our eyes off our wool customers and as a result it came as a complete surprise when in two years our major customers, the USSR and China, changed and bought next to nothing. Meanwhile, nobody told the farmers. They kept on producing. Can you imagine losing the majority of your customers in two years, doubling your production and not being able to predict any part of it? Even if we didn't know about market research, what about industrial spying?' This has a lot to do with the Australian's basically trusting, naive nature; he does not expect to be deceived or let down. In business, all too often, he can be a sitting duck.

Australia has also made the classic mistake of failing to upgrade into value-added products, rather than just exporting raw primary commodities and produce, and this too has played a role in the wool disaster. In the old days, raw wool went out to England and returned to Australia as a made-up garment (now the same applies to wool sent out to China); Australian iron ore goes to Japan and returns in a made-in-Japan car. This has been bad for the balance of payments. Fundamentally, Australia is still 'digging it up', growing it or farming it, from coal and natural gas to canola oil and dairy products. But too rarely, making it. Former Prime Minister Kevin Rudd's declared hopes of fostering a thriving car manufacturing industry in Australia, preferably focused on environmentally-friendly hybrids and other innovations, was probably the way to go, but unfortunately a world recession hit before he could get off base with this one.

The State of the Economy

The nation's trade balance (for merchandise) made a dramatic turnaround from past multi-billion dollar deficits into a surplus of close to 17 billion Australian dollars during 2010-2011, with China the largest trading partner, notching up over A$100 billion of total trade. The Current Account Balance is in the red to the tune of US$33 billion. Total (gross) foreign debt is around A$1,365 billion, equivalent to 94.7 per cent of GDP, about 80 per cent of it attributable to private-sector borrowing. This ranks Australia 13th on the global external debt scoreboard, with the USA at the top.

Unemployment is around 5 per cent, compared with the above 7 per cent average recorded from the 1970s up to 2010. However, the casualisation of the labour force often seen in mature post-industrial economies continues, in the form of widespread part-time, casual, temporary or contract employment affecting about 25 per cent of the workforce. Women workers (72 per cent of part-timers in 2007) and the young are particularly affected. This effectively can disguise further unemployment, as well as adversely impacting on general economic and administrative efficiency. It also promotes a general feeling of unease and social insecurity, as well as disloyalty, among workers, while making it impossible for families to plan or commit ahead, and discouraging employers from investing in skills training. This precarious scenario has led to an apt new term for the new proletariat, the "Precariat", coined by British economist Professor Guy Standing in his 2011 book *The Precariat: The New Dangerous Class* . Others just call this system 'flexible' and say it is essential to modern economies. As the *Sydney Morning Herald* commented in 2012, if you add to the 25 per cent another 4 per cent for fixed-term contractors and 10 per cent for independent contractors, often dependent on one client, you get a floating sector accounting for a massive 40 per cent of the Australian workforce.

The Fair Work Australia body administers the provisions of the Labor government's Fair Work Act of 2009, including the minimum wage of A$ 15.51 per hour or A$ 589.30 per week. Wage rises were set at 3.4 per cent in the required annual wage review of 2011. Hours worked have eased in recent years as the economy has improved, to about an average of 35 hours a week. Employers from more free-wheeling economies need to be aware that in Australia, there are laws against "Unfair Dismissal" of workers, coupled with a special dismissal code applicable to small businesses.

Wheelers and Dealers

Australia's businessmen are much more 'real' today than they were in the 1980s. A whole breed of 'smart-guys' got its comeuppance after a decade of heady euphoria during the 1980s.

Names like Alan Bond (English-born former sign-painter), Christopher Skase (Qintex group of companies), John Elliott (Elders-IXL), and others were all powers in the land, and national heroes—yesterday.

Today, most of these multimillionaires are ruined or discredited, or both, with debts in the billions of Australian dollars, former emperors with no clothes but the debts on which their empires were founded. (Although the irrepressible Bond seems to be on a comeback path). Their main tactic had been to use the tax deductibility of the interest payable on their borrowings, which they had used to acquire companies— and to make money by selling off their appreciated assets later. It was, as *The Australian* remarked, 'a stark reminder that money needs to be earned'. In Western Australia and in Victoria, the problem was governments fancying themselves as businessmen, taking on what should have been entrepreneurial projects in partnership with businessmen, while in Queensland, it was corruption and dirty tricks generally.

The survivors of the business fallout are big fish such as media magnates James Packer, Kerry Stokes and Rupert

Murdoch (hiding his Australian birth under an American passport). These days, the resource giants and miners feeding the Chinese behemoth tend to top the A-list. The *Business Review Weekly* (BRW)'s annual *Rich 200* list for 2010–11 showed a woman at no 1, Gina Rinehart, heiress to her father the late Lang Hancock's iron-ore empire in Western Australia (A$ 10.31 billion); low-profile South Africa-born Israeli commodities trader Ivan Glasenberg at no 2 (Glencore International, A$ 8.80 billion); Fortescue Metals Group chairman Andrew "Twiggy" Forrest at third place (A$ 6.18 billion); Queensland miner and resources investor Clive Palmer fifth (Mineralogy, A$ 5.05 billion),

Eminent Queenslanders have appeared in court, right up to the level of the former premier, Sir Joh Bjelke-Petersen. In 1991, after an 89-day trial, the former state police commissioner, Sir Terence Lewis, was found guilty of 15 bribery counts between 1978 and 1987 in connection with a protection racket shielding gambling and prostitution rings.

followed closely by retail tycoon Frank Lowy (Westfield shopping-centre properties (A$ 4.98 billion) and James Packer (Crown casinos and Consolidated Media, A$ 4.16 billion), sixth and eighth respectively.

When doing business in Australia, you need to be aware of the scars left by all the bad news of the past.

Australian business circles now are sobered, conservative and cautious, wary of risk or any form of debt. Witness the strength of Australia's banks in recent years compared with their European and American counterparts; witness also the Labor government's almost hysterical insistence on balancing the national Budget to achieve a surplus in 2011–12 even if it risked slowing the economy.

Boom-Bust

Up to the 1990s, the Australian economy, including subdivisions like the property market, characteristically displayed a strongly cyclical boom-bust pattern.

It is still not clear whether this pattern is really over, as some economists believe—certainly property has still shown great volatility and has powered ahead in an almost alarming way, making housing in Australia's key cities Sydney, Melbourne, Brisbane, Adelaide and Perth "severely unaffordable" in the

2011 data gathered internationally by the US consultancy Demographia: "Australia exhibited the worst housing affordability of any national market outside Hong Kong. There were no affordable markets in Australia in 2011 and the overwhelming majority of markets were severely unaffordable." The median house price nation-wide is now around half a million Australian dollars, upwards (especially in Sydney). Part of the national psychology which has contributed to this cycle is the Australian gambling instinct, which easily matches that of those other well-known punters, the Chinese. The gambling obsession stems both from Irish traditions in Australia's colonial beginnings and from the boredom of life in the remote countryside back in the old days: for a bit of excitement, the Australian would bet on anything that moved, and still does.

The government derives considerable tax revenue from this national weakness. In 2006, state and local government gambling tax revenue amounted to close to A$ 5 billion, Australians are legally permitted to gamble on horses, dogs, numbers games such as Lotto (you can just trot down to the newsagent's and ask for your '12-game Slikpik for Saturday Lotto' like I do, if you don't want to dream up your own permutations of numbers) and the football Pools, as well as on slot-machines or 'one-armed bandits' ('pokies') in some states. You place your gee-gee, doggie or other sporting bet through the government's local TAB (Totalisator Agency Board) office.

National gaming takings amount to about A$ 15.5 billion a year, with almost 60 per cent of that coming from poker and other gaming machines Australian gamblers lose about A$ 19 billion a year on various types of gambling recreation.

Casino Culture

Residual puritanism delayed the introduction of (legal) casinos until the first was opened in 1973, in the Tasmanian capital of Hobart. Today they exist in all states, numbering 13 in all. One casino game you probably will encounter for the first time when in Australia is the old outback game of 'Two-Up'. It is based on spinning two coins and betting whether they will fall as two heads or two tails. The simple zinc Two-Up sheds still stand on the fringes of goldrush towns like Kalgoorlie, reminding us of how basic recreational facilities were in pioneer days.

The casinos are crammed full with 'ordinary Australians'. The atmosphere is rarely as classy as at the French counterparts, for example, although there will be private gaming rooms for very special customers, of course.

Turning Things Upside Down

Australia is now going through an economic revolution every bit as turbulent as a war. Sacred cows of all kinds are being sent crashing to the ground, or at least being chipped away at—the welfare state, the power of the unions, protectionism, state enterprise …

Much of the action, ironically, began under the auspices of an increasingly right-of-centre Labor government, in power from 1983, perhaps because Labor was the party most likely to be able to persuade the average Australian worker to go along with it. As the 1980s turned into the 1990s, Australia briefly overheated, then began to enter 'the recession we had to have' to prevent Australia from becoming a 'banana republic', to use two of former Prime Minister Paul Keating's phrases. Small wonder the unpopular Keating earned for himself the sobriquet 'The Grim Reaper'. After the election of John Howard's conservative Liberal Party government in 1996, all the expected conservative measures were gradually put in place, including tighter control of welfare and tax reform, looser individual 'Workplace Agreements' also known as 'WorkChoices', instead of mandatory conditions for workers; the virtual removal of 'unfair dismissal' appeal protection for sacked workers. Privatisation was also a Liberal leitmotif and the proposed sale of the major, formerly national monopoly, telecoms player Telstra has been a bone of much contention in Australia. But under the Labor government since late 2007, the Workplace Agreements have been scrapped. The current industrial relations regime is known as Fair Work Australia. As might be expected, it is more favourable to employees; for example, the concept of "unfair dismissal" has been restored.

The Global Financial Crisis of 2007-'09 now looks like a minor interruption to the general upward trend, possibly thanks to former Labor Prime Minister Rudd's input of expensive cash stimulus programmes at the time: Australia remains a rich country mostly getting richer, with a real economic buzz, particularly as China gears its economy upwards and keeps up its large orders for Australian commodities – so much so that the economy has forced the Government into much greater investment in apprenticeship programmes, and an accelerated programme for skilled worker immigration.

One of the indices that Australians watch the most nervously is the home-loan interest rate, which is now around 6 per cent, with cash rates much lower at 3.75 per cent—retail banks churlishly have not been passing on the independent Reserve Bank of Australia recommendations for lower interest rates.

To summarise recent economic history, I quote a US State Department briefing in late 2004:

'Australia commenced a basic reorientation of its economy in the 1980s and has transformed itself from an inward looking, import-substitution country to an internationally competitive, export-oriented one.' The problem ahead for the Australian economy is simply that it is no longer a single economy: it now has two tiers, with the resources and mining sector "going gang-busters" as Aussies would say, on the up and up, while almost all other industries, notably retail, tourism and manufacturing are either stagnant or declining, smarting from a high Australian dollar, high prices and low consumer confidence. The mining boom's gains have not been evenly distributed through the economy: many ordinary Australians see only rising prices and a declining quality of life arising from it. Many businesses are struggling with the increasing cost of credit, while consumers are nervously reining in their spending, with one eye to the financial instability in Europe and in the banking sector particularly. The resources sector's dependence on China's economic health is worrying. Chinese and other foreign investors' current interest in acquiring vast stretches of Australian agricultural land, often to convert its use to mining, is another worry, a possible threat to the nation's future food security.

Nonetheless, in many ways, the Australian economy today, recession-proof so far, is the envy of the world. In 2011, it was the fastest growing advanced economy in the world. The International Monetary Fund also pronounced in April 2012 that it would be the world's best performer over the near future. The expected growth rate for 2012 was 3.25 per cent, with early indications suggesting even 4 per cent or more. The 2012–13 Budget has been carefully engineered into a projected modest A$ 1.5 billion surplus, delivery of which will be a feat considering the actual blowout of the preceding year's Budget to an A$ 44.4-billion deficit.

Poverty Think

'Life is not meant to be easy' said the former Liberal prime minister Malcolm Fraser in 1971. Most Australians remember, and quote, this phrase ruefully nowadays. Funnily enough, despite general economic growth, the gap between the rich and the poor is widening rapidly in Australia and the old classless egalitarian model of Australian society is under severe pressure as a result. There is an army of semi-employed, part-time and contract workers that is doing it tough, on very low earnings, many of them women, quite a few single parents.

I had never heard of 'lay-bys' until I went to Australia. A sure sign of a cash-strapped people, they are extended hire-purchase arrangements, interest-free, privately contracted between shopkeeper and customer. So if you fancy a mechanical doll for your little daughter's Christmas present, you can go into the shop in September and ask for a 'lay-by'. The doll will be kept aside for you and you will go into the shop every month to pay off a fixed sum, until you have paid for it and can take it home.

Then there are the busy, informal neighbourhood swap and second-hand markets, usually at weekends, where the elderly and desperate selling their family heirlooms for a song are sprinkled among the younger traders simply out to make a buck. And the 'op shops' selling second-hand goods are popular with almost everybody, including yours truly. There is a strong tradition also of informal groups, both in the suburbs and the countryside, using barter of services and goods instead of money. At this level, the cash economy has disappeared. Instead people are saying 'You babysit for me this Friday and I'll mow your lawn on Sunday,' or 'I'm a trained secretary, so I'll type out your letters; you're a trained electrician, so after that you can fix my light switch.'

Australia is still comparatively rich, but many have fallen by the wayside. It is as well to remember this when dealing with Australians—remember that they may be hiding real distress, never assume they have money.

Scientific Excellence

Australia has sworn to transform its national slogan from 'The Lucky Country' to 'The Clever Country'. It is already well set on that path. Australian achievements in science and technology are well documented, among the best known being in computer software, telecommunications, medicine and biotechnology—and perhaps also the much-maligned cardboard and foil wine-cask.

Migrants tend to pack an enormous amount of electrical gadgetry when they move house to Australia, in the belief that they won't be able to get as good or as cheap electronics in Australia. They should pause to check this one out first, however, as often the Australian technology (and design) is superior, and the price either similar or only marginally higher.

Like other countries before her, however, Australia is still making the mistake of failing to link academic research properly with the private sector for implementation. Two important bodies involved in the promotion of research and development are the CSIRO or Australian Commonwealth Scientific and Industrial Research Organisation, which dates back to 1926, and the Australian Research Council. If it were not for CSIRO's work on giving wool new properties such as being shrink-proof and capable of permanent pressing, the Australian wool industry would have collapsed much earlier, in the 1950s, when synthetics first began to gain popularity. But the CSIRO has been forced in recent years to seek linkage with, and funding from, the private sector by the Federal Government's decision to slash its own funding for the organisation.

It is generally agreed that, if Australia is to reduce her dependence on primary products, her politicians and businessmen must do much more to support the country's undoubted talent for areas such as biotechnology and information technology.

THE TAX MAN COMETH...

If I really knew all the ins and outs of Australian tax, I doubt I would be writing this book. I would be sitting back and enjoying my enormous wealth. Because everybody in Australia wants to understand the Australian tax system. Few do.

Coping with Australia's Byzantine tax regulations is a national industry. The situation is very grey indeed and it is entirely possible to get totally contradictory counsel from different accountants and tax consultants, as well as from the Australian Taxation Office (ATO) itself. On the other hand, the system is not quite as cruel as outsiders have branded it: consider the generosity of items such as Low Income Tax Offset, the Mature Age Workers Offset and the Medical Expenses Offset, all of which may reduce your income tax if you are a low-earner, ageing, and paying substantial medical bills.

Suffice it to say that one of the first things you are supposed to do on arrival in Australia, particularly if you have a job or want one, is to apply for a Tax File Number. If you have a formal, conventional job, you will probably be put on the Pay As You Go or PAYG system whereby your tax will be deducted automatically from your monthly pay and if you have overpaid, you will have the pleasure of a rebate cheque from the ATO after you have submitted your income tax return form to them. The law requires you to keep your tax records for five years in case the ATO wants to backtrack with queries, perish the thought. There has been a single taxation policy operated at the Federal level since 1942.

For more information, visit the ATO at http://www.ato.gov.au

The GST Revolution

The Liberal Party lost an election on the Goods and Services Tax issue (the equivalent of the UK Value Added Tax) in 1993 but rode to victory on this dark horse in 1996. What exactly changed the voters' minds is a mystery to most observers. Perhaps they just hated the then Premier Paul Keating's lofty manner more than the GST, who knows.

The GST levies 10 per cent on just about everything except fresh food, hospital services, education, charitable funds and farmed farmland. This does not necessarily imply price rises though the general outlook points to mild inflation. While all this is bothersome to the consumer, what has caused even more ructions is the impact on small business of the system requiring everyone (except employees) to register for an Australian Business Number (ABN) bracketed as his or her GST registration number. Not having an ABN clearly quoted on your invoice risks a blanket top tax rate of 47 per cent.

This was partly a ploy to bring in from the cold small businesses operating in the twilight zone, often transacting in cash and avoiding tax—but there is a still a 'black economy' working underground, nevertheless. Taxi drivers, for example, must have an ABN regardless of their turnover. Technically, those with a turnover below A$ 50,000 do not fall into the compulsory GST net, but voluntary registration for the system might be wise. Many big businesses prefer not to deal with contractors who are not registered for GST, since if you do not charge them for GST, they then cannot claim GST outputs to offset against their own GST collections that must be rendered to government.

Businesses must file with the Tax Office a regular Business Activity Statement charting GST collected and due to the government and claiming credits on GST paid to suppliers to reduce the tax which must be remitted to the Government. Here are some simplified pointers on tax matters. Get an advisor and keep every piece of documentary evidence you can obtain for each of your financial transactions, including a log for your car use.

- **Tax File Numbers**
  If you are a tax resident (and it can be interesting defining exactly when this is—as Arthur Andersen, a consultancy expert, says, 'There is no clear-cut answer as to when a person becomes or ceases to be a tax resident'), you are required by law to apply for a Tax File Number. The onus is on you to do so.
- **Tax Residency**
  As mentioned above, the situation is not very clear.

However, a person present in Australia for more than 183 days in a tax year may be considered a tax resident. A person who usually lives in Australia, and in particular maintains a residence there, may be considered a tax resident irrespective of the time he or she actually spends there. Permanent Resident status obviously could be another factor defining the tax resident.

- **The Tax Year**
  Australia's tax year runs from 1 July to 30 June the following year, not on a calendar year basis.

- **Residents**
  If you are a tax resident, Australia taxes you on your worldwide income, regardless of whether it derives from, or is remitted to, Australia, unless it has already been taxed in the source country; there are quite a lot of tax agreements with other countries that allow offsetting against foreign tax paid but you need to have all the paperwork, receipts etc, to prove that this foreign tax has been paid, and then submit it to the ATO.

- **Non-Residents**
  If you are a non-resident, you will be taxed only on assessable Australian-sourced income.

- **Overseas Employment**
  A tax resident who has worked in a foreign country for a continuous period of 91 days or more will be fully exempted from Australian tax, providing he has been taxed in the other country. This exemption applies only to money derived from employment, however.

- **Overseas Income**
  Income earned by Australian companies resident in low-tax countries will be attributed to their parent companies and taxed on an accrual basis, except in a list of 61 'comparable-tax countries'. But if the comparable-tax country taxes at a low, concessional rate, accrual tax will still apply.

- **Capital Gains**
  There is no capital gains tax on profits from the sale of your first/main home ('principal residence') in Australia, even if you have been overseas for some time (providing you have not used it to earn rental income during your absence). If

you have been renting it out, the capital gains tax exemption applies only for a maximum period of six years' absence from the country. Even if you sell off a second home bought as an investment, providing you time that sale carefully, for instance at least 12 months from purchase, capital gains tax can be mitigated quite substantially, and you can offset many expenses against it. Generally speaking, there are no taxes on capital or wealth per se.

- **Raids**

  The Australian tax authorities regularly implement rigorous audits on taxpayers' accounts, often within a single professional group (e.g. all builders this year, all performing artists next year etc), more or less at random and with only minimal forewarning. This is when you may really need all that substantiation documentation, for five years back.

- **Tax-free Threshold**

  Recent government policy relaxation and streamlining have brought a much more generous tax-free threshold of A$ 18,200 (it was a mere A$ 6,000 before 2012), meaning that low income-earners below this level have not even needed to file a tax return as of tax year 2012–13. In 2015–16, the threshold will again rise to A$ 19,400. Combined with the A$ 445 Low Income Tax Offset, this makes the tax system relatively easy on the low-income earner. Over the tax-free threshold, up to A$ 37,000 income, you will pay 19 cents for each $1 over A$ 18,200. But once you have income of A$ 37,001 up to A$ 80,000 to assess, you will be liable for a fixed payment of A$ 3,572 plus 32.5 cents for each $1 over A$ 37,000. In the A$ 80,001-A$ 180,000 bracket, you will pay A$ 17,547 plus 37 cents for each $1 over A$ 80,000, and in the top bracket over A$ 180,000, you will pay A$ 54,547 plus 45 cents for each $1 over A$ 180,000.

- **Rates**

  These are local government taxes, which vary according to the property you own and the services you enjoy. When buying a house, it is well to check on the level of rates being levied by your future local Council, since some can be quite high.

DIY AUSTRALIA, A TO Z

For Sale or Rent: Continent, quiet, secluded neighbourhood off the beaten track, all round panoramic ocean views, magnificent gardens but some irrigation needed for parts of property (suit handyman); no dwellings but huge potential; many native fauna species on property available as pets or food; traditional owners very obliging; suit pioneer couple wishing to get away from it all. First to see will colonise!

EVERY SOCIETY HAS A HIDDEN MENU OF TOPICS—people, events, things—with which all members of that society are supposed to be familiar. Such knowledge serves as a sort of password or passport proving that you are indeed an insider, or almost, and so allows you to enter that society.

Australia is no exception. To help you get your foot past more than just the door, here is a grab-bag of information that once internalised, should allow you to bluff your way through dinner parties, cocktail party small talk and even job interviews, without asking the fatal questions 'Who?' or 'What?'

I am deliberately excluding any names or events which have been adequately dealt with in earlier chapters, so exclusion from this chapter naturally does not imply that the missing name or event is somehow unimportant.

Official Name
Commonwealth of Australia.

Capital
Canberra (*No, not Sydney, like you thought!*), located in its own separate territory, Australian Capital Territory (ACT).

Flag
Blue background with the Union Jack (upper left hand corner) and a single star on the left, and the Southern Cross on the right.

National Anthem

Advance Australia Fair.

God Save The Queen!—the British National Anthem is played as 'the Royal Anthem' in Australia at any occasion at which members of the royal family or their representative, the Governor-General of Australia or her state-based equivalent, is present.

Waltzing Matilda—the third-level, unofficial Australian anthem.

National Colours

Green and gold.

Official Language

English.

Time Zones

There are three time zones in Australia: Western, Central and Eastern.

Using Perth as a benchmark (apologies to easterners), the Western Australian capital is eight hours ahead of Greenwich Mean Time in England, and two hours behind Australia's eastern states; it's in the same time zone as Hong Kong, Bali (Indonesia), Singapore and Malaysia. But during Summer Time (October-March), Daylight Saving kicks in for the eastern states of New South Wales, Victoria, South Australia, Tasmania, and the Australian Capital Territory. With no Daylight Saving regime in Western Australia (the conservative 'sandgropers; of WA voted Daylight Saving down in a 2009 referendum), Queensland or the Northern Territory, these states then fall an extra hour behind the eastern states during summer, making Perth three hours behind in the summer.

The Northern Territory and South Australia, in the Central zone, are one and a half hours ahead of Perth.

Telephone Codes

The international dialling code is 61 followed by one of the four regional codes; but note that when you are calling from outside the country, these codes do not have the '0' in front that they must have when calling from inside Australia. Hence '02' for the Sydney area becomes just '2' when calling from outside Australia. So to dial Sydney number 4444-5555 from abroad, you would dial 61-2-4444-5555. (Australian fixed line numbers are all 8-digit).

Note also that when calling an Australian mobile phone number from outside the country, you should again drop the first '0' of the number (most Australian mobiles begin with a '0'). Additionally, you do *not* need to use a regional code prefix for the mobile—so when dialling an Australian mobile, you will use a number such as 61-444-555-666, whereas from inside Australia, that number is 0444-555-666.

Regional Codes

- 02   New South Wales (e.g. Sydney–NSW) and Australian Capital Territory (e.g. Canberra–ACT)
- 03   Victoria (e.g. Melbourne–Vic) and Tasmania (e.g. Hobart–Tas)
- 07   Queensland (e.g. Brisbane–Qsld)
- 08   South Australia (e.g. Adelaide–SA), Western Australia (e.g. Perth–WA), and the Northern Territory (e.g. Darwin–NT) including the Broken Hill area

---

Land
The island continent of Australia, comprising the two land masses of mainland Australia and the island state of Tasmania to its far south, sits in the southern hemisphere with the Indian Ocean to the west and the South Pacific Ocean to the east.

Area
Total: 7,686,850 sq km (2,967, 909.4 sq miles).
Land: 7,617, 930 sq km (2,941,299.2 sq miles).
Water: 68,920 sq km (26,610.2 sq miles).

Highest Point
Mount Kosciuszko in New South Wales (2,229 m / 7,312.9 ft).

Lowest Point

Lake Eyre (16 m or 53 ft below sea level), in Central Australia, spread across parts of the states of South Australia, Northern Territory and Queensland.

Major Rivers

Murray River, Darling River, Murrumbidgee Rivers.

Climate

The climatic range is wide, from arid to semi-arid climates in the centre to tropical and monsoonal in the north, and 'Mediterranean' to temperate weather in the east and south. The highest temperature ever recorded was 53.1°C (127°F) at Cloncurry, Queensland, in 1889, but in northern and central parts of the continent, temperatures such as 45°C (113°F) are quite common in the summer.

Natural Resources

Australia is 'filthy rich' when it comes to minerals, precious metals and gems: bauxite, coal, copper, diamonds, gold, opals, iron ore, lead, mineral sands, natural gas, nickel, petroleum, silver, tin, tungsten, uranium, zinc.

Population

By May 2011, the resident population of Australia had risen to 22.9 million mark. The population is expected to increase to between 30.9 and 42.5 million people by 2056, and to between 33.7 and 62.2 million people by 2101. As of 30 June 2006, Australia's Indigenous population was estimated at 517,000 people, or 2.5 per cent of the total Australian population.

Population Density

Population density in the vastness that is Australia is low, at only about 2.6 persons per square kilometre. About 27 per cent (June 2010) of the population is now overseas-born (compared with only 10 per cent in 1947).

Population Centres

The largest cities, in order of population size, are Sydney (over

4 million), Melbourne (over 3.8m), Brisbane (over 1.8m), Perth (over 1.5m) and Adelaide (over 1m). Almost 64 per cent of the population is concentrated in the main capital cities, making Australia a very urbanised nation.

Religion
Roman Catholic and Anglican Christianity dominate, together with other forms of Christianity but almost 19 per cent of the population claims 'No Religion' according to the 2006 Census. Some 5.6 per cent are affiliated with non-Christian faiths, the three most common being Buddhism (2.1 per cent of the population), Islam (1.7 per cent) and Hinduism (0.7 per cent). Of these, Hinduism has experienced the fastest proportional growth since 1996, more than doubling to 150,000, followed by Buddhism which doubled to 420,000.

Administrative Divisions
Six states: New South Wales, Queensland, South Australia, Tasmania, Victoria, and Western Australia.

Two territories: Australian Capital Territory and Northern Territory.

There are also some external territories: Norfolk Island, the Cocos Islands, Christmas Island, Macquarie Island and Australian Antarctica (between 45 degrees south and 160 degrees east).

The Capital Cities
Canberra is the federal capital, in Australian Capital Territory. State capitals: Sydney, New South Wales; Melbourne, Victoria; Brisbane, Queensland; Perth, Western Australia; Adelaide, South Australia; Hobart, Tasmania; Darwin, Northern Territory.

Government Structure
Australia has a federal system of government, with a Commonwealth and six State parliaments, and representative councils in the Australian Capital Territory and Northern Territory (which are not states).

With the Queen of Australia and her representative, the Governor-General, at the top—and an Executive Council to advise the Governor-General—to give Cabinet decisions legal force, major political decisions and most real government are in the hands of the Federal Prime Minister and his Cabinet. The power of the Federal Government is limited by the Australian Constitution, which cannot be changed except by a referendum vote.

In current politics, the 'Westminster model' is more or less in force, with government faced by an Opposition in Parliament. Glossing over subtleties, there is at present in effect a two-party system, with the Australian Labor Party currently holding government (2010 General Election), and the Liberal Party in opposition, together with its usual coalition ally the National Party (although this alliance is weakening). The strongest minority party is the Greens, and since the tumultuous 2010 General Election, they have shared the balance of power with three Independents, partnering the Australian Labor Party. Hence the ALP government holds only minority government until the GE to be called by November 2013. Voting is compulsory for all Australians over 18 years old, except for the Aboriginals who may choose whether or not to register on the electoral roll.

The 150-seat federal House of Representatives is the equivalent of Britain's House of Commons, elected every three years, while the Senate acts as an 'upper house' representing State interests and reviewing legislation, elected every six years (ACT and NT, three years).

State government mirrors this structure, each state with its own royally-approved Governor, its own Premier and Cabinet, its own constitution, an upper house called the Legislative Council (elected for twice the period of the lower house) and a lower house called either the Legislative Assembly or the House of Assembly (elected for four years, except in Queensland).

The Northern Territory (self-governing since 1978) and Australian Capital Territory (a federal government territory, with self-government more or less imposed on it against the will of most residents) have a single house of parliament—the Legislative Assembly—which is elected for four years, and the head of the majority party is called the Chief Minister, while the Queen's representative is called the Administrator.

Head of State

Her Majesty Queen Elizabeth II, represented by Australia's first-ever female Governor-General, the exotically named Quentin Bryce, appointed by the new Labor government in April 2008; the elegant Queenslander and former barrister would make a splendid Head of State, many feel, should Australia become a Republic. However, this seems unlikely before Queen Elizabeth II passes away, since she is personally still very popular, as amply demonstrated during her official visit to Australia in October 2011

Head of Government

The Prime Minister (British/Welsh-born Julia Gillard of the Australian Labor Party since August 2010, Australia's 27th Prime Minister and the first female in the seat, following her controversial replacement, virtually by 'internal Party coup', of the sitting Labor PM Kevin Rudd who had been elected following the long 'reign' of PM John Howard for the Liberal Party, 1996-2007).

Elections

Every three years—2007, 2010 etc. The main system of voting used is the Preferential system.

Currency

The Australian dollar—decimal since 1966—consists of 100 cents. There are 1 and 2 dollar coins, and five notes of 5, 10, 20, 550 and 100 denominations, all polymer (plastic) since 1992, an Australian technological innovation. The 'Aussie dollar' has floated free on exchange markets since December 1983.

Gross Domestic Product (GDP)

GDP: US$ 1,507.4 billion (2011, IMF forecast).
Per capita GDP: US$ 66,984 (2011, IMF forecast).

Products and Industries

Barley, cattle, chemicals, food processing, fruit, industrial and transportation equipment, mining, poultry, sheep, sugarcane, steel, wheat.

Exports
Alumina, coal, metal ores and minerals, e.g. gold and iron ore, crude petroleum, natural gas, agricultural produce (incl. meat, wheat, wool), transport equipment. US$ 284.1 billion (2010).

Imports
Cars and other passenger vehicles, computers and office machines, crude oil and petroleum products, medicaments (including veterinary), telecommunication equipment and parts. US$ 25.3 billion (2010).

Current Account Balance
US$ 30.4 billion deficit (2010 est.).

Budget Deficit
A$37 billion (2011-2012 fiscal year forecast).

Unemployment Rate
5.5 per cent (2011-2012 forecast).

Total Stock of Foreign Direct Investment in Australia
US$ 436 billion (July 2010).

NAME-DROPPING
Phillip Adams
Urbane liberal columnist, arts-world personality, and pioneer of Australian cinema, Adams presides over ABC Radio National's *Late Night Live* programme, writes for *The Australian* newspaper, and relishes his self-appointed role as the scourge of the right wing.

Julian Assange
Certainly a famous Australian, many would say a great one, but the Australian government appears to be in two minds about that. Assange, essentially a computer hacker,

programmer and political Internet activist, is the founder-editor of WikiLeaks, a daring foray into whistle-blowing online journalism that fearlessly publishes political leaks and secret documents, thus enraging governments, especially in the USA. At the time of writing, he awaits his fate, pending possible extradition from Britain to Sweden, to face (apparently technical) rape charges that allegedly could lead to his extradition to the US to face possibly far more serious charges regarding US military intelligence secrets.

'The Bali Nine'

This is the tag used to refer to nine Australians convicted in the Indonesian courts of the attempted smuggling of 8.3 kg (18 lb) of heroin onto the Indonesian island of Bali in April 2005. They received sentences varying from life imprisonment to 20 years, and in the case of two, Andrew Chan and Myuran Sukumaran, death. The case is ongoing, and forms part of a mosaic of similar irritations between Indonesia and Australia.

The Bali Bombers

Three Indonesians who spearheaded the lethal bomb attack on tourist havens in Bali in October 2002, killing 202 people, including 88 Australians. They were executed by firing squad in November 2008.

Sir Edmund Barton

The first Prime Minister of Australia at the formal Federation of its States in 1901 and leader of the Protectionist party, Barton held power thanks to the Australian Labor Party's support. He resigned his position in 1903, returning to his original career as a High Court judge. I pop this one in just for the hell of it; if you know this factoid, you will be well ahead of most 'dinky-di' Aussies!

Alan Bond

English migrant rags-to-riches business tycoon, declared bankrupt in 1992, a legend for delivering the coveted America's Cup yachting trophy to Australia in 1983. In 2000, he was released from four years in prison for shady business deals but he continues to build a new fortune, almost incredibly reappearing in *BRW* (*Business Review Weekly*) magazine's annual 'Rich 200' list in 2008.

Sir Don Bradman
Australian-born cricketer, a brilliant batsman whose record of 452 runs not out in 1930 survived until 1994. Knighted in 1979, he died in February 2001. He is frequently referred to admiringly as 'The Don'.

Martin Bryant
The disturbed lone gunman who massacred 35 innocents at Port Arthur in Tasmania, 28 April 1996, provoking the government to sweeping gun-control law reforms. He got 35 life-terms in jail.

Quentin Bryce
Curiously named for a woman, this gracious lady is the very first female Governor-General of the Commonwealth of Australia, appointed by Kevin Rudd's Labor government in 2008, immediately following her five years' service as Governor of the State of Queensland—she was born in the Queensland capital of Brisbane in 1942. She is a distinguished lawyer with a strong record of human rights advocacy.

Brian Burke
Former premier of Western Australia (1983–1987), he keeps on popping up again in brand new scandals, having been jailed for his role in the notoriously free-wheeling, greedy 'W.A. Inc.' era of the 1980s. In his more recent career as a political lobbyist, his excessive influence on the WA State Government (Labor, under Premier Alan Carpenter) became so outrageous that the Labor Government lost the 2008 state election partly as a result.

Julian Burnside
This distinguished barrister, a QC, has been involved with several high-profile court cases centring on human rights, such as the 2001 'Tampa case' on the rights of 'boat-people' refugees seeking asylum.

Harry Butler

'National Living Treasure', former Australian of the Year (1979) and in 2012, awarded the Officer in the Order of Australia honour, Dr Harry Butler was a 'TV naturalist' celebrity of the 1970s-'80s and now puts his nature conservation expertise and passion to very practical use as a valued environmental management consultant for resources projects such as the oil and gas giant Chevron's A$43-billion gas project on Western Australia's Barrow Island. He believes industry and conservation can coexist, given proper management.

Peter Costello

Most famous for what he nearly became, but did not—i.e. Prime Minister of Australia. Australia's longest serving Treasurer in Prime Minister John Howard's Liberal Party government (1996–2007), Costello was constantly thwarted by Howard in his obvious ambition to take the top job. His bitterness over this has emerged clearly, see his 2008 book . Now working for the World Bank, his views are still regularly sought by the media.

Tim Costello

Yes, Peter Costello's brother. A former Baptist Minister, he is recognised as one of Australia's leading campaigners for social justice, and heads World Vision Australia, a relief agency dedicated to alleviating global poverty.

Janet Holmes à Court

Widow of multi-millionaire business deal-maker Robert Holmes à Court, she inherited his mantle after his death in 1990 and proved to be his equal as a businesswoman. Today she is a noted patron of the arts.

Graham Farmer

Arguably Australia's most famous 'footy' player, this Western Australian Aboriginal star was at his peak in the 1950s. The Graham Farmer Freeway in Perth is named after him.

Cadel Evans

Tenacious professional racing cyclist who won the élite Tour de France race in 2011 after several unsuccessful tries, all the more admirable for his age at the time, 34.

'The Dismissal'

Refers to the dramatic demise of the Whitlam government in 1975; see the entry for 'Khemlani' below.

Tim Flannery

Outspoken environmentalist, bushman, TV celebrity, best-selling author and distinguished scientist (zoology, palaeontology), 'Australian of the Year' in 2007, Flannery is a man of our times. He is currently Australia's Climate Change Commissioner, besides his post as a Professor at Australia's Macquarie University. Read his books, *The Future Eaters* (1994), *The Weather Makers* (2005) and *Here on Earth*, and watch his DVDs, *Two Men in a Tinnie* (2006) and *Two in the Top End* (2008), real edutainment.

Andrew Forrest

Also known as "Twiggy" ('Forrest', trees, geddit?), Forrest is Australia's third richest man (*BRW* magazine's 2011 *Rich 200* list), with a mining fortune from his Fortescue Metals Group of A$ 6.18 billion.

Professor Germaine Greer

Internationally known for her feminist writings (notably *The Female Eunuch*, 1970) and also for her very considerable scholarly oeuvre in the field of English Literature, this expatriate Australian academic is sometimes disliked by fellow Australians for her vociferous 'knocking' of her home country from her new base in England, where she has lived since the 1960s. However she is much courted by the media for her strong opinions.

Dr Mohammed Haneef

The 'Haneef case' of 2007 was a serious immigration and security bungle. Indian-born Dr Haneef, working in

Queensland, was wrongfully detained for more than three weeks on poorly grounded suspicions of terrorism links under the then Howard Liberal government. In 2010, Haneef was awarded compensation estimated at A$1 million, apparently in exchange for shutting up about his treatment.

Rolf Harris

This Perth-born octogenarian entertainer and painter just keeps on going. He is a much- loved Aussie icon (even more so in Britain, where he now lives), best remembered for his bouncy 1950s hit song *Tie Me Kangaroo Down, Sport*. In 2012 he added the Officer in the Order of Australia honour to his substantial collection of 'gongs' (medals).

Bob Hawke

The 'Silver-haired Bodgie' (a complex Aussie slang term most often used to refer to sharply-dressed but possibly 'dodgy' 1950s-type teddy boys), once a forceful and charismatic union leader, was Labor's Prime Minister of Australia 1983–1991 and is still affectionately regarded for his colourful personality and personal life. Read his biography, see this book's *Further Reading* list at end.

Lleyton Hewitt

The world's Number One male professional tennis player in 2001, at the age of 20, Australian-born Hewitt still plays but by 2011 was ranked only 187th after battling various health problems.

David Hicks

Adelaide-born in 1975, Muslim convert Hicks has been a cause celèbre in Australia ever since he was captured in Afghanistan in December 2001, having trained with the Al-Qaeda-linked Taliban government there, and subsequently detained at the USA's notorious post-'9/11' Guantanamo camp, until early 2007. He plea bargained, accepted a charge of 'providing material support for terrorism' and served the nine remaining months of his suspended seven-year sentence in Australia. His treatment by the American authorities was, and still is, highly controversial in Australia. Read his autobiography *Guantanamo: My Journey* (2010).

Harold Holt

Australia's Prime Minister in 1966, believed drowned while swimming off Victoria in 1967. As his body was never recovered, mystery lingers, amid all kinds of crazy folklore about what might have happened to him.

Fred Hollows

'Australian of the Year' 1990 although New Zealand-born, ophthalmologist Hollows worked to bring sight through eye-surgery to the developing world, including Aboriginal Australia. He died of cancer in 1993, but the Fred Hollows Foundation and his wife Gaby carry on his work.

Steve Hooker

A consistent gold medallist, including at the Beijing Olympics of 2008, Hooker is an outstanding pole-vaulter who has topped 6.6 metres (21.6 feet) making him the world's second best in history.

Stephen Hopper

Botanists Professor Hopper is among Australia's most dedicated nature and plant conservationists. Following his success as Director of King's Park and Botanic Gardens in Perth, he scaled the top of the botanical career ladder with his appointment in 2006 as the first non-British Director of the iconic mother of all botanic gardens, England's Royal Botanic Gardens of Kew. He was awarded Australia's highest honour, Companion in the Order of Australia, in 2012 and, now in his 60s, is moving on to an academic post at the University of WA's southern coastal campus in Albany.

Steve Irwin

A famous 'larrikin' Aussie (see Glossary), conservationist adventurer, TV celebrity and director of Queensland's Australia Zoo, Irwin met his bizarre death in 2005 via a stingray's barb while filming underwater off the Great Barrier

Reef. The natural successor to former 'Crocodile Dundee' Paul Hogan, Irwin was known as 'The Crocodile Hunter.' His American-born widow Terri and their precocious star of a daughter Bindi (born 1998) continue Irwin's legacy at his Zoo.

Alan Joyce

The daring Irish-Australian A$5 million-a-year CEO of Australia's putative national flag-carrier airline Qantas Airways (the world's second oldest airline, founded in Queensland in 1920) alias 'The Flying Kangaroo', was far from flavour of the month for many Aussies in 2011. He then announced his intention to slash some 1,000 Australian jobs in the airline and translocate many aspects of the airline overseas, particularly to Asia. Some asked whether Qantas "still called Australia home", in reference to the airline's famous advertising theme song. Joyce's announcement provoked rolling strikes among airline and airport workers, culminating in his own unprecedented grounding of the entire Qantas fleet worldwide in October 2011. Both airline and workers were then forced into industrial arbitration by the government's Fair Work process.

Kamahl

Extremely popular with 'middle Australia', from tiny tots to grandmas, this very successful Indian-descent singer who came originally from Malaysia is an Australian institution, although now somewhat passé.

Paul John Keating

Australia's Labor Prime Minister 1991-1996, notable for his transformation of the Australian economy (he floated the Aussie dollar), for his drive to bring Australia closer to Asia, his street-fighter invective in Parliament, and his penchant for antique French clocks and smart suits. He shone so brightly on the 'big picture' international stage that the average Australian voter decided he was forgetting home, and so kicked him out.

Ned Kelly

Legendary 'bushranger' (bandit) of Victoria in the 1870s, famous for his 40-kg home-made suit of armour. In 1880, he was hanged for murder. Lionised in Australian folklore as a kind of Robin Hood, he stands for the ancient Irish hatred of the English and for the generally uneasy relationship between Australians and policemen or other authority figures. Do read Peter Carey's *The True Story of the Kelly Gang* (2001).

Tirath Hassaram Khemlani

Mysterious Sindhi middleman said to have brokered an A$ 4-billion Middle Eastern loan for Prime Minister Gough Whitlam's government. Revelation of the loan provoked a constitutional crisis, which led to the Queen's representative Governor-General Sir John Kerr's dismissing Whitlam's government in 1975 ('The Dismissal'). Many Republican Australians have since used this incident to illustrate how the British monarch can undermine Australia's independence.

Crown Princess Mary of Denmark

Born in Tasmania as plain and simple Mary Donaldson, this charming and stylish woman struck lucky when she fell in love with a handsome Danish yachtsman whom she met in a Sydney bar during the 2000 Olympic Games in Sydney. Little did she realise—until a little later—that he was none other than Crown Prince Frederik of Denmark. The wedding was in May 2004. And so they lived happily ever after, with four children, a son born in 2005, a daughter born in 2007, and twins, a son and a daughter, born in 2010. Aussies are totally 'rapt' with Mary, who has achieved 'Princess Diana' status with them, upstaging even the British Royal Family.

Robert Gordon Menzies

Australia's longest-serving Prime Minister 1939–1941 and 1949–1966 and the founder of the Liberal Party. An icon of the old 'Anglo' Australia with an accent to match, he died in 1978. He is still infamous for his oft-quoted fawning reference to Queen Elizabeth II of Great Britain/Australia in

1963, echoing an Elizabethan poet: *"I did but see her passing by, and yet I love her till I die"*.

Rupert Murdoch

Already notorious, he needs hardly any introduction, but just to remind you: this celebrated octogenarian media mogul was Australian-born, from Melbourne, before he became American and set out to rule the world. His News Ltd company owns plenty media in Australia, including the first and still only national daily, *The Australian*.

Ian MacNamara

Known to Australians as 'Macca', he hosts ABC Radio's folksy *All Over Australia* programme on Sunday mornings (particularly popular in rural Australia) and is known for his dedication to Australia's 'core values'.

James Packer

Heir to the media empire founded by his redoubtable father Kerry Packer (of Consolidated Press, who also pioneered one-day cricket matches), now re-focusing on casino and other gaming investments worldwide, and listed among *BRW* magazine's top 10 richest Australians, at No. 8, with A$ 4.16 billion.

Sally Pearson

Rising Aussie sports-star Pearson (born in 1986) excelled in the 100 metres women's hurdles at the 2011 World Championships in Athletics, winning with the fourth fastest time in history, 12.28 seconds, and breaking the Australian national record.

John Pilger

This expatriate Australian writer, journalist and commentator is the bane of the right-wing, of politicians generally worldwide, and of dishonest or lazy fellow journalists. Resident in London, he remains an incisive observer of the Australian scene, as in his book *A Secret Country* (1992).

Phar Lap
A race-horse known to almost every Australian. A consistent winner, notably in the 1930 Melbourne Cup event, he was found dead in April 1932. Speculation on the causes continues.

Gina Rinehart
Heiress to the mining (chiefly iron ore) empire founded by the late Lang Hancock of Western Australia (Hancock Prospecting), listed by *BRW* magazine in 2011 as the richest person in Australia, with a A$10.31-billion fortune. The bitter soapie of her own children's court case against her, over her management of the family trust, rolls on.

Geoffrey Robertson
Impressive Australian-born but Oxford-educated (England) barrister dedicated to defending human rights issues in particular, both at home and abroad, and one of the leaders of the republican movement.

Professor Brian P. Schmidt
In 2011, American-Australian astrophysicist Schmidt, attached to the Australian National University, became the first Australian scientist since 1915 to win a Nobel Prize, and the nation's 12th-ever Nobel winner. Together with two other scientists, he shared the Nobel Prize for Physics, for their work on distant supernovae and their discovery that the universe is not only expanding but expanding at an accelerating rate.

Peter Singer
Controversial Australian philosopher and committed vegetarian known internationally for his radical views on euthanasia and as the 'Father of Animal Liberation' (see his 1975 book *Animal Liberation*. He works as a Professor of Bioethics at Princeton University, USA, is also part-time Laureate Professor at the University of Melbourne, and despite the controversy his views often stir, was awarded Australia's highest honour, Companion in the Order of Australia, in 2012.

Dick Smith

A successful entrepreneur and serial adventurer, founder of a thriving electronic goods chain, Smith uses his money to fund a series of hobbies, from publishing to aviation and exploration, or for plain philanthropy.

Professor Fiona Stanley

A heart-warming Australian heroine, Australian of the Year 2003. Stanley will have a A$ 2-billion, cutting-edge new hospital in Western Australia named after her, opening in 2014, in recognition of her tireless work first in the field of childhood illnesses and more recently, in the tough arena of Aboriginal health.

Kerry Stokes

Media tycoon, chairman of Seven West Media which includes the dominant West Australian Newspapers in Western Australia and Seven Media's several TV channels.

Samantha, "Sam", Stosur

Ranked seventh in the world, Sam is among Australia's best professional tennis players, winner of the 2011 US Open Singles title. She was born in 1984.

Dame Joan Sutherland

Internationally acclaimed and celebrated, this remarkable Australian soprano opera singer, once dubbed "La Stupenda" by an impressed Italian audience of cognoscenti, sadly passed away in October 2010.

Malcolm Turnbull

The urbane former leader of the conservative Opposition (Liberal Party), September 2008-December 2009 (usurped by the current leader, Tony Abbott), is believed by many to be still standing in the wings waiting on his chance for a comeback before the 2013 General Election. His views on climate change and a carbon price are known to be at variance with those of the more sceptical Abbott. A former journalist and high-profile lawyer, he is also an ex-banker and businessman who has amassed considerable personal wealth.

Shane Warne

Retired Aussie cricketer hailed as the greatest spin-bowler of all time, but unfortunately even better known for his 'sexting' compulsion and his engagement in 2011 to marry sexy British actress Liz Hurley.

Dr Fiona Wood

Named 'Australian of the Year' in 2005, Dr Wood is the English-born, now Western Australian plastic surgeon specialising in the treatment of severe burns injuries, who is famous for her saving of more than 20 severe cases (up to 92 per cent burned) resulting from the terrorist bombings of Bali tourist havens in October 2002, treated by her at the Royal Perth Hospital. See also her entry in our panel on Inventors & Innovators (above), for her invention of 'spray-on skin'.

INVENTORS & INNOVATORS

Australia has long had the reputation of being extraordinarily creative and inventive, but not so good at developing and marketing her inventions. Be that as it may, the list of internationally significant Australian inventions and discoveries makes impressive reading. Here is just a small sample:

- **Square Kilometre Array Telescope (SKA), Australia /New Zealand & S. Africa**

  The world's biggest, most sensitive and most powerful deep-space telescope probe, the A$2-billion, one square-kilometre SKA, will be partly located at northern Western Australia's Murchison Radio-Astronomy Observatory, north-east of Geraldton town, a shared project with New Zealand and South Africa. Construction starts in 2016 and full operation by 2024.

- **Cervical Cancer Vaccine, Professor Ian Frazer**

  Scottish-born, Melbourne-based immunologist who in 2006 pioneered the first vaccine (best known as *Gardasil*) against Human Papilloma Virus, cause of many cervical cancers. His Chinese co-researcher Jian Zhou sadly died in 1999. Frazer was awarded Australia's highest honour, Companion of the Order of Australia, in 2012.

- **Stomach Ulcer Bacterium, Dr Barry Marshall and Dr J Robin Warren**
  Australian-born and Western Australia-based, these researchers won the 2005 Nobel Prize for their 1980s discovery that the bacterium *Helicobacter pylori* caused stomach ulcers.

- **'Spray-on Skin', Dr Fiona Wood**
  In 1992, British-born Dr Wood, based at the Royal Perth Hospital in Western Australia, together with scientist Marie Stoner, initiated development of a 'spray-on' skin replacement for serious burns victims, much faster than traditional skin-culturing and grafting.

- **Plastic Bank Notes, CSIRO & RBA**
  The Australian Commonwealth Scientific & Research Organisation and the Reserve Bank of Australia created the world's first polymer bank note with the first plastic A$10 note, issued in 1988, Australia's Bicentenary. Printing Australia, part of the RBA, is now printed these highly durable, waterproof notes for many other countries.

- **Dual-flush Toilet, Bruce Thompson**
  In 1980, Thompson, then working with South Australia's Caroma company, devised the water-saving dual-flush toilet so familiar worldwide today.

- **Bionic Ear, Professor Graeme Clark**
  Australian-born Clark led a University of Melbourne team that developed the 'Bionic Ear', inserting the first cochlear implant into a patient's ear to restore hearing in 1978.

SELECTED ACRONYMS

ABC   Australian Broadcasting Corporation.

ABN   Australian Business Number.

ACA   Australian Consumers' Association.

ACCC   Australian Competition & Consumer Commission.

ACT   Australian Capital Territory, capital Canberra.

ACTU   The Australian Council of Trade Unions, believed to be crucial underpinning for the Australian Labor Party.

AFL   Australian Football League (Aussie Rules football).

ALP   Australian Labor Party.

AMA   Australian Medical Association.

ANU   Australian National University.

ANZAC   Australian & New Zealand Army Corps (coined in World War I, pronounced 'Anzack').

ASIC   Australian Securities and Investment Commission, the primary regulator for companies, investors, share market etc.

ASIO   Australian Security Intelligence Organisation (pronounce like a real word, 'Ayzeeoh'). Australia's official intelligence outfit.

ASX   Australian Stock Exchange.

ATO   Australian Taxation Office.

AusAID   Australian Agency for International Development, the Government aid unit.

BAS   Business Activity Statement.

BSB   Bank-State-Branch number. You will need this number for bank transactions such as electronic funds transfer. It is the number which clearly identifies exactly which bank/branch your account is with. You will find it, a six-digit number expressed in two separated sets of three numbers, printed immediately to the left of your account number, and to the right of the cheque number, at the bottom of your cheques, just about in the centre.

CCC   Corruption & Crime Commission, known as the 'Triple C'.

COB   Close of Business (which in Australia means 5pm).

EST   Eastern Standard Time in the eastern states, i.e. 10 hours ahead of Greenwich Mean Time (and 2 hours ahead of Western Australia's time zone), except in summer, when daylight saving moves it ahead another hour.

GST   Goods and Service Tax, a consumption tax first imposed in 2000, currently standing at 10%.

MCG   Melbourne Cricket Ground.

NSW   State of New South Wales, capital Sydney.

NT   Northern Territory, capital Darwin.

OBE   Outcomes-Based Education, a free-wheeling modern form of curriculum that is still at the centre of heated controversy in Australia, particularly in certain states such as Western Australia.

PAYG   Pay As You Go income tax.

QSLD   State of Queensland, capital Brisbane.

RSL   Returned Services League, an influential ex-servicemen's association traditionally associated with crusty conservatives and diehard chauvinistic nationalists, but recently showing signs of catching up with the times.

SA   State of South Australia, capital Adelaide.

SBS   The Special Broadcasting Service, established to serve ethnic minorities. SBS TV now does far more than this, offering excellent world news coverage and quality documentaries and movies.

TAB   Totalisator Agency Board—go to their nearest shop, or register an account and bet online at http://www.tab.com.au/ for your annual Melbourne Cup horse-racing flutter.

TAFE   Technical and Further Education—Tafe colleges are the alternative, and sometimes a gateway, to university. Pronounced like a real word, 'Tayfe'.

TAS   State of Tasmania, capital Hobart.

TGIF   Thank God it's Friday!

VIC   State of Victoria, capital Melbourne.

WA   State of Western Australia, capital Perth.

CULTURE QUIZ

Can you be Australian enough to merge into the background?
Here are a few test situations to try yourself out.

SITUATION 1

The Australian office you work with is having some problems
with a document in French which needs translating. You have
a post-graduate degree in French language and literature.
Do you:

Ⓐ Announce the fact loud and clear and proceed to do the
translation?

Ⓑ Keep quiet until some else says, "Hey, Bill knows a bit of
French, doesn't he?" and asks you to do it?

Ⓒ Offer rather tentatively to do the translation, saying, "Look,
I'm not sure I can handle it, but let me take a look at it,"
and then translate, but deliberately take a little more time
that you really need, and include a few mistakes which
the boss can spot, to make him feel proud?

Comments

Of the three options, **Ⓒ** is definitely the most Australian. The
idea is not to stand out too much, not to excel too obviously—
not to risk becoming a tall poppy asking to be mown down.
However, **Ⓑ** is a good alternative, while **Ⓐ** is definitely not on.
Oh, and if by any chance you get a promotion as a result of
this performance, remember not to throw a party to celebrate
it—that would be crowing too much.

SITUATION 2

You've landed a date with this gorgeous Australian blonde
at last. Do you:

Ⓐ Take her to the most expensive restaurant in town to wine
and dine her, opening the car door and the restaurant
door for her, as well as pulling out her chair for her,
and pay the whole bill before escorting her right to her
front door?

B Take her to a medium or low-budget restaurant, let her largely fend for herself and split the bill with her before seeing her to her own car or taxi so that she can drive herself home?

C Take her to the local footy match after a quick fish-and-chips snack at the neighbourhood takeaway?

Comments

Choice **B** is probably right for the first date. Falling over yourself to charm her as in **A** will probably alarm her and convince her you 'want to get into her knickers' as the saying goes. On the other hand, choice **C** is just too Aussie male for a real date, although it is an option by no means unheard of or untried among Aussie males. You can step up the charm on subsequent dates if you like, once she gets used to your foreign ways.

SITUATION 3

The chairman of an important business associate company in Australia, whom you have never met, has written to you for some information which he says he needs 'soonish'. Do you:

A Compose a letter beginning, 'Dear Sir, with reference to yours of the 18th inst, re data required...' etc., and fax it forthwith, mailing the original by express airmail?

B Put it in your KIV tray for a few days and then answer it by ordinary airmail, writing, 'Dear Joe, it's been a bit of a problem finding what you need, but no worries, this should be about right...'?

C Forget about it?

Comments

Option **A** will do you little good, maybe some harm, while **B** is correct and non-threatening in terms of over-efficiency. It is quite essential that you address your correspondent by his first, given name to get the right Australian tone. If possible, do remember to include a few spelling mistakes. Option **C**, while it does occur, is just too unfriendly for an Australian.

SITUATION 4

Just to prove you can speak the lingo, now translate this short passage (courtesy of writer Frank Devine's 'That's Language' column in *The Australian Magazine*, 28–29 May 1994, then circulated nationally with *The Weekend Australian* newspaper, a marvellous source of information for all Australia-watchers):

'At Chrissie, me and my sister went to Brizzie to see our rellies. I got an eleckie blankie for a prezzy and she got some lippy. We both got sunnies and pushies. For brekky, we had mushies and chocky bikkies.'

Answer

'At Christmas, me and my sister went to Brisbane to see our relatives. I got an electric blanket for a present and she got some lipstick. We both got sunglasses and pushbikes. For breakfast, we had mushrooms and chocolate biscuits.'

DOS AND DON'TS

DO

- Respond in like manner to friendly comments made to you in passing by strangers—it is quite normal for Aussies to talk to people they don't know. It's rude to cold shoulder them.

- Accept that strangers and new acquaintances will use your first name, and do likewise yourself—it's a subtle signal of equality.

- Take seriously and obey all warning signs on beaches and if local experts or lifeguards say get out of the water, get out!

- Apply full lane discipline and signalling etiquette when driving—no zig-zagging without signalling—and give way graciously, while minimising the use of the horn.

- Take the local drink-driving blood alcohol limit seriously and get someone else to drive on that night out.

- Talk about sport and learn to enjoy a beer with the boys in the pub if you are male.

- Pay your share of the bill at restaurants and bars.

- Bring a bottle of booze or some food with you when you are invited to a party or dinner.

- Refer to anyone who does not appear to be married to their companion, but is obviously living with them, (whether heterosexual or homosexual) as that person's 'partner'. (In fact, you can use this term even for their legally wedded spouse—'husband' and 'wife' are so last century).

- Rein in any prejudices you may harbour about homosexuals, women in society and feminists, or the unemployed—it is definitely not done in polite Australian circles to display public animosity to any of these (although you may hear plenty in other circles).

- Acquire knowledge of a few 'Strine' phrases to get you through daily life with some understanding of what is going on (but note a 'Don't' below that also applies to this knowledge).

- Learn to do things for yourself; Australia is a do-it-yourself society, and labour is costly.
- Equip yourself immediately with outdoors gear such as a picnic blanket, 'esky' (cooler-box), folding chairs, folding parasol, picnic basket and plastic table-ware and cutlery—you're not an Aussie if you don't picnic outdoors during summer; likewise for the backyard 'barbie' (barbecue)—better buy one now, or at least a modish free-standing electric grill.
- Hand over your parking coupon with unused but already paid time on it to a fellow motorist about to park; that's the sharing Australian spirit, and it also indicates in true Aussie style that you are not about to let the authorities get away with taking the common man's hard-earned cash.

DON'T

- Even try to be smart or funny or to hoodwink Australian Customs and Immigration officers; especially, do NOT try to smuggle in food or plants.
- Overreact to bad language, insults or rude gestures, just return them in kind and in good humour and then forget it.
- Take disagreement personally. Don't hold grudges or brood after a healthy Aussie argument; it's all part and parcel of the normal rough and tumble of Australian life.
- Raise over-serious issues such as race or religion at relaxed social functions.
- Launch into discussions or jokes about cultural or racial differences before checking who is who in any social gathering—Australia is multi-cultural and multi-racial so you can't always be sure exactly what everyone's background may be nor how you may offend. Remember for example that many Aboriginals can look almost white.
- Talk about money, particularly your own money, on social occasions .
- Throw money around, buying everyone in sight dinner or beers; Aussies hate to feel indebted.

- Assume you should tip, at the hairdresser's, in a restaurant etc.—it's often offensive outside of the tourism industry context.
- Dress too sharply at relaxed social functions—learn to be creatively shabby sometimes.
- Assume that throwing lots of Strine phrases like 'G'day, mate!' around will bring you instant love; some Aussies resent outsiders appropriating their lingo like this—you have to win your right to use the language over time.
- Expect Aussies to be impressed by big flashy cars, opulent homes and career success; they are not impressed by that, all they want to know is, are you a good bloke at a party or a pleasant woman with heart.
- Publicly compare things in Australia negatively with things 'back home'.
- Complain—about the heat, about people, about Australia— since 'whingeing' is a cardinal sin in get-on-with-it Australia.
- Ask personal questions such as 'What's your salary like?', 'Why aren't you married?'
- Expect Australian-reared children and teenagers to be quiet and deferential to you as an older person or even as their teacher or parent.
- Try to bargain prices down at most retail establishments.
- Go into the deep countryside/outback on a driving or trekking trip without studying local conditions, taking a map and basic supplies (especially water and spare petrol), and informing local police or rangers of your itinerary. Outside of the suburbs, it can be tough territory.
- Flatter people excessively or offer to serve them too much—Aussies detest obsequiousness.
- Smoke anywhere without asking permission. Most Aussies assume it is impolite to smoke inside someone else's house and automatically step out into the backyard to smoke even without asking.
- Cast aspersions on, or engage in over objective analysis of, those who have served in wars such as World Wars I and II, and certainly not sacred cows such as the defeat at Gallipoli in 1915.

- Use politically incorrect phrases such as 'cripple' or 'handicapped', still less 'spastic', for the disabled, 'abo' for Aboriginals etc, in polite company. Learn as quickly as possible which are the no-nos.
- Attempt to jump queues or blatantly use connections/position in any way to influence outcomes in your favour—the egalitarian Aussie will slap you down even harder. (The operative word here is 'blatantly,' however. A lot of this goes on behind closed doors, but you mustn't be caught out.)
- Invite people, or accept invitations, to 'tea' or 'dinner' without checking carefully what they mean by that term. Many Aussies refer to the main evening meal when they say 'tea' and lunch when they say 'dinner'.
- Talk about yourself too much, unless asked.
- Be too much of a goody-goody when it comes to obeying government and other rules and regulations or, at least, don't reveal that you are. Cheat a little on your bus tickets or something. Aussies admire rebels.
- Underestimate the Australian sun and risk of skin cancer. Don't bake in the sun for more than 30 minutes maximum. Hats, UV-protected 'sunnies' (sunglasses), cover-ups and the highest possible sun protection factor sunscreen lotion (e.g. SPF 30) are musts, even in winter sun.
- Start any fires anywhere, including at home, without first studying current fire warnings and wind conditions and checking for permission to do so. Avoid lighting fires in the summer.

GLOSSARY

Akubra	The classic broad-brimmed Aussieman's hat, now very chic, once the headgear of rural folk. Good ones don't come cheap, either.
Arvo	Afternoon. 'See you this arvo.'
Barbie	The barbecue pit in your back garden, the centre of all social action during the Australian summer. Barbies are also barbecue parties serving charcoal-cooked meats and salads, always in the open air.
Bathers	Bathing costume, swimming costume, (also known as 'togs' or 'cozzie').
Battler	A quintessentially Aussie concept, fronting a philosophy of life. The battler is the little man, the underdog struggling to survive, often in conflict with the top dog. He or she is always a hero.
Beaut	Great! Also common is 'Beauty!', pronounced 'B-you-dee!'
Bell	'Give us a bell tomorrow'—please phone tomorrow.
Bickies	Bucks, money. 'I reckon I could earn big bickies on this deal, mate.'
Bludger	A bludger is anyone who sponges off anyone else, someone who never buys his round of drinks, and in the case of dole-bludging, someone living off the state's unemployment benefits.
Blue	A quarrel, a row, or else, a blunder.

Bodgie	The Australian equivalent of a Teddy Boy in the 1950s. Former Prime Minister Bob Hawke has been dubbed 'The Silver Bodgie' for looking like a leftover Teddy Boy at times earlier in his political career, complete with loud jackets and sideburns, albeit silvering ones.
Bucketing	To get or 'cop' a bucketing, is to be reviled, strongly criticised. The phrase recalls the pre-flush toilet days when human excreta were collected in buckets; in other words, when you get 'bucketed', you get a bucket of shit poured over you.
Buckley's Chance	No chance. Origins of this phrase are obscure, but it's certainly of early 19th century date and Buckley clearly was a very unlucky man. This is also used more concisely, as 'You've got Buckley's of winning this bet, mate!'
Budgie Smugglers	Er, this is embarrassing, but typically, and topically, Australian. 'Budgie Smugglers' are those old-fashioned skimpy male swimming trunks that tightly hug the genitalia. The resulting manly bulge is jocularly referred to by Aussies as 'a budgie' (a bird) stuffed into the trunks. This blushworthy term enjoys revived currency at present only because the Putin-esque, outdoorsy Liberal party (Opposition) leader Tony Abbott, when recently competing in a triathlon event, daringly fronted up on TV in the aforementioned garb, much to the nation's mirth (and some female admiration, it must be said).
Bunyip	A mythical and not always friendly Australian creature entrenched in childhood stories, often found around waterholes.

Cark it	To die. Strictly informal usage. It would be rude and flippant to suggest your best friend's father has just 'carked it'.
Catchya	For 'Catch you later' (i.e. see you later), a common farewell phrase.
Chook	A chicken.
Chuck a wobbly	Have a fit, lose your temper. See also, 'Spit the dummy.'
Chunder	To vomit, the word deriving from a warning on board ship to those unfortunates happening to stand below the seasick, 'Watch under!'
Clayton's	A Clayton's thing is a false or 'bluff' thing, not the real thing. From a non-alcoholic drink of the same name—a drink that's not a drink.
Cobber	Fondly believed by many to be one of the most typical Aussie slang words, referring to a friend, this word is in fact just about dead in the Australian dialect, completely overtaken by 'Mate'.
Cocky	Originally, a smallholder farmer from the smallholder's propensity to grow crops, only to have them eaten up by pest cockatoos. Used for cockatoos as well.
Crook	Sick or ill, badly done or formed, not right.
Crust	Your bread and butter, livelihood. The question 'What does he do for a crust?' is quite common.
Dag	Derogatory. A dag (the word being derived from the filthy matted wool at the hind end of a sheep) is someone who's awful in some way, whether badly dressed, pretentious or boring.

Daks/ Strides	Men's trousers. 'Daks' originates from a brand-name.
Dingbat	A weirdo, someone eccentric or deranged.
Dinkum	Most famously used in the fuller expression 'Fair dinkum', meaning 'Honest, it's the truth!' It refers to the 'real thing.' 'Dinky-di' is a more intense version of this.
Dob In	To inform on someone, to betray, especially a friend, workmate or neighbour.
Drongo	A hopeless loser, a stupid or clumsy person. After a horse in the 1920s which persistently failed to win a single race.
Drum	Information, the latest news, the inside story. 'What's the drum on that takeover proposal, Pete?'
Dunny	A legendary item of Australiana, the outdoors WC (toilet, lavatory) shed, pretty rarely encountered in cities nowadays, but in the countryside, still, anything goes.
Esky	Portable cooling box used to carry food and drink (more importantly, beer) to picnics on the beach or in the park, etc. Derived from the original trade name, 'Eskimo'.
Flat Chat/ Flat Tack	Flat out, stretched to the limit, very busy.
The Fremantle Doctor	A West Australian phrase referring to the welcome cool breeze blowing from Fremantle to Perth on a hot afternoon, sometimes shortened to just 'The Doctor'.
Full Bottle	Fully informed, well up in. 'Henry's not full bottle on this issue, so let's call Reggie instead.'

Furphy	A rumour or false report. It arose from soldiers' tall-tale telling while sitting around water carts (servicing the latrines) branded with the manufacturer's name, 'Furphy'.
Get on your bike	Better hurry up, then.
Globe	Where other English-speakers might buy a bulb or a light-bulb, Aussies always ask for a 'globe'.
Gong	Medal, award or badge of authority. 'So who got the gongs at the Oscars then?'
Grog	Booze, liquor. Any alcoholic drink, but usually beer.
Guernsey	A symbol of acceptance, from a type of sweater, and the team jersey you get on selection for a footy team.
Jackaroo/ Jackeroo	Usually a young city-slicker working on a sheep or cattle station in the rough outback to get first-hand experience of farming. A jackeroo's life is almost synonymous with toughing it out.
Jarmies	Pyjamas (Pajamas).
Joey	A baby kangaroo.
Lakkies	Rubber bands (from 'elastics').
Larrikin	A rowdy no-gooder, a hooligan, a mischievous youth, a trouble-maker. But also a scallywag with a golden heart.
Lolly/Lollies	An abbreviation from 'Lollipop', it means any sweet or candy, especially brightly coloured ones.
Nong	A fool or simpleton.

Ocker	The ultimate, uncultured Australian boor. He is almost certain to be found wearing shorts and thongs, is characteristically jingoistic and insular when confronted with other races, creeds or cultures or indeed, any culture at all. Thankfully, his tribe is dwindling very quickly.
Poofter	A derogatory term for male homosexuals, very commonly used, probably to reaffirm what Australian men see as their central macho identity.
Pooh	Shit. 'Oh, the cat's just done a pooh on the carpet,' or 'Oh dear, looks like I'm in the pooh with my boss again!'
Prang	As in 'My son went and pranged the car again.' Only for minor car accidents, dents and so on.
Rack Off	Push off, get lost.
Rage	This has very recently acquired the meaning of 'to party wildly'. You may well be invited to 'go rageing' at the weekend; do not be alarmed, this is probably an invitation to visit a few discos.
Ratbag	An eccentric or stupid person. Gradually coming to have a very general derogatory meaning.
Ringer	An outstanding performer. Originally the best shearer in the sheep-shearing shed. But in northern Australia, it usually only refers to a cattle muster.
Ripper	Similar to 'beaut', this means 'terrific!' 'What a ripper night we had!'.

Roo-bar	A large and solid structure made of metal bars attached to the front of Australian cars. Any car driving out of the city needs this fixture to cope with kangaroos bounding into the headlights on country roads at twilight or night. A collision with a kangaroo will otherwise result in far more serious damage to you and your car than to the 'roo itself!
Root	A dangerous one for Americans, this one. Americans may use it to mean cheering on their favourite sports team—'I was rooting for the Mets'—but in Strine it refers only to sexual intercourse, being the equivalent of 'screw'. You have been warned.
Rort	What the Americans and British know as a 'scam'—a fraudulent scheme or stunt; to con or cheat.
Sandgropers	Natives of Western Australia, because their state is largely desert sand; this is also the name of a wee sand-burrowing beastie that lives permanently in the soil feeding off the base of plants.
Sangers	Sandwiches.
Sea-change	Mid-life crisis or retirement urge to move house from the city/suburbs to the coast and a sea-view, ostensibly for a more gracious lifestyle. See 'Tree-change' below.
Secret Women's Business	Those rituals and secrets within an Aboriginal group that are taboo to men. White men have now fought back and the new phrase 'Secret Men's Business' is often jocularly used by all Aussies.
Shonky	Dubious, fraudulent, charlatan.

Shout	Both a noun and a verb. A shout is a round of drinks, for which someone has to pay. 'When my shout came round, I did the honours. But the whole evening, he never shouted one drink!'
Sledgeing	Systematic personal abuse and insult, usually among competing sportsmen on the sports field, most recently among cricketers.
Smoko	Short for a 'smoke', it has come to mean all features of a break from work, for a smoke, for tea and sandwiches.
Snags	Sausages.
Specky	Australian for 'Cool', derived from 'Spectacular.' Often downplayed in true Aussie fashion, even further from the original, by using the qualifier 'pretty': "Yeah, it was a pretty speccy day for me, winning a million bucks on Lotto and all."
Spit the dummy	Same as 'Chuck a wobbly', see above. Graphically recalls a baby's tantrum, spitting out its dummy. Used humorously or mockingly: "When I told the boss to get stuffed, she really spat the dummy!"
Spruik (verb) / Spruiker (noun)	A weird one, this, apparently of unknown origin but used as far back as 1902. It looks South-African-Dutch, doesn't it? It means (verb) to advertise something loudly and vigorously as if selling on a street market and canvassing for customers. 'She used the child's school report to spruik the child's genius all over town.'
Sticky Beak	A graphic word for the nosey parker, he or she who sticks his or her nose into things. It can also be used as a verb.

Stubby	When not a small beer bottle, a pair of tight, short shorts for men. Rarely an attractive sight.
Super	Superannuation – old-age pension and retirement income savings nest-egg achieved by putting aside a (small, compulsory) proportion of employees' salaries in a selected superannuation fund (matched by a compulsory contribution from their employer). Extra voluntary contributions to super, e.g. via the "salary sacrifice" mechanism, may reduce your overall income tax level, since voluntary contributions attract a lower rate of tax.
Swag	In the past, the ill-gotten goods carried by a thief or vagabond, but today used of any traveller's quite legitimate bags and baggage. 'Here, you can rest your swag here while you come inside.'
Tart	This sounds offensive to English ears, since it would normally refer to a prostitute. But in Australia, it just refers to any young, and usually pretty, woman. It is actually a contraction of the affectionate 'sweetheart'.
Too right!	I couldn't agree more.
Tree-change	Mid-life crisis or retirement urge to move house from the city/suburbs inland to wooded bushland in the countryside, ostensibly for a more gracious, more eco-friendly and gentler lifestyle. See 'Sea-change' above.

Two-up	A traditional Australian gambling game based on spinning two coins and betting whether they will fall as two heads or two tails. A two-up gambling den is often referred to as a 'Two-up School', but even Australia's most respectable casinos feature this game, which originated in the pioneer outback.
Wag	To skip something, drop out or play truant. 'My daughter's been wagging school for weeks, the head teacher just told me.'
Whinger	Anyone who complains too much instead of getting on stoically with being a battler like the rest of Australia. 'Poms'—the British—are supposed by Australians to have developed whingeing into a fine art.
Willy Willy	Not what you are thinking of at all. This is a sudden mini-whirlwind that circles the dust around you, often encountered in dry and dusty Australia.
Wowser	A killjoy, one who lectures, a puritan. The wowsers would like everything to close on Sundays.
Yakker	Not to be confused with 'yacker' (a talker), this word means 'work'.
Yard	A general term used for the land at the back of your house, whether it is in fact a garden or a paved area.
Youse	Probably of Irish origin, substitutes for 'you'. 'Youse blokes is OK,' or 'One of youse, come over here.' Considered by many to be a bit 'low' but commonly heard for all that.

SOME IDIOMATIC PHRASES

I'll give it a go; I'll give it a burl.
- I'll try, never mind if it doesn't work, but I'm sure it will… This mindset, while optimistic, can however lead to amateurism when it comes to the more precise technologies.

I don't know her from a bar of soap.
- I haven't the faintest idea who she is.

I suppose it's better than a poke in the eye with a burnt stick.
- It's better than nothing. As *The Bulletin* weekly magazine put it in 1974, this is the Australian way of expressing ecstasy.

I'll just pencil it in for Monday, then.
- By this, the Aussie speaker means he will tentatively jot this appointment down in his diary for Monday. But it's tentative: remember, you can erase pencil easily! But it does mean you have some sort of a prior claim, a reservation on his/her time. It's also typically old-technology for an Aussie to refer to (and even to use) pencils—you won't catch him/her 'inputting'!

Don't come the raw prawn with me.
- Don't try to bluff me, to put one over me.

Good onya!
- Good for you, well done! Often abbreviated to 'Onya!'

In like Flynn.
- To seize an opportunity with enthusiasm, especially a sexual one. It derives from the energetic romantic exploits of the Australian-born (Tasmanian) Hollywood hero of 1930s movies, Errol Flynn.

A cut lunch and a water-bag.
- An old bushman's way of saying 'It's a long way.' 'You're going there? Well, it's a cut lunch and a water-bag for sure.'

I'll be in that; I'm up for that.
- I'm pretty keen to do that, alright.

SOME COMMON ABORIGINAL WORDS

Billabong	A waterhole.
Boomerang	The curved Aboriginal hunting weapon that returns to its owner after hitting its target, making sophisticated use of aerodynamics.
Corroboree	A festive gathering, a get-together, usually with music and dance.
Humpy	An Aboriginal bark hut, classically a temporary dwelling erected by nomads, now any rough hut or shelter.
Walkabout	The habit ingrained in Aboriginal culture, of temporary migration from one's home base, for an unplanned period of time and often without a specific goal in mind. Used now of anyone who disappears mysteriously for a while to be alone or to escape something. 'Can't find Bill anywhere, musta gone walkabout.'

SOME COMMON DIMINUTIVES

Bevvies	Alcoholic drinks (beverages).
Brickie	Bricklayer.
Chrissie	Christmas.
Cozzie	Swimming costume.
Deli	Delicatessen shop or counter.
Divvie	Dividend.
Footy, Footie	Australian Rules Football.
Journo	Journalist.
Muso	Musician.

Pokie	Poker machines, in pubs, clubs and casinos. 'Playing the pokies' is a favourite Aussie pastime but currently controversial. In 2011, Independent parliamentarians tried to use their control of the balance of power to push the Labor government to legislate for pokie gambling controls, but narrowly failed. This remains a major political issue.
Prezzie	Present, gift.
Sickie	Taking sick leave off work. Often used jokingly, on the understanding that it is just a way of getting off work. 'Your party's on Thursday morning? No worries, I'll just take a sickie and I'll be there.'
Tassie	Tasmania. Pronounced 'Tazzie'.
Tinnie/tinny	A can of beer, but also a small open metal boat (as in environmentalist Tim Flannery's TV edutainment series *Two Men in a Tinnie*).
U-ie	A U-turn, when driving a vehicle.
Uni	Where others might say 'varsity' (antique British) or 'U', the Aussies say 'Uni' for University.

SELECTED RHYMING SLANG

Bag of Fruit	Suit.
Butcher's	For Butcher's Hook—Look ('I'll just take a butcher's at the baby for a minute').
Chevy Chase	Face. (An interesting potential source of confusion for Americans, this one, as a well-known comic film actor in the USA is also named Chevy Chase.)

424 CultureShock! Australia

Dog and Bone	Telephone.
Khyber Pass	Arse.
Plates	For Plates of Meat = Feet.
Pot	For Pot and Pan = Old Man = Dad.
Steak and Kidney	Sydney.
Titfer	For Tit for Tat = Hat.
Trouble and Strife	Wife.

TERMS OF ABUSE

'Dickhead' (originally obscene but now weakened by over-use), 'Drongo' and 'Boofhead' are some of the most popular insults commonly hurled at various offenders for various 'crimes'. The body language and context of the moment will tell you whether they are truly being applied to you aggressively, or perhaps semi-affectionately. A series of colourful phrases describe someone who is mentally not all there, 'off their rocker', with my favourite being 'Oh, that one, she's a sandwich short of a picnic alright!'

TERMS OF ENDEARMENT

Complete strangers, e.g. friendly shop assistants, will commonly address you as 'Darl', short for 'Darling', or the more familiar London-style 'Love'. Those closer to you may even call you 'Possum' or 'Hun', for 'Honey'.

TERMS OF EXCITEMENT

When very pleased, an Aussie may declare that he/she is 'Stoked' (used to mean 'high'), 'Rapt' or 'Happy as Larry'.

RESOURCE GUIDE

Australia is very good at providing information: every library, health clinic and tourist centre seems to be crammed with helpful brochures and leaflets. The federal structure of the country means that many services have a single central reference point, such as a phone number, often in Canberra or Sydney, which then directs you on to the exact information point in the state where you are; or else services are replicated in each state. There are also plenty of dial-in phone help lines.

Use Your Phone Directory

Do not neglect to consult your local phone directory which you will find is full of useful information, some of it very helpfully indexed. Local tourism authority information lines and websites are also useful.

- International call access code: 0011
  Put this before the country/area codes for the foreign number you are contacting.
- If you want to have the duration and cost of your call played back to you, dial 0012 instead.
- From outside Australia, dial 61 for Australia, followed by the area code. Do not use the '0' in the area code, which applies only when you are inside Australia. For example, to dial Perth in Western Australia from Singapore or London, you dial 61-8-Perth phone number.

Area Codes

Australian Capital Territory	02
New South Wales	02
Northern Territory	08
Queensland	07
South Australia	08
Tasmania	03
Victoria	03
Western Australia	08

- Phone numbers with the 1800 prefix offer free calls, while calls to a 13 or 1300-prefix number entail only the cost of a local call. These numbers cannot be called from outside Australia.
- Mobile phone numbers are prefixed with 04, followed by two digits and the subscriber's number, dialled in full, e.g. 0412-xxx-xxx.
- The 190 prefix on indicates an information service incurring a special charge, usually anything from A$ 0.38–5.50 a minute.

Abbreviated Form

You will find that most Australians list telephone numbers under the abbreviation 'Ph.' for "Phone", rather than 'Tel' for 'Telephone'.

- Directory Enquiries
  Tel: 12456 or 1223 for local numbers
         1225 for international numbers
         1234 for search and information service.

IMPORTANT TELEPHONE NUMBERS

- Emergencies (Police/Fire/Ambulance)
  Australia-wide—for life-threatening or time-critical emergencies only:
  - 000   from a land line
  - 112   from a mobile
  If you have hearing difficulties, dial 1800-555-677 to get a relay to 000.

- Emergency translation
  Tel: 1300 655 010

- Urgent assistance at a major Australian airport
  131 AFP (131 237)

- For less urgent police matters
  Tel: 13-1444

- Crime Stoppers line
  Tel: 1800-333-000
  To report anything you know that could help the police solve a crime that has already been committed.

Crisis
For all kinds of crises and distress, including fire, flood, storm damage etc, your local State Emergency Service (SES) or Fire & Emergency Service will provide sterling assistance—find them in the local White Pages phone directory.

'Lifeline' provides crisis counselling on
Tel: 13-1114, Australia-wide, particularly regarding suicide.
- In Perth, there are also the
  - Samaritans
    Tel: (08) 9381-5555
  - Crisis Care help-line
    Tel: (08) 9223-1111, 1800-199-008
- In Melbourne
  - Crisis Care
    Tel: 1800-177-135
Go to http://www.mindframe-media.info/site/index.cfm?display = 104614 for a list of many more.

Search & Rescue
Tel: 1800-641-792 (maritime)
       1800-815-257 (aviation)
This should be reserved for major emergencies—for example, your friends have disappeared while hiking wilderness, rock-climbing or sailing the high seas.

National Security Hotline (report suspicious activity that may relate to terrorism): 1800-123-400

Telephone Services
Australian telephone services are de-regulated for competition, but still with essentially a duopoly split between:
- Telstra, the original government server, now privatised
  Website: http://www.telstra.com

428 CultureShock! Australia

- Optus
  Website: http://www.optus.com.au

Several other phone companies, such as AAPT, Vodafone, Virgin, 3, etc also operate. Small charges apply to most telephone services.

General Information
- National Time
  Tel: 1900-931-240
- Wake Up/Reminder: 1 2454 (Telstra: A$1/84 booking + 71.5 cents callback fee).
- Weather (All States): 1196, or 1900-926-161 (A$ 0.77 cents per minute for the 1900 call).
- White Pages (Phone Directory): 1800-810-211
  Website: http://www.whitepages.com.au
- Yellow Pages (Business Director): 13 23 78
  Website: http://www.yellowpages.com.au
- 'Where Is' Enquiries: 1800-819-471

WEB TIPS
A few starting points on the Internet, with information on Australia:

Aboriginal Australia
- Australians for Native Title and Reconciliation (ANTaR)
  Website: http://www.antar.org.au
- Aboriginal Australia
  Website: http://www.aboriginalaustralia.com
See also Department of Families, Housing, Community Services & Indigenous Affairs: http://www.facs.gov.au/
- SBS TV's revealing 'First Australians' documentary film series
  Website: http://www.sbs.com.au/firstaustralians/

Culture & The Arts
- Australia Council for the Arts
  Website: http://www.ozco.gov.au
- Australian government culture and recreation portal
  Website: http://www.cultureandrecreation.gov.au

Employment & Social Welfare

- Centrelink
  Website: www.centrelink.gov.au
- Fair Work Australia
  Website: http://www.fwa.gov.au/
- Fair Work Ombudsman
  Website: http://www.fairwork.gov.au/pages/

Government

- Federal Government gateway
  Website: http://www.australia.gov.au/
- Prime Minister of Australia
  Website: http://www.pm.gov.au
- Department of Foreign Affairs and Trade
  Website: www.dfat.gov.au/
- Austrade (trade & investment)
  Website: http://www.austrade.gov.au

Media

- *The Australian* newspaper
  Website: http://www.theaustralian.com.au
- *The Age* newspaper
  Website: http://www.theage.com.au
- *Sydney Morning Herald* newspaper
  Website: http://www.smh.com.au
- *Australian Financial Review* newspaper
  Website: http://afr.com
- *Australian Broadcasting Corporation* (ABC) radio/TV
  Website: http://www.abc.net.au/
- *Special Broadcasting Service* (SBS) radio/TV
  Website: http://www.sbs.com.au/
- *Crikey.com*, independent & alternative news & commentary
  Website: http://www.crikey.com.au/

Migration, Citizenship & Travel

- Department of Immigration & Citizenship
  Website: http://www.immi.gov.au
- *Beginning A Life in Australia*–key Immigration Department
  briefing brochure on everything you have to know,

essential download.
Website: http://www.immi.gov.au/living-in-australia/settle-in-australia/beginning-life/
- SBS TV's 'Immigration Nation' documentary series
Website: http://www.sbs.com.au/immigrationnation/
- Australian Customs & Border Protection Service
Website: http://www.customs.gov.au
- Tourism Australia
Website: http:// www.australia.com

Natural Environment & Science
- Environment Australia (Department of the Environment)
Website: http://www.environment.gov.au/
- Commonwealth Scientific & Industrial Research Organisation (CSIRO)
Website: http://www.csiro.au

Reference/General Information
- National Library of Australia
Website: http:www.nla.gov.au
- Australian National University (ANU), Canberra
Website: http://www.anu.edu.au
- Australian Bureau of Statistics
Website: www.abs.gov.au/
- Australia to 2050: future challenges – The Intergenerational Report 2010
Website: http://archive.treasury.gov.au/igr/igr2010/report/pdf/IGR_2010.pdf
Interesting overview of Australia's future and government planning for it, including aspects of the economy, climate change, immigration and the ageing population.

HEALTH EMERGENCIES
- 24-hour Health Advice
Tel: 1800-022-222
- Medicines Line
Tel: 1300-888-763
- Health Info Line: 1300-135-030

For a full list of hospitals, state-by-state, and other useful information: Website: http:// www.drsref.com.au

Medical Services

The Online Medical Dictionary is full of information about medicine in general and the Australian medical scene in particular: http://www.mydr.com.au/tools/dictionary.asp

For quick medical treatment, especially overnight or on holidays or weekends, you need an on-call Locum doctor. Here are some contacts:

- Australian Capital Territory/Canberra
  Tel: (02) 6288-1711 or 1300-422-567
- New South Wales/Sydney
  24-hour Hotel Doctor Service
  Tel: (02) 9962-6000
- Northern Territory/Darwin:
  24-hour medical crisis counselling
  Tel: (08) 8922-7156
- Queensland/Brisbane
  Tel: 1800-80-2622
- South Australia/Adelaide
  State Emergency Service
  Tel: 132-500 or 000
- Western Australia/Perth
  Tel: (08) 9328-7111/ 9328-0553

First Aid Online

- If you have time, there is some excellent Australian first aid briefing at: http://www.parasolemt.com.au

Hospitals

- Brisbane
  Royal Brisbane Hospital (University of Queensland)
  Tel: (07) 3636-8111
- Canberra
  - Canberra Hospital
    Tel: (02) 6244-2222
  - Calvary Hospital
    Tel: (02) 6201-6111

- Melbourne
  Royal Melbourne Hospital
  Tel: (03) 9342-7000
- Perth
  - Royal Perth Hospital
    Tel: (08) 9224-2244;
  - Princess Margaret Hospital for Children
    Tel: (08) 9340-8222
- Sydney
  - Royal North Shore Hospital
    Tel: (02) 9926-7111
  - Sydney Children's Hospital
    Tel: (02) 9382-1111
  - St Vincent's (public) Hospital
    Tel: (02) 8382-1111

Dental Emergencies
- Melbourne
  Tel: (03) 9341-0222, (07) 9341-1040
- Perth
  Tel: (08) 9346-7626 / 9383-1620 / 9221-2777
- Sydney
  Tel: (02) 9906-1660, (08) 9369-7050

Poisons Information Centre
Tel: 13-1126 (Australia-wide)
You can use this number for serious bites (by snakes, for instance) or stings (e.g. by jelly-fish, known to Aussies as 'stingers')

Other Medical Helplines
- Asthma Australia
  Tel: 1800-645-130
- Diabetes Australia
  Tel: 1300-136-588

Medical Insurance & Treatment

Visitors from Finland, Norway Italy, Malta, the Netherlands, New Zealand, Sweden, the UK and the Republic of Ireland have reciprocal health rights with Australia's Medicare authority and can register with any Medicare office.
Tel: 13-2011 (information line)

Pharmacies

24-hour or 7-day pharmacies are plentiful in Australia:

Perth

- Beaufort St Pharmacy, Mt Lawley
  Tel: (08) 9328-7775
- Bell's Drive-In
  Tel: (08) 9328-5762
- Fremantle Drive-in Pharmacy
  Tel: (08) 9335-9633
- Forrest Chase Pharmacy
  Tel: (08) 9221-1691

Sydney

Try the Kings Cross & Oxford Street night-life areas, e.g.
- Darlinghurst Prescription Pharmacy
  Tel: (02) 9361-5882
- Wu's Pharmacy
  Tel: (02) 9211-1805
- Pharmacy Guild's Emergency Prescription Service 24 hrs
  Tel: (02) 9467-7100

Melbourne

- Tambassis Pharmacy, Brunswick
  Tel: (03) 9387-8830
- Leonard Long Pharmacy, Prahran
  Tel: (03) 9510-3977
- My Chemist, Brunswick
  Tel: (03) 9386-1000

Translating & Interpreting Service (TIS)
Tel: 13-1450, Australia-wide.
If you cannot speak English well, you can get help in your chosen language.

Legal Aid Information
- Western Australia: 1300-650-579.
- Victoria: (03) 9269-0120/ 1800-677-402
- New South Wales: 1300-888-529

For more info, National Legal Aid: www.nla.aust.net.au/

Lost Property Services
At the airport:
- Melbourne,
    - Traveller's Information Service
      Tel: (+61 3) 9297-1062 / 9338-4401
    - Lost property
      Tel: (+61 3) 9297-1805
      Email: lost@easygo.com.au
- Sydney
    - T1 International Terminal
      Tel: (+61 2) 9667-9583
      Email: sit.reception@syd.com.au
    - T2 Domestic Terminal
      Tel: (+61 2) 9352-7450
    - T3 Qantas Domestic Terminal
      Tel: (+61 2) 9952-9312
- Perth
    - Terminals 1 (international) & 3 (domestic)
      Tel: (+61 8) 9478-8503
    - Terminal 2 (Qantas & Jetstar domestic)
      Tel: (+61 8) 9270-9504

Resources for the Disabled
Australia is exceptionally sensitive to the needs of the disabled and almost every website or information service provides targeted information for the disabled user. Even websites for national parks and nature reserves offer trail guides etc. for disabled trekkers. So never be afraid to ask.

Your two best information clearing houses are:

- Government website: http://australia.gov.au/people/ people-with-disabilities
- Centrelink
  Tel: 13-2717
  Website: http://www.centrelink.gov.au

To solve transport and many other problems, call the

- Commonwealth Carelink Centres
  Tel: 1800-052-222
- Assistance with disability, sickness and carers' enquiries
  Tel: 13-2717

And just imagine, so sensitive is Australia to the needs of the elderly and incontinent etc that the government has assembled a website dedicated to mapping and describing all of Australia's public toilets—what a boon! Go to http:// www.toiletmap.gov.au/

- Spinal Cord Injuries Australia (formerly The Australian Quadriplegic Association)
  Tel: 1800-819-775 if outside Sydney
          (02) 9661-8855 in Sydney
  Email: office@scia.org.au
  Website: http://www.scia.org.au/
- *Easy Access Australia* is a travel guide for disabled travellers by wheelchair-bound Bruce Cameron that offers good state-specific information (512 pp, A$ 27.45), first published 1995 and updated since. Available at bookshops or via email: bruceeaa@vicnet.net.au or through the post at PO Box 218 Kew, Vic 3101, Australia. See also http:// www.easyaccessaustralia.com.au/contact/

EMBASSIES

The key diplomatic posts are located at full embassies, in Canberra, Australian Capital Territory. Other locations, including state capitals, mostly host only consulates.

Australian Capital Territory (Canberra)

- Canada (High Commission)
  Tel: (02) 6270-4000
  Website: www.australia.gc.ca
- China
  Tel: (02) 6273-4780
  Website: http://au.china-embassy.org/eng/
- France
  Tel: (02) 9268-2400
  0419 015 294 (emergencies only)
  Website: www.ambafrance-au.org/
- Germany
  Tel: (02) 6270-1911
  Website: www.canberra.diplo.de/
- India (High Commission)
  Tel: (02) 6273-3999, (02) 6225-4928
  Website: www.hcindia-au.org/
- Indonesia
  Tel: (02) 6250-8600
  Website: www.kbri-canberra.org.au/
- Japan
  Tel: (02) 6273-3244
  Website: www.au.emb-japan.go.jp/
- Malaysia
  Tel: (02) 6120-0300
  Website: www.malaysia.org.au/main.html
- New Zealand (High Commission)
  Tel: (02) 6270-4211
  Tel: 1300 559 535 (passports, birth certificates etc)
  Website: www.nzembassy.com/australia
- Singapore (High Commission)
  Tel: (02) 6271-2000
  Website: www.mfa.gov.sg/canberra/
- United Kingdom (High Commission)
  Tel: (02) 6270-6666
  Website: http://ukinaustralia.fco.gov.uk/en/
- United States of America
  Tel: (02) 6214-5600
  Website: http://canberra.usembassy.gov/

AIRLINES

- American Airlines
  Tel: (07) 3329-6060
- British Airways
  Tel: 1300-767-177
- Qantas Airways
  Tel: 13-1313
- Singapore Airlines
  Tel: 13-1011
- Thai International Airways
  Tel: 1300-651-960
- Malaysia Airlines
  Tel: 13-2627
- Emirates
  Tel: 130-030-3777
- Virgin Blue Airlines
  Tel: 13-6789
- Jetstar
  Tel: 131-538
- Tiger Airways
  (03) 9999-2888

FURTHER READING

THE 'HARD CORE'
The Lucky Country. Donald Horne. Australia: Penguin Books Australia, 1988 (revised).
- This is the definitive study and should be your 'Bible' on Australia; it hardly seems outdated to me, even today.

Down Under ('In A Sunburned Country' in the US). Bill Bryson. London, UK: Black Swan, 2001; New York, USA: Broadway, 2001.
- Lighthearted, witty, readable account of the Australia and why it is the way it is.

Reinventing Australia: the Mind and Mood of Australia in the 90s. Hugh Mackay. Sydney, Australia: Angus & Robertson, 1993 (revised edition).
- There also several others by Hugh Mackay, such as *Generations* on baby-boomers in Australia, 1997.

Advance Australia... Where? Hugh Mackay. Australia: Hachette, 2007.
- Seasoned Australia-analyst Mackay resolutely demolishes the old myths (like that hoary old one, that Australians don't work hard), and paints a disturbing picture of everything from Australian credit card debt to rampant materialism, decreasing egalitarianism and diminishing tolerance.

A Short History of Australia. Manning Clark, Australia: Penguin Books Australia, 1996 (4th edition).
- The big historical picture, right up to the 1980s. (The full version, *A History of Australia,* comes in six volumes.)

The Fatal Shore. Robert Hughes, London, UK: Vintage, 2003; New York, USA: Vintage, 1998.
- Sobering detail on the terrible years of convict transportation to Australia.

The Australians: In Search of an Identity. Ross Terrill. London, UK: Bantam,1987; New York, USA: Simon & Schuster, 1987.

A Secret Country. John Pilger. London, UK: Vintage, 2004; New York, USA: Knopf Publishing, 1991.
- A thought-provoking assessment of the darker side of contemporary Australia, touching on politics, business, sociology and the environment.

The Future Eaters: An Ecological History of the Australasian Lands and People. Tim Flannery. New York, USA: Grove Press 2002.
- A distinguished Sydney-based research scientist looks at the human relationship with the land of Australia and the impact on its unique ecology.

The Weather Makers. Tim Flannery. Text Publishing, 2005.
- A classic on man-made climate change and its impact on the Australian environment.

Renovation Nation, Our Obsession with Home. Fiona Allon, University of New South Wales Press, 2008.
- This insightful book suggests that the Great Australian Dream of home ownership may have gone too far, distorting Australian lives with the pursuit of capital gains and debt-servicing, and may reflect deep insecurities on a national level.

Watching Brief, reflections on Human Rights, Law and Justice. Julian Burnside. Scribe Publications, 2007. (ISBN 9781921215490)
- Distinguished Australian human rights lawyer Julian Burnside offers deep insight into the state of justice and democracy in modern Australia.

Underbelly: The Gangland War. John Silvester & Andrew Rule. Australia: Floradale Press, 2004/2008.
- The recent television series based on this book caused a

sensation in Australia (and was banned in Victoria for fear of prejudicing ongoing court cases) because it transparently was not fiction but rather, based solidly on the hard-edged reality of Melbourne's organised crime underworld.

The Little Aussie Fact Book. Margaret Nicholson. Australia: Penguin Books Australia, 2002. (21st century edition)
- Everything you could ever want to know about anything Australian, in neat concise form, pocket-sized.

A Dictionary of Australian Colloquialisms. G A Wilkes. Sydney, Australia: Sydney University Press, 1978/1985.
- A flashlight in the maze of 'Strine'.

The Australian National Dictionary: A Dictionary of Australianisms on Historical Principles. Ed. W S Ramson. Melbourne, Australia: Oxford University Press, 1989.

The Macquarie Dictionary of Australian Quotations. Eds. Stephen Torre & Peter Kirkpatrick. Sydney, Australia: The Macquarie Library, 1990.

The Penguin Australian Encyclopaedia. Ed. Sarah Dawson, Melbourne, Australia: Viking/Penguin Books, 1990.
- A crash course in Australia.

The Book of Australia, an almanac. Hodder & Stoughton, Sydney 1990/reprinted.

The Macquarie Book of Events. Ed. Bryce Fraser. Sydney, Australia: The Macquarie Library, 1990.

ON ABORIGINAL AUSTRALIA
Aboriginal Australia & the Torres Strait Islands. Australia: Lonely Planet Publications, 2001.

Another Country. Nicolas Rothwell. Melbourne: Black Inc, 2007.
- Rothwell demonstrates his unparalleled understanding of that other Australia 'out back', perhaps the only 'real'

Australia—the desert lands and wildly beautiful terrain of the Centre and the far North, Aboriginal culture and so much more—in this stirring collection of essays and sketches.

First Australians. Rachel Perkins, Marcia Langton. Melbourne University Publishing, 2008. (ISBN 0522853153)
- Linked with the pathbreaking SBS documentary series telling the Australian Aboriginal story from the Aboriginal point of view.

Whitefella Jump Up. Germaine Greer. Profile Books, 2004.
- One of Australia's most famous, and most provocative, expatriate writers, slams the white settler record in Australia.

My Place. Sally Morgan. Western Australia: Fremantle Arts Centre Press, 2000.
- A personal search for lost Aboriginal 'roots'.

The Other Side of the Frontier: Aboriginal Resistance to the European Invasion of Australia. Henry Reynolds. Victoria, Australia: Penguin Books Australia, 1990.
- White settlement of Australia seen from the other side, by the Aboriginals.

That Deadman Dance. Kim Scott. Australia: Picador, 2010.
- A winner of the prestigious Miles Franklin book award, this poetic novel tells the story of first contact between the white settlers of Western Australia in the early 1800s and the indigenous peoples. It's surprisingly upbeat, writing from the standpoint of both the black and the white players.

The Chant of Jimmie Blacksmith. Thomas Keneally. Sydney, Australia: Angus & Robertson, 2002; New York, USA: Penguin Books, 1989.
- A novel dramatically depicting the Aboriginal plight.

The Songlines. Bruce Chatwin. London, UK: Vintage, 1998; New York, USA: Penguin, 1988.
- This mystical work tells of the ancient paths travelled by

the Aboriginals while singing the songs of their ancestors.
My People. Kath Walker. Australia: Jacaranda Wiley, 1981.
- Collected verse by this established, campaigning Aboriginal poet.

Charles Perkins: A Biography. Peter Read. Australia: Penguin Books Australia, 2001; New York, USA: Viking, Australia 1990.

Being Whitefella. Ed. Duncan Graham. Western Australia: Fremantle Arts Centre Press, 2001.
- Essays by thinking whites on their relationships with the Aboriginals.

MULTICULTURAL AUSTRALIA
Unpolished Gem. Alice Pung. Melbourne: Black Inc, 2006.
- Growing up in a Cambodian refugee family in suburban Footscray, with a foot in two worlds. Alice's strength is her ability to step back from her own culture and see it with ironic but affectionate and knowledgeable, observant Australianised eyes.

Growing Up Asian in Australia. Alice Pung (Ed.). Melbourne: Black Inc, 2008.
- Anthology of assorted essays by very different first- and second-generation Asian migrants to Australia, enjoyable, humorous, insightful.

Diaspora: The Australasian Experience. Ed. Cynthia Vanden Driesen. New Delhi: Prestige Books, 2006.

You will find more of interest in this rich area of Australian life, on the website http://www.multiculturalaustralia.edu.au/

And in Bibliographies:
A Bibliography of Australian multicultural writers. Sneja Gunew (Ed). Victoria: Deakin University, 1992.

Australian writing: ethnic writers 1945–1991. Annette Robyn Corkhill. Melbourne: Academia Press, 1994.

Diversity and Diversion: An Annotated Bibliography of Australian Ethnic Minority Literature. Peter Lumb & Anne Hazelle (eds). Melbourne: Hodja, 1983.

Ethnic Writings in English from Australia: A Bibliography. Lolo Houbein. Working Papers, Australian Literary Studies, University of Adelaide, 1984.

MORE HISTORY AND CURRENT AFFAIRS

The Tyranny of Distance. Geoffrey Blainey. New South Wales, Australia: Pan Macmillan Australia, 2001.

- How the geography and sheer vastness of Australia have shaped the country's history. For more historical insight, try also Blainey's *Triumph of the Nomads*, a history of ancient Australia, *The Rush That Never Ended* and *A Land Half Won.*

A Fortunate Life. A B Facey. Victoria, Australia: Penguin Books Australia, 1985.

- The moving autobiography of a completely ordinary white Australian, born in 1894, who helped pioneer the harsh West, survived Gallipoli, saw and experienced the lot.

For the Term of His Natural Life. Marcus Clarke. Gloucerstershire, UK: Nonsuch Publishing, 2005; New York, USA: HarperCollins Publishers, 2002.

- A pioneering novel of colonial times depicting the horrors of Australia as a penal colony.

The Horne Trilogy: *The Education of Young Donald; Confessions of a New Boy; Portrait of an Optimist.* Donald Horne. Victoria, Australia: Penguin Books Australia, 1988.

- An intellectual autobiography and indirectly an intellectual history of three decades in Australia.

Robert J Hawke: A Biography. Blanche d'Alpuget. New York, USA: Penguin Books, 1985.

- This substantial warts-and-all biography of Australia's

second-longest-serving prime minister, up to his first election victory in 1983, paints a revealing picture of Australian political life.

WOMEN IN AUSTRALIA

Damned Whores and God's Police. Ann Summers. Victoria, Australia: Penguin Books Australia, 1975.
- A startling and revealing feminist history of Australia.

Tracks. Robyn Davidson. London, UK: Picador, 1998; New York, USA: Vintage, 1995.
- An incredibly brave desert solo trek in which the camels star as much as this intrepid female explorer.

Pioneer Women of the Bush and Outback. Jennifer Isaacs. Australia: Lansdowne, 1990.
- The women pioneers' story—European, Chinese, Aboriginal—as researched through archival records.

No Place for a Nervous Lady. Ed. Lucy Frost. Australia: University of Queensland Press, 1999.
- The letters and diaries of 13 white women struggling with 19th century Australia.

FICTION / LITERATURE

The Hunter. Julia Leigh. Australia: Penguin Books, 1999.
- A new movie starring Willem Dafoe based on this eco-thriller about a mercenary hunter roaming the wilderness of Tasmania, is now in the pipeline (2011). An obsessive loner, the hunter has been hired by a biotech company to search for the elusive last 'Tasmanian Tiger' (or Marsupial Wolf, ostensibly extinct since about the 1930s)—the legendary Thylacine—so that its DNA can be marketed commercially.

The Eye of the Storm. Patrick White. Australia: Jonathan Cape, 1973.
- White is a giant of the Australian literary canon and this novel about the dying but still destructively scheming

matriarch of a neurotic wealthy family is one of his best. The magnificent eponymous movie released in 2011 and directed by respected Australian film-maker Fred Schepisi accurately reflects the book, with luminous performances by Geoffrey Rush, Judy Davis and Charlotte Rampling, among others. Read also White's *Voss* (1957) and *The Tree of Man* (1955).

Don's Party. David Williamson, New South Wales, Australia: Currency Press, 1978.
- A novel of rumbustious postwar, pre-Whitlam Australia in the raw.

Oscar & Lucinda. Peter Carey. London, UK: Faber & Faber, 2004; New York: USA: Vintage, 1997.
- Like White's works, a difficult, dense piece of writing which yields magic if you concentrate. This novel won the Booker McConnell prize for fiction. Try also his *True History of the Ned Kelly Gang* (Random House, 2000), a gripping account of the life of the 19th-century Irish-Australian bandit Ned Kelly, skilfully written in Kelly's own illiterate voice..

A Town Like Alice. Nevil Shute. London, UK: House of Stratus, 2000; New York, USA: Ballantine, 1987.
- This wartime romance of an Englishwoman and an Aussie soldier tells much about Australia.

The Thorn Birds. Colleen McCulloch. New York, USA: Avon Trade, 2005.
- An epic family 'dynasty' romance, through the generations of an Irish-Australian family. Some 20 million copies of the book have been sold.

The Fortunes of Richard Mahony. Henry Handel Richardson. Australia: Penguin Books Australia, 2008.
- This Australian classic begun in 1917 and set in the gold-mining boom of 19th century Australia, is actually a trilogy. A rich human drama, the book is acclaimed as an important contribution to the Australian literary canon.

Cloudstreet. Tim Winton. New York, USA: Scribner, 2002.

- Like many Aussies, this celebrated West Australian novelist is in love with beaches, boating, surfing and the sea. Winner of the Miles Franklin book award. Read also his *Dirt Music* (Picador and Scribner, 2003) and *Breath* (Hamish Hamilton, 2008).

The Slap. Christos Tsiolkas. Australia: Allen & Unwin, 2008.

- Winner of the Commonwealth Writer's Prize 2009. The author is an Australian of Greek descent, as partly mirrored in the book. The characters in this book are often repellent but admittedly the plot does reflect certain aspects of Australian suburban life, and also modern Australian child-rearing practices (i.e. you will be taken to court for physically disciplining a wayward child). And being a truly Australian novel, the story revolves around an incident at a backyard family 'barbie' (barbecue)...On a soapie sort of level, the 2011 ABC TV series based on the book was riveting, well-acted drama.

Remembering Babylon. David Malouf. Australia: Vintage, 1994 (first published 1993).

- Malouf, an Australian of Lebanese and English-Jewish descent, is another giant of Australian literature and all of his novels deserve attention. This one set in early-settler Australia, is another in the genre of reflections on white contact with Aboriginal Australians. The book was a winner of several awards, including the Commonwealth Writers Prize and the Los Angeles Times Book Prize. Read also his *An Imaginary Life* (1978).

The Secret River. Kate Grenville. Australia: Text Publishing, 2005.

- First volume of a trilogy: *The Lieutenant* (2008); *Sarah Thornhill* (2011). Another fascinating colonists vs Aboriginals story set in 19th century pioneer Australia, elegantly written by the accomplished Grenville.

AUSTRALIANA: BUSH BALLADS AND SATIRE

The Best of Henry Lawson. Henry Lawson. Australia: Angus & Robertson, 1981.
- Favourite bush ballads and poetry.

The Prose Works of Henry Lawson. Australia: Angus & Robertson, 1948/1980s.

Collected Verse. A B 'Banjo' Paterson. Australia: Angus & Robertson, 1993.

The Songs of a Sentimental Bloke. C J Dennis. UK: Kessinger Publishing Co, 2004.

Australian Bush Ballads. Eds. Douglas Stewart & Nancy Keesing. Australia: Angus & Robertson, 1986.

Great Australian Legends. Frank Hardy (in association with Truthful Jones). Australia: Hutchinson, 1988.

CULTURE SHOCK & HUMOUR

How to Survive Australia. Robert Treborlang. Sydney, Australia: Major Mitchell Press, 2005 (9th edition).

How to be Normal in Australia. Robert Treborlang. Sydney: Major Mitchell Press, 1999 (8th edition).

They're a Weird Mob. Nino Culotta (John O'Grady). Sydney, 1957.
- A big hit at the time, this is a lighthearted account of early migrants' lives.

Australian Language & Culture. Australia: Lonely Planet Publications Pty Ltd, 1994/2007.

My Gorgeous Life, An Adventure. Dame Edna Everage (alias Barry Humphries). London, UK: Mandarin, 1995.
- To quote a *Weekend Australian* review: 'Scorned at school for her mauve hair, little Edna eventually triumphs as an international megastar.' A spoof, of course.

The Life and Death of Sandy Stone. Barry Humphries. London, UK: Penguin Book Ltd, 1991.
- Moribund suburban Australia captured with lugubrious accuracy.

Keating: 'Shut Up and Listen and You Might Learn Something!' Compiler Edna Carew, New Endeavour Press, Sydney 1990.
- True sayings of the former Treasurer. It was a toss-up whether to categorise this book under Humour, Current Affairs, or what ...

AT HOME AND OUTDOORS
Traditional Australian Cooking. Shirley Constantine, McPhee Gribble/Penguin Books Australia, 1991.
- Replete with fascinating social history, this is more than a cookery book, but it is also that.

Australian Bushcraft: A Guide to Survival and Camping. Richard Graves. Australia: New Holland Publishers, 1989 (3rd edition).

Stay Alive, A Handbook on Survival. Maurice Dunlevy, Canberra: Australian Government Publishing Service, 1997.

Bushwalking in Australia. John Chapman and Monica Chapman. Melbourne, Australia: Lonely Planet Publications, 1997.

What Bird Is That?: Classic Guide to the Birds of Australia. Neville W. Cayley. Ed. Alec H Chisholm. Australia: HarperCollins, 1991.
- The classic birdwatcher's field guide.

The Slater Field Guide to Australian Birds. Peter Slater, Pat Slater and Raoul Slater. Australia: New Holland Publishers, 2003.
- Very clear colour illustrations in this handy small-and-tall guidebook.

ABOUT THE AUTHOR

Ilsa Sharp is uniquely well positioned to explain culture shock in Australia. She comes to the subject from many different directions: British-born, she has worked as a journalist in South-east Asia, chiefly in Singapore, since 1968. She holds a degree in Chinese Studies from Leeds University, England, and is married to a Singaporean-Tamil. In 1989, she and her husband became migrants to Western Australia, and a new love affair with Australia began.

Ilsa is the author of several books ranging from histories of Raffles Hotel (1982/1986), the Singapore Cricket Club (1986/1993), the national lottery, Singapore Pools (1998) and Land Transport (2005), in Singapore, and a privately commissioned Indonesian family history (1992) and the history of the Eastern & Oriental Hotel in Penang, Malaysia (2008), to wildlife/nature books such as *Green Indonesia* (Oxford University Press, 1994) and the story of the Singapore Zoological Gardens (1994). An active environmentalist in Asia since the 1970s, she has also worked as manager of public relations and marketing (1998–2000) for Greening Australia (Western Australia), a non-governmental organisation dedicated to the conservation and renewal of native vegetation. She is now a freelance writer.

INDEX

Titles in the CultureShock! series:

Argentina	Hawaii	Sri Lanka
Australia	Hong Kong	Shanghai
Austria	Hungary	Singapore
Bahrain	India	South Africa
Beijing	Ireland	Spain
Belgium	Italy	Sri Lanka
Berlin	Jakarta	Sweden
Bolivia	Japan	Switzerland
Borneo	Korea	Syria
Bulgaria	Laos	Taiwan
Brazil	London	Thailand
Cambodia	Malaysia	Tokyo
Canada	Mauritius	Travel Safe
Chicago	Morocco	Turkey
Chile	Munich	United Arab
China	Myanmar	Emirates
Costa Rica	Netherlands	USA
Cuba	New Zealand	Vancouver
Czech Republic	Norway	Venezuela
Denmark	Pakistan	
Ecuador	Paris	
Egypt	Philippines	
Finland	Portugal	
France	Russia	
Germany	San Francisco	
Great Britain	Saudi Arabia	
Greece	Scotland	

For more information about any of these titles, please contact any of our Marshall Cavendish offices around the world (listed on page ii) or visit our website at:

www.marshallcavendish.com/genref